# SOURCES IN IRISH ART

D0420625

# SOURCES IN IRISH ART
# A READER

Fintan Cullen

CORK UNIVERSITY PRESS

First published in 2000 by
Cork University Press
Cork
Ireland

British Library Cataloguing in Publication Data
A CIP catalogue record for this book is available from the British Library.

Library of Congress Cataloging-in-Publication Data

Cullen, Fintan
    Sources on Irish art : a reader / by Fintan Cullen
        p.      cm.
    Includes bibliographical references and index.
    ISBN 1-85918-154-6 (alk. paper) -- ISBN 1-85918-155-4 (pbk. : alk. paper)
    1. Arts, Irish--Sources 2. Arts, Modern--18th century--Ireland--Sources. 3. Arts,
    Modern--19th century--Ireland--Sources. 4. Arts, Modern--20th century--Ireland--
    Sources. I. Title

    NX546.A1 C85  2000
    709'.415--dc21

                                                                              00-029026

ISBN 1 85918 154 6 [Hardback]
ISBN 1 85918 155 4 [Paperback]

Typesetting by Red Barn Publishing, Skeagh, Skibbereen

Printed in Great Britain by MPG Books Ltd., Bodmin, Cornwall

# CONTENTS

## Section I   Word and Image

Introduction                                                    28

## *Aesthetic Viewpoints*

## Section II   Making and Viewing

## Display

## Section III    Creating Histories

# ACKNOWLEDGEMENTS

First and foremost thanks must be extended to all those copyright-holders who have granted permission for texts to be reproduced here and edited where necessary. Acknowledgement is also extended to the copyright-holders and owners of the art works reproduced in these pages.

In helping with enquiries and giving guidance when necessary I am extremely grateful to the following: Richard Aylmer, Eileen Black, Colin Cruise, Tom Duddy, Luke Gibbons, Josephine Guy, Anne Hodge, Catherine Marshall, Diana Norman, Sheila O'Connell, Joe O'Donnell, Niamh O'Sullivan, Gerald Parsons, Robert Towers and Jeremy Wood. At different times, Gabriele Neher and Sergio Benedetti assisted me in translating Hugh Douglas Hamilton's letters to Canova (entry 29) and I am also grateful to the Editor of Circa Art Magazine for information on back issues of that journal.

I am grateful to the University of Nottingham for granting me study leave in Spring 1998 to work on this anthology and to Cork University Press for covering the travel costs involved. Personnel at the following libraries were always helpful: the British Library, London, the National Library of Ireland, Dublin, University College Dublin Library, Trinity College Dublin Library, the National Irish Visual Arts Library, at the National College of Art and Design, Dublin, and most especially the Reference Desk and Inter Library Loan office at the University of Nottingham Library.

As always my family have been a great source of encouragement. My sincerest acknowledgement is to Felicity Woolf.

Fintan Cullen
February, 2000

# LIST OF ILLUSTRATIONS

# INTRODUCTION: IDENTIFYING SOURCES

In 1750, commenting on George Berkeley, Bishop of Cloyne, Charles Smith, the pioneer of Irish topographical writing, wrote that,

> His present lordship successfully transplanted the polite arts, which heretofore flourished only in a warmer soil, to this northern climate. Painting and musick are no longer strangers to Ireland, nor confined to *Italy*. In the episcopal palace at *Cloyne* the eye is entertained with a great variety of good paintings as well as the ear with concerts of excellent musick. There are some pieces by the best masters, as a *Magdalen of Sir Peter Paul Rubens*, some heads by *Van Dyck* and *Kneller*, besides several good paintings performed in the house, an example so happy, that it has diffused itself into the adjacent gentlemen's houses, and there is at present a pleasing emulation raised in this country, to vie with each other in these kinds of performances.[1]

And yet a few years later, while touring Ireland, the English traveller Richard Twiss was struck by the paucity of outward signs of civilization:

> In regard to the fine arts, Ireland is yet comparatively behindhand with the rest of Europe, partly owing to the unsettled state which that island was in during the civil wars and commotions, which to a reflecting traveller offers matter of wonder that it is even so forward. Out of Dublin and its environs, there is scarcely a single capital picture, statue or building to be found in the whole island. Neither is music much cultivated out of the above limits, to any degree of perfection; so that nothing is expected in making the tour of Ireland, beyond the beauties of nature, a few modern-antiquities, and the ignorance and poverty of the lowerclass of inhabitants.[2]

We are offered here two conflicting views of the state of patronage and collecting in mid-eighteenth-century Ireland. The question is not a case of which one to believe, rather that Ireland was contested territory that evoked different responses from visitors and inhabitants alike. The aim of this anthology of sources on the visual arts is to alert the student of Irish art and Irish culture in general to the attention paid to the visual over the past three hundred years.

The focus of this anthology is on texts from the eighteenth to twentieth centuries. The earliest text included is an extract from Berkeley's Italian

Journal of 1717 (entry 1) while the most recent piece is a 1995 essay by
Fionna Barber on the contemporary artist, Alice Maher (entry 23; fig. 12).
The time frame for the book is roughly from the foundation of the Dublin
Society in 1731 to the setting up of the Irish Museum of Modern Art in
Dublin in 1990. Although Berkeley's trip to Rome predates the founding of
the Dublin Society, his close friendship with such supporters of the Society
as Samuel Madden (entry 24; fig. 13) and his own subsequent interest in the
institution warrants his appearance. Equally, some of the more recent entries,
including the piece on Alice Maher, were published after the establishment
of IMMA, but conveniently refer to artists whose work is represented in that
institution's permanent collection (entries 23 and 54; figs. 12 and 30, respectively).[3] The seventeenth century and earlier are excluded not because they
do not offer rich material, for example, the catalogues of the Ormonde collection or the late sixteenth-century inventory of Lord Kildare's seat at
Maynooth Castle,[4] but because such documents are too singular to offer sufficiently varied viewpoints.

By nominally starting with the foundation of the Dublin Society, the user
of this volume is supplied with a narrative impetus that takes one through
three centuries of an increasing awareness of the visual in Irish society.
Although it may seem perverse, that narrative has not influenced the layout
of the book as it has been felt that a thematic arrangement offers greater
insights into the subject. Such a format allows the user to make specific com-
parisons over time; for example, one can chart the development and relative
success of native subject matter in Irish visual production from the exclusivist, nationalist demands of Thomas Davis in the 1840s (entry 8) to the more
complex iconography of artists such as Alice Maher (entry 23; fig. 12) or
Willie Doherty (entry 52; fig. 28) as discussed by Fionna Barber and Joan
Fowler, respectively. As the accompanying 'Presentation and Editing of Texts'
and the introductions to each of the three sections explain, the texts are
arranged in such a way that one can happily avoid, if one wants, the telling
of a story.

In tracing a documentary-based history of Irish involvement in the visual
arts, this book is initially indebted to the precedent set by the 'Sources and
Documents' series published by Prentice-Hall a generation or more ago,
which made available a wide range of material from 1400 B.C. to the mid-
twentieth century. Although certain volumes were dedicated to such illustrious cultures as ancient Greece and Rome or Renaissance Italy, only one
volume concentrated on a specific nation in the modern sense, *American Art,
1700–1960* (1965). The general premise set by John McCoubrey in his
preface to that volume still holds true and can be easily applied to the
example of Ireland, the subject of this book:

The literature of our painting and sculpture has no counterparts to the influential doctrines of Winckelmann, the journals of Delacroix, or the manifestos that marked the major developments of European painting from Courbet's realism to Breton's Surrealism. It reflects rather a discontinuous, unsystematic development that makes the orderly presentation of its history difficult and the usual terminology awkward.[5]

With the exception of Edmund Burke (entry 2), Ireland has not produced a major theoretician of art and thus, to someone new to Irish Studies, many of the names that appear in this reader will be unknown. Great names such as George Berkeley and W.B. Yeats do appear (see entries 1, 10 and 36) but, as with McCoubrey's volume, this book is more concerned with identifying a series of national and at times more specifically local discourses, as opposed to attempting to rewrite the history of European art history.

Unlike the task faced by McCoubrey in the 1960s, an added difficulty for Ireland is that of identifying existing discourses, either historical or contemporary. One of the problems with Irish visual material is deciding on the Irishness of an object, an artist or an aesthetic viewpoint. Many of the sources cited in this book could just as easily appear in an anthology of British commentary on art. A decade ago, Seamus Deane, speaking on behalf of his fellow editors, addressed this issue in his General Introduction to *The Field Day Anthology of Irish Writing*,

> Part of the significance of this work for us has been the recognition of the power of the English canonical tradition to absorb a great deal of writing that, from a different point of view, can be reclaimed for the Irish tradition. Such acts of annexation and reclamation are integral to the assertion of cultural authority and confidence, but the assumptions on which they are based are frail indeed. Therefore, we consider ourselves to be engaged in an act of definition rather than in a definitive act.[6]

In using passages from Edmund Burke's celebrated *Philosophical Enquiry into the Origin of our Ideas of the Sublime and Beautiful*, which first appeared in 1759 (entry 2), this anthology is not claiming exclusive Irish rights to the thoughts of this Irish-born commentator. Equally, Burke's letters to the Irish artist James Barry (entry 28), written as they were from London to his protégé in Rome, could be used in a generalized discussion of the relationship between an English-based patron and an artist in the mid-eighteenth century. Other eighteenth-century sources, such as Daniel Webb on taste in Italian painting (entry 3) or Barry (entry 5) on the development of the arts in these islands as well as Anthony Pasquin's biographical compilations of the 1790s (entry 15) or the Earl of Charlemont's letters to William Hogarth (entry 26) where he apologizes for late payment for a portrait (fig. 16), could be used to enliven the study of the visual arts in Britain and indeed they have.[7] Certain texts included here, most particularly Burke's *Enquiry* and perhaps Berkeley's travel journals, are not hard to find in university libraries, but the vast majority of extracts have not been anthologized before and, apart from the texts that were published in the last generation or so, many are difficult to locate. Thus, what is being attempted here is a reassembling of some well-known texts with others of little renown so as to reorientate the material into an Irish context. In reminding the reader that Burke and Barry were born in Ireland and that this nation and its concerns, be they colonial status, Roman Catholicism, Republicanism or whatever, continued to feature in their writings, allows us to consider their discussions of the visual arts in a new light.

Anthony Pasquin's dictionary-like entries on a wide range of Irish artists have the honour of being the first attempt to broadcast the legitimacy of an Irish visual culture. But by birth Pasquin was English and he spent most of his life as a hack journalist and satirist in London. His inclusion in this volume together with other non-Irish contributors perhaps needs a word of explanation. The close political and cultural relationship between Ireland and Britain demands that the study of the visual arts as it affected the smaller nation takes full account of the contribution of visiting artists, patrons or commentators. In compiling this anthology of sources, no exclusivist agenda has been in operation; rather, the emphasis is on suggesting as wide a range of useful material as possible. As with Pasquin, more than a few of the authors of entries included were British: for example, John Parker (entry 25), an English history painter whom the Irish peer Lord Charlemont appointed as his agent in Rome and who kept him informed of the many acquisitions made on his behalf, most of which ended up in Charlemont's various splendid Dublin residences. The Scottish painter, David Wilkie, visited Ireland for only a matter of weeks one summer in the mid-1830s (entry 7), yet he wrote letters describing the painterly delights of the west of Ireland while Elizabeth Thompson, Lady Butler (entry 11), is included because she happened to marry a Catholic Irishman and became interested enough in her husband's country to paint a number of topical themes (fig. 3). Also to be found in this volume is William Godwin (entry 16), the well-known English radical writer, who wrote a fascinating account of the early-nineteenth-century Irish painter William Mulready, while the equally English radical artist, Benjamin Robert Haydon (entry 31), makes an appearance due to the fact that he recorded both on canvas and in his diaries an encounter with Daniel O'Connell.

As will be seen from the few examples cited in this introduction, the entries included focus in the main on the history of and attitudes towards the art of painting in Ireland from the eighteenth to the late twentieth centuries. Other visual media do appear, from book illustration (entry 18; figs. 8–9), antique sculpture (entries 1 and 25), church decoration (entry 35) and the range of techniques utilized by contemporary artists (for example, entries 23 and 52; figs. 12 and 28), but painting and drawing dominate the examples chosen. Comparable anthologies to this one could well be produced on other aspects of Irish visual and material culture from cinema in Ireland to architecture, design and the applied arts.

The selection of material has been as much a case of identifying Irish interest as of attempting to chart an Irish theoretical tradition in the discussion of the visual arts. Added to all of this is the problem of recognizing the Irishness of an art object and the relevancy of the discourse that surrounds it. A recent example will explain this dilemma.

## WHO OWNS IRISH ART?

The story of Seamus Heaney's refusal to be anthologized in a 1982 volume of contemporary British verse resurfaced in 1999 with the suggestion that Heaney might be appointed British Poet Laureate to succeed his friend Ted Hughes. In September 1983, responding to his inclusion in *The Penguin Book of Contemporary British Poetry*, Heaney published a verse letter addressed to the editors of the anthology.[8] In 'An Open Letter',[9] Heaney complained that his identity had been questioned, even if

> . . . doubts, admittedly, arise
> When somebody who publishes
> In *LRB* and *TLS*,
>     *The Listener* –
> In other words, whose audience is,
>     Via Faber,
>
> A British one, is characterised
> As British. But don't be surprised
> If I demur, for, be advised
>     My passport's green.

Heaney 'footered' and 'havered' but in the end wrote his letter of disagreement: 'I regret / The awkwardness. / But British, no, the name's not right.'[10] Irish literary confidence received a welcome charge from Heaney's now famous refusal to be accepted as British. By contrast, accounts of the

British establishment's cultural appropriation of Irish visual culture are not so well recorded – nor have they benefited from a Nobel Laureate's pen.

In 1997, a very fine late-eighteenth-century pastel by the Irish portraitist Hugh Douglas Hamilton was bought by the Victoria and Albert Museum, London (fig. 17).[11] The pastel is dated to 1788–90 and had been in private ownership, in England, for two hundred years. It was offered for sale to the J. Paul Getty Museum in Malibu, California, at a price of over half a million pounds sterling. The Victoria and Albert Museum in London requested a British government deferral of the export licence on the basis that the object was of intrinsic British interest. Although the pastel was executed in Rome by an Irish artist and portrays an Italian sculptor and another Irish painter, the Victoria and Albert Museum, in 1998, eventually won the deferral and with the assistance of the National Art Collections Fund bought the drawing for the nation.

In acquiring the pastel, the Victoria and Albert Museum denied the object its Irish significance. By boldly declaring it to be a major British object, the museum ignored not only the artist's Irish origins, but also its wider European associations. In terms of the relevancy of the affair to this volume, the documentation that accompanied the purchase of the Hamilton pastel allows us to comment on the peripheral role that Irish art frequently has to play internationally.

In 1997, the British Government Department for Culture, Media and Sport produced a news release announcing the possible loss of this pastel to the British nation unless half a million pounds was to be found. The release never once mentioned Hamilton's origins nor his position as a leading Irish artist of the late eighteenth century. Similarly unacknowledged was Hamilton's well-documented friendship with Canova. Instead, the release emphasized, understandably in the context of attracting British support for the pastel to stay in the United Kingdom, Canova's close relationship with any number of British patrons and his influence on British taste, particularly in the culture of the Grand Tour. Omitted entirely from the news release and from the eventual *Report of the Reviewing Committee on the Export of Works of Art* was any reference to the Irish dimension of Hamilton's pastel.[12] If one wishes to be cynical, one could surmise that when a work is of high aesthetic quality it can be British but if not it can remain Irish!

The pastel shows the celebrated Italian sculptor Antonio Canova in his studio with an early version of his famous marble group, *Cupid and Psyche* (now in the Musée du Louvre, Paris). Turning from his carving, and still holding his mallet and chisel, the sculptor has paused to talk to the Irish artist and dealer Henry Tresham, who stands on the right. Hamilton lived in Rome for many years and was a close friend of Canova's and certainly knew Tresham well.

The British Government based its deferral of an export licence for the Hamilton on the Waverley Criteria, established in 1950 in order to consider and advise on an export policy of single works of art. The Reviewing Committee on the Export of Works of Art applies the following questions to objects[13]:

•    Is the object so closely connected with our history and national life that its departure would be a misfortune?
•    Is it of outstanding aesthetic importance?
•    Is it of outstanding significance for the study of some particular branch of art, learning or history?

In its submission to the Reviewing Committee, the Victoria and Albert Museum maintained that the pastel should be retained because it was part of British heritage. The pastel, the museum argued, 'was made at the time when the new neo-classical style was replacing the Rococo in Britain and symbolized the crucial role of the Grand Tour in the construction of British national life . . . The pastel, more than any other single picture, could be seen as summing up this country's love affair with Canova, with Italy and with neo-classical sculpture in the late-eighteenth century.'[14]

In highlighting the tale of the acquisition by the Victoria and Albert Museum of this pastel, I have no wish to questions its aesthetic quality – the concern of the second of the Waverley Criteria.[15] Nor do I wish to question that this group portrait belongs to the study of the culture of the Grand Tour or the social history of the representation of artists – or the important if understudied history of the pastel medium. (Such issues are covered by the third Waverley criterion, which is concerned with the significance of a work for 'the study of some particular branch of art, learning or history'.)[16] Instead, I will focus on the first Waverley criterion and the issue of British heritage. I want to stress that in advocating the purchase of this drawing by the national collections of the United Kingdom, the museum was reluctant to acknowledge an Irish connection. In maintaining that the pastel satisfied the first Waverley criterion, and thus was part of 'our' history and national life, British curators played an understandable but questionable game of cultural appropriation. Personally, I am not concerned with the emotional argument of where the pastel should be exhibited; one hopes that good Irish art can be appreciated in Malibu, London or Dublin. But in view of the facts, is it legitimate to argue that *Antonio Canova in his Studio with Henry Tresham and a Plaster Model for the 'Cupid and Psyche'* is a purely British work of art?

The artist Hugh Douglas Hamilton (1740–1808) was Irish-born and trained. One of the leading pupils of the Dublin Society Schools in the mid-eighteenth century (see entry 30) and a leading portraitist in the closing years of that century (see entries 42–3), Hamilton is a major Irish artist.[17] Ostensibly the pastel celebrates the creation of the sculptured group of *Cupid and Psyche;* however, the intimate nature of the composition and the delicate medium of pastel suggest a more personal intention. In the 1780s, as Canova rose rapidly in celebrity to become one of Rome's leading contemporary artists, he struck up a close friendship with the older Irish artist, Hugh Douglas Hamilton, who lived in Italy from at least 1782 to 1792. Produced towards the close of Hamilton's Italian sojourn, the pastel can be read as an elaborate and technically masterful personal memento of a close friendship and a stimulating period in the Irish artist's career. Technically, one of the most innovative aspects of this large pastel is that Hamilton drew Canova's and Tresham's portraits on separate pieces of paper from the surrounding composition. This may have been done so that the artist could maintain an up-to-date representation of his associates, a further indication of Hamilton's determination to record an important series of friendships. On returning to Ireland, Hamilton wrote a number of letters to Canova in which he frequently lamented having left Italy and the friends and companions he had known there (see entry 29).

The Canova/Tresham pastel can thus be seen, not as 'a symbol of the outstanding importance of the Grand Tour and Canova in British national life and on the development of neo-classical taste in sculpture in England',[18] but rather as a statement of an international friendship forged by at least two Irishmen (if we include Tresham) and a leading Italian artist of the late eighteenth century. The 'Irish' dimension of the pastel has been long recognized, even if ignored by the Victoria and Albert Museum. Anne Crookshank and the Knight of Glin included it in their ground-breaking exhibition, *Irish Portraits, 1660–1860,* held at the National Gallery of Ireland, the National Portrait Gallery, London, and the Ulster Museum, Belfast, from 1969 to 1970. These same scholars discussed it in their equally important survey, *The Painters of Ireland,* while the pastel appears in full colour on the dust cover as well as inside their more recent *The Watercolours of Ireland: Works on Paper in Pencil, Pastel and Paint, c. 1660–1914.*[19]

The discussion of Irish historical art has advanced a great deal since the days of Sir Ellis Waterhouse, who in 1953, as director of the Barber Institute of Fine Arts at the University of Birmingham, wrote his still easily available book, *Painting in Britain, 1530–1790.*[20] The so-called Celtic Fringe did not fit into Waterhouse's great canonical spread of artists and movements. Instead, 'Painting in Scotland in the Eighteenth Century' is the title of a brief chapter at the end of his volume – followed by a even briefer piece on pastellists, amongst whom he includes Hamilton.[21] In the last twenty-five years, surveys on Irish art, as well as a steady stream of monographs on Irish artists and themes in Irish art, have challenged such neglect of Irish visual representation.

But especially in Britain, an uncertainty about the cultural placement of Irish visual artists prior to the establishment of the Free State persists.

A successful nineteenth-century London-based Irish artist such as Daniel Maclise (see entry 18) may have attempted to eradicate his Irishness – not caring a 'sixpence for his native country', according to a contemporary, and even changing his name from McClise to MacClise and to the 'unproblematic' Maclise.[22] As can be judged in more recent general accounts of the artist, such self-repudiation of nationality as well as Maclise's long working life in London have helped to eradicate a general awareness of his Irish origins.[23] But, in the 1870s, as entry 18 shows, Maclise's first biographer, the Cork barrister W. Justin O'Driscoll, was at pains to demonstrate through a lengthy discussion of the artist's illustrative work that his hero was 'the twin star of [Thomas] Moore' (see figs. 8 and 9).

The political and cultural interdependence that continues to define the relationship between Britain and Ireland should encourage us to guard against unthinking artistic appropriation. Hugh Douglas Hamilton's pastel is now easily accessible in a major London museum, but such ownership should not obscure its Irish dimension.

The aim of this anthology is to assist in eradicating such confusions. The existence of a range of sources that deny the Victoria and Albert Museum's appropriation of Hamilton as a British artist needs greater exposure. In organizing this book around a series of themes, 'Aesthetic Viewpoints', 'Patronage and Education' as well as 'Display', artists such as Hamilton and many like him can be seen to have been discussed within an Irish context. This is, of course, not to deny that Hamilton along with James Barry, Daniel Maclise and many more recent Irish artists cannot also be discussed in a British or European context. Hamilton's letters to his friend Canova (entry 29) are of interest from a European viewpoint, as they show the international connections between artists in the late eighteenth century, but they also inform us about artistic conditions in Dublin. Entry 30, an extract from the playwright John O'Keeffe's *Recollections*, tells us of Hamilton's youthful talent as a pastellist, information that can be used to highlight the popularity of that artistic medium in these islands throughout the eighteenth century. O'Keeffe's account also sheds light on the seriousness of the Dublin Society as a training ground for young talent in many spheres, thus strengthening our knowledge of Enlightenment Ireland (fig. 18). Finally, the various references to Hamilton's paintings in Dublin diaries and newspaper reviews around the year 1800 (entries 41–3) confirm his central position as a leading Irish artist who painted everyone, both leading members of the establishment (fig. 22) and radicals such as Lord Edward Fitzgerald. But such diary entries and newspaper reports should also be of interest to the student of western portraiture in the late eighteenth century, for they reveal the tensions operating within a usually conservative medium when challenged by international radicalism.[24]

Given the wide range of texts included, this book, as stated at the beginning of the introduction, can be read as an anthologized documentation of art in Ireland from the foundation of the Dublin Society Schools in the early eighteenth century (entry 24, fig. 13, and entry 27) up to the Arts Council's 1979 report written by Ciarán Benson (entry 40), which called for schools to 'prepare critical audiences for the arts' or the demand by Declan McGonagle, in 1990, soon before his appointment as founding director of the Irish Museum of Modern Art (entry 14), that more attention be given to 'local culture'. However, on another level, the arrangement of these texts need not be read as a narrative but as a contribution to Irish aesthetic thought. Richard Kearney has reminded us of the colonial and racial stereotypes of the 'thoughtless Celt', and the contested existence of an Irish mind.[25] It is hoped that these fifty-four extracts (although admittedly not all by Irish writers) will alert the student of Irish studies to a neglected discourse and encourage further investigation into the relationship of the Irish to the art of the visual.

## NOTES

1    Charles Smith (c. 1715–62), *The Antient and Present State of the County and City of Cork*, 2 vols., Dublin, 1750, vol. 1, pp. 146–7. For Smith see Seamus Deane (gen. ed.), *The Field Day Anthology of Irish Writing*, 3 vols., Derry, Field Day, 1991, vol. 1, pp. 974–5, 1008.

2    Richard Twiss, *A Tour in Ireland in 1775 with a View of the Salmon Leap at Ballyshannon*, London, 1776, pp. 10–11. For a recent discussion of Twiss, see Cal Hyland and James Kelly, 'Richard Twiss's *A Tour of Ireland in 1775* (London, 1776) – The Missing Pages and Some Other Notes', *Eighteenth-Century Ireland/Iris an dá chultúr*, 1998, vol. 13, pp. 52–64.

3    Irish Museum of Modern Art, *Catalogue of the Collection, 1991–1998*, Dublin, 1998; see the accompanying Select Bibliography for references to 'Permanent holdings of Irish visual material'.

4    See Anne Crookshank and the Knight of Glin, *The Painters of Ireland, c. 1660–1920*, London, Barrie and Jenkins, 1978, pp. 19–20, and idem, *Irish Portraits, 1660–1860*, London, Paul Mellon Foundation, 1969, pp. 11–12.

5    John McCoubrey, *American Art, 1700–1960*, Englewood Cliffs, New Jersey, Prentice-Hall, Inc., 1965, viii.

6    *Field Day Anthology*, vol. 1, xix–xx.

7    See the individual entries for references to subsequent use made of these documents.

8    Blake Morrison and Andrew Motion (eds.), *The Penguin Book of Contemporary British Poetry*, Harmondsworth, 1982. A version of this account of the Hamilton pastel first appeared in *Éire-Ireland*, Fall/Winter 1998 and Spring 1999, vol. 33, Nos. 3 &4, vol. 34, No.1, pp. 15–21.

9    *An Open Letter* originally appeared as a Field Day Pamphlet, No. 2 (Derry, 1983). It was republished in Field Day Company, *Ireland's Field Day*, London, Hutchinson,

1985, pp. 23–9, quotation, 25. Until recently, Republic of Ireland passports were coloured green; they are now a standard European Union purple.

10    Ibid., pp. 24 and 29; to footer: from the Irish, 'to act in a bungling manner', T. P. Dolan (ed.), *A Dictionary of Hiberno-English,* Dublin, Gill & Macmillan, 1998, p. 112; to haver: Scottish dialect, 'to hesitate', *Oxford English Dictionary.*

11    For Hamilton see entries 29, 42 and 43.

12    Department of Culture, Media and Sport, *Export of Works of Art, 1997–98: Forty-Fourth Report of the Reviewing Committee (Cm 4056),* London, The Stationery Office, 1998, pp. 20–1.

13    Ibid., p. 15.

14    Ibid., pp. 20–1.

15    For a discussion of Hamilton's pastel, see Fintan Cullen, 'Hugh Douglas Hamilton's Letters to Canova,' *Irish Arts Review,* vol. 1, no. 2, Summer 1984, p. 32.

16    The Hamilton pastel was recently included in the exhibition, Andrew Wilton and Ilaria Bignamini, eds., *Grand Tour: The Lure of Italy in the Eighteenth Century,* London, Tate Gallery, 1996, p. 72.

17    See Anne Crookshank and the Knight of Glin, *The Painters of Ireland, c. 1660–1920,* London, Barrie and Jenkins, 1978, pp. 91–4, and Fintan Cullen, 'The Oil Paintings of Hugh Douglas Hamilton', *Walpole Society,* 50, 1984, pp. 165–208.

18    *Export of Works of Art,* p. 20.

19    Anne Crookshank and the Knight of Glin, *The Watercolours of Ireland: Works on Paper in Pencil, Pastel and Paint, c. 1660–1914,* London, Barrie and Jenkins, 1994, p. 71.

20    Ellis Waterhouse, *Painting in Britain, 1530–1790,* New Haven and London, Yale University Press, 1994.

21    Ibid., pp. 335–6.

22    See Fintan Cullen, *Visual Politics: The Representation of Ireland, 1750–1930,* Cork University Press, 1997, pp. 42–3, and an unpublished 1841 letter from Frederick William Burton to George Petrie, Burton Archive, National Gallery of Ireland.

23    The fullest late-twentieth-century account of Maclise is the Arts Council of Great Britain, *Daniel Maclise,* London, 1972; although Irish portraits and subject pictures are discussed, not enough is made of the artist's origins.

24    For more on this see Fintan Cullen, 'Radicals and Reactionaries: Portraits of the 1790s in Ireland', in Jim Smyth, ed., *Revolution, Counter Revolution and Union: Ireland in the 1790s,* Cambridge University Press, forthcoming.

25    Richard Kearney, *The Irish Mind: Exploring Intellectual Traditions,* Dublin, Wolfhound Press, 1985, pp. 7–9.

# PRESENTATION AND EDITING OF TEXTS

This anthology of sources on Irish art contains 54 entries, ranging from the early eighteenth century to the late twentieth century. The entries have been divided into three main sections:

*Word and Image*
*Making and Viewing*
*Creating Histories.*

The first two of these are divided into two subsections; each containing extracts taken from the eighteenth century to the present day. The final section, *Creating Histories*, is made up of six lengthy extracts from contemporary texts.

Section I, *Word and Image*, is divided into two sections: 'Aesthetic Viewpoints' and 'Focus on the Individual'. The first offers a range of judgements on art as well as theoretical views ranging from philosophers such as George Berkeley to the poet and political commentator Thomas Davis to the present director of the Irish Museum of Modern Art. The 'Focus on the Individual' section moves from Anthony Pasquin's late-eighteenth-century dictionary of artists through a high Victorian celebration of the émigré artist Daniel Maclise to a close analysis of the works of such contemporaries as Louis Le Brocquy and Alice Maher. Section II, *Making and Viewing*, is equally divided in two, offering a range of documents informing us on 'Patronage and Education' and 'Display'. The emphasis here is on the nuts and bolts aspects of art provision in Ireland from the setting up of the Dublin Society Schools in the mid-eighteenth century to recent, late-twentieth-century government attitudes to the arts. Public and private patronage is highlighted just as personal reactions to display are juxtaposed with published statements in journals and newspapers. Finally, Section III, *Creating Histories*, supplies the reader with judicious extracts from half a dozen seminal essays and books which have appeared over the past quarter century, each offering us a more rigorous approach to the discussion of Irish visual imagery than had been available prior to the 1970s.

Each of the three sections carries an introduction as does each extract. Original notes accompanying texts have, on occasion, been maintained as endnotes. These are indicated by the annotation [Orig. note.] and sometimes have been edited. Most extracts carry explanatory endnotes, written by the compiler of this anthology. These serve two purposes, to identify and provide a context for some of the many references in the texts and to indicate further readings on the subject.

The choice of texts has been dictated by historical interest rather than by comprehensiveness. An artist such as Jack Yeats has received far more critical attention than, say, the eighteenth-century portrait painter Hugh Douglas Hamilton. Given that, in Ireland, Yeats is continuously in the public eye, it was decided that he warranted less space in a reader such as this than an artist who still awaits a full monograph. This has resulted in the inclusion of one critical essay on Yeats by Ernie O'Malley (entry 20) and the exclusion of an equally interesting piece on the artist by the art historian and critic Thomas MacGreevy and even the well-known comments on the artist by Samuel Beckett; both of these latter pieces of writing have been recently discussed in a study on Yeats.[1] The corollary of all of this is that MacGreevy appears elsewhere in the anthology as a commentator on modernism in Ireland in the 1920s (entry 46). Sources on Hamilton, by contrast, are not so easy to find without access to a specialist library. To a degree, Hamilton has been used as an exemplum of a successful eighteenth-century Irish artist and references to him appear in a number of entries (see 29, 30, 41–3).

So as to maintain diversity and deter overloading in any one section, the author has decided to emphasize a theme at one particular period at the expense of another historical period. For example, less material on patronage is offered for the twentieth century than for the eighteenth and nineteenth centuries, largely due to the relative richness of the literature on modern artists over their pre-twentieth-century counterparts. At the same time, in Section I, part 2, where the focus is on the individual artist, five out of the nine extracts are from twentieth-century examples with only one from the eighteenth century. The choice here was clear: a consciousness of Irish art was in full evidence in the twentieth century compared with the 1790s, when Pasquin's *An Authentic History of the Progress of Painting . . . in Ireland* (entry 15) was compiled. Pasquin's text is one of the few dictionaries of the period to include Irish references; by contrast, for the twentieth century, the compiler has a host of published artists' autobiographies to choose from, together with a wealth of public exhibitions and accompanying critical catalogues.

The title of a document given in the Contents page or on the top of the entry is the title of the piece as it first appeared either in published or unpublished form. The present source of the document, if published, is cited in the introduction to the entry. An example will clarify this: entry 1 is an extract from George Berkeley's diary of his visit to Italy in 1717. Owing to the fact that there is no self-contained edition of Berkeley's travel journals, the diary extract included here is taken from the section, 'Journals of Travel in Italy', in A.A. Luce and T.E. Jessop's *The Works of George Berkeley, Bishop of Cloyne* (1955), the full citation appearing at the end of the introduction to the extract.[2]

Titles of books and newspapers are given in italics, for example, Burke's *Philosophical Enquiry into the Origin of our Ideas of the Sublime and Beautiful* (entry 2) or Daniel Webb's *Inquiry into the Beauties of Painting* (entry 3), etc. Single quotation marks apply to titles of articles and poems, for example, Thomas Davis's essays (entry 8) or Mainie Jellett's explanation of how she discovered Modernism (entry 12), while as with the above example of George Berkeley, the fully cited sources for all sections of larger works, articles and poems are given in the entry introduction. In the absence of a title, descriptive headings without quotation marks have been given, for example, Richard Mansergh St George's crazy letter of the mid-1790s (entry 4) or

David Wilkie's more sober letters of the mid–1830s (entry 7). The term 'from' preceding a title signifies that a specific extract has been taken from a longer text. When 'from' does not appear the full text has been included. When a text has been edited, deletions are indicated by square brackets with ellipsis [. . .].

Thirty illustrations accompany the selection of texts. These have been chosen according to two main criteria: to illustrate an art object being specifically discussed in a text or on occasion to portray a likeness of the author of a particular entry. Entries 11 and 24 can act as examples for each. Elizabeth Thompson's *Eviction* of 1890 (fig. 3) was painted as the result of an incident observed by the artist in Co. Wicklow, a story she recounts in her 1922 autobiography (entry 11). An important Irish philanthropist, Samuel Madden (entry 24) is remembered as a supporter of the Dublin Society's Drawing Schools in the first half of the eighteenth century. The author of an essay advocating the awarding of prizes to students, the clergyman is shown in Richard Purcell's fine mezzotint after an original portrait by Robert Hunter (fig. 13) seated in his study surrounded by paintings and books. On a number of occasions more than one illustration accompanies an entry (16, 18, 25). In the case of the Mulready section (entry 16), three plates have been taken from the original William Godwin text (figs. 4–6) which would be less useful without these early drawings by the Irish artist. Similarly, in the extract from W. Justin O'Driscoll's *Memoir of Daniel Maclise*, the emphasis is on the description of a number of the artist's literary illustrations, in this case to Sydney Owenson's *Life of Salvator Rosa* and Tom Moore's *Melodies* (figs. 7–9).

## NOTES

1    See Bruce Arnold, *Jack Yeats*, New Haven and London, Yale University Press, 1998, pp. 205–6, 280–4, 326–7.

2    For discussion of Berkeley's travel writings see Edward Chaney, *The Evolution of the Grand Tour: Anglo-Italian Cultural Relations since the Renaissance*, London and Portland, OR, Frank Cass, 1998, chapter 13. For an Italian edition of the journals see T.E. Jessop and M. Fimiani (eds.), *George Berkeley: Viaggio in Italia*, Naples, 1979.

# SECTION I

## WORD AND IMAGE

INTRODUCTION

This section highlights the relationship between the image and the written word. It is divided into two subsections, 'Aesthetic Viewpoints' and 'Focus on the Individual', the emphasis being on the reasoning behind the creation of art in general and on the bond that connects practice and the specificity of the life of the artist involved.

AESTHETIC VIEWPOINTS

One of the most dominant concerns of writers on the visual arts in Ireland from the eighteenth century to the present day has been the discussion of the relationship between art and the nation. From Samuel Madden in the 1730s and Thomas Campbell in the 1760s (who feature in Section 2, 'Making and Viewing', entries 24 and 27) to Thomas Davis in the 1840s (entry 8) and on to present-day museum officials (entry 14), attempts have been made to direct Ireland's involvement with the visual. Madden and Campbell were interested in the logistics of setting up viable academies to train artists while a century later Davis was suggesting (entry 8b) a list of subjects that might redirect Irish artists towards a fuller awareness of their national duty. Attempts to define a national art preoccupied many in the nineteenth century and indeed well into the twentieth century. In the 1820s Sydney Owenson, later Lady Morgan (entry 6), equated the wild spirit of an Italian seventeenth-century artist with the subject-matter of her own Irish novels, while a few years later George Petrie (entry 9) was unequivocal in visualizing emphatically what 'Ireland' is, 'a dark and ruined castle, seated on some rocky height, or the round tower, with its little parent church, in some sequestered valley'. The late twentieth century had more distractions to contend with than the untroubled vision of Petrie. Tom Duddy (entry 13) outlines the problems many Irish artists and Irish art critics have had in relation to mainstream modernism and the overdominant pull of a universalist aesthetic. To Declan McGonagle (entry 14), the answer is not difficult, turn to the local, a word that he would like to see moved up the art agenda.

In reading George Berkeley's Italian journal (entry 1), we notice the highly subjective reactions of an early-eighteenth-century Anglican priest to classical Rome and Renaissance and Baroque Italian art. In offering us intriguing non-Catholic insights to Roman art though his Italian journal, Berkeley may be contrasted with the painter James Barry (entry 5), who wrote from a firmly Romanist frame of mind. Writing some sixty years later in his *Inquiry into the Real and Imaginary Obstructions to the Acquisition of the Arts*, a pamphlet published in 1775, Barry stresses the importance of religion as a key to patronage and the production of art, a view strengthened after many years of living in Rome. It is not until the early twentieth century that we again pick up this connection between art and the spiritual. W.B. Yeats (entry 10) and Mainie Jellett (entry 12) for different reasons turn to the art of China for spiritual guidance, seeking as Jellett says, 'the inner principle and not the outer appearance'.

Edmund Burke's great *Philosophical Enquiry* (entry 2), which first appeared in 1757, is an intensely personal probing of his own responses to poetry and to aesthetics in general.[1] The section included here discusses clearness and obscurity, where Burke compares poetry and painting, deciding that 'poetry with all its obscurity, has a more general as well as a more powerful dominion over the passions than the other art'. Burke's *Enquiry* went though fifteen editions in English in the author's lifetime and one of the later editions may well have fallen into the hands of the deeply troubled Richard Mansergh St George, an Irish landowner who in the mid-1790s wrote a fascinating letter (entry 4) to an as yet unknown artist, requesting a portrait that as described would have all the hallmarks of a Burkian definition of Obscurity. Burke describes Milton's image of Satan as 'crouded and confused', while Mansergh St George conjures up a picture that is also a 'dreadful and strange apparition'.

## FOCUS ON THE INDIVIDUAL

This second subsection of 'Word and Image' turns our attention towards the individual artist. The nine entries focus on just eight Irish artists from the eighteenth century to the present day. James Barry features twice as he is the subject of Anthony Pasquin's short biographical account (entry 15) as well as being the focus of Francis Sylvester Mahony's lengthy satire (entry 17).

This subsection could well have taken over the whole anthology. Lives of individuals and celebratory accounts of artists, not surprisingly, still dominate the historiography of Irish art. Equally, it will come as no surprise that biography features elsewhere in the volume, for example, the playwright John O'Keeffe's reminiscences of attending the Dublin Society Schools in the mid-eighteenth century (entry 30) or the artist-based focus of the work of Anne Crookshank and the Knight of Glin (entry 51; fig. 26). The point of the subsection is to highlight the diversity of forms that colour this concern with biography.

When examined critically, artists, all too often, do not lead lives but satisfy myths. These can be described positively or negatively. Starting with Anthony Pasquin in the 1790s (entry 15), we see in this compilation of Irish artists' lives a focus on one or two character traits for each of his subjects. Barry, for example, is cantankerous and difficult. Here anecdote overtakes fact, a formula used with excessive zeal by Francis Sylvester Mahony, the author of *The Reliques of Father Prout* (entry 17). In Mahony's account, Barry is again seen as aggressive and deeply egotistical, the victim of what Terry Eagleton sees as Mahony's carnivalesque mind, the main features of which are the author's 'abrupt lurchings from the erudite to the everyday, from pokerfaced pedantry to knockabout humour'.[2]

Less negative myth-making colours William Godwin's account of the Irish child prodigy William Mulready (entry 16; figs. 4–6) and W. Justin O'Driscoll's life of Daniel Maclise (entry 18; figs. 7–9). In Godwin's story, racial, economic and familial disadvantages are overcome to produce 'an *Artist*', while O'Driscoll resorts to uncritical celebration. Equally, in the twentieth century, Ernie O'Malley can be insightful in his comments on the form of Jack Yeats's work but, given the former IRA man's own personal investment in a West of Ireland idyll, he cannot but celebrate Yeats's romantic subject matter (fig. 10).

The subject of artists' autobiographies in the modern era is an area in need of some scholarly attention. From the late nineteenth century onwards, numerous British artists, many with Irish connections, such as Lady Butler (entry 11), produced accounts of their careers and were soon followed by their Irish colleagues.[3] Irish-born artists such as Henry Jones Thaddeus and William Orpen as well as John Lavery (entry 19) and Paul Henry (entry 21) are but four of the small band of anecdotally-led self-reflections produced in the first half of the twentieth century.[4] In the two examples included here, myth-making dominates. Lavery, the son of a wine-merchant, casts a gentlemanly amateurish air over his portrait business as he moves effortlessly from dinner with Winston Churchill to painting the dead Michael Collins. Equally, Paul Henry writes of his Gauguin-like isolation on Achill Island during the same troubled period in Ireland's history without once mentioning that his wife, Grace Henry, also a painter, was with him all the time.

Richard Kearney's and Fionna Barber's essays on Le Brocquy and Maher (entries 22 and 23) offer alternative approaches to writing on individual artists. Both authors, as is also the case with Luke Gibbons and Catherine Nash (entries 53 and 54) in the final section, place their subjects firmly within a cultural context and probe a variety of traditions in search of explanations for the finished work. In analysing Le Brocquy's Irishness, Kearney refers to the painter's clear debt to a Celtic visual tradition but pushes that further and explores similarities to James Joyce's fragmented vision (fig. 11). Alice Maher offers Fionna Barber the opportunity to explore an Irish imagination fully in touch with a greater European tradition of subversion and confrontation. The gender imagery in Maher's art (fig. 12) has echoes of surrealism but as Barber shows it also needs to be discussed in relation to the formation of an Irish feminist consciousness.

## NOTES

1    See *The Writings and Speeches of Edmund Burke: I, The Early Writings*, eds. T.O. McLoughlin and James T. Boulton, Oxford, Clarendon Press, 1997, p. 2.

2    Terry Eagleton, *Crazy John and the Bishop and Other Essays on Irish Culture*, Cork University Press, 1998, p. 192.

3    Another British example is *The Reminiscences of Frederick Goodall*, London and Newcastle on Tyne, 1902, pp. 27–33.

4    H.J. Thaddeus, *Recollections of a Court Painter*, London, 1912; W. Orpen, *Stories of Old Ireland and Myself*, London, Williams and Norgate, Ltd., 1924; another is Beatrice, Lady Glenavy's *Today We Will Only Gossip*, London, Constable, 1964.

*Aesthetic Viewpoints*

— 1 —

# George Berkeley, 'First Journal in Italy', 1717

Considered Ireland's greatest philosopher, George Berkeley (1685–1753) was educated at Trinity College Dublin and ordained an Anglican priest in 1710. In 1713 he made his first visit to Italy, travelling only as far south as Florence. His second visit began in November 1716, with Berkeley leaving England for Italy in the company of his pupil St George Ashe, the son of the Bishop of Clogher and Vice-Chancellor of Trinity College Dublin. The tour lasted from 1716 to 1720 and is thought to have been the most extensive British or Irish tour of this period.[1] As a committed Hellenist Berkeley was keen to see examples of original Greek architecture and thus visited Sicily as well as Naples and Rome. In this extract describing his first days in Rome, it is worth noting Berkeley's dimissal of the Byzantine mosaics at S. Paolo fuori le Mura and his delight in the Greek statuary in the Palazzo Farnese while later in the same day, he even has some words of praise for the Baroque sculptor, Gian Lorenzo Bernini, whose *Apollo and Daphne* (1622–5) he viewed in the Villa Borghese. During his travels in Italy, Berkeley kept four pocket notebooks where he commented, at length, on art and architecture and offers the most sustained example of an early eighteenth-century Irishman's fascination with the visual. When reading Berkeley's observations on Roman Catholic art and customs, one must remember that he was, first and foremost, an Anglican cleric.

Source: *The Works of George Berkeley, Bishop of Cloyne*, eds., A.A. Luce and T.E. Jessop, VII, London, Thomas Nelson and Sons, Ltd., 1955, pp. 247–9 (The original journal is in the British Library, Add Ms, 39307)

## JANUARY 9, 1717

Our first visit this day was to the Sepulchre of Cestius.[2] This building is pyramidal, of great smoothed pieces of marble. A considerable part of it is now underground, but what appears is about a hundred foot in length, each side of the square basis, and about a hundred and fifty the side of the pyramid. There is a chamber within in which there have been not many years ago several antique figures painted in fresco. They are now defaced and the entrance made up. This monument lies between the Mons Aventinus and the Mons Testaceus. Having viewed the Sepulchre of Cestius, we ascended the Mons Testaceus, from whence we had a fair prospect of Rome. This mount was formed in the time of old Rome by the Potters, who had this place appointed them for heaping together their rubbish, to prevent their choking the Tiber. You see the mount to be made up of bits of broken potsherds. After this we went along the Via Ostiensis (of wch we cou'd still see some remains) to St Paul's Church.[3] By the wayside we saw a chapel with a bas-relief representing the parting embrace between S: Peter and S: Paul. The inscription tells you this is the spot where those Holy martyrs were parted as they went to their martyrdom, the one (S: Peter) turning to the right to Montorio, the other going to the Tre Fontane. S: Paul's church, wch stands above a mile out of the towne, was built by Constantine; there are nevertheless two ranges of noble Corinthian pillars on both sides of the great Isle, that seem too elegant for that age in which the arts were much on the decline. Probably they belonged to some more ancient building. On the floor of this church we saw a Column of white marble in shape of a Candlestick, for wch purpose it had been made in Constantine's time. It was all over adorned with very rude sculpture. Under the great altar there lie one half of the bodies of S: Peter and S: Paul (the other half being under the great altar of S: Peter's). The rude painting and Mosaic deserves no regard. I must not forget that this Church is very rich in indulgences. We read in an inscription on the wall, that an indulgence of above 6000 years was got by a visit to that church on any ordinary day, but a plenary remission on Christmas and three or four other daies. I asked a priest that stood by, whether by virtue of that remission a man was sure of going straight to Heaven without touching at Purgatory, in case he shou'd then die. His answer was that he certainly wou'd. From this Church we went to that of the three Fountains, four miles from Rome southward.[4] This is a small church built in the place where S: Paul was beheaded. They shew'd us in a Corner of the Church the very pillar of white marble on which his head was cut off. The head, say they, made three leaps, and a fountain sprung up at each leap. These fountains are now shewn in the Church, and strangers never fail to drink of them, there being an indulgence (I think) of a hundred years attending that function. The altar piece of this Church is finely painted by Guido Reni.[5] At a small distance from this Church there is another called Scala Cœli,[6] from a Vision of S: Bernard's, who, say they, as he was celebrating mass in this place saw Angels drawing the souls in Purgatory up to Heaven. This vision we saw painted in the Church. Underneath they tell you are interred 10303 Christian soldiers with the Tribune Zeno, who were picked out of the Roman Army and martyrd in this place. All these odd things are not only told by the monks or friars, but inscribed in marble in the Churches.

## JANUARY, 10, 1717

Mr Hardy, the Abbate Barbieri, Mr Ashe, & I went this morning to see the Famous Farnesian Palace. The gallery so much spoken of proved smaller than I expected, but the painting is excellent, it is all over done in fresco by Annibal Carache.[7] Here and in other parts of the Palace we saw several fine Antique Busts and Statues. The principal are the Hercules commonly called the Farnesian Hercules, the Flora, the Bust of Caracalla, the flesh whereof is wonderfully soft and natural, and an admirable groupe of Zetus, Amphion, Antiope, Dirce, and a Bull all out of one stone, done by two R[h]odians.[8] The two young men, Sons of the Theban King, tie Dirce to the Bull's horns in order to precipitate her into a well (as the Inscription on a tablette hung by the statue tells you). The Bull and the men are incomparably well done, but there is little expression in the face of Dirce wch makes me suspect the head to be modern. The easiness, the strength the beauty, and the muscles of the Hercules cannot be too much admired. The drapery of the Flora is admirable, & the bust of Antoninus Caracalla is flesh & blood. Nothing can be softer. In the afternoon we drove out of town through the porta Collatina, leaving Lucullus's gardens on the left hand and Sallustius's on the right. We got by three a clock of our reckoning to the Villa Borghese. The outside and gardens we had seen before; we spent this afternoon in viewing the Apartments; the greatest part of the pictures are copies. I remember some good ones of Corregio, and the famous Battel of Constantine by Julio Romano. In the apartments of this villa we saw several excellent statues; those most remarkable of the Antique are the Hermaphrodite, the Gladiator, and, on the outside of the wall, that of Curtius on horseback leaping into the Cavern. I must not forget three statues of Bernini in these apartments, that raise my idea of that modern statuary almost to an equality with the famous ancients – Apollo and Daphne, Æneas with Anchises on his shoulders, David going to fling the stone at Goliath. The grace, the softness, and expression of these statues is admirable. In our return we took a walk round part of the walls of the City. Both walls and Turrets were pretty entire on that side. They have stood since Justinian's time, having been built by Bellisarius. We enter'd the city at the porta Viminalis, steped into the Victoria, a beautiful church incrusted with ornaments of the richest stones, as Jallo Antico, Verde antico, Jaspers, &c.⁹ In this are hung up trophies taken from the Turks. After this, we paid a second visit to Dioclesian's Baths, admiring the lofty remains of that stupendous Fabrick, which is now possessed by the Carthusians.¹⁰ In the pavement of the Church, made out of the standing part of the baths, we saw a meridian line (like that of Bologna) drawn by the learned Bianchini.

## NOTES

1    John Ingamells, *A Dictionary of British and Irish Travellers in Italy, 1701–1800*, New Haven and London, Yale University Press, 1997, p. 81, and Edward Chaney, 'George Berkeley's Grand Tours: The Immaterialist as Connoisseur of Art and Architecture', in his *The Evolution of the Grand Tour: Anglo-Italian Cultural Relations since the Renaissance*, London and Portland, Frank Cass, OR, 1998, pp. 314–65. Chaney comments at length on Berkeley's diary observations.

2    Pyramid of Gaius Cestius, *c.* 12 B.C., set in the Aurelian wall next to Porta San Paolo.

3    S. Paolo fuori le Mura, 4th Century Basilica, destroyed by fire in 1823 and rebuilt.

4    San Paolo alle Tre Fontane.

5    *Crucifixion of St Peter*, 1604–5, now in the Vatican Museums.

6    Santa Maria Scala Coeli.

7    Palazzo Farnese, now the French Embassy; frescoes made by Annibale Carraci, 1597–1600.

8    Mainly now in the Museo Nazionale, Naples.

9    S. Maria della Vittoria. Ten days later Berkeley returned to this church to admire Bernini's *St Teresa in Ecstasy*.

10   S. Maria degli Angeli; converted by Michelangelo into a church in 1563.

# — 2 —

# Edmund Burke, *A Philosophical Enquiry into the Origin of Our Ideas of the Sublime and Beautiful*, 1759

Primarily remembered as a London-based statesman attached to the Whig interest, Burke (1729–97) was also the author of one of the most influential eighteenth-century treatises on aesthetics. Descended from a Catholic family, he was born in Dublin but was involved in Westminster parliamentary life from the mid-1760s onwards. While still a student at Trinity College Dublin, and perhaps inspired by an interest in painting, he conceived the basic arguments of *A Philosophical Enquiry*, although it was not published until 1757 (and then anonymously). His interest in painting also persuaded him, some years later, to finance the Irish artist James Barry's sojourn in Rome (see entry 28). The extract included here from the *Enquiry* discusses the difference between clearness and obscurity, as well as the differences between poetry and painting. The confident tone of Burke's arguments, which so inspired the young James Barry, are also found in his *Essay on Taste*, which appeared with the second edition of the *Enquiry*, published in 1759.[1]

Source: Edmund Burke, *A Philosophical Enquiry into the Origin of our Ideas of the Sublime and Beautiful*, ed. James T. Boulton, rev. ed., Oxford, Basil Blackwell, 1987, pp. 18–20, 60–64. Some of Boulton's original notes have been included.

## ESSAY ON TASTE

Now as the pleasure of resemblance is that which principally flatters the imagination, all men are nearly equal in this point, as far as their knowledge of the things represented or compared extends. The principle of this knowledge is very much accidental, as it depends upon experience and observation, and not on the strength or weakness of any natural faculty; and it is from this difference in knowledge that what we commonly, though with no great exactness, call a difference in Taste proceeds. A man to whom sculpture is new, sees a barber's block, or some ordinary piece of statuary; he is immediately struck and pleased, because he sees something like an human figure; and entirely taken up with this likeness, he does not at all attend to its defects. No person, I believe, at the first time of seeing a piece of imitation ever did. Some time after, we suppose that this novice lights upon a more artificial work of the same nature; he now begins to look with contempt on what he admired at first; not that he admired it even then for its unlikeness to a man, but for that general though inaccurate resemblance which it bore to the human figure. What he admired at different times in these so different figures, is strictly the same; and though his knowledge is improved, his Taste is not altered. Hitherto his mistake was from a want of knowledge in art, and this arose from his inexperience; but he may be still deficient from a want of knowledge in nature. For it is possible that the man in question may stop here, and that the masterpiece of a great hand may please him no more than the middling performance of a vulgar artist; and this not for want of better or higher relish, but because all men do not observe with sufficient accuracy on the human figure to enable them to judge properly of an imitation of it. And that the critical Taste does not depend upon a superior principle in men, but upon superior knowledge, may appear from several instances. The story of the ancient painter and the shoemaker is very well known. The shoemaker set the painter right with regard to some mistakes he had made in the shoe of one of his figures, and which the painter, who had not made such accurate observations on shoes, and was content with a general resemblance, had never observed.[2] But this was no impeachment to the Taste of the painter, it only shewed some want of knowledge in the art of making shoes. Let us imagine that an anatomist had come into the painter's working room. His piece is in general well done, the figure in question in a good attitude, and the parts well adjusted to their various movements; yet the anatomist, critical in his art, may observe the swell of some muscle not quite just in the peculiar action of the figure. Here the anatomist observes what the painter had not observed, and he passes by what the shoemaker had remarked. But a want of the last critical knowledge in anatomy no more reflected on the natural good Taste of the painter, or of any common observer of his piece, than the want of an exact knowledge in the formation of a shoe. A fine piece of a decollated head of St John the Baptist was shewn to a Turkish emperor; he praised many things, but he observed one defect; he observed that the skin did not shrink from the wounded part of the neck.[3] The sultan on this occasion, though his observation was very just, discovered no more natural Taste than the painter who executed this piece, or than a thousand European connoisseurs who probably never would have made the same observation. His Turkish majesty had indeed been well acquainted with that terrible spectacle, which the others could only have represented in their imagination. On the subject of their dislike there is a difference between all these people, arising from the different kinds and degrees of their knowledge; but there is something in common to the painter, the shoemaker, the anatomist, and the Turkish emperor, the pleasure arising from a natural object, so far as each perceives it justly imitated; the satisfaction in seeing an agreeable figure; the sympathy proceeding from a striking and affecting incident. So far as Taste is natural, it is nearly common to all.

A PHILOSOPHICAL ENQUIRY INTO THE ORIGIN OF OUR IDEAS OF THE SUBLIME AND BEAUTIFUL

*Section IV*
Of the difference between CLEARNESS and OBSCURITY with regard to the passions

It is one thing to make an idea clear, and another to make it *affecting* to the imagination. If I make a drawing of a palace, or a temple, or a landscape, I present a very clear idea of those objects; but then (allowing for the effect of imitation which is something) my picture can at most affect only as the palace, temple, or landscape would have affected in the reality. On the other hand, the most lively and spirited verbal description I can give, raises a very obscure and imperfect *idea* of such objects; but then it is in my power to raise a stronger *emotion* by the description than I could do by the best painting. This experience constantly evinces. The proper manner of conveying *the affections* of the mind from one to another, is by words; there is a great insufficiency in all other methods of communication; and so far is a clearness of imagery from being absolutely necessary to an influence upon the passions, that they may be considerably operated upon without presenting any image at all, by certain sounds adapted to that purpose; of which we have a sufficient proof in the acknowledged and powerful effects of instrumental music. In reality a great clearness helps but little towards affecting the passions, as it is in some sort an enemy to all enthusiasms whatsoever.

*Section [IV]*
The same subject continued
There are two verses in Horace's art of poetry that seem to contradict this opinion, for which reason I shall take a little more pains in clearing it up. The verses are,

> *Segnius inritant animos demissa per aurem*
> *Quam quae sunt oculis subjecta fidelibus.*[4]

On this the abbe du Bos founds a criticism, wherein he gives painting the preference to poetry in the article of moving the passions; principally on account of the greater *clearness* of the ideas it represents.[5] I believe this excellent judge was led into this mistake (if it be a mistake) by his system, to which he found it more conformable than I imagine it will be found to experience. I know several who admire and love painting, and yet who regard the objects of their admiration in that art, with coolness enough, in comparison of that warmth with which they are animated by affecting pieces of poetry or rhetoric. Among the common sort of people, I never could perceive that painting had much influence on their passions. It is true that the best sorts of painting, as well as the best sorts of poetry, are not much understood in that sphere. But it is most certain, that their passions are very strongly roused by a fanatic preacher, or by the ballads of Chevy-chase,[6] or the children in the wood, and by other little popular poems and tales that are current in that rank of life. I do not know of any paintings, bad or good, that produce the same effect. So that poetry with all its obscurity, has a more general as well as a more powerful dominion over the passions than the other art. And I think there are reasons in nature why the obscure idea, when properly conveyed, should be more affecting than the clear. It is our ignorance of things that causes all our admiration, and chiefly excites our passions. Knowledge and acquaintance make the most striking causes affect but little. It is thus with the vulgar, and all men are as the vulgar in what they do not understand. The ideas of eternity, and infinity, are among the most affecting we have, and yet perhaps there is nothing of which we really understand so little, as of infinity and eternity. We do not any where meet a more sublime description than this justly celebrated one of Milton, wherein he gives the portrait of Satan with a dignity so suitable to the subject.

> He above the rest
> In shape and gesture proudly eminent
> Stood like a tower; his form had yet not lost
> All her original brightness, nor appeared
> Less than archangel ruin'd, and th' excess
> Of glory obscured: as when the sun new ris'n
> Looks through the horizontal misty air
> Shorn of his beams; or from behind the moon
> In dim eclipse disastrous twilight sheds
> On half the nations; and with fear of change
> Perplexes monarchs.[7]

Here is a very noble picture; and in what does this poetical picture consist? in images of a tower, an archangel, the sun rising through mists, or in an eclipse, the ruin of monarchs, and the revolutions of kingdoms. The mind is hurried out of itself, by a croud of great and confused images; which affect because they are crouded and confused. For separate them, and you lose much of the greatness, and join them, and you infallibly lose the clearness. The images raised by poetry are always of this obscure kind; though in general the effects of poetry, are by no means to be attributed to the images it raises; which point we shall examine more at large hereafter. But painting, when we have allowed for the pleasure of imitation, can only affect simply by the images it presents; and even in painting a judicious obscurity in some things contributes to the effect of the picture; because the images in painting are exactly similar to those in nature; and in nature dark, confused, uncertain images have a greater power on the fancy to form the grander passions than those have which are more clear and determinate. But where and when this observation may be applied to practice, and how far it shall be extended, will be better deduced from the nature of the subject, and from the occasion, than from any rules that can be given.

I am sensible that this idea has met with opposition, and is likely still to be rejected by several. But let it be considered that hardly any thing can strike the mind with its greatness, which does not make some sort of approach towards infinity; which nothing can do whilst we are able to perceive its bounds; but to see an object distinctly, and to perceive its bounds, is one and the same thing. A clear idea is therefore another name for a little idea. There is a passage in the book of Job amazingly sublime, and this sublimity is principally due to the terrible uncertainty of the thing described. *In thoughts from the visions of the night, when deep sleep falleth upon men, fear came upon me and trembling, which made all my bones to shake. Then a spirit passed before my face. The hair of my flesh stood up. It stood still,* but I could not discern the form thereof; *an image was before mine eyes; there was silence; and I heard a voice, – Shall mortal man be more just than God?*[8] We are first prepared with the utmost solemnity for the vision; we are first terrified, before we are let even into the obscure cause of our emotion; but when this grand cause of terror makes its appearance, what is it? is it not, wrapt up in the shades of its own incomprehensible darkness more aweful, more striking, more terrible, than the liveliest description, than the clearest painting could possibly represent it? When painters have attempted to give us clear representations of these very fanciful and terrible ideas, they have I think almost always failed; insomuch that I have been at a loss, in all the pictures I have seen of hell, whether the painter did not intend something ludicrous. Several painters have handled a subject of this kind, with a view of assembling as many horrid phantoms as their imagination could suggest; but all the designs I have chanced to meet of the temptations of St Anthony, were rather a sort of odd wild grotesques, than any thing capable of producing a serious passion. In all these subjects poetry is very happy. Its apparitions, its chimeras, its harpies, its allegorical figures, are grand and affecting; and though Virgil's Fame,[9] and Homer's Discord,[10] are obscure, they are magnificent figures. These of figures in painting would be clear enough, but I fear they might become ridiculous.


## NOTES

1    For some recent discussion of the relevance of Burke's *Enquiry* to Irish aesthetics, see Joep Leerssen, *Mere Irish and Fíor-Ghael Studies in the Idea of Irish Nationality, its Development and Literary Expression prior to the Nineteenth Century*, Cork University Press, 1996, pp. 67–76, and Luke Gibbons, 'Topographies of Terror: Killarney and the Politics of the Sublime', *The South Atlantic Quarterly*, 95:1, Winter 1996, pp. 23–44.

2    This story is told of the Greek painter Apelles, in Pliny, *Historia Naturalis*, XXXV, 84–5. It also appears in Roger De Piles, *Abregé de la vie des peintres* (Paris, 1699), pp. 125–6. This work was translated into English in 1706; a second edition in 1744 may have been Burke's source. A contemporary reference to the story of Apelles is found in Johnson, *Rambler*, No. 4 (31 March 1750). [Orig. note.]

3    The painter in this story was Gentile Bellini (*c.* 1421–1508). The story appears in Carlo Ridolfi, *Le Maraviglie Dell'Arte* (Venice, 1648), I, 40, and also in De Piles, *Abregé de la vie des peintres,* pp. 250–1 (English translation, 1744, p. 158). Burke does not quite complete the story: the Emperor, Mahomet II, to prove the validity of his criticism, ordered a slave to be beheaded so that Bellini might see how the skin shrank back from the wound. [Orig. note.]

4    *De Arte Poetica*, II, 180–1. [Translated, 'Less vividly is the mind stirred by what finds entrance through the ears than by what is brought before the trusty eyes', Horace, *Satires, Epistles, Ars Poetica*, trans. H. Ruston Fairclough, London, Heinemann, 1966, p. 465.] [Orig. note.]

5    *Réflexions critiques sur la poësie et sur la peinture* (Paris, 6th edn, 1755), I, 416 ff. [Orig. note.]

6    Addison had written on *Chevy Chase* in *Spectator*, Nos. 70 and 74. [Orig. note.]

7    *Paradise Lost*, I, 589–99. [Orig. note.]

8    *Job*, IV, 13–17. [Orig. note.]

9    *Aeneid*, IV, 173 ff. [Orig. note.]

10    *Iliad*, IV, 440–5. [Orig. note.]

# — 3 —

# Daniel Webb, *An Inquiry into the Beauties of Painting*, 1760

A critic and theorist, Webb (1719?–98) was born in Limerick and studied at Oxford. In 1760 he published *An Inquiry into the Beauties of Painting*, the first of a number of theoretical studies on art. It was followed by *Remarks on the Beauty of Poetry* (London, 1762; Dublin, 1764). In 1755 Webb was in Italy where he purchased what he purported to be 'two Albani's, a copy of Coregio [*sic*] by Carache [*sic*], and a . . . Parmegianino [as well as] a capital piece by Julio Romano'.[1] While in Rome, Webb befriended the Dresden-born artist Anton Raffael Mengs (1728–79). Mengs painted Webb's portrait and shared many of his theories on art with his Irish friend, including granting him access to the manuscript of *Gedanken über die Schönheit* ('Thoughts on Beauty', published in 1762). Later, that other great Rome-based theorist, Johann Joachim Winckelmann (1717–68), was to accuse Webb of plagiarism, saying that *The Beauties of Painting* was similar to Mengs's text in its views on Raphael. In time, Webb was widely read; Diderot admired him as did James Barry, while three German editions of *The Beauties of Painting* appeared in 1771.[2] Webb stated that he wrote *The Beauties of Painting* for 'young travellers, who set out with much eagerness, and little preparation; and who, for want of some governing object to determine their course, must continually wander, misled by ignorant guides, or bewildered by a multiplicity of directions'.[3] The book is arranged, as was fashionable with theoretical discourses, as a dialogue, in this case between plain 'A' and 'B'. It covers seven areas of concern ranging from 'Our Capacity to Judge of Painting', 'The Antiquity and Usefulness of Painting', 'Of Design', 'Of Colouring', 'Of the Clear Obscure' and, as in this extract, 'Of Composition'. This section from Dialogue 7 shows Webb's preference for the controlled classicism of Raphael and Leonardo over the elegance of the seventeenth-century Baroque painters.

Source: Daniel Webb, *An Inquiry into the Beauties of Painting and into the Merits of the Most Celebrated Painters, Ancient and Modern*, London, 1760, pp. 136–40

A.   History Painting is the representation of a momentary drama: we may therefore, in treating of composition, borrow our ideas from the stage;

and divide it into two parts, the scenery and the drama. The excellence of the first, consists in a pleasing disposition of the figures which comprise the action. However trifling the pleasure we receive from this may appear to some, it is certain, that it is founded on nature, and of course must merit our attention. If we look on a clear night on a starry sky, our eyes presently fix on those parts, where the stars are (if I may so term it) grouped into constellations. The mind, indifferent to a loose unideal dispersion, seeks for something of system and economy; and catches at every image of contrivance and design. Perhaps too, there may be something of harmony in a particular arrangement of objects; similar to that, which strikes us, on the correspondence of sounds, or flatters us, in the union of colours.

B.    Whatever the principle may be, we cannot doubt of the effect. The eye charmed with the elegant distribution of a Lanfranc, or Pietro di Cortona, looks with coldness on the scattered compositions of a Domenichino; and often wishes for something more flattering in those of the great Raphael.[4]

A.    Your observation, so far as it touches Raphael, shews the necessity of a distinction in this place. The disposition, of which we have been speaking hitherto, is purely picturesque: But there is a second kind, which we may call the expressive. When many persons are present at an action, in which they are interested, it naturally sets them in motion, their movements will depend on their characters and feeling; anger, love, or astonishment, shall with propriety be expressed by single figures; whilst others shall be collected into parties, or groupes, to communicate their fears, doubts, beliefs, and the like. Thus, in that inimitable picture by Leonardo da Vinci, when Christ, at supper with his disciples, declares, that one of them shall betray him; they all instantly take the alarm.[5] One of the youngest, rising from his seat, his hands crossed on his breast, looks at Christ with an action full of love and attachment to his person; the zealous and impatient St Peter, throws himself a-cross two or three others, and whispers to the beloved disciple, who is next to Christ; no doubt, to ask his master who it should be. The rest are divided into parties, reasoning and disputing on their different sentiments. It is easy to perceive that the artist, intent on giving a full expression to the sentiments and passions becoming the occasion, considered the disposition of his picture merely as it tended to explain or add force to his principal action. This will ever be the case with the greatest painters: they may set a just value on the scenery of their piece, but never sacrifice to that the expression of their subject. When Christ gives the keys to Peter, nothing is more natural, than that the disciples should all crowd together, to be witnesses of an action which so much concerned them. This disposition is true and excessive, but by no means picturesque: Raphael was too wise to flatter the eye at the expense of the understanding; yet where they could both be indulged with propriety, his composition was no less picturesque than expressive. In his St Paul preaching at Athens, the disposition in general is not only pleasing, but the groups are well imaged, and happily connected.[6] In short, the true difference between these artists, is this, with Raphael and Leonardo da Vinci, disposition is an accessory; with Lanfranc and Pietro di Cortona, it is not only a principal, but comprehends too often the whole merit of the picture.

## NOTES

1    Letter to Lord Huntingdon, quoted in John Ingamells, *A Dictionary of British and Irish Travellers in Italy, 1701–1800*, New Haven and London, Yale University Press, 1997, p. 983. The actual paintings by Francesco Albani (1578–1660), Annibale Carracci (1560–1609), Francesco Parmigianino (1503–40) and Giulio Romano (c. 1492–1546) have not been traced.

2    Steffi Roettgen, *Anton Raphael Mengs, 1728–1779, and his British Patrons*, London, Zwemmer/English Heritage, 1993, p. 18. See also Johann Dobai, *Die Kunstliteratur des Klassizismus und der Romantik in England*, 4 vols., Berne, 1975, II, pp. 718–34, and *The Works of James Barry*, ed. Edward Fryer, 2 vols., London, 1809, I, p. 373.

3    Daniel Webb, *An Inquiry into the Beauties of Painting and into the Merits of the Most Celebrated Painters, Ancient and Modern*, London, 1760, vi.

4    Giovanni Lanfranco (1582–1647), Pietro da Cortona (1596–1669), Domenichino (1581–1641) and Raphael (1483–1520).

5    Leonardo da Vinci (1452–1519), *Last Supper*, Sta. Maria delle Grazie, Milan, 1497.

6    Here Webb is referring to two Raphael compositions of 1515, *The Giving of the Keys* and *St Paul at Athens*, tapestry designs for the Sistine Chapel in the Vatican; the cartoons for both are in the Victoria and Albert Museum, London.

$$- \ 4 \ -$$

# Richard Mansergh St George,
# letter to an artist, early 1790s

Written in the early 1790s, this letter to an unidentified artist describes a portrait which seems never to have been painted. The letter was composed by
Richard Mansergh St George (1756/9–98), a Galway landowner, who in
1791 or 1792 lost his wife, Anne Stepney, perhaps in childbirth, leaving him
with two small boys. For reasons that become obvious in the text, the letter
may have been sent to the well-known Swiss-born artist Henry Fuseli
(1741–1825), but no record of a painting by that artist corresponds to St
George's demands. The only known portrait of St George is Hugh Douglas
Hamilton's fine full-length in the National Gallery of Ireland which dates
from about 1796–8 (see entry 43 for a contemporary review of this painting).[1] The letter is a fascinating exercise in the fashionable late-eighteenth-
century Gothic sensibility and, in the context of the troubled 1790s in
Ireland, it reflects aspects of Terry Eagleton's definition of the Protestant
Gothic, where 'nothing lent itself more to the genre than the decaying gentry in their crumbling houses, isolated and sinisterly eccentric, haunted by
the sins of the past . . . For Gothic is the nightmare of the besieged and
reviled . . . of a minority marooned with a largely hostile people to whom
they are socially, religiously and ethnically alien.'[2] In early 1798 St George
was brutally murdered by a gang of intruders.

Source: St George's letter is in a private collection; a copy is on file in the
National Gallery of Ireland.[3]

My Dear Sir,

   I wish my meaning could be conveyed to you without my expressing it.
You can never believe That a picture is important to the future welfare of my
Children and to other objects of equal moment[;] you will conceive either
That I am mad or That I affect to be extraordinary – This being the age of
affectation God knows I affect nothing. – Infamy or celebrity is equal to Me
– assuredly equal except as they relate to my Children – The fact is I have lost
all – the balm of Life, the vital principle is destroyd.[4] [I] would give millions,

if I possessed Them to feel what Grief [is] as I have heard people talk of it – I want a Crisis – Two more beautiful and promising babes perhaps never blessed a Father[.] I am grateful for the blessing – but there's a dreadful subtlety – real as it is subtle – They are [a] blessing as a man of reason and religion I am convinced and acknowledge[.] They are so but The blessing affords Me not happiness, not comfort, not a moments ease, nor diversion of Thought but agony to madness[;] yet I woud pour out my blood in Thanks my Life in torture drop by drop were it acceptable to the God who I adore and love more in misfortune than in the most properous and flattering moments of my Life – They leave me on wednesday the Eldest for Inoculation and in the state of my health and mind and the Long absence in a Country insalutory to Me which my affairs necessarily occasion[.] It is at least probable I may see them no more[;] yet I part with them with as much indifference almost as I shoud separate myself from Their pictures, tho their future happiness [and] Education employd my Thoughts in moments I wish to God I could forget and produced volumes of Instructions to Their Guardians in the Intervals of Convulsive fits, in Intervals more terrible and painful to Me –

To what purpose is all This –? To possess you If possible with the Infinite Loss I have sustained the Infinite superior value of what I have been deprived of, and Thence by a simple deduction of the Importance to me at least or rather my children of the picture which you alone can paint – If I were a Prince my history would interest nations and ages – and perhaps Create Painters and Poets – This looks like pretence of being an Extraordinary person – o God That I could but for Three hours in 24 be at Ease and the most Obscure of mankind – I have not one second of Ease – No Effort nor medicine no trick can procure it – I take laudanum by advice – I try to divert thoughts pain by every method every one proposes – I take snuff – I walk till I am fatigued[,] read write weary myself drink wine – but in vain – I resist. – I give way – sit quiet [–] run from room to room[,] from seat to Seat[,] talk with Servants[,] look out at the window[,] out the door[,] Eat against appetite, but I can not as I have in the pain of the body obtain momentary Ease by change – I can not weep – I have tried mechanical means to do it – This (jargon as it is) has too much the air of description for real suffering – But it is (and painful is the Expression) To Impress you how important to me the Picture I mentioned.

I am urged by the Most powerful motives That actuate human nature, I mean human Nature sublimed and rendered exquisitely sensible by Education and habits and circumstances peculiar as mine – by a nervous and too susceptible frame by disease calamity and Reflection of neglected duties and affections ill rewarded. I am urged I say by These and many more powerful motives, affection, sympathies, Regrets[,] Providence towards my Children &cc to Leave behind me The Circumstances of my Life from 16 years old – Instructions shall be given to my Executors &c That The Volumes containing it shall not till they arrive at a Certain age be taken out of the place where they shall be deposited – and given Them to read – or rather The Key given them – They [shall] not [be] solicited or urged to Read them – None having previously seeen them – the Volumes I mean.

This has a Strange romantic air – but there is coud [sic] you see the whole a meaning not extravagant or unwise or frivolous in this – No frivolous mystery – but how shall I impress you with This – ? Now to the point[.] The dreadful[5] Picture (which I will never see) you are to paint for my children and Posterity shall not be seen (nor known) to any Person till they arrive at mature years.

In the Mansion house I shall build a room where it shall be deposited, so as to be preserved from injury of time and weather in which I shall advise with you. Instructions shall be left so managed that the time I may reasonably conceive their most impressionable and most permanently so, without any previous intimation of it, suddenly The Images of their Father and Mother may appear to Them in the terrible circumstances I have conveyed to you. I have a material purpose in this which may be frustrated perhaps, it depends on their nature, but I conceive This dreadful and strange apparition may by a sudden and powerful impulse (inducing them eagerly to read the history contained in the volumes which shall be deposited in a Trunk in the room with the Picture of which they shall have had no previous intimation) produce the effects I wish for and hourly fill my thoughts. [. . .]

Here is a novel circumstance you will say. I cannot help it but I have purposes of important Reality to effect by it. Ten minutes conversation with you would explain and elucidate my meaning more than volumes in writing could[.] I endure the pain of expressing such conceptions methodically and considerately as a man should do who writes or speaks to be understood, but this would be to near burning iron in one's hand [. . .] all I expect knowing you that these hints, scattered wildly and in agony before you, you will collect my meaning. I have this hope also, you are not born in equal times. (This is no time to flatter) I mean the times and that you well know are not appropriate to you – and better, or should I say, greater times may arrive, lesser cannot, I conceive therefore (for where ourself does not blend or unite nothing great is ever done nor can be done.) that your fame will unite with my purpose. I have said I will never see the Picture because I know the pain from the terrible original, it may appear strange, but having as it were transferred the Image to you, it will cease to haunt me I feel the more I think I have impressed you with it that I am delivered from it, otherwise I believe, my dear Sir, it would drive me into madness and kill me [. . .] Let me for Gods sake finally as to my part get through it –

There was a circumstance, not imaginary, Dr Brain assured me he perceived the same sometime before the fatal end of all a cold damp vapour from the living which came in gales circuitously (not like a breath) as from a vault – O God. The Lungs destroyed – all hollow within – O God – This may be useful to you, not to paint but a terrible circumstance that would excite a kind of horror in a poet would urge as it were sympathetic madness a painter like you to produce some strange and unconceived circumstance in painting analogous to that which belongs more to poetry. [. . .]

These are not words to express myself – but the circumstance is too terrible. You will conceive it – Thank God This is done – I will take another sheet. Now My very Dear Sir I feel more composed.

If I should have health enough to return to England, on these hereto we may speak without the dreadful deliberate pain of opening such a subject. In case I should die, (I think I am dying, That is the arrow in my side), I shall leave instructions with my executors that Henry Fusile is to be paid the price he demands for a Picture concerning which he has my instructions; (without mentioning what the subject of the Picture is) and I shall also add that Henry Fusile has my instructions concerning the disposal of the Picture, of which no Person is to enquire, and I inform my executors not to mention this circumstance nor to ask any questions of H. Fusile nor require the Picture of him.

I shall take means to prevent any conjectures of extravagance relative to this. I shall transmit to you instructions how to dispose of the Picture. This understanding is in Case of my Death previous to our conversing on the subject and your painting my face etc from the sad original.

If I die before this, a miniature painted here, more like than miniatures usually are, shall be transmitted to you, also a Drawing in black chalk as large as reality, made at Naples by Clerk considered like. Pope, the Actor in Half Moon Street, has made from this a Coloured Crayon Picture which is in his possession – why he thought my face worthy as in a Gallery I don't know. Besides you will have access to the Picture by Gainsborough of me which you have seen. This when a youth. The black Chalk and Crayon when I was several years younger, but from your remembrance probably of my face and your Imagination you will make a sufficient historical resemblance conceiving the expression of convulsive horror and Incurability, Delirium I should say, in my countenance![6]

I could conceive the blessed Dying Countenance close to mine was some supernatural Creature that had torn my wife from me. This was what I now recollect: the dreadful suggestion – and I attempted to destroy or contend with it – O God – The Ghastly Morning seen gleaming on us . . . all windows open and doors . . . conceive me by care and years grown haggard – my hair and beard are white as snow – and I am an aged man in appearance, though just advancing on middle age . . . The blessed countenance I would perpetuate you will see at Romney's, painted three weeks after the physicians informed me of the fatal symptoms.[7]

If I live, you will have a proper model for that dreary subject. I am daily visited with convulsive attacks – three this very day – melted down also by nightly hallucinations and dreadful visions and suggestions – sudden delirium also – yesterday one terrible to recollect – and many more a few days previously –

Dr Brain says they will not settle into melancholy madness as I apprehended by reason of what is the most painful of all affecting human nature.

NOTES

1    See Fintan Cullen, *Visual Politics: The Representation of Ireland, 1750–1930*, Cork University Press, 1997, pp. 104–15.
2    Terry Eagleton, *Heathcliff and the Great Hunger: Studies in Irish Culture*, London and New York, Verso, 1995, pp. 188–9.
3    The letter has also been published by David H. Weinglass, ed., *The Collected English Letters of Henry Fuseli*, Millwood, NY, London and Nendeln, Liechtenstein, Krauss International Publications, 1982, pp. 66–71.
4    'gone' has been deleted.
5    'sad' has been deleted.
6    References here are possibly to John Clerk (1728–1812), an amateur artist and son of John Clerk of Penicuik, Scotland; Alexander Pope (1763–1835), a Dublin-trained pastellist and miniaturist, was in London by the 1780s. The Gainsborough is not recorded.
7    St George's wife, Anne Stepney, was painted by Romney in July/August 1791, see H. Ward and W. Roberts, *Romney: A Biographical and Critical Essay with a Catalogue Raisonne of his Works*, 1904, vol. 2, p. 138. In the painting she appears with one of her sons. The painting is now in the Heckscher Museum, Huntington, New York, and is reproduced in Fintan Cullen, 'Hugh Douglas Hamilton, "painter of the heart" ', *Burlington Magazine*, CXXV, July 1983, p. 419.

# — 5 —

# James Barry, *Works*, 1809

Barry (1741–1806) is one of the most important painters that Ireland has produced yet his dedication to history painting and an art of high moral intent left him in constant penury and seriously undervalued by his contemporaries. Born in Cork, he came under the patronage of Edmund Burke and studied in Italy for a number of years (see entry 28). Returning to London in 1771, he spent the next thirty years attempting to inculcate British taste with a respect for the ancients and the great names of the Italian Renaissance. He did this with both his brush and his pen. As a writer, Barry published numerous public letters and pamphlets as well as delivering lectures to the students of the Royal Academy where he was Professor of Painting. As a Catholic, his attachment to Rome was constant. Living in late-eighteenth-century London he encountered little toleration for his religion associated as it was with despotism and absolutism. The first extract from his writings included here, a chapter from *The Inquiry into the Real and Imaginary Obstructions to the Acquisition of the Arts in England*, highlights the importance of religion in his thought and work. Written on his return to London, *The Inquiry* (1775) dismisses an argument put forward by, among others, Johann Joachim Winckelmann (1717–68), the great German connoisseur and theorist of classical Greece, that Britain's temperate climate prevented the development of a visual tradition comparable to that of the Mediterranean countries. In his counter-attack, Barry gives the role of religion a more central position in the history of European development.[1]

In time, Barry's preoccupation with religion and national themes surfaced in his discussion of his series of murals in the Great Hall of the Society for the Encouragement of Arts, Manufactures and Commerce, in central London.[2] In the second extract from his writings, Barry's letter to the society in 1793, he discusses the main painting of his cycle, *Elysium and Tartarus or the State of Final Retribution*, explaining why it is populated with philosophers and Christians. Barry describes changes he has made to the original design and points out the error he had originally made in giving the Quaker William Penn (1644–1718) the claim for religious toleration in North America when the award should have gone to Cecil Calvert, 2nd Lord Baltimore, a Roman Catholic (1606–1675) with an Irish title (fig. 1).[3]

Barry was always serious, as his friend and editor Edward Fryer commented in his Preface to Barry's *Works*, 'Mr Barry's views were invariably fixed to one great point – to give the fine arts elevation by directing them to ethical and national purposes, and to this end, the efforts of his pencil were a constant commentary on the text which his pen produced.'[4]

Source: *The Works of James Barry, Esq., Historical Painter,* ed. Dr Edward Fryer, 2 vols., London, 1809, vol. 2, pp. 210–14 (Barry's footnotes have been omitted); pp. 447–50 and 457–9

A) *The Inquiry into the Real and Imaginary Obstructions to the Acquisition of the Arts in England, 1775*

'The Introduction of Superior art in England prevented by the accidental change of religion.'

Now we have shewn to what causes we might properly ascribe the rise, success, and different perfections of art in the countries where it had existed; let us turn ourselves to the British dominions; and if it be evident that the same opportunities and advantages did not concur to favour our acquisition of the arts, but on the contrary that everything was diametrically opposite, we can therefore, with every colour of reason and truth exculpate that climate and that genius which were never put to a fair trial of the extent of their powers. It will appear that the accidental circumstance of the change of religion, which happened just at the time we should have set out in the arts, gave us a dislike to the superior and nobler parts; the subjects of Christian story, which might be generally understood and felt, were then prohibited, so that, except landscape, portrait, and still life, every thing else was either unintelligible or uninteresting to the people at large: the artists were then naturally led to practise only the baser and lower branches. The farther they advanced in these, the wider they wandered from the truth and dignity of art; and we should, no doubt, have gone on past all hope of recovery, had it not been for another accident, as little connected with climate as the former; I mean our cultivation of Greek, Italian, and French literature, where we unavoidably acquired something of a just taste for the fine arts: but as we were at the same time growing up amidst the corruptions of debased art, infections variously communicated, have hitherto exceedingly retarded our progress, and it is not over likely that they will be very soon totally removed.

Francis I and Henry VIII lived in the same time; and, with respect to the arts, the two countries of England and France were in the same state of ignorance and barbarism; their buildings were Gothic; they both painted upon glass; and it is hard to say which of them was the worst in their monuments of sculpture. But Francis had been in Italy, from whence he brought to his own country many monuments of sound art for his people to form themselves by. With this view he invited L. da Vinci, Rosso, Primaticcio, Nicolo del Abate, Cellini,[5] and many other great artists into his service. By his order Battista della Palla was stripping Florence of all the pictures, sculptures, &c. that he could possibly come at, as well antiques as those of the most distinguished moderns.[6] Antonio Mini, the scholar of M. Angelo, carried into France with him at this time the greatest part of Angelo's designs and cartoons, two cases of models, &c. the only remaining entire copy of that famous cartoon of M. Angelo which was destroyed in the insurrection at Florence, went also into France. [. . .] Raffael, besides other pictures, painted his Transfiguration for France, and the picture that was excuted in competition with it, of the resurrection of Lazarus, by M. Angelo and Seb. Del Piombo was actually sent there, and is now in the collection at the Palais-Royal.[7]

Thus painting and sculpture, which were grown to a state of maturity in Italy, were in this state introduced into France in the same manner as the good taste of architecture was into the state of Venice, which is the reason why in those places there have been so few intermediate artists between their periods of barbarism and perfection.

Whilst Francis was thus taken up with introducing the arts into his kingdom, our Henry was engaged in warm controversies with Luther, and afterwards with the pope. Toto del Nunciata, Rovezzano, and Holbein came over from England, and the Reformation came over also: the history of this Reformation, the general ferment and collision of religious opinions, the pulling down of pictures, images, &c. and the setting fire to them by public authority – in short, the whole spirit and activity of the nation turned into this channel; for four reigns successively present a very different kind of picture from that of France. It was then exceedingly idle (to say nothing worse) in the Abbe Du Bos[8] to overlook all this, and to consider the arrival of Holbein[9] in England as a proper foundation on which he candidly supposes the natives, if they had any genius, must have raised a superstructure. Why did he not choose to recollect that such a superstructure was then the abomination of our people, and that they were every day proscribing, decrying, and objecting to it, in their controversies with the other nations of Europe? To say the truth, the Christian church, at the time of the Reformation, appears to have been so much heated by the disputes, that neither of the parties, as well as the Reformers as the Catholics, seemed to have been the least disposed to do any sort of justice to the fine qualities of the other; every thing was warped by passion and hatred, and the arts, which were the honour and ornament of Italy at that time, could not by consequence escape being criminated and unfortunately spurned and trampled under the feet of reformers.

Attempts were made in the beginning of the reign of Charles I to introduce arts and elegance into the kingdom, and much was done in the way of
making a collection; but what followed soon after shewed, but too convincingly, how little the public in general were disposed to cultivate national art,
until this zeal for religious canting and reformation had spent itself. It is then
no great matter of wonder that the English were remarkable for nothing but
portraits, and that Vandyke, Lely, &c.[10] who had been born and educated in
great historical schools abroad, were better qualified to succeed in this, or any
other branch of the art, than a few scattered ignorant natives, who were never
educated for it.

About the reign of queen Anne and George I our religious jarring, and its
political consequences, were much subsided; all parties had by this time pretty
well ground off their asperities, they grew tired of ill-humour, and ashamed
of rusticity; and as the arts came to be sought for and considered as an acquisition to our elegancies, it looked something like a favourable outset. But
national art was now, generally speaking, imperfect and unformed; the hands
so lately freed from the manacles of reformation were but little fitted to the
purpose for which they were now wanted; hence it was, that although some
small part of this demand for art has of late years flowed naturally into the
hands of the natives, and has been the means of so rapid an improvement
since, as is, I believe, without example in the history of any other people; yet
the main body of this stream has unfortunately taken another course, and is
wasting itself away in the watering of decayed roots and the young suckers
that sprout from them. In short, our demands for art have principally tended
to multiply the importation of foreign pictures, statues, and all other things
that go under the denomination of virtu.

B) *A Letter to the Rt. Hon. The President, Vice Presidents . . . of the
Society for the Encouragement of Arts, Manufactures, and Commerce, John Street, Adelphi,* **1793**

[. . .] In this new design, which consists of King Alfred and the other legislators, where Lycurgus is looking over the Pacific Code of Laws which is
considered as the ultimatum of legislation for a mixt people, I have instead
of Penn, placed those laws in the hands of Caecilius, Lord Baltimore [fig. 1],
whom Alfred leans on, and is as it were, exultingly producing, and who is
affectionately looking back upon Alfred and pointing to him as the real
source from whence issued the old common law, of which this code of Maryland is but an extension suited to the occasion of many instead of one people.

1      James Barry, *Lord Baltimore and the Group of Legislators*, 1793

As after all William Penn must be allowed the merit of having copied this excellent pacific example, I have honourably placed him with his Pensylvanian [sic] code next to Calvert, which keeps up an agreeable diversity in the forms, and is an additional weight to the moral of this part.

In order to remove any prejudice which sincere and zealous christians of any communion, may have to the doctrine of the political equality of all religious sects which is here so warmly recommended as the wisest and the best maxim of government for a mixt people; it may be right to observe, that it can very well subsist with the most rigid idea of the immutable characteristic of christian verity. Religious orthodoxy may go on without being obliged to any concessions, or to assume any new appearance of any thing vague, uncertain, indifferent, or in the least degree more tolerant than before. [. . .] Having put in this caveat, I shall proceed to observe that although this group of legislators forms but a small part of the subject of the Elysium, yet as the figures are two feet high, it will make as large a print as that of the entire subject, and besides the advantage it affords in the enlarged size of the figures of this principal group, it furnishes also an agreeable opportunity of distinguishing in a more satisfactory and conspicuous manner another group which links in with the upper part of these figures, and is not less connected with them in the picturesque arrangement than in the concatenation of the sentiment.

This upper group, consisting of those exalted truly Christian dispositions, who were disposed to labour in conciliating, doing away difference, and restoring the primitive unity and peace of the Christian church, begins with pope Adrian, who is seen over Lycurgus at a little distance, and by his action may be supposed to express to Grotius, Father Paul, and the others that remarkable wish to reduce the temporalities of the papacy to the apostolic simplicity if it might obtain this pacific reconciliation. The figure on the right of Adrian is Chichele, Archbishop of Canterbury, in the reign of Henry the fifth and sixth, who was so illustrious for the truly christian piety and fervour with which he asserted and maintained the rights and liberties of the church of England against foreign and domestic encroachments. The next to him is Reginald Pole, the last English cardinal, and, as far as my knowledge extends, the first writer, who to the new fangled doctrines of *the divine right and irresistible power of kings, and the passive obedience of subjects,* opposed those sacred *rights of the people,* from whence he nobly derives the delegated, legitimate powers which give sanction and just authority to the exercise of royalty. Standing next to him is Mariana, the Jesuit, who has discussed that question more at length. [. . .] The capuchin friar who is next Mariana and Cardinal Pole, was introduced to fill up the chasm, and lead the eye on to that vigorous assertor and defender of every valuable right, Paul Sarpi the Venetian friar. The next characters are Dr Benjamin Franklin, Barnevelt, Grotius, and

Bishop Berkeley. The pacific graceful virtues so conspicuous in Berkeley, that corrective for the shallow infidelity which would obtrude itself for philosophy, makes him a becoming part of this company. [. . .][12]

Nothing can be more false, mischievous, and irreconcileble with fact, than the impertinent philosophy of Montesquieu, which would insinuate that the catholic religion is more agreeable to a monarchy and the protestant to a republic.[13] Can we forget that Italy was, before the reformation, a country of republics, containing a greater number of free governments than was any where else to be found, or at anytime, in the same extent of territory? Can we forget also that the popish cantons of Switzerland are the most democratical, and that the slavish notions taught in the homilies and other writings of the reformers, concerning the divine right of kings, and the passive obedience of subjects, have been opposed by Milton, Locke, Sidney, and others, with arguments borrowed from popish writers. For the honour of the eighteenth century, the time is at last come, when from the necessary wise policy of emancipating the catholics of Ireland and uniting and making the most of all our people, after the loss of America, we have now no longer any occasion for distorting or suppressing facts, in order to hold forth such a horrid scarecrow of popery, slavery, wooden shoes, and ignorance, as should coincide with the left-handed, wicked policy adopted by our fathers, in order to keep that country divided, wrecked, and dependent. [. . .]

I could not withold my feelings in this letter from running out into some length upon the subject of religion; it has been the parent of arts in all ages, and it is almost impossible for a man to think of anything else at this time, when he can go nowhere without meeting in the streets of this great metropolis such numbers of the poor and venerable clergy of the country of our next neighbour, driven here for protection and shelter. Who could withhold himself from enquiring into whatever might be connected with, and might tend to alleviate the horrors and distresses of such a scene; how far it might have been expedient to have gone such desperate lengths, and how long that expediency might or ought to continue? besides, the object of the group of legislators, and that pacific, christian uniformity, which employed the attention of the other group, of pope Adrian, father Paul, Grotius, Berkeley, and the others, naturally led to and incorporated with any thing which could be said on so interesting a subject.

## NOTES

1    For a discussion of Barry's writings see John Barrell, *The Political Theory of Painting from Reynolds to Hazlitt*, New Haven and London, Yale University Press, 1986, chapter 2.

2    See William L. Pressly, *The Life and Art of James Barry*, New Haven and London, Yale University Press, 1981, chapter 4.

3    For discussion of the Irish background to this painting see Luke Gibbons, 'A Shadowy Narrator: History, Art and Romantic Nationalism in Ireland, 1750–1850', in *Ideology and the Historians*, ed. Ciaran Brady, Dublin, The Lilliput Press, 1991, pp. 99–127 and entry 53 of this *Reader*. For Baltimore see John J. Silke, 'The Irish Abroad in the Age of the Counter-Reformation, 1534–1691,' in *A New History of Ireland*, ed. T.W. Moody, F.X. Martin and F.J. Byrne; vol. III, *Early Modern Ireland, 1534–1691*, Oxford, Clarendon Press, 1976, p. 600.

4    *The Works of James Barry, Esq., Historical Painter*, ed. Dr Edward Fryer, 2 vols., London, 1809, vi.

5    Italian artists: Leonardo da Vinci (1452–1519), Rosso Fiorentino or Giovanni Battista Rosso (1494–1540), Francesco Primaticcio (1504/5–70), Niccolò dell' Abbate (*c.* 1512–71), Benvenuto Cellini (1500–71).

6    Giovanbattista della Palla (*c.* 1485–1531), Florentine agent for Francis I.

7    Michelangelo Buonarroti (1475–1564) and Raffaello Sanzio, known as Raphael (1483–1520); the latter's *Transfiguration* is now in the Pinacoteca, Vatican Museums, while the *Raising of Lazarus* by Sebastiano del Piombo (1485–1547) is in the National Gallery, London.

8    Abbé Jean Baptiste Du Bos, *Réflexions critiques sur la posie et sur la peinture*, 1719.

9    Hans Holbein the Younger (1497/8–1543), in England from 1526 to 1527 and 1532 to his death; on Henry VIII's payroll from 1536.

10   Sir Anthony Van Dyck (1599–1641) and Sir Peter Lely (1618–80), Flemish and Dutch, respectively.

11   Lycurgus, Spartan lawmaker, possibly lived between 1000–776 B.C.; chronicled in Plutarch's *Lives*, see vol. 1, Loeb Classical Library edition, London, 1914. The Quaker, William Penn did not colonize what became Pennsylvania until 1681, many years after Calvert had introduced religious toleration in Maryland. Alfred (849–99), King of Wessex from 871, is supposed to have united England while also translated Pope Gregory I's *Pastoral Rule*, a guide to co-operation between bishops and kings.

12   Adrian VI, Dutch-born prelate (1459–1523), who was pope for only twenty months (1522–23) but is credited as having been the first of the sixteenth-century reforming popes. Not to be confused with Nicholas Breakspear, an Englishman who held the papacy as Adrian VI, from 1154 to 1159, and granted Ireland to English kings. Hugo Grotius (1583–1645), Delft-born jurist who propogated a theory of international law. Father Paul Sarpi (1552–1623), a Venetian who attacked Church hypocrisy and corruption. Henry Chichele (1361–1443), Archbishop of Canterbury, who grew estranged from the papacy. Reginald Pole (1500–58), the last Roman Catholic archbishop of Canterbury. Juan de Mariana (1536–1624), a Jesuit who in *De Re rege et regis institutione* (Toledo, 1599), infamously defended regicide, as he saw power as lying ultimately in the people. Benjamin Franklin (1706–90), American businessman, politician and natural philosopher. Johan van Oldenbarnevelt (1547–1619), Dutch statesman, central figure in forging peace between Protestant Dutch Republic and Catholic Spain. George Berkeley, see entry 1. For further discussion of these references, see Gibbons, 'A Shadowy Narrator' and entry 53.

13   Charles de Secondat Montesquieu (1689–1755), a leading Enlightenment thinker who espoused a natural law, author of the famous *Lettres persanes*, 1721.

— 6 —

# Sydney Owenson (Lady Morgan), *Life and Times of Salvator Rosa*, 1824

The novelist Sydney Owenson (*c.* 1776–1859), later Lady Morgan first encountered art in the picture galleries of Kilkenny Castle.Viewing the famed collection of paintings belonging to the Butler family, she was to claim that it was here that 'I first became acquainted with that master mode of express-ing the human form divine in all its phases! This was my first contact with high art, and awakened a passion for its noble powers which in after life broke forth in my life of Salvator Rosa, of all my works the most delightful to myself in its execution.'[1] It has been suggested that Owenson was attracted to the work of the seventeenth-century Italian painter, Rosa (1615–73), because his wild landscapes reminded her of the scenery of the west of Ireland.[2] Her 1824 study of *Rosa* was the first art historical biography written by an Irish person as well as being the first full-length biography in English of a foreign artist.[3] It began as a novel but turned into a biography, and she used original sources, such as seventeenth-century biographies and Rosa's letters, none of which had ever before appeared in English. It has to be acknowledged that Morgan indulges in a number of fictional passages, the most sustained of which is an account of the artist's sojourn with a group of banditti in the mountains of the Abruzzi. Recent comment on the *Life of Rosa* has claimed that Lady Mor-gan 'never omits an opportunity to draw analogies between Ireland and Italy' while also suggesting that her hero takes on 'many of the traits ascribed to romantic outcasts in her own Irish novels'.[4] In time Lady Morgan's book was to suggest themes to a wide range of artists, including some Irish painters such as James Arthur O'Connor and Daniel Maclise (see entry 18 and fig. 7).[5]

Source: Sydney Owenson, Lady Morgan, *The Life and Times of Salvator Rosa*, 2 vols., London, 1824, vol. 1, pp. 114–19

⸱

The stronghold of this singular order had long been in the Abruzzi. There amidst 'Rocks, caves, lakes, fens, bogs, dens, / And shades of death,' they held with their families a wild and precarious, but not a joyless existence; while occasionally they were brigaded into separate bands, and distributed, under

the protection of the government, among the towns and cities of the kingdom, or garrisoned the domestic fortresses of the factious Neapolitan barons,
and others of the same rank, who lived in perpetual hostility with that rul-
ing power, by which they were perpetually distrusted and oppressed. Many
of these haughty nobles (themselves flying from the circles of their native
metropolis) exercised the old trade of the Italian fourusciti and reclaimed
their ancient rights as feudatory princes over the adjacent country. Upon
these occasions they were sometimes joined, and sometimes opposed, by the
banditti of the Abruzzi, as the interests or the feelings of these formidable
outlaws led them to embrace or to reject their cause.

The conflicts of unregulated interests, and of lawless but powerful voli-
tions – the stern elevation of character, reckless of all human suffering, beyond
all social relations – the play of strong antipathies, and operation of strong
instincts – the fierce rebuff of passions, wild as they were nurtured – the
anatomy of the mixed nature of man, laid bare, and stripped of all disguise,
were subjects of ennobling study to one who saw all things as a philosopher
and a poet – one who was prone to trace, throughout the endless varieties of
external forms, the deep-seated feelings that produced and governed their
expression. In the fierce guerrilla warfare of the Abruzzi, between the Spanish and German troops and the mountain-bands, may be traced the leading
character of that vast and wondrous battle-piece[6] which is destined to be the
study of successive generations of artists; and to the necessities of the outlaw's
life we are indebted for many of those singular groupings and views of violence and danger, which form the subjects not only of the pencil, but of the
graver, of Salvator Rosa.

There is one engraving which, though evidently done *à colpo di pennello*,
seems so plainly to tell the story of the wandering artist's captivity, that it may,
as an historic fact, if not as a *chef-d'œuvre* of the art, merit a particular description. In the midst of rocky scenery appears a group of banditti, armed at all
points, and with all sorts of arms. They are lying, in careless attitudes but with
fierce watchfulness, round a youthful prisoner, who forms the foreground figure, and is seated on a rock, with languid limbs hanging over the precipice,
which may be supposed to yawn beneath. It is impossible to describe the
despair depicted in this figure: it is marked in his position, in the droop of his
head, which his nerveless arms seem with difficulty to support, and in the
little that may be seen of his face, over which, from his recumbent attitude,
his hair falls in luxuriant profusion (and the singular head and tresses of Salvator are never to be mistaken). All is alike destitute of energy and of hope,
which the fierce beings grouped around the captive seem, in some sentence
recently pronounced, to have banished for ever. Yet one there is who watches
over the fate of the young victim: a woman stands immediately behind him.

Her hand stretched out, its forefinger resting on his head, marks him the subject of a discourse which she addresses to the listening bandits. Her finger which is erect, is composed of those bold straight lines, which in art and nature constitute the *grand*. Even the fantastic cap or turban, from which her long dishevelled hair has escaped, has no curve of grace: and her drapery partakes of the same rigid forms. Her countenance is full of stern melancholy – the natural character of one whose feelings and habits are at variance, whose strong passions may have flung her out of the pale of society, but whose feminine sympathies still remain unchanged. She is artfully pleading for the life of the youth, by contemptuously noting his insignificance. But she commands while she soothes. She is evidently the mistress, or the wife of the Chief, in whose absence an act of vulgar violence may be mediated. The youth's life is saved: for that cause rarely fails to which a woman brings the omnipotence of her feelings.[7]

## NOTES

1    *Lady Morgan's Memoirs*, 2 vols., eds. W. Hepworth Dixon and Geraldine Jewsbury, London, 1863, vol. 1, p. 117.

2    Mary Campbell, *Lady Morgan: The Life and Times of Sydney Owenson*, Pandora, London, 1988, p. 33. For the scale of the original Ormonde collection, see the inventories in *Historical Manuscripts Commission, Ormonde MSS*, new series, vol. 7, Hereford, 1912, pp. 501–9; for what Owenson might have seen, see *Catalogue of the Ormonde Collection of Pictures which will be exhibited in the Museum*, Kilkenny, 1840, and *Catalogue of the Pictures at Kilkenny Castle*, Kilkenny, 1875. More recently see Jane Fenlon, 'The Ormonde Picture Collection', *Irish Arts Review*, 16, 2000, pp. 143–49.

3    Michael Kitson in *Salvator Rosa*, London, Arts Council, 1973, p. 16.

4    Luke Gibbons, 'Between Captain Rock and a Hard Place: Art and Agrarian Insurgency,' in *Ideology and Ireland in the Nineteenth Century*, eds. Tadhg Foley and Seán Ryder, Dublin, Four Courts Press, 1998, p. 25. See also Jonathan Scott, *Salvator Rosa: His Life and Times*, New Haven and London, Yale University Press, 1995, pp. 229–30. Scott points out that many of the more romantic passages are taken from Bernardo De Dominici's *Vite de' Pittori* . . . , vol. 3, Naples, 1763, which includes a life of Salvator.

5    See *Salvator Rosa*, 1973, pp. 73–87, and Arts Council of Great Britain, *Daniel Maclise*, National Portrait Gallery, London, and National Gallery of Ireland, Dublin, 1972, pp. 60–62.

6    Morgan notes that this work is now in the 'Musée, at Paris'; now known as *Battle Scene*, Musée du Louvre, Paris, see *Salvator Rosa*, 1973, pp. 28–9.

7    Describes 'Four Warriors and a Youth' from the *Figurine* series, a set of sixty-one prints of 1656, see *Salvator Rosa*, 1973, plate 20.

## — 7 —

# David Wilkie, letters from Ireland, 1835

In the late summer of 1835 the successful Scottish-born artist Sir David Wilkie (1785–1841) visited Ireland and toured the country for a little over a month. The pictorial outcome was two large oils, *The Peep-O-Day Boy's Cabin, in the West of Ireland* (Tate Gallery, London) and *The Irish Whiskey Still* (National Gallery of Scotland, Edinburgh), exhibited at the London Royal Academy in 1836 and 1840, respectively. Wilkie also produced numerous drawings (fig. 2) as well as writing a number of letters to friends in England describing his journey and his opinions on Ireland.[1] The first of the two letters included here dates from 30 August 1835 and was sent from Limerick to the prominent London physician Sir William Knighton (1776–1836). The second letter (of a fortnight later, 12 September 1835), written from Edgeworthstown, Co. Longford, is addressed to Wilkie's artist-friend William Collins (1788–1847) and although it includes similar observations to the first letter, it elaborates on Ireland's painterly qualities.

Sources: Letter 1: Mitchell Library, University of Glasgow, Ms 308895;[2] Letter 2:

2     David Wilkie, *Study for 'The Irish Whiskey Still'*, 1835

Allan Cunningham, *The Life of Sir David Wilkie*, 3 vols., London, Murray, 1843, III, pp. 106–7

## LETTER 1

[. . .] awakened next morning about 6 in the bay of Dublin. The scene that presented on landing, so repugnant to the philanthropist, is to the painter most highly interesting, Velazquez, Murillo, and Salvator Rosa would here find the fit objects of their study.[3] The misery did not strike me; it was apparently not felt by the people themselves, whose condition is, after all, what the more advanced societies have gone through, in their progress to refinement. [. . .] the town [. . .] of Dublin, with its splendid squares and public buildings, is essentially English, still the mass of the population, has a Spanish and Italian look, and one is only surprised that with their appearance their habits and their faith, they should yet be our own people and speak our own language. [. . .] at Dublin [. . .] I was occupied in visiting convents, chapels, and the haunts of the lower classes; [. . . then] started with two friends per mail, directly westward, till we met the Atlantic at Lord Sligo's domain called Westport. We then proceeded southward through the wild mountainous district of Connemara to Galway, a region of which the inhabitants are said to be descended from a colony of Spaniards to whom they still bear a marked resemblance. Here the impression produced by the aspect of these people and their cabins made is not to be described. In a state of primeval simplicity, honest, polite, and virtuous, with so few wants that even the children run about the cabins unclad, realizing to a fervid imagination an age of poetry, yet which the poetry of our times has not described, and which to painting is perfectly new and untouched. Indeed I would say that a future painter, after he has seen and studied, all that has been done by the Greeks and Italians, should see such a state of life as a basis for his imagination to work upon, and I would venture to recommend that Mr Knighton should, in the course of his studies, see Ireland at a future time with such a view.
The costume of the district we have travelled through, he would find a perfect model. Dublin has the disadvantage, that, the lower classses, wear only the cast-off clothes, in rags, of their fashionable superiors: but in Connaught and Connemara, the clothes particularly of the women are the work of their own hands; and the colour they are most fond of is a red they dye with madder, which as petticoat, jacket, or mantle, brightens up the cabin or landscape, like a Titian or Giorgione.[4] Indeed, the whole economy of the people furnishes the elements of the picturesque. They build their own cabins, fabricate their own clothes, dig their own turf, catch their own salmon, and plough

their own fields, bringing into their confined dwellings, a confused variety of implements not to be described.

So remarkable are the scenes I have seen that I am wondering it has not long before been the object of research among painters – true, to the politician and to the patriot, much is seen with pity and regret, still the Irish peasantry are a rising and not a declining people, and as their good qualities must lead to future improvement, their present most simple and pastoral condition, if properly recorded, must in all times be subject of legitimate interest to the painter, the poet and the historian. The place I have not yet seen in Ireland is that strangers mostly visit, the Lakes of Killarney; for these I proceed tomorrow [. . .] I naturally wish to see you [. . .] to show you the subjects I have picked up here, with the question, whether any can be set about before next year's Exhibition, as I find an Artist who paints in Watercolour has just been a week before me, here, and I feel quite afraid, that other Artists will soon be coming the same road.

## LETTER 2

What one has often so much difficulty in contriving for a picture, and imagining for a poetical description, may, in the western provinces of Ireland, be found ready made to one's hands; and what is more, between ourselves, it is *untouched and new*. The question that you will naturally ask is, whether it will be applicable to *your* art, and whether it would be worth your while to visit Ireland. This has been present to my mind; and on all the occasions of seeing coast and harbour scenery, I have thought of you; but when I tell you the ships and boats, the sea and hills, are the same as in England, and that sailors in Ireland are not to be distinguished from those of the opposite shore, that there is but little life peculiar, excepting the female costume, the cabins, the pigs, and naked children, perhaps you will see but little to induce you to visit Ireland; still, though your sea or lake subjects here could not be distinct from England, yet the rustic life that you paint would be here found in perfection, and being of that simple kind, with all its wildness and poverty, it is an approach to pastoral life, which, with all its homeliness, is best adapted to grandeur and poetical effect.

This indeed I am perfectly satisfied of, as you I am sure will be, that if Ireland has been overlooked and forgotten by the votaries of our art, it will not remain so much longer. A pursuit requires but a beginning: Irish artists will, from the curiosity of strangers, begin to think themselves of painting their own country, and the craving of the public for variety, and the publishers for new thoughts, will send over some who have exhausted the Rhine, and Italy,

Spain and Barbary, *to do* Ireland at last, as a card for which a public interest is already made. In my journey I was preceded by an artist in aquareil, who I doubt not has some such object in view.

## NOTES

1    See Fintan Cullen, *Visual Politics: The Representation of Ireland, 1750–1930*, Cork University Press, 1997, chapter 4.
2    See also Lindsay Errington, *Work in Progress: Sir David Wilkie: Drawings into Paintings*, Edinburgh, National Gallery of Scotland, 1975, pp. 21–3.
3    Three seventeenth-century painters, Velazquez (1599–1660), Murillo (1617–82) and Rosa (1615–73).
4    Two sixteenth-century Venetian painters, Titian (c. 1487/90–1576) and Giorgione (c. 1476/8–1510).

# — 8 —

# Thomas Davis, 'National Art' and 'Hints for Irish Historical Paintings', 1843

In 1842 the poet and writer Thomas Davis (1814–45) together with John Blake Dillon (1816–66) and Charles Gavan Duffy (1816–1903) founded *The Nation*, a newspaper which became the organ of the Young Ireland movement. Concerned with defining Irish identity and propagating a form of cultural nationalism, the Young Irelanders initially supported Daniel O'Connell's Repeal movement. *The Nation* published many of Davis's poems including such popular ballads as 'A Nation Once Again', along with numerous literary, historical and political essays. Two such essays are included here, both dating from 1843, their focus being on the definition and content of a distinctly Irish national art. The first essay discusses the relevance of a national art and how it can be achieved in mid-nineteenth-century Ireland. The second piece is less an essay than a list. Davis cites a range of historical events which could be painted by Irish artists and in the process shows his prodigious learning.[1] For a further example of Davis's art criticism, see entry 44B.

Source: *Essays Literary and Historical by Thomas Davis*, D.J. O'Donoghue, ed., Dundalk, Dundalgan Press, 1914, pp. 119–23, 112–15[2]

## A) 'NATIONAL ART'

No one doubts that if he sees a place or an action he knows more of it than if it had been described to him by a witness. The dullest man, who 'put on his best attire' to welcome Caesar, had a better notion of life in Rome than our ablest artist or antiquary.

Were painting, then, but a coloured chronicle, telling us facts by the eye instead of the ear, it would demand the Statesman's care and the People's love. It would preserve for us faces we worshipped, and the forms of men who led and instructed us. It would remind us, and teach our children, not only how these men looked, but, to some extent, what they were, for nature is consistent, and she has indexed her labours. It would carry down a pictorial history of our houses, arts, costume, and manners to other times, and show the dweller in a remote isle the appearance of countries and races of his contemporaries.

As a register of *facts* – as a portrayer of men, singly, or assembled – and as a depicter of actual scenery, art is biography, history, and topography taught through the eye.

So far as it can express facts, it is superior to writing; and nothing but the scarcity of *faithful* artists, or the stupidity of the public, prevents us from having our pictorial libraries of men and places. There are some classes of scenes – as where continuous action is to be expressed – in which sculpture quite fails, and painting is but a shadowy narrator.

But this, after all, though the most obvious and easy use of Painting and Sculpture, is far indeed from being their highest end.

Art is a regenerator as well as a copyist. As the historian, who composes a history out of various materials, differs from a newspaper reporter, who sets down what he sees – as Plutarch differs from Mr Grant, and the Abbé Barthelemy from the last traveller in India[3] – so do the Historical Painter, the Landscape composer (such as Claude or Poussin) differ from the most faithful Portrait, Landscape, or Scene Drawer.

The Painter who is a master of composition makes his pencil cotemporary with all times and ubiquitous. Keeping strictly to nature and fact, Romulus sits for him and Paul preaches. He makes Attila charge, and Mohammed exhort, and Ephesus blaze when he likes. He tries not rashly, but by years of study of men's character, and dress, and deeds, to make them and their acts come as in a vision before him. Having thus got a design, he attempts to realise the vision on his canvas. He pays the most minute attention to truth in his drawing, shading, and colouring, and by imitating the force of nature in his composition, all the clouds that ever floated by him, 'the lights of other days', and the forms of the dead, or the stranger, hover over him.

But Art in its highest stage is more than this. It is a creator. Great as Herodotus and Thierry are, Homer and Beranger are greater.[4] The ideal has resources beyond the actual. It is infinite, and Art is indefinitely powerful. The Apollo is more than noble, and the Hercules mightier than man. The Moses of Michael Angelo is no likeness of the inspired law-giver, nor of any other that ever lived, and Raphael's Madonnas are not the faces of women. As Reynolds says, 'the effect of the capital works of Michael Angelo is that the observer feels his whole frame enlarged'.[5] It is creation, it is representing beings and things different from our nature, but true to their own. In this self-consistency is the only nature requisite in works purely imaginative. Lear is true to his nature, and so are Mephistopheles, and Prometheus, and Achilles; but they are not true to human nature; they are beings created by the poets' minds, and true to *their* laws of being. There is no commoner blunder in men, who are themselves mere critics, never creators, than to require consistency to the nature of us and our world in the works of poet or painter.

To create a mass of great pictures, statues, and buildings is of the same sort of ennoblement to a people as to create great poems or histories, or make great codes, or win great battles. The next best, though far inferior, blessing and power is to inherit such works and achievements. The lowest stage of all is neither to possess nor to create them.

Ireland has had some great Painters – Barry and Forde, for example, and many of inferior but great excellence; and now she boasts high names – Maclise, Hogan, and Mulready.[6] But their works were seldom done for Ireland, and are rarely known in it. Our portrait and landscape Painters paint foreign men and scenes; and, at all events, the Irish people do not see, possess, nor receive knowledge from their works. Irish history has supplied no subjects for our great Artists; and though, as we repeat, Ireland possessed a Forde and Barry, creative Painters of the highest order, the pictures of the latter are mostly abroad; those of the former unseen and unknown. Alas! that they are so few.

To collect into, and make known, and publish in Ireland the best works of our living and dead Artists is one of the steps towards procuring for Ireland a recognised National Art. And this is essential to our civilisation and renown. The other is by giving education to students and rewards to Artists, to make many of this generation true representers, some of them great illustrators and composers, and, perchance, to facilitate the creation of some great spirit.

Something has been done – more remains.

There are schools in Dublin and Cork. But why are those so neglected and imperfect? and why are not similar or better institutions in Belfast, Derry, Galway, Waterford, and Kilkenny? Why is there not a decent collection of casts anywhere but in Cork, and why are they in a garret there? And why have we no gallery of Irishmen's, or any other men's, pictures in Ireland?

The Art Union has done a great deal. It has helped to support in Ireland artists who should otherwise have starved or emigrated; it has dispersed one (when, oh when, will it disperse another?) fine print of a fine Irish picture through the country, and to some extent interested as well as instructed thousands.[7] Yet it could, and we believe will, do much more. It ought to have Corresponding Committees in the principal towns to preserve and rub up old schools of art and foster new ones, and it might by art and historical libraries, and by other ways, help the cause. We speak as friends, and suggest not as critics, for it has done good service.

The Repeal Association, too, in offering prizes for pictures and sculptures of Irish historical subjects, has taken its proper place as the patron of nationality in art; and its rewards for Building Designs may promote the comfort and taste of the people, and the reputation of the country.[8] If artists will examine the rules by which the pictures, statues, and plates remain their property, they will find the prizes not so small as they might at first appear. Nor should they, from interest or just pride, be indifferent to the popularity and fame of success on national subjects, and with a People's Prizes to be contended for. If those who are not Repealers will treat the Association's design kindly and candidly, and if the Repealers will act in art upon principles of justice and conciliation, we shall not only advance national art, but gain another field of common exertion.

The Cork School of Art owes its existence to many causes.[9]

The intense, genial, and Irish character of the people, the southern warmth and variety of clime, with its effects on animal and vegetable beings, are the natural causes.

The accident of Barry's birth there, and his great fame, excited the ambition of the young artists. An Irishman and a Corkman had gone out from them, and amazed men by the grandeur and originality of his works of art. He had thrown the whole of the English painters into insignificance, for who would compare the luscious commonplace of the Stuart painters, or the melodramatic reality of Hogarth, or the imitative beauty of Reynolds, or the clumsy strength of West, with the overbearing grandeur of his works.[10]

But the *present* glories of Cork, Maclise and Hogan, the greater, but buried might of Forde, and the rich promise which we know is springing there now, are mainly owing to another cause; and that is, that Cork possesses a gallery of the finest casts in the world.

These casts are not very many – 117 only; but they are perfect, they are the first from Canova's moulds, and embrace the greatest works of Greek art. They are ill placed in a dim and dirty room – more shame to the rich men of Cork for leaving them so – but there they are, and there studied Forde, and Maclise, and the rest, until they learned to draw better than any moderns, except Cornelius and his living brethren.[11]

In the countries where art is permanent there are great collections – Tuscany and Rome, for example. But, as we have said before, the highest service done by success in art is not in the possession but in the creation of great works, the spirit, labour, sagacity, and instruction needed by the artists to succeed, and flung out by them on their country like rain from sunny clouds.

Indeed there is some danger of a traditionary mediocrity following after a great epoch in art. Superstition of style, technical rules in composition, and all the pedantry of art, too often fill up the ranks vacated by veteran genius, and of this there are examples enough in Flanders, Spain, and even Italy. The schools may, and often do, make men scholastic and ungenial, and art remains an instructor and refiner, but creates no more.

Ireland, fortunately or unfortunately, has everything to do yet. We have had great artists – we have not their works – we own the nativity of great living artists – they live on the Tiber and the Thames. Our capital has no school of art – no facilities for acquiring it.

To be sure there are rooms open in the Dublin Society, and they have not been useless, that is all. But a student here cannot learn anatomy, save at the same expense as a surgical student. He has no great works of art before him, no Pantheon, no Valhalla, not even a good museum or gallery.

We think it may be laid down as unalterably true that a student should never draw from a flat surface. He learns nothing by drawing from the lines of another man – he only mimics. Better for him to draw chairs and tables, bottles and glasses, rubbish, potatoes, cabins, or kitchen utensils, than draw from the lines laid down by other men.

Of those forms of nature which the student can originally consult – the sea, the sky, the earth – we would counsel him to draw from them in the first learning; for though he ought afterwards to analyse and mature his style by the study of works of art, from the first sketches to the finished picture, yet, by beginning with nature and his own suggestions, he will acquire a genuine and original style, superior to the finest imitation; and it is hard to acquire a master's skill without his manner.

Were all men cast in a divine mould of strength and straightness and gallant bearing, and all women proportioned, graceful, and fair, the artist would need no gallery, at least to begin his studies with. He would have to persuade or snatch his models in daily life. Even then, as art creates greater and simpler combinations than ever exist in fact, he should finally study before the superhuman works of his predecessors.

But he has about him here an indifferently-made, ordinary, not very clean, not picturesquely-clad people; though, doubtless, if they had the feeding, the dress, and the education (for mind beautifies the body) of the Greeks, they would not be inferior, for the Irish structure is of the noblest order.

To give him a multitude of fine natural models, to say nothing of ideal works, it is necessary to make a gallery of statues or casts. The statues will come in good time, and we hope, and are sure, that Ireland, a nation, will have a national gallery, combining the greatest works of the Celtic and Teutonic races. But at present the most that can be done is to form a gallery.

Our readers will be glad to hear that this great boon is about to be given to Irish Art. A society for the formation of a gallery of casts in Dublin has been founded.

It embraces men of every rank, class, creed, politics, and calling, thus forming another of those sanctuaries, now multiplying in Ireland, where one is safe from the polemic and the partisan.

Its purpose is to purchase casts of all the greatest works of Greece, Egypt, Etruria, ancient Rome, and Europe in the middle ages. This will embrace a sufficient variety of types both natural and ideal to prevent imitation, and will avoid the debateable ground of modern art. Wherever they can afford it the society will buy moulds, in order to assist provincial galleries, and therefore the provinces are immediately interested in its support.

When a few of these casts are got together, and a proper gallery procured, the public will be admitted to see, and artists to study, them without any charge. The annual subscription is but ten shillings, the object being to interest as many as possible in its support.

It has been suggested to us by an artist that Trinity College ought to establish a gallery and museum containing casts of all the ancient statues, models of their buildings, civil and military, and a collection of their implements of art, trade, and domestic life. A nobler institution, a more vivid and productive commentary on the classics, could not be. But if the Board will not do this of themselves, we trust they will see the propriety of assisting this public gallery, and procuring, therefore, special privileges for the students in using it.

But no matter what persons in authority may do or neglect, we trust the public – for the sake of their own pleasure, their children's profit, and Ireland's honour – will give it their instant and full support.

## B) 'HINTS FOR IRISH HISTORICAL PAINTINGS'

National art is conversant with national subjects. We have Irish artists, but no Irish, no national art. This ought not to continue; it is injurious to the artists, and disgraceful to the country. The following historical subjects were loosely jotted down by a friend. Doubtless, a more just selection could be made by students noting down fit subjects for painting and sculpture, as they read. We shall be happy to print any suggestions on the subject – our own are, as we call them, mere hints with loose references to the authors or books which suggested them. For any good painting, the marked figures must be few, the action obvious, the costume, arms, architecture, postures historically exact, and the manners, appearance, and rank of the characters strictly studied and observed. The grouping and drawing require great truth and vigour. A similar set of subjects illustrating social life could be got from the Poor Report, Carleton's, Banim's, or Griffin's Stories, or better still, from observation.[12]

The references are vague, but perhaps sufficient.[13]

The Landing of the Milesians – Keating, Moore's Melodies.

Ollamh Fodhla Presenting his Laws to his People. Keating's, Moore's, and O'Halloran's Histories of Ireland – Walker's Irish Dress and Arms, and Vallencey's Collectanea.

Nial and his Nine Hostages – Moore, Keating.

A Druid's Augury – Moore, O'Halloran, Keating.

A Chief Riding Out of his Fort – Griffin's Invasion, Walker, Moore.

The Oak of Kildare – Moore.

The Burial of King Dathy in the Alps, his thinned troops laying stones on his grave – M'Geoghegan, 'Histoire de l'Irlande' (French edition), Invasion, Walker, Moore.

St Patrick brought before the Druids at Tara – Moore and his Authorities.

The First Landing of the Danes – See Invasion, Moore, etc.

The Death of Turgesius – Keating, Moore.

Ceallachan tied to the Mast – Keating.

Murkertach Returning to Aileach – Archæological Society's Tracts.

Brian Reconnoitring the Danes before Clontarf.

The Last of the Danes Escaping to his Ship.

O'Ruarc's Return – Keating, Moore's Melodies.

Raymond Le Gros Leaving his Bride – Moore.

Roderick in Conference with the Normans – Moore, M'Geoghegan.

Donald O'Brien Setting Fire to Limerick – M'Geoghegan.

Donald O'Brien Visiting Holycross – M'Geoghegan.

O'Brien, O'Connor, and M'Carthy making Peace to attack the Normans – M'Geoghegan, Moore.

The Same Three Victorious at the Battle of Thurles – Moore and O'Conor's Rerum Hibernicarum Scriptores.

Irish Chiefs leaving Prince John – Moore, etc.

M'Murrough and Gloster – Harris's Hibernica, p. 53.

Crowning of Edward Bruce – Leland, Grace's Annals, etc.

Edgecombe Vainly Trying to Overawe Kildare – Harris's Hibernica.

Kildare 'On the Necks of the Butlers' – Leland.

Shane O'Neill at Elizabeth's Court – Leland.

Lord Sydney Entertained by Shane O'Neill.

The Battle of the Red Coats – O'Sullivan's Catholic History.

Hugh O'Neill Victor in Single Combat at Clontibret – Fynes Moryson, O'Sullivan, M'Geoghegan.

The Corleius – Dymmok's Treatise, Archæological Society's Tracts.

Maguire and St Leger in Single Combat – M'Geoghegan.

O'Sullivan Crossing the Shannon – Pacata Hibernia.

O'Dogherty Receiving the Insolent Message of the Governor of Derry – M'Geoghegan.

The Brehon before the English Judges – Davis's Letter to Lord Salisbury.

Ormond Refusing to give up his Sword – Carte's Life of Ormond.

Good Lookers-on – Strafford's Letters.

Owen Conolly before the Privy Council, 1641 – Carey's Vindiciæ.

The Battle of Julianstown – Temple's Rebellion, and Tichbourne's Drogheda.

Owen Roe Organising the Creaghts – Carte, and also Belling and O'Neill in the Desiderata Curiosa Hibernica.

The Council of Kilkenny – Carte.

The Breach of Clonmel – Do.

Smoking Out the Irish – Ludlow's Memoirs.

Burning Them – Castlehaven's Memoirs.

Nagle before the Privy Council – Harris's William.

James's Entry into Dublin – Dublin Magazine for March 1843.

The Bridge of Athlone – Green Book and Authorities.

St Ruth's Death – Do.

The Embarkation from Limerick – Do.

Cremona – Cox's Magazine.

Fontenoy – Do.

Sir S. Rice Pleading against the Violation of the Treaty of Limerick – Staunton's Collection of Tracts on Ireland.

Molyneaux's Book Burned.

Liberty Boys Reading a Drapier's Letter – Mason's St Patrick's Cathedral.

Lucas Surrounded by Dublin Citizens in his Shop.

Grattan Moving Liberty – Memoirs.

Flood Apostrophising Corruption – Barrington.

Dungannon Convention – Wilson, Barrington.

Curran Cross-Examining Armstrong – Memoirs.

Curran Pleading Before the Council in Alderman James's Case.

Tone's First Society – See his Memoirs.

The Belfast Club – Madden's U.I., Second Series, vol. I.

Tone, Emmet, and Keogh in the Rathfarnham Garden.

Tone and Carnot – Tone's Memoirs.

Battle of Oulart – Hay, Teeling, etc.

First Meeting of the Catholic Association.

O'Connell Speaking in a Munster Chapel – Wyse's Association.

The Clare Hustings – Proposal of O'Connell.

The Dublin Corporation Speech.

Fathew Mathew Administering the Pledge in a Munster County.

Conciliation – Orange and Green.

The Lifting of the Irish Flags of a National Fleet and Army.

## NOTES

1    For a recent discussion of Davis's 'Hints', see Joep Leerssen, *Remembrance and Imag-ination: Patterns in the Historical and Literary Representation of Ireland in the Nineteenth Century*, Cork University Press, 1996, p. 149. Half a century earlier, Joseph Cooper Walker was probably the first to publish such a list, see his *Outlines of a Plan for Pro-moting the Art of Painting in Ireland: with a List of Subjects for Painters drawn from the Romantic and Genuine Histories of Ireland*, 1790.

2    O'Donoghue's edition includes other relevant essays such as 'Historical monuments of Ireland', 'Art Unions', etc. The extracts included here first appeared in *The Nation* on December 2, 1843 and July 29, 1843, respectively.

3    Plutarch (before 50–after 120 AD), Roman historian, whose *Lives* consists of over twenty paired biographies of Greek and Roman historical figures. James Grant (1802–79), a prolific journalist and travel writer. Jean Jacques Barthélemy (1716–93), French scholar and *abbé* who popularised an interest in Greek antiquity. Claude Gelleé, called Lorraine (1600–82) and Nicolas Poussin (1594–1665), French landscape painters.

4    Herodotus (c. 490–80 B.C–425 B.C.), author of *The Histories*, accounts of Greek conflicts with Persia. Augustin Thierry (1785–1856), French historian and philos-pher, famous for his *History of the Norman Conquest in England*, 1824. Homer (c. 700 B.C.), author of the *Iliad* and the *Odyssey*. Pierre Jean de Béranger (1780–1857), French poet and writer of songs.

5    Not a verbatim quotation, from Discourse 5, 1772, see Sir Joshua Reynolds, *Dis-courses on Art*, ed. Robert R. Wark, New Haven and London, Yale University Press, 1975, p. 83.

6    James Barry (1741–1806), Samuel Forde (1805–28), Daniel Maclise (1806–70), John Hogan (1800–58) and William Mulready (1786–1863).

7    This is possibly a reference to Frederick William Burton's *The Blind Girl at the Holy Well*, engraved by Henry Thomas Ryall in 1841, see Eileen Black, 'Practical Patri-ots and True Irishmen: The Royal Irish Art Union, 1839–59', *Irish Arts Review*, 14, 1998, pp. 140–6.

8    See Jeanne Sheehy, *The Rediscovery of Ireland's Past: The Celtic Revival, 1830–1920*, London, Thames & Hudson, 1980, pp. 37–9.

9    See Peter Murphy, *The Crawford Municipal Art Gallery*, Cork Vocational Education Committee, 1991, pp. 2–6.

10    Gilbert Stuart (1755–1828), William Hogarth (1697–1764) and Benjamin West (1783–1820)

11    Peter von Cornelius (1783–1867), German painter. For the casts see Murray, *Crawford Municipal Art Gallery*, pp. 196–7 and passim.

12    Davis is referring to three major writers of fiction, William Carleton (1794–1869), John Banim (1798–1842) and Gerald Griffin (1803–40).

13    The following are some of the references Davis cites: James Mageoghegan, *Histoire de l'Irlande ancienne et moderne, tirée des monuments les plus authentiques*, 3 vols., Paris, 1758–62; Thomas Moore, *Melodies*, 1807–34; Thomas Leland, *The History of Ireland from the invasion of Henry II with a preliminary discourse on the ancient state of that kingdom*, 3 vols., Dublin, 1773; Walter Harris (ed.), *Hibernica, or, some antient pieces relating to Ireland*, 2 vols., Dublin, 1747–50; Geoffrey Keating, *Forus feasa ar Éirinn: The history of Ireland*, ed. Dermod O'Connor, 1723; Fynes Moryson, *An Itinerary written by Fynes Moryson Gent.*, 1617; John Dymmok, 'A treatice of Ireland' (ed. R. Butler for the Irish Archaeological Society). *Tracts relating to Ireland 2* (1842), pt. 1; Mathew Carey, *Vindiciae Hiberniae: or, Ireland Vindicated*, Philadelphia, 1819; John Temple, *The Irish Rebellion*, London, 1646; Charles H. Teeling, *Personal Narratives of the Irish Rebellion of 1798*, London, 1828; Edward Hay, *History of the Insurrection in the County of Wexford, AD 1798*, Dublin, 1803; R.R. Madden, *The United Irishmen, their Lives and Times*, vol. 1, London, 1842; Jonah Barrington, *Personal Sketches of His Own Times*, 3 vols., Paris, 1827–32.

— 9 —

# George Petrie, from William Stokes, *Life and Labours in Art and Archaeology of George Petrie,* 1868

Trained as a watercolour artist in Dublin, George Petrie (1790–1866) became one of the great Irish antiquarians of the nineteenth century. As Librarian for the Royal Irish Academy, he purchased important early manuscripts and initiated serious research into Irish antiquities. In 1845 he published his lavish *Ecclesiastical Architecture of Ireland*, which contributed to a heated mid-century debate on the 'vexed question' of the nature of Irish round towers.[1] In 1857 he was briefly President of the Royal Hibernian Academy. Two extracts from his writings are included here, both being examples of what Petrie's biographer, William Stokes (1804–1878), referred to as 'word painting'. The extracts describe early ecclesiastical sites and reflect the kind of Irish landscape that

Petrie admired, dotted as it was with ancient ruins or with colourful peas-
antry and thus exhibiting, again as Stokes observed, a 'national character'.[2]
The first example of Petrie as 'word painter' is a letter to the Royal Irish Art
Union, *c.* 1838, discussing a watercolour of the monastic site at Clonmacnoise, which Petrie had produced in the 1820s and reworked *c.* 1838. The
Royal Irish Art Union eventually purchased the watercolour for 100 guineas.[3]
The second extract is also from the 1830s and is a description of Monaster-
boice in County Louth. It originally appeared in the *Irish Penny Journal*, 'a
cultural and historical magazine for the middle classes'.[4]

Source: William Stokes, *The Life and Labours in Art and Archaeology of George Petrie,
LL.D.*, London, 1868, pp. 15 and 71–2

My Dear Sir, I beg to acquaint you that I am now ready to place in the
hands of the Committee of the Royal Irish Art Union my picture of Clonmacnoise, and I have also to beg that you will do me the kindness to express
to that truly patriotic body my deep sense of gratitude, not only for the honour conferred upon me by their very liberal purchase of my work, but for
their considerate kindness in allowing me such ample time to endeavour to
make it, as far as my humble abilities could do so, in some degree worthy of
their approbation, and conducive to their enlightened objects. I cannot,
indeed, flatter myself that my labours have been to any large extent successful; but I trust, at least, that it will be apparent that I have not failed from any
want of patient exertion, or anxious desire to give satisfaction. I trust also that
it will be apparent that my aim was something beyond that of the ordinary
class of portrait landscape, and, therefore, more difficult of attainment. It was
my wish to produce an Irish picture somewhat historical in its object, and
poetical in its sentiment – a landscape composed of several of the monuments
characteristic of the past history of our country, and which will soon cease
to exist, and to connect with them the expression of human feelings equally
belonging to our history, and which are destined to a similar extinction.
In short, I desired to produce a picture which might have an interest and
value, not merely pictorial, beyond the present time, and thus connect my
name with that of the Art Union Association, and with the history of art in
Ireland. And, with this feeling, I did my best to adhere to local as well as general truth at whatever cost to the pictorial attraction of the work, and to adopt
such a treatment of effect as might conduce to the sentiment of the picture
without unfitting it for the purpose of a popular print, if it should ever be
deemed worthy to be engraved.
[. . .]

To the observing and imaginative traveller, our island must present a great number of peculiarities of aspect which will not fail to excite his notice, and impress themselves indelibly upon his mind. The scantiness of wood – for its natural timber has nearly all disappeared – and the abundance of water, are two of the characteristics that will most strike him; and, next to these, the great extent of prospect usually afforded to the eye in consequence of the undulating character of its surface. Sparkling streams are visible everywhere, and shining lakes and noble rivers come into view in rapid succession; while ranges of blue mountains are rarely wanting to bound the distant horizon. The colours with which nature has painted the surface of our island are equally peculiar. There is no variety of green, whether of depth or vivid brightness, which is not to be found covering it. They are hues which can be seen no where else in equal force; and even our bogs, which are so numerous, with all their mutations of colour – now purple, and anon red, or brown, or black, by their vigorous contrasts, give additional beauty and life to the landscape, and assist in imparting to it a sort of national individuality. Our very clouds have, to a great degree, a distinctive character – the result of the humidity of our climate; they have a grandeur of form and size, and a force of light and shadow, that are but rarely seen in other countries: they are *Irish clouds*, at one moment bright and sunny, and in the next flinging their dark shadows over the landscape, and involving it in gloomy grandeur. It is this striking force of contrast in almost everything we look at, that the peculiarity of our scenery chiefly consists; and it appears to have stamped the general character of our people with those contrasting lights and shades so well exhibited in our exquisite and strongly-marked national music, in which all varieties of sentiment are so deeply yet harmoniously blended, as to produce on the mind effects, perhaps, in some degree saddening; but, withal, most delightfully sweet and soothing. A country marked with such peculiarities is not the legitimate abode of the refined sensualist of modern times, or the man of artificial pleasure and heartless pursuits, and all such naturally remain away from it or visit it with reluctance; but it is the proper habitation of the poet, the painter, and, above all, the philanthropist; for nowhere else can the latter find so extensive a field for the exercise of the godlike feelings of benevolence and patriotism.

Yet, the natural features of scenery and climate which we have pointed out, interesting as all must admit them to be, are not the only ones that confer upon our country the peculiar and impressive character which it possesses. The relics of past epochs of various classes; the monuments of its Pagan times, as revealed to us in its religious, military, and sepulchral remains; the ruins of its primitive Christian ages, as exemplified in its simple and generally unadorned churches, and slender round towers – the more splendid monastic edifices of later date, and the gloomy castles of still more recent times – these are everywhere present to bestow historic interest on the landscape, and bring the successive conditions and changes of society in bygone ages forcibly before the mind; so that an additional interest, of a deep and poetical nature, is thus imparted to views in themselves impressive, from their picturesque and wild appearance. So perfect, indeed, is this harmony of the natural and artificial characteristics of Irish scenery, so comprehensively do both tell the history of our country, to which nature has been most bountiful, and in which, alas! man has not been happy, that if we were desirous of giving a stranger a true idea of Ireland, and one that would impress itself on his mind, we should conduct him to one of our green open landscapes, where the dark and ruined castle, seated on some rocky height, or the round tower, with its little parent church, in some sequestered valley, would be the only features to arrest his attention; and of such a scene we should say emphatically, 'This is Ireland!'

## NOTES

1    See Joep Leerssen, *Remembrance and Imagination: Patterns in the Historical and Literary Representation of Ireland in the Nineteenth Century*, Cork University Press, 1996, pp. 108–56.

2    William Stokes, *The Life and Labours in Art and Archaeology of George Petrie, LL.D.*, London, 1868, p. 395.

3    *The Last Circuit of Pilgrims at Clonmacnoise*, pencil and watercolour, National Gallery of Ireland, see Fintan Cullen, *Visual Politics: The Representation of Ireland, 1750–1930*, Cork University Press, 1997, p. 133.

4    Leerssen, *Remembrance*, p. 114.

# — 10 —

# W.B. Yeats, 'Art and Ideas,' 1913

In his early prose writings, including his personal letters, William Butler Yeats (1865–1939) frequently cited his admiration for the Pre-Raphaelites. Later, in the essay 'Art and Ideas', written in 1913 and published in a collection of essays entitled *The Cutting of an Agate*, Yeats discussed his gradual movement away from the aestheticism of his youth to a more unified view of the role of art, where life and thought are integrated.[1] In the preface to this collection, the poet states of how he 'wrote the greater number of these essays . . . [when he] was busy with a single art, that of a small, unpopular theatre'.[2] Real life was thus impinging on his imaginative world and Pre-Raphaelitism had to be reassessed. The change in Yeats's aesthetic taste is reflected in the fact that he begins the essay by remembering a visit to the Tate Gallery to view the work of the Pre-Raphaelite painter John Everett Millais (1829–96), while towards the end he refers to a photograph of a Paul Gauguin (1848–1903) painting which 'hangs over my breakfast-table'.

Source: W.B. Yeats, *Essays and Introductions*, London, Macmillan & Co. Ltd, 1961, pp. 346–55

Two days ago I was at the Tate Gallery to see the early Millais's, and before his *Ophelia,* as before the *Mary Magdalene* and *Mary of Galilee* of Rossetti that hung near, I recovered an old emotion.[3] I saw these pictures as I had seen pictures in my childhood. I forgot the art criticism of friends and saw wonderful, sad, happy people, moving through the scenery of my dreams. The painting of the hair, the way it was smoothed from its central parting, something in the oval of the peaceful faces, called up memories of sketches of my father's on the margins of the first Shelley I had read, while the strong colours made me half remember studio conversations, words of Wilson, or of Potter perhaps, praise of the primary colours, heard, it may be, as I sat over my toys or a child's story-book. One picture looked familiar, and suddenly I remembered it had hung in our house for years. It was Potter's *Field Mouse.*[4] I had learned to think in the midst of the last phase of Pre-Raphaelitism and now I had come to Pre-Raphaelitism again and rediscovered my earliest thought. I murmured to myself, 'The only painting of modern England that could give pleasure to a child, the only painting that would seem as moving as *The Pilgrim's Progress* or Hans Andersen.' 'Am I growing old,' I thought, 'like the woman in Balzac, the rich bourgeois ambitious wife, who could not keep, when old age came upon her, from repeating the jokes of the concierge's lodge where she had been born and bred; or is it because of some change in the weather that I find beauty everywhere, even in Burne-Jones's *King Cophetua,*[5] one of his later pictures, and find it without shame?' I have had like admiration many times in the last twenty years, for I have always loved those pictures where I meet persons associated with the poems or the religious ideas that have most moved me; but never since my boyhood have I had it without shame, without the certainty that I would hear the cock crow presently. I remembered that as a young man I had read in Schopenhauer that no man – so unworthy a thing is life seen with unbesotted eyes – would live another's life, and had thought I would be content to paint, like Burne-Jones and Morris under Rossetti's rule, the Union at Oxford, to set up there the traditional images most moving to young men while the adventure of uncommitted life can still change all to romance, even though I should know that what I painted must fade from the walls.

Thereon I ask myself if my conception of my own art is altering, if there, too, I praise what I once derided. When I began to write I avowed for my principles those of Arthur Hallam in his essay upon Tennyson.[6] Tennyson, who had written but his early poems when Hallam wrote, was an example of the school of Keats and Shelley, and Keats and Shelley, unlike Wordsworth, intermixed into their poetry no elements from the general thought, but wrote out of the impression made by the world upon their delicate senses. They were of the aesthetic school – was he the inventor of the name? – and could not be popular because their readers could not understand them without attaining to a like delicacy of sensation and so must needs turn from them to Wordsworth or another, who condescended to moral maxims, or some received philosophy, a multitude of things that even common sense could understand. Wordsworth had not less genius than the others – even Hallam allowed his genius; we are not told that Mary of Galilee was more beautiful than the more popular Mary; but certainly we might consider Wordsworth a little disreputable.

I developed these principles to the rejection of all detailed description, that I might not steal the painter's business, and indeed I was always discovering some art or science that I might be rid of: and I found encouragement by noticing all round me painters[7] who were ridding their pictures, and indeed their minds, of literature. Yet those delighted senses, when I had got from them all that I could, left me discontented. Impressions that needed so elaborate a record did not seem like the handiwork of those careless old writers one imagines squabbling over a mistress, or riding on a journey, or drinking round a tavern fire, brisk and active men. Crashaw could hymn Saint Teresa in the most impersonal of ecstasies and seem no sedentary man out of reach of common sympathy, no disembodied mind and yet in his day the life that appeared most rich and stirring was already half forgotten with Villon and Dante.

This difficulty was often in my mind, but I put it aside, for the new formula was a good switch while the roads were beset with geese; it set us free from politics, theology, science, all that zeal and eloquence Swinburne and Tennyson found so intoxicating after the passion of their youth had sunk, free from the conventional nobility borne hither from ancient Rome in the galley that carried academic form to vex the painters. Among the little group of poets that met at the Cheshire Cheese I alone loved criticism of Arthur Hallam's sort, with a shamefaced love – criticism founded upon general ideas was itself an impurity – and perhaps I alone knew Hallam's essay, but all silently obeyed a canon that had become powerful for all the arts since Whistler, in the confidence of his American *naïveté,* had told everybody that Japanese painting had no literary ideas. Yet all the while envious of the centuries before the Renaissance, before the coming of our intellectual class with its separate interests, I filled my imagination with the popular beliefs of Ireland, gathering them up among forgotten novelists in the British Museum or in Sligo cottages. I sought some symbolic language reaching far into the past and associated with familiar names and conspicuous hills that I might not be alone amid the obscure impressions of the senses, and I wrote essays recommending my friends to paint on chapel walls the Mother of God flying with Saint Joseph into Egypt along some Connacht road, a Connemara shawl about her head, or mourned the richness or reality lost to Shelley's *Prometheus Unbound* because he had not discovered in England or in Ireland his Caucasus.

I notice like contradictions among my friends who are still convinced that art should not be 'complicated by ideas' while picturing Saint Brandan in stained glass for a Connemara chapel, and even among those exuberant young men who make designs for a Phallic Temple, but consider Augustus John lost amid literature.

But, after all, could we clear the matter up we might save some hours from sterile discussion. The arts are very conservative and have a great respect for those wanderers who still stitch into their carpets among the Mongolian plains religious symbols so old they have not even a meaning. It cannot be they would lessen an association with one another and with religion that gave them authority among ancient peoples. They are not radicals, and if they deny themselves to any it can only be to the *nouveau riche,* and if they have grown rebellious it can only be against something that is modern, something that is not simple.

I think that before the religious change that followed on the Renaissance men were greatly preoccupied with their sins, and that to-day they are troubled by other men's sins, and that this trouble has created a moral enthusiasm so full of illusion that art, knowing itself for sanctity's scapegrace brother, cannot be of the party. We have but held to our ancient Church, where there is an altar and no pulpit, and founded, the guide-book tells us, upon the ruins of the temple of Jupiter Ammon, and turned away from the too great vigour of those who, living for mutual improvement, have a pulpit and no altar. We fear that a novel enthusiasm might make us forget the little round of poetical duties and imitations – humble genuflexions and circumambulations as it were – that does not unseat the mind's natural impulse, and seems always but half-conscious, almost bodily.

Painting had to free itself from a classicalism that denied the senses, a domesticity that denied the passions, and poetry from a demagogic system of morals which destroyed the humility, the daily dying of the imagination in the presence of beauty. A soul shaken by the spectacle of its sins, or discovered by the Divine Vision in tragic delight, must offer to the love that cannot love but to infinity, a goal unique and unshared; while a soul busied with others' sins is soon melted to some shape of vulgar pride. What can I offer to God but the ghost that must return undisfeatured to the hands that have not made the same thing twice, but what would I have of others but that they do some expected thing, reverence my plans, be in some way demure and reliable? The turning of Rossetti to religious themes, his dislike of Wordsworth, were but the one impulse, for he more than any other was in reaction against the period of philanthropy and reform that created the pedantic composure of Wordsworth, the rhetoric of Swinburne, the passionless sentiment of Tennyson. The saint does not claim to be a good example, hardly even to tell men what to do, for is he not the chief of sinners, and of how little can he be certain whether in the night of the soul or lost in the sweetness coming after? Nor can that composure of the moralists be dear to one who has heard the commandment, that is for the saint and his brother the poet alike, 'Make excess ever more abundantly excessive', even were it possible to one shaken and trembling from his daily struggle.

We knew that system of popular instruction was incompatible with our hopes, but we did not know how to refute it and so turned away from all ideas. We would not even permit ideas, so greatly had we come to distrust them, to leave their impressions upon our senses. Yet works of art are always begotten by previous works of art, and every masterpiece becomes the Abraham of a chosen people. When we delight in a spring day there mixes, perhaps, with our personal emotion an emotion Chaucer found in Guillaume de Lorris, who had it from the poetry of Provence; we celebrate our draughty May with an enthusiasm made ripe by more meridian suns; and all our art has its image in the Mass that would lack authority were it not descended from savage ceremonies taught amid what perils and by what spirits to naked savages. The old images the old emotions, awakened again to overwhelming life, like the gods Heine tells of, by the belief and passion of some new soul, are the only masterpieces. The resolution to stand alone, to owe nothing to the past, when it is not mere sense of property, the greed and pride of the counting-house, is the result of that individualism of the Renaissance which had done its work when it gave us personal freedom. The soul which may not obscure or change its form can yet receive those passions and symbols of antiquity, certain they are too old to be bullies, too well-mannered not to respect the rights of others.

Nor had we better warrant to separate one art from another, for there has been no age before our own wherein the arts have been other than a single authority, a Holy Church of Romance, the might of all lying behind all, a circle of cliffs, a wilderness where every cry has its echoes. Why should a man cease to be a scholar, a believer, a ritualist before he begin to paint or rhyme or to compose music, or why if he have a strong head should he put away any means of power?

Yet it is plain that the casting out of ideas was the more natural, misunderstanding though it was, because it had come to matter very little. The manner of painting had changed, and we were interested in the fall of drapery and the play of light without concerning ourselves with the meaning, the emotion of the figure itself. How many successful portrait-painters gave their sitters the same attention, the same interest they might have given to a ginger-beer bottle and an apple? and in our poems an absorption in fragmentary sensuous beauty or detachable ideas had deprived us of the power to mould vast material into a single image. What long modern poem equals the old poems in architectural unity, in symbolic importance? *The Revolt of Islam, The Excursion, Gebir, Idylls of the King*, even perhaps *The Ring and the Book*, which fills me with so much admiring astonishment that my judgment sleeps, are remembered for some occasional passage some moment which gains little from the context. Until very lately even the short poems which contained as clearly as an Elizabethan lyric the impression of a single idea seemed accidental, so much the rule were the 'Faustines' and 'Dolores' where the verses might be arranged in any order, like shot poured out of a bag. Arnold when he withdrew his *Empedocles on Etna*, though one had been sorry to lose so much lyrical beauty for ever, showed himself a great critic by his reasons, but his *Sohrab and Rustum* proves that the unity he imagined was a classical imitation and not an organic thing, not the flow of flesh under the impulse of passionate thought.

Those poets with whom I feel myself in sympathy have tried to give to little poems the spontaneity of a gesture or of some casual emotional phrase. Meanwhile it remains for some greater time, living once more in passionate reverie, to create a *King Lear*, a *Divine Comedy*, vast worlds moulded by their own weight like drops of water.

In the visual arts, indeed, 'the fall of man into his own circumference' seems at an end, and when I look at the photograph of a picture by Gauguin, which hangs over my breakfast-table, the spectacle of tranquil Polynesian girls crowned with lilies gives me, I do not know why, religious ideas. Our appreciations of the older schools are changing too, becoming simpler, and when we take pleasure in some Chinese painting of an old man meditating upon a mountain path, we share his meditation, without forgetting the beautiful intricate pattern of the lines like those we have seen under our eyelids as we fell asleep; nor do the Bride and Bridegroom of Rajput painting, sleeping upon a housetop, or wakening when out of the still water the swans fly upward at the dawn, seem the less well painted because they remind us of many poems. We are becoming interested in expression in its first phase of energy, when all the arts play like children about the one chimney, and turbulent innocence can yet amuse those brisk and active men who have paid us so little attention of recent years. Shall we be rid of the pride of intellect, of sedentary meditation, of emotion that leaves us when the book is closed or the picture seen no more; and live amid the thoughts that can go with us by steamboat and railway as once, upon horseback, or camel-back, rediscovering, by our reintegration of the mind, our more profound Pre-Raphaelitism, the old abounding, nonchalant reverie?

## NOTES

1    See Elizabeth Bergmann Loizeaux, *Yeats and the Visual Arts*, New Brunswick and London, Rutgers University Press, 1986, pp. 122–3.

2    W.B. Yeats, *Essays and Introductions,* London, Macmillan, 1961, p. 219.

3    Painted in 1851–2, still in the Tate Gallery, London, as are the two Dante Gabriel Rossetti watercolours, nos. 2859 and 2860, respectively.

4    Frank Huddlestone Potter (1845–87), *Little Dormouse*, Tate Gallery. The painting represents a small girl with a stirring bowl. Potter was a friend of the poet's father, John Butler Yeats (1839–1922). The Yeats family owned the painting for many years, see W. B. Yeats, 'Reveries over Childhood and Youth', in *Autobiographies*, London, Macmillan, 1955, pp. 44–5. Reproduced in colour, Loizeaux, *Yeats and the Visual Arts*, Figure III. George Wilson (1848–90) was a watercolourist friend of Yeats's father.

5    Edward Burne-Jones (1833–98), *King Cophetua and the Beggar Maid*, 1884, Tate Gallery.

6    An early influence on Yeats, see R.F. Foster, *W.B. Yeats: A Life, I: The Apprentice Mage, 1865–1914,* Oxford University Press, 1997, p. 99.

7    This thought, which seemed a discovery, was old enough. Balzac derides in a story a certain Pierre Grassou who attained an immense popularity by painting a Chouan rebel going to his death. [Orig. note.]

— 11 —

# Elizabeth Thompson, Lady Butler,
## *An Autobiography,* 1922

The English artist Elizabeth Thompson (1846–1933) was one of the most successful women painters of the Victorian period. Her interest in Irish subject-
matter was brief but sincere; she was married to an Irishman, Major Sir William
Butler, a colonial officer. Thompson's versatility and capacity to attempt a wide
range of subjects is shown in her autobiographical accounts of the background
of many of her paintings. Discussion of some of her most well-known Irish
works appear in the same chapter as memories of painting the colourful 24th
Dragoons at Dinan in Brittany and an account of the exotic subjects to be
found during a lengthy sojourn in Egypt. In the extract included here, the artist
describes the evolution of her Irish painting, *Evicted* (1890, fig. 3), which depicts
a lone woman who has been removed from her house, a burnt-out shell that
frames her against a wild mountainous Wicklow background.[1]

3     Elizabeth Thompson, Lady Butler *Eviction,* 1890

Source: Elizabeth Thompson, *An Autobiography*, London, Constable & Co. Ltd., 1922, pp. 199–200

We went to live in Ireland from Dinan, in 1888, under the Wicklow Mountains, where the children continued their healthy country life in its fullness. The picture I had painted of the departing dragoons went to the Academy in 1889, and in 1890 I exhibited 'An Eviction in Ireland', which Lord Salisbury was pleased to be facetious about in his speech at the banquet, remarking on the 'breezy beauty' of the landscape, which almost made him wish he could take part in an eviction himself. How like a Cecil![2]

The 'eighties had seen our Government do some dreadful things in the way of evictions in Ireland. Being at Glendalough at the end of that decade, and hearing one day that an eviction was to take place some nine miles distant from where we were staying for my husband's shooting, I got an outside car and drove off to the scene, armed with my paints. I met the police returning from their distasteful 'job', armed to the teeth and very flushed. On getting there I found the ruins of the cabin smouldering, the ground quite hot under my feet, and I set up my easel there. The evicted woman came to search amongst the ashes of her home to try and find some of her belongings intact. She was very philosophical, and did not rise to the level of my indignation as an ardent English sympathiser. However, I studied her well, and on returning home at Delgany I set up the big picture which commemorates a typical eviction in the black 'eighties. I seldom can say I am pleased with my work when done, but I *am* complacent about this picture; it has the true Irish atmosphere, and I was glad to turn out that landscape successfully which I had made all my studies for, on the spot, at Glendalough. What storms of wind and rain, and what dazzling sunbursts I struggled in, one day the paints being blown out of my box and nearly whirled into the lake far below my mountain perch! My canvas, acting like a sail, once nearly sent me down there too. I did not see this picture at all at the Academy, but I am very certain it cannot have been very 'popular' in England. Before it was finished my husband was appointed to the command at Alexandria, and as soon as I had packed off the 'Eviction', I followed, on March 24th, and saw again the fascinating East.

## NOTES

1    See Paul Usherwood and Jenny Spencer-Smith, *Lady Butler, Battle Artist, 1846–1933*, Alan Sutton and the National Army Museum, London, 1987, pp. 94–5.

2    *Evicted* was exhibited in the Royal Academy of Arts in London in 1890. Robert

Gascoyne-Cecil, third Marquess of Salisbury (1830–1903) was Prime Minister from 1885 to 1892 and from 1895 to 1902.

# – 12 –

# Mainie Jellett, 'My Voyage of Discovery', 1943

The daughter of a respectable Dublin Protestant family, Mainie Jellett (1897–1944) is celebrated as the main instigator of abstract painting in Ireland. After training in Dublin and London, she began her first lessons with the cubists André Lhote (1885–1962) and Albert Gleizes (1881–1953) in Paris in 1921. Two years later she was exhibiting abstract paintings in Dublin. A theorist and an inveterate propagandist for her cause, Jellett produced numerous essays and gave many lectures and broadcasts. She died in her forties, having helped establish the Irish Exhibition of Living Art.[1] 'My Voyage of Discovery', the piece included here, first appeared in the *Dublin Art Handbook*, 1943, as 'Definitions of My Art'. Here, Jellett defines her work in succinct terms, 'we sought the inner principle and not the outer appearance'; she also stresses the Irish dimension to her experiments, her interest in 'rhythmic forms' having been influenced by Celtic art. Jellett's discussion of such relationships between the modern and the ancient Irish is picked up again in the 1960s and 1970s, see entries 13, 22 and 48.

Source: Mainie Jellett, *The Artist's Vision: Lectures and Essays on Art*, ed. Eileen MacCarvill, Dundalk, Dundalgan Press Ltd., 1958, pp. 47–51.

My Voyage of Discovery from student to professional painter and teacher has been stormy and varied. At least three times I have gone through major revolutions in my work, style and ideas, and more or less started afresh.

I studied in Ireland till I was eighteen, then went to London and studied under Walter Sickert (first revolution), where for the first time drawing and composition came alive to me, and with Sickert's help I began to understand the work of the Old Masters. Sickert being in the direct line of French impressionist painting was an excellent stepping stone to my next revolution, Paris and Lhote's Studio. This was my first encounter with modern French painting; though I had admired and appreciated it in London and wherever I had come in contact with it, the ideas behind it I had only partially understood.

In Lhote's Studio, where we worked on modified cubist theories, my eyes were again opened to the glories of the Old Masters. I have always maintained, and will continue to do so, that the further I progressed on my voyage towards the extremes of modern painting, the greater became my appreciation of the Old Masters. With Lhote it was the great Masters of the Renaissance and Rubens; later when I advanced deeper into the cubist and non-representational schools it was the Italian primitives, 11th, 12th and 13th century painting, the sculpture and architecture of Europe and Celtic art which influenced me. With Lhote I learnt how to use natural forms as a starting point towards the creation of form for its own sake; to use colour with the knowledge of its great potential force, and to produce work based on a knowledge of rhythmical form and organic colour, groping towards a conception of a picture being a creative organic whole, but still based on realistic form. I worked on these lines and developed a great deal but felt I had not gone as far as I wanted on the way to the full understanding of the extreme forms of non-representational art.

Then came my third revolution, and this was produced by my becoming a student of Albert Gleizes, one of the original members of the cubist group and one who has produced the purest and most austere form of non-representational work. I went right back to the beginning with him, and was put to the severest type of exercise in pure form and colour, evolved on a certain system of composition. I now felt I had come to essentials, and though the type of work I had embarked upon would mean years of misunderstanding and walls of prejudice to break through, yet I felt I was on the right track. I worked in close contact with Gleizes and his ideas for a considerable time, but with intervals between each period when I came back to Ireland to work out the ideas I had gleaned in France and to continue my teaching of private students.

Though my main work was non-representational, I never completely abandoned realistic work. We never as a group turned from Nature – we could not; our aim was to delve deeply into the inner rhythms and constructions of natural forms to create on their pattern, to make a work of art a natural creation complete in itself like a flower or any other natural organism, based on the eternal laws of harmony, balance and ordered movement (rhythm). We sought the inner principle and not the outer appearance.

After my first contacts with Albert Gleizes my work for some time was severely non-representational and still at an experimental stage. Then by slow degrees and much work I gained a wider and more emotional power of expression. The harmonic study of colour had become a very intense factor in the work, and this, allied with the previous concentrated study of form, produced a background from which ideas began to germinate.

Another very strong influence on my work was Oriental Art, and particularly Chinese Art. I went to London with the express purpose of seeing and studying the Winter Exhibition of Chinese Art at Burlington House in 1935–36. This made a profound impression upon me and helped to form an approach to landscape painting, which I have used in varied forms ever since.

In recent years my work roughly tends to divide itself into three categories:

(i)     Non-representational painting based on some emotional contact received from nature or experience, but first born in the mind.

(ii)    Non-representational work based on Christian religious subjects treated symbolically without realism.

(iii)   Realistic landscape treated in a manner inspired by Chinese Art, and direct realistic studies for exercises and reference.

The last time I saw Albert Gleizes, his talks to me on painting were in this vein: a painting, like a human being, must be made up of two elements, body and soul. The body in the picture being the material element, the emotion derived from a poetic idea, a religious subject, some contact with nature, which has started the artist's imagination working; the soul is the power of the artist to work this material into a creative whole which lives as an organic entity complete in itself, and lifts the material element into an inner world controlled by an inner rhythm and harmony aspiring towards the eternal.

I believe that a work of art is something that is born in the mind and in the innermost emotions; it may lie dormant in the deep recesses of the artist's consciousness till the moment strikes for its release and realisation in material form, but for it to live there must be the almost sub-conscious creative urge which brings it into being.

I believe in the organic and elemental force of colour and the necessity to use colour constructively and with a sense of its power and the laws governing it.

I believe in the necessity of a highly developed sense of craftsmanship; every artist should be capable of executing adequately whatever job he is entrusted with. An artist should be a competent worker as he was in the periods when the Guild system operated; he should have an honest standard of workmanship like any competent worker in other walks of life. The idea of an artist being a special person, an exotic flower set apart from other people, is one of the errors resulting from the industrial revolution, and the cause of artists being pushed out of their lawful position in the life and society of the present day.

Artists as a whole are people with certain gifts more highly developed than the majority, but for this very reason their gifts are vitally important to the mental and spiritual life of that majority. Their present enforced isolation from the majority is to be deplored and, I believe, is one of the many causes which has resulted in the present chaos we live in.

The art of a nation is one of the ultimate facts by which its spiritual health is judged and appraised by posterity, and in many cases when all else has disappeared the clue to a whole civilisation may be traced through fragments of pottery, sculpture, or other artistic manifestations which may remain.

I believe in the truth of the ideals which inspire what is commonly called 'the Modern Movement' in art. This movement has been a means of purification and revitalisation of the art of the late 19th and the 20th centuries. It has shaken the materialism of the so-called academic traditition and has shown those who were alive enough to see, where the true traditions lie. It has shown the futility of merely copying the great works of the past and, by so doing, fondly imagining a tradition was being carried on. It has demonstrated with clarity and success that the only way to carry on a live tradition is to understand and venerate the great works of the past and to realise the unchanging artistic laws behind them, laws which must be reinterpreted by each period in turn so as to express its needs and character.

In so doing it is producing an art representative of the present period. I do not say it is a great art because I do not consider the present period is capable of producing a great art. A time when one civilisation is in its death throes and a new civilisation is struggling for birth is not a period to produce great art, but it is a period in which new foundations can be placed and everlasting truths re-expressed in forms adapted to the present time. That, I feel, 'the Modern Movement' in art is doing, and has done.

France has been the centre of this movement. There has not been much chance for Irish people to see many examples of its work in their own country. From time to time, through the kindness of private owners, some of these works in Irish private collections have been shown on loan; some to exhibitions organised by 'Contemporary Pictures', Dublin. There are several examples which have been presented to Dublin and are in the Municipal Collection in Charlemont House, Parnell Square. Amongst them are pictures by Bonnard, Utrillo, Picasso, Lurçat, and a fine example of the work of Rouault, now in Maynooth College [fig. 25].[2] In private collections there are a number of representative works by some of the leading painters of the modern French school, and I hope that eventually these works may pass into our national collections.

A picture to me is primarily the harmonious filling of a space with rhythmic forms, the subject being of secondary importance.

This was the root ideal of ancient Celtic, or what we call Early Irish Christian art, of Eastern art, and of European art from the Christian Era to the early Renaissance. Following on the Renaissance came the materialistic idea, though it was only by degrees (in the 19th century, as a matter of fact) that the artistic standard is changed from spiritual to material.

The surface is my starting point, my aim is to make it live.

The surface on which a painter works can be either wall, panel, canvas or paper; the primary truth of that surface is its flatness.

I wish to preserve that flatness and to oppose Renaissance perspective.

I recognise a natural perspective of colours and forms, for example, the power of certain colours to dominate others and to come nearer the eye; and of forms by their placing in the composition having the same effect, but this I recognise as natural perspective which can be organised in the general composition, its effects nullified if desired by careful arrangement of colour and form.

A picture to me is a mobile living object with an organisation controlled by a definite rhythm and like any natural organisation, flowers, trees, human beings, complete in itself.

I do not deny nature. I would not; but I wish to copy nature not in her external aspects but in her internal organisation; to create as far as my human power will let me as nature is created.

I wish my pictures to be as perfect organisations of form and colour as it is in my power to make them.

My pictures are first conceived in my mind and then worked out according to the laws of colour, the formal composition and rhythmic movement peculiar to the surface and shape I am filling.

The organisation of a picture of this kind is somewhat similar to the orchestration of a musical composition which is first conceived in the mind and then is presented to the world through the medium of sound organised by the laws of harmony and counterpoint.

Conceived in the mind, my picture becomes a concrete fact, an interpretation of the original mental conception through the medium of form and colour, controlled by the laws of composition.

A picture should be capable of producing an emotional reaction on the spectator entirely on its merits as a colour organisation and formal composition without a realistic appeal.

## NOTES

1    See Bruce Arnold, *Mainie Jellett and the Modern Movement in Ireland*, New Haven and London, Yale University Press, 1991.

2    This is a reference to Georges Rouault's *Christ in His Passion*, which eventually
     entered the collection of the Municipal Gallery of Modern Art, Dublin. See also
     entry 47.


# — 13 —

# Tom Duddy, 'Irish Art Criticism – A Provincialism of the Right?', 1987

An earlier version of this article appeared in *Circa Art Magazine*, an important source for the discussion of the visual arts in Ireland since its foundation
in 1981. Originally edited from Belfast, *Circa* has always attempted a
comprehensive cross-border approach to coverage of the visual arts. Duddy,
a lecturer in philosophy at the National University of Ireland, Galway, here
offers an assessment of recent art criticism in Ireland. He has taken the title
of his essay from a comment by the modernist critic Brian O'Doherty (see
entry 49). Since its first appearance, Duddy has made minor changes to the
text; the notes for the article have been maintained but the accompanying
illustrations have been left out.

Source: *Circa Art Magazine*, no. 35, July/August 1987, pp. 14–18


Many of our most influential art critics, when attempting to say what is distinctively Irish about Irish art, are much more likely to answer in terms of geography, landscape, and weather than in terms of history and economic realities.
An exemplary version of the geographical approach can be found in Frances
Ruane's introduction to *The Delighted Eye* catalogue in which she maintains
that the recurrence of the rural landscape as a motif in Irish painting is 'probably the most important element' that distinguishes Irish art from the international mainstream.[1] Her basic argument is that Ireland is a fundamentally
different place from New York or Los Angeles, that Irish artists remain fundamentally different as a result of their rootedness in a remote and unique landscape, and that Irish artists consequently opt for subjects, treatments, and media
that express their unique location. Irish artists are more likely to adapt the irregular organic shapes of a hillside than they are to register, say, the hard-edged

geometry of machines or machine parts. The work of Colin Middleton, Camille Souter, Barrie Cooke, Brian Bourke, and Maria Simmonds-Gooding may appear expressionistic or abstract in varying degrees, as if all these artists were under the influence of modernist values, but in fact the sources of their inspiration lie elsewhere.[2] The countryside and the landscape, rather than any close acquaintance or sympathy with the work of artists from abroad, remain the primary points of departure: 'Agricultural roots, conservatism, an obsession with the past, and a passion for indirect statement shape the way [the Irish artist] expresses himself visually.'[3] Even the Irish artist's preference for 'natural' media such as oil-paint, water-colour, wood, and stone is considered an expression of a conservative sensibility, a sensibility that is conservative because it is shaped and sustained by a natural – i.e., rural – environment.

Brian Fallon, though suspicious of attempts to identify national characteristics in art, nonetheless assigns a good deal of importance to place and the individual artist's response to it. In a catalogue essay on Tony O'Malley he has shown an anxiety to look past signs of foreign influence and uncover evidence of something local and native as well as individually distinctive. Submitting to international influences is not the way out of provincialism, in Fallon's view. On the contrary, trucking to international fashion is usually the trademark of an endemically provincial culture. But lest anyone imagine that the rejection of provincialism implies the rejection of locality or place, Fallon quotes with approval Peter Lanyon's distinction between being parochial and 'being local and rooted'. Comparing O'Malley with Lanyon – whom he describes as 'a born internationalist', – he suggests that one cannot overstress 'the sense of place both [artists] shared, the consciousness of having roots in their own region'.[4] He concludes that however much a certain kind of fashionable, journalistic rationalism may ridicule such things as the Celtic nature mystique, such factors remain 'a reality which obstinately surfaces in the most disparate works of art'.[5]

Even one of Ireland's leading 'internationalist' critics, Dorothy Walker, will not let an orthodox modernist formalism have its way with our Irish artists. After alluding to the fact that 'atmospheric' painting is often held to be peculiarly Irish and that such painting 'undoubtedly represents frequent weather conditions', she goes on to insist that there is an underlying structural basis in Irish art which has persisted since prehistoric times, 'a paradoxically informal formalism which can be seen as far back as the great carvings at Newgrange'.[6] She can find in Felim Egan 'dark background colours which represent the surface of the ancient stone.'[7] And she finds Charles Tyrrell using abstract painting to express his particular statement of 'the recurring Irish combination of formalism allied to natural or organic materials'.[8] In other words, even those artists most sympathetic to formalist ideas remain true to a native organic impulse, remain capable of a natively instinctive response to local shapes, textures, and materials – an impulse and a response which are, moreover, symptomatic of an underlying collective genius whose identity extends all the way back into the prehistoric past.

Meteorological versions of the geographical aesthetic may be found in the writing of a surprising number of critics. Brian O'Doherty, in one of his texts for *The Irish Imagination* catalogue, maintains that hosts of modern Irish artists have evolved a 'poetic' genre in painting, an 'atmospheric mode' – a genre or mode which is largely a response to the Irish landscape and the Irish light, especially Ireland's long twilights.[9] Even a radical critic like John Berger has not been immune to bewitchment by the language of landscape and weather. Consider this piece of meteorological eroticism on Jack B. Yeats:

> Yeats seems too 'mobile', over-spontaneous, until one has watched the west coast of Ireland. And watched is the word, for the land-scape there is a fast series of events, not a view – an unchanging structure. The land is as passive as a bog can be. The sky is all action. I am told that the sky is similar in California . . . But in Ireland the sky is a dancer, tender and wild alternately, and then furious, ripping her clothes and parading her golden body to get just one glimmer of response from the peat. And she gets it . . . And it is this wild dancing and wilder response that Yeats has painted.[10]

And Cyril Barrett, in his contribution to the 14th AICA Congress of the International Association of Art Critics (on the theme of international influences on local art communities), found that Irish artists, even when registering international influences, nonetheless manage to convey the Irish countryside and its light and atmosphere. It is as though the Irish landscape moulds its people and artists alike, moulding the artists indeed to such an extent that it finds its way inevitably into their work. Superficially, the paintings of Patrick Scott may look like informal abstracts, 'yet, in fact, they convey the colours, the atmosphere, the lights (dawn, sunset), the flora, the heat or dampness of an Irish heath or bog in a way that no naturalistic painting could'.[11]

## LOCALITY AND THE NATIVE IMPULSE

The need to place, localise, regionalise, naturalise, root, and generally 'countrify' Irish artists has been accompanied by a comparable need to identify 'a strong native impulse', a native genius which is ultimately explicable in terms of an elective affinity between the sensibility of the individual artists and certain special qualities immanent in the Irish landscape. Localism, posed as the salvation of Irish artists, rides pillion to Brian O'Doherty's suggestive observation that the best Irish artists display 'an independence that is not obtuse, avoiding the provincialism of the right (nationalism) and the provincialism of the left (modernism)'.[12] The future of Irish art does not lie with either provincialism but with 'the successful local artists'. The localness of these artists, however, is not just a matter of living in a particular place, even a natural, rural place. It is something deeper than that, something that must make its presence visible in the work of art itself, in the subjects the artists paint, in the styles they adopt, in the materials they use. Being local means being defensively or pro-actively local; it means offering resistance to influences from other localities, especially non-Irish, non-rural, 'international' localities.

Being local also means avoiding the embrace of big movements or schools and remaining an uncompromised, virginal individual. In his 14th Congress paper Cyril Barrett makes the point explicitly: 'The Irish artists of the 1970s are individual artists. There is no-one anywhere who works like Seamus Coleman, Patrick Scott, Robert Ballagh, Michael Craig-Martin, Colin Harrison and Brian King.'[13] Brian Fallon likewise is of the view that what matters in the long run is not whether an artist works in a 'national' or 'international' style, but his own personal stature. Many artists may need the stimulation of the city but 'others mature in relative isolation or in relatively provincial centres'.[14] The more removed the artist is from the urban centre, the safer she is, it seems, from the sources of influence; the more likely she is to remain close to nature and to remain therefore in a state of pristine native individuality. The thinking here is rather reminiscent of Rousseau's romantic vision of the original state of nature when savage man not only wandered in the forests without industry or society but did so more or less alone, without the need of interactive or communicative skills more elaborate than those of the crow or monkey. Nature, native genius, locality, place, and physical distance – distance from urbanity, complication, and influence – are concepts which cluster together here to form a romantic vision of the sources of ethnic artistic identity.

It is arguable that the tendency of Irish art critics to impose a naturalistic or nativistic content and ethos on Irish art, specifically to read off landscape motifs or signs of the Celtic past from an apparent diversity of images, is a conservative and protectionist one – protectionist in the measure that it will not allow for completely new things, for timely development and change, for constructive influence from abroad. More specifically, it will not allow Irish art to be really abstract, or abstract in the way that other people's art is abstract. In attempting to fix a particular identity for Irish art, this visual ideology suggests, in an almost racialistic sense, that the sensibility of Irish people, artists and public alike, is not disposed to express itself in conceptual, formal, or abstract modes, and that Irish art specifically does not lend itself to interpretation in such modes. This assumption of a pathological reluctance or inability on the part of the Irish to deal with concepts, or to construct and paint in abstract modes, need not be linked to Suzi Gablik's questionable hypothesis that progress in art is progress towards ever-increasing conceptualization.[15] We may take it, however, that the ability to abstract in visual art is just a particular exercise of the ability to abstract in perception and knowledge generally. The notion that the Irish eye is focussed only on the particular, the local, and the immediately natural is not a compliment to either the extreme beauty of the natural object or to the extreme receptivity of the Irish eye. Rather, it is an insult to the Irish eye and the Irish mind. These faculties, as they are locally embodied, cannot seem to see further than *this* curve of hillside, *this* angle of cutaway bog, *this* segment of dancing sky. To be unable to abstract from the particular indicates a weakness of intellect and imagination, not a power of perception. It might be claimed here that it is simply the sheer beauty of the particular which overwhelms eye and mind, but this claim only compounds the insult – to be helplessly taken in by the beauty of the object suggests not only intellectual weakness but moral weakness as well, a weakness of the will and of character.

The hypothesis of landscapism, coupled with the hypothesis of the native impulse or the hypothesis of the underlying tradition, may be conservative and protectionist in a more political sense – in the sense that it fails to acknowledge the crucial roles played by dominant visual ideologies, by centrally-sponsored avant gardes, by the uneven distribution of cultural as well as economic capital, by the uneven dissemination of trend-setting galleries, dealers, critics, and art journals. Romantic concepts of place, atmosphere, native sensibility, native impulse, local genius, and the Celtic imagination are given priority over such 'dirty' materialistic concepts as economy, market, commodity, visual ideology, conspicuous consumption, and the sorts of useful explanatory terms used by historians like Hadjinicolaou and sociologists like Bourdieu.[16] Drawing almost exclusively from a store of romantic notions, the idealists, nativists, transcendental regionalists, and informal formalists seem to have decided that Ireland can stand alone culturally, indeed can do no other than stand alone, exploiting its insularity and relative isolation, celebrating the unsullied impulses of its local geniuses, and inviting its artists to look no further than native tradition for their sources of inspiration. This means that certain unpleasant realities are not recognised, let alone dealt with.

One of the less pleasant consequences of insularity and marginalisation is that very few artists who remain in Ireland can hope to achieve greatness or have greatness thrust upon them. Greatness has connotations not only of excellence and originality but also of marketability, scale and scope of publicity, level of conspicuous consumption, and degree of influence enjoyed by supporting patrons, critics, and connoisseurs. The aesthetic merit of the work of art itself has to hold its own in the context of such all-pervasive and powerful variables. Irish critics, however, may have done Irish artists a disservice by promoting delusions of grandeur, by suggesting that a work produced in Ireland ultimately enjoys the same prospects as one produced in New York – by pursuing, in other words, a line of interpretation and advocacy which ignores the ruder and baser realities that ground our cultural lives and our cultural work.

Acknowledging such realities need not lead to cynicism or despair. It does not follow that because provincial status is not a great virtue that therefore it must be a great vice. The relevant point here may be stated in terms of right and obligation. The right to remain obscure and local in the remoter provinces of the art-world demands the obligation to face up to and identify the consequences of doing so. There are perhaps more obligations for critics to meet than there are for artists. Artists, no matter where they are located, no matter how 'local' they are, may do all sorts of things in the name of creativity; critics, because they are obliged to take the overview, do not have the same liberty. Provincialism is some kind of option for artists; for critics, however, it is at best a right that has to be argued for.

## O'Doherty's Provincialisms Revisited

To the problem of marginalisation, then, artists have been providing their own individual answers, as is their creative wont. The critics have still to give a satisfactory response. By squinting through the distorting lens of a particular visual ideology and by ignoring the dirtier social, economic, and historical contexts in which art is produced, the critics have too often spoken the romantic language of landscape and nativism, and have too often come uncomfortably close to promoting an ethnicist, even racialistic, notion of artistic identity. Hence the charge made here that some critics at least have been tempted towards a provincialism of the right as far as critical values are concerned, especially when attempting to say what is distinctive about Irish art.

This is not to say that O'Doherty's original distinction between a provincialism of the right and a provincialism of the left is unproblematic. The main problem with it lies in the nature of the polarisation itself. Once you introduce a polarisation towards either end of a continuum, it is very difficult to think in terms of 'a third way'. The best you can hope for is an ambivalent position somewhere along that polarised continuum. O'Doherty thinks that by advocating localism he is steering safely clear of his two provincialisms, but in fact he has simply moved a safe distance from one provincialism – namely, the provincialism of the left – and has backed into the only available alternative on the continuum, namely, the provincialism of the right. His localism is just another version of nationalism – nationalism writ small – since the local-ism that is under approval in this case is a distinctively Irish localism.

For the sake of the argument being pursued here, however, we are going to stay with O'Doherty's polarities and risk making an impertinent recom-mendation. Perhaps our critics should experiment with a provincialism of the left, albeit in a sense rather different from O'Doherty's original formulation. A provincialism of the left in our revised sense would not mean an uncriti-cal internationalism (which nobody could wish to promote anyway) but an historically realistic, even materialistic, understanding of local art production. The difference between a provincialism of the right and a provincialism of the left is that the former gives undue weight to ahistorical factors, such as nature and locality, while the latter would give due weight to historical and economic realities. Nicos Hadjinicolaou once argued that the question, 'What is beauty?' should be replaced by the more realistic or materialistic question, 'By whom, when, and for what reason was this work thought beautiful?'[17] Questions like 'What is art?' or 'What is great art?' or even 'What is distinc-tive about Irish art?' could be re-interpreted in the same way, giving rise to a new realism about art – a kind of 'dirty realism', if you will. In general, any attempt to isolate the purely artistic elements of art from all the other rag-and-bone elements – location of art market, size of market, size of museum budget, level of conspicuous consumption, dominant visual ideology – would be seen as unduly idealistic and romantic.

Such acknowledgement of all the material circumstances would help crit-ics resist the temptation to reach for the easy semiology of either Celtic nat-uralism or Celtic formalism. A provincialism of the left – a sustained realism about the local conditions in which art is produced and marketed – might, for example, relieve critics and art historians of the need to establish grand con-tinuities between the present and the distant past. It might relieve a respected historian of the need to say, for example, that Mainie Jellett, despite her Cubist training, 'shows a flat, linear and colouristic quality which takes up an ancient thread'.[18] It might not be necessary for a respected critic to identify one of the themes of Irish art as that of 'focusing on elements that tie contemporary man to the ancients'.[19] Or for a respected artist to make the extraordinary statement that 'no pictures of any value concerned with the real problem of picture-making have been made in Ireland since the Book of Kells'.[20]

## A PROVINCIALISM OF THE LEFT?

How then might one attempt a realistic or 'materialistic' account of how and why Irish art is different from art produced elsewhere? In other words, how might one attempt an account that pays due attention to what's going on in the market-place? One way is to look at the poignant and often telling relationship between art, money, and life – that is to say, between the artist who needs to live and the potential buyer who can provide the means of life in a free enterprise economy. (Lest such an approach should be thought to presuppose an 'alien' ideology, such as Marxism or historical materialism, it is worth noting that one of the critics cited above has already had recourse to what we are calling a materialistic or simply realistic analysis. Brian O'Doherty, in the same text in which he wrote of the determining influence of landscape and light, also wrote briefly but informatively of the important role played in Dublin in the forties and fifties by Victor Waddington's gallery in South Anne Street.[21]) The small art-buying community in Ireland is part of the international art-market, since no modern market can insulate itself from global forces and currents. This small community knows the exchange-value of whatever commodity it deals in, including works of art, but it tends to lack initiative, to lack the knowledge and confident visual ideology of the centrally-positioned international patrons and dealers. This is not due to any native lack of taste or sensibility but mainly to a lack of access to regular trend-setting exhibitions and museums, and to the whole complex *milieu* of connoisseurship and influential patronage.

And this simple material fact may have had consequences for developments in the local art-world, including developments at the practical on-canvas level of content and style. Artists in Ireland, unlike their critical counterparts, recognised, if only implicitly, the limitations of their potential patrons and public. They took due account of the fears and the modestly informed sensibilities and expectations of their potential buyers – and produced accordingly. Hence, in the modernist period artists were able to blur the edges of the object but without losing it entirely in the medium. (Patrick Collins's remark, 'You destroy your object, yet you keep it . . .'[22] could be taken as the motto of this approach, though Collins himself attributed such creative destruction to the Celtic imagination.) Artists availed of the opportunity to become more or less non-figurative and sometimes virtually abstract but softly, softly. They were in general able to mediate creatively between the new pressures from abroad and the guarded receptivity of their patrons at home. This delicate and often inspired appeal to the wary sensibilities of the conservative Irish art-lover may have contributed more to the 'atmospheric mode' of several decades of Irish painting than did the influence of climate, ancient tradition, or the Celtic imagination.[23]

In other words, the atmospheric mode, the organic style, and the emergent, residual, or fractured object may be the creative response of an embattled artist caught between a rock and a hard place – between the rock of an avant-gardist international modernism and the hard place of marginalised and underdeveloped local patronage. (It must be borne in mind that the connoisseurs and patrons of a provincial art-world, and not just the artists, may also be marginalised – perhaps even more so than the artists.) The fact that this represents a kind of compromise for artists themselves is not relevant, creatively speaking. One way of understanding creativity, after all, is to see it as, among other things, a kind of problem-solving activity. It involves solving not only technical problems but also problems of influence and marginalisation. Irish artists have in many cases developed impressive solutions to these problems. Too many critics, however, talk and write as if there was no problem, as if Irish artists had in fact fewer problems than their counterparts in the influential international centres – as if they just act naturally as a matter of course, blissfully spinning their lyrical, natively expressive narratives.

A provincialism of the left, then, acknowledges the distinctive position of Ireland and Irish culture but sets out to give more than a geographical or quasi-racialistic account of that distinctiveness. There is nothing in itself wrong with references to landscape, tradition, or ancient craftsmanship, as long as such things are not 'mystified' and as long as equal weight is given to the more historical, ideological, and economic sorts of extra-artistic factors, i.e., the dirtier material sorts of factors. Without reference to such factors, any account of the distinctiveness of Irish art, where it *is* distinctive, will be incomplete. A mode of explanation and criticism which is narrowly idealistic, or which is based on a quest for a narrowly protectionist sort of nativism or naturalism, should be avoided, if only because there may be an element of truth in Herbert Read's assertion that 'decadence is usually associated with the growth of naturalism'.[24] The sort of naturalism we are questioning here, however, is not a particular style produced by artists but a visual ideology produced by critics – an ideology which has blinkered the vision of critics who should permit themselves to see more and know more.

## NOTES

1    Frances Ruane, *The Delighted Eye: Irish Painting and Sculpture of the Seventies*, Dublin, 1980, unpaginated. [Orig. note.]
2    For accounts of many of these artists and others referred to later in the article see Dorothy Walker, *Modern Art in Ireland*, Dublin, The Lilliput Press, 1997, passim.
3    Ibid. [Orig. note.]
4    Brian Fallon, *Tony O'Malley*, Belfast, and Dublin, Arts Council of Ireland and Arts Council of Northern Ireland, 1984, p. 35. [Orig. note.]
5    Ibid., p. 38. [Orig. note.]
6    Dorothy Walker, 'Traditional Structures in Recent Irish Art', *The Crane Bag*, vol. 6, no. 1, 1982, p. 41. [Orig. note.]

7      Ibid., p. 42. [Orig. note.]

8      Ibid. [Orig. note.]

9      Brian O'Doherty, Introduction to *The Irish Imagination, 1959–71*, Dublin, 1971, p. 11. [See entry 49 for text of O'Doherty's Introduction.] [Orig. note.]

10     John Berger, *Selected Essays and Articles*, Harmondsworth, 1972, p. 57. [Orig. note.]

11     Cyril Barrett, 'The "Internationalism" of Irish Art, 1943–73', in *Proceedings of the 14th Congress of AICA*, Dublin, 1983, p. 51. [Orig. note.] [For an example of Barrett's work see entry 50.]

12     O'Doherty, 'The Native Heritage', in *The Irish Imagination*, p. 20. [Orig. note.]

13     Barrett, 'The "Internationalism" of Irish Art, 1943-73', in *Proceedings of the 14th Congress*, p. 54. [Orig. note.]

14     Fallon, *Tony O'Malley*, p. 29. [Orig. note.]

15     See Suzi Gablik, *Progress in Art*, London, 1976. [Orig. note.]

16     See Nicos Hadjinicolaou, *Art History and Class Struggle*, London, 1978, and Pierre Bourdieu, *Distinction: A Social Critique of the Judgement of Taste*, London, 1984. [Orig. note.]

17     Hadjinicolaou, *Art History*, p. 183. [Orig. note.]

18     John Turpin, 'Colonialism and the Visual Arts in Ireland', in *Proceedings of the 14th Congress*, p. 38. [Orig. note.]

19     Ruane, *The Delighted Eye*, unpaginated. [Orig. note.]

20     Michael Farrell, *Artists' Statements*, Dublin, 1979, p. 20. [Orig. note.]

21     O'Doherty, *The Irish Imagination*, p. 10. O'Doherty makes the point that Waddington created the first stable of Irish artists and also created for these artists 'an audience which he educated with a series of small-scale international shows' (p.10). [Orig. note.]

22     Frances Ruane, *Patrick Collins*, Dublin, 1982, p. 23. [Orig. note.]

23     Cf. O'Doherty's observation that 'a suggestive form of painting with a particular atmospheric complexion' was 'a product of the interaction of artists and audience' in the forties and fifties (*The Irish Imagination*, p. 11). [Orig. note.]

24     Herbert Read, *The Philosophy of Modern Art: Collected Essays*, London, 1964, p. 264. That Read might in fact have supported a provincialism of the right is suggested by his startling reference to a Celtic strain in the English race 'pressing us on, in Matthew Arnold's words, "to the impalpable, the ideal". . .' [Orig. note.]


— 14 —

# Declan McGonagle, 'Looking Beyond Regionalism', 1990


This essay was originally delivered as the opening address of the Annual Conference of the Association of Art Historians held at Trinity College Dublin in

1990. The theme of the conference was 'Regionalism: Challenging the Canon'; it was the first occasion that the British-based association held a non-UK conference and it also marked the largest gathering of art historians in Ireland. At the time of its delivery, McGonagle was running the Orchard Gallery in Derry; he was subsequently appointed founding Director of the Irish Museum of Modern Art.

Source: *Circa Art Magazine*, no. 53, September–October 1990, pp. 26–27

The first thing we have to do is question and expand upon the idea of regionalism itself. I wonder if regionalism is not a necessary part of the canon we are supposed to be challenging – that is, something defined by the centre. If we define ourselves as being regional are we not accepting the set of definitions which puts the centre at the top of the hierarchy and the regional somewhere below, implying an acceptance of the hierarchy itself and the relationships of power within it?

Yet we know that social formations exist beyond geographical and political boundaries. Regionalist thinking overrides locality and actually becomes part of the centralist confirmation of privilege and power, which will always require a depoliticisation of art and culture and the removal of social meaning lest the hierarchy is actually challenged. I would suggest that we look beyond regionalism to locality as a way of challenging the canon.

Until recently, in the context of these islands, a particular socio–economic system was unquestionably at the top of the hierarchy with all other regions having degrees of diminishing value, ending with the ultimate periphery – a place like Northern Ireland in general, and Derry in particular. While this marginalisation has, historically, taken very dramatic forms, in Derry the principle is present everywhere.

It's my view that art deserves a future only in as much as it addresses and goes beyond the dominant set of colonial relationships that still apply in terms of class, gender, race in these islands and elsewhere. Colonisation is only successful when the colonised colonise themselves, legislating for themselves, socially and culturally, on behalf of the coloniser and rendering the meaning of their own culture invalid.

In such circumstances local culture is distorted and marginalised, resulting in the cultural parodies of the Irish leprechaun and Scottish tartan. Taken from their original social context and meaning they are made safe for the coloniser. The culture of locality, by contrast, is rooted in process and is problematic. An emphasis on process connects it with some of the most significant developments in contemporary art this century.

By definition the culture of locality is embedded within its audience. In fact, the idea of a separated audience doesn't apply. Where the process of mediation is connected to the context and can develop a sense of the world without invalidating the local or the vernacular a new vocabulary is possible. Such a vocabulary can be read locally and internationally; it breaks the presumption of metropolitan knowledge and local ignorance; engages with those processes already present in the society; empowers and enables the otherwise dispossessed. It is actually in those places which have been excluded historically where social structures may be in a state of flux – that cultural intervention is not only possible but necessary and where new models will develop.

This cannot be done without engaging with the importance of place, its meaning and its universality, and that requires a definition of regionalism as part of the canon to be challenged.

I have been involved in projects with artists which set out to address these issues. Some of the projects took place in central London – right beside the seat of power. I regard London as just another locality, albeit massively loaded with characteristics which mark it out as a very particular place. In that place culture already engages those characteristics of place and power. The annual Trooping the Colour engages with meanings deeply embedded in the physical and psychological fabric of Whitehall in Central London as surely as the annual Orange marches articulate and activate the City Walls in Derry. Both the Orange marches and Trooping the Colour are very sophisticated forms of triumphalist image-making, but one is hugely validated over the other. And that is even within a continuous tradition of Loyalism, never mind the negative value attached to anti-state public image-making, which, according to the current canon of media representation, should not be allowed into contemporary history at all.

Derry was one of the first places in Ireland to experience Town Planning according to modes of 17th century English social and economic thinking. The City Walls, which are still intact, were built in the early 1600s on behalf of the Guilds of the City of London as a condition of gaining extensive areas of land. Derry became the fortified town of Londonderry because of its strategic importance as a back door to England for continental enemies. Despite their age the walls cannot be consigned to Tourism or to settled history because they are still charged with their original meanings. To Loyalists they are a powerful symbol of the survival of Protestantism in Ireland. In this context there is no such thing as history. The past is present in very particular form in Derry and Northern Ireland but its underlying principles are connected to the heart of the constitutional monarchy which provides a spine to the status quo in British society.

It is therefore incorrect to describe what is going on in Derry and Northern Ireland as marginal, particularly after the last year in Europe where very similar questions of identity and power have resurfaced along old lines which pre-date many nation states. Derry is a concentrated sign of the radiating relationships between two communities, Northern and Southern Ireland, and between England and Ireland. It could be said that 'The Walled City' represents a modernist idea laid over a particular social context. Within The Walls: the coloniser; power; attached to the centre; in history. Without The Walls: the colonised people of locality; native; no power; not part of history.

For this colonial equation to work what is required is for the coloniser to devalue the native culture 'outside the Walls', to render it invisible because it is not defined as culture. Because if you are not in history how can your art be in art history?

From our standpoint how then could culture avoid reflecting these relationships in the social environment within which it is made and mediated? This image of a walled city, designed in the centre but applied in the locality, is part of an imposition of a sort of rationalism – culture over nature – a view of the world which puts a small number of mainstream European cultures at the top of the hierarchy leading history. It was their duty to raise other cultures, to bring them into history; to turn Irishmen into Englishmen, Irishmen who were otherwise not part of the universal conversation, who were 'beyond the pale'.

This rationalist idea that history had a goal, that progress was consistent and inevitable and led by mainstream cultures, is essentially religious myth disguised as secular thought. It defines others as disabled and not as whole people adapted to another sensory mode. It is underpinned by the belief that only white western culture could carry out the work of history; so only the western world was in history; so only western art was in art history. This idea is deeply embedded within our social environment, from the edge to the centre, almost to the point of invisibility; it forms the basis of most public art in our cities.

There is an increasing loss of faith in history, in its linear progression and in modernism, where the essential considerations were formal; formal solutions to formal problems in which the cognitive, the aesthetic and the ethical were separated, their interaction denied, with the result that art was disconnected from the social and detached from locality. If we look at the very powerful model of MOMA in New York it has always defined those values acceptable to it as universal, and those not as marginal. Of course this empowers the metropolitan and disenfranchises the local. In application it involves not just the critical promotion of abstract over figurative art but the projection of abstracted art – art which is disengaged from society, disconnected from the local or the particular – as universal. This practice devalues and sub-ordinates other cultural practices. On the one hand you have the 'real thing'; on the other, you have ethnic art, feminist art, community art. The universal is defined as not specific to locality, gender, race or nationality.

I believe that principle works against the interests of art, artists and any identifiable community, but it seems to me that a new agenda is under discussion which counteracts the emphasis on metropolitan knowledge and local ignorance, an emphasis which is dependent on an inconsistent defini-tion of people as consumers of cultural products rather than participants in a cultural process. Locality is the word and idea I would like to move up this agenda.

*Focus on the Individual*

— 15 —

# Anthony Pasquin, *An Authentic History of Professors of Painting . . . in Ireland,* 1796

Anthony Pasquin (1754–*c.*1821) was the alias of the Englishman John Williams, a hack journalist, satirist and occasional art critic. His *Authentic History of the Artists of Ireland*, also known as *An Authentic History of the Professors of Painting, Sculpture, & Architecture in Ireland*, is the first full-scale account of the visual arts in Ireland. Pasquin includes some 190 biographies of both British and Irish artists, though these are not arranged alphabetically and many are short and not very factual. One of the more substantial entries is an account of the émigré artist James Barry (1741–1806), which is included here, together with an extract from Pasquin's introduction. The dependence on anecdote over factual information defines Pasquin's approach to biography and he uses the genre so as to make a satirical attack on his subjects. Williams's other writings include his pseudo–play *The Royal Academicians: A Farce* (1786), which offers yet another parody of Barry under the guise of 'Jemmy O'Blarney', while in 1793 he published the *Life of the late Earl of Barrymore,* 'one of the wildest and most profligate bucks of the age'.[1] Three years later, Pasquin published *Memoirs of the Royal Academicians; Being an Attempt to Improve the National Taste* with *An Authentic History of Painting in Ireland* as a companion volume.

Source: *An Authentic History of the Professors of Painting, Sculpture, & Architecture in Ireland*, London, 1796, pp. 5, 7, 48, see also facsimile reprint edited by R.W.

Lightbown, with *Memoirs of the Royal Academicians; Being an Attempt to Improve the National Taste*, London, Cornmarket Press, 1970.

The following imperfect Essay is the issue of all my researches, during the last twenty-one years of my existence, assisted by the oldest and most intelligent among the Artists of Ireland. I have published it, to rescue, as far as I am able, the Professors of Painting, Sculpture, and Architecture, in our sister kingdom, from oblivion; and to strengthen the propensies of the wise and powerful, in their habits of protection and encouragement towards the Muses and their retainers. It is an extraordinary truth, that neither *Leonardo da Vinci*, *Vasari*, the *Abbe Winkelman*, the *Abbe de Bos*, *Felibien*, *Algorotti*, or any other eminent foreign author on the Arts, have mentioned Ireland in their performances; and only *Bassan* among the recent moderns.[2]

The *Fine Arts* have never been cultivated in Ireland, with that strong attention and encouragement which is necessary to produce *eminent* Professors: there are two reasons which may be adduced to apologize for this unfortunate truth; *viz.* the poverty of the nation, and the consequent want of illumination in the general orders of its inhabitants. Though Ireland has become proverbial for her wit and her bravery, she appears to me to want that portion of confederation and perseverance, which is incontestibly expedient to the furtherance and completion of such an object. — PAINTING, SCULPTURE, and ARCHITECTURE, are the offspring of Luxury, and the concomitants of refinement; and were never known to flourish greatly, where Nature was unadulterated, or Society enfeebled by penury: those impressive and alluring ladies must be pampered, or they will sicken; if not perish.

Previous to the commencement of this century, the Polite Arts were so little known in Ireland, as to elude human research. It is a theme on which none of their authors treat, who have any authority with mankind; and of which, I believe, they were nearly wholly ignorant. The likenesses or effigies of their kings and powerful men, which were stamped upon the current metal of the hour, as pecuniary obligations, or tokens of value, formed the chief organ which might lead them to a contemplation or admiration of the efforts of art. If any vagrant Professor sojourned among them at an earlier period, his labours are either forgotten or demolished by time. Their ideas of carving in stone and wood, and the branches of chalcography, were antecedent to their knowledge of colours; as many rude examples remain in their cathedrals and sepulchres, illustrative of holy writ, and commemorating their heroes, which must have been executed in the earlier ages of Christianity.

The Fine Arts knew not the pleasure of being embraced willingly in Ireland, until the Society of Arts, Manufactures, and Commerce, was established in Dublin; and this great and wise measure was principally effected by the *Duke of Leinster, Lords Charlemont, Portarlington, Powerscourt,* and *Conyngham; Mr Latouche, Mr Caldbeck, Mr Tisdall, Mr Stewart,* &c. – and as the noble pride which attracts itself to honourable examples is highly communicative, the list of Subscribers in a short period amounted to several hundreds of the primary characters of the nation: yet, the encouragement which even they afforded to the Polite Arts, though comparatively ample, was not sufficient. Their Academy is rather destructive than otherwise; as it annually vomits forth an immense pictorial fry, who fall short of their expected attainments; as, commonly speaking, they are surreptitiously imitative, and unqualified claimants upon Fame and Patronage; their talents are immature, and their lives replete with disappointment and sorrow. Thus, in this particular department of their vast undertaking, I think the Society has been more injurious than beneficial; as it is not in the disposition of a human being to bless those who create an appetite, without having the ability to administer sustenance. But it is not the students of every empire that can resort for consolation or energy to an *Augustus*, a *Mecænas*, an *Alexander*, the *Tuscan Cosmo, Charles Stuart,* or the *Tenth Leo.* Yet, let me recollect, while I am bringing our sister kingdom to her purgation, that Britain, with more power, has less ardour; and, though her taste is purer, her vain love of portraiture consumes her regards for sublimity. These remarks must be understood as applying to the comparative state of general patronage in either country, and not to the state of the Professors.

Considering Ireland as a nation, she possesses a more than ordinary portion of genius; but that genius is exemplified in an aptitude of merriment according with momentary social desires, and conducive to the sublimation of hilarity; rather than in those progressive stages of endeavour, which lead the struggling mind to an established excellence. Irishmen are generally speaking too mercurial in their propensities for the habitudes of profound thinking. The impulse of their souls is such, as would lead them to the protection of the whole Parnassian choir; but the contagion of their manners poisons that wholesome principle: the seeds of their action are fraught with the noblest qualities; but the issue from that seed is too repeatedly blighted by the elements of custom; they have some enlightened and philosophic men among them, who have done much towards suppressing the remnants of barbarism, which are even now too prevailing; but their efforts are not effectual; hence the good taste of the country is limited, and not equal to the maintenance of the higher orders of imitative merit: they are more prompt and brilliant than Englishmen; but do not so repeatedly weigh causes with consequences; and that man who wishes to become exemplary as an artist, must connect his understanding with his fancy, and assign to each an equal dominion over his time and labour.

[...]

JAMES BARRY, R.A. The origin of this gentleman was unpropitious; his father was a bricklayer in Cork; and the professor of painting was wont to carry the hod: he emanated upon the general eye, by painting a sign of Neptune, for a whiskey shop in that city; and which was a production so uncommon for a lad situated as he was, that *Dr Longfield* immediately put his ample wing over him, and rescued him from meanness, penury, and oblivion.

When this inconstant man had returned from Italy, and was much depressed in circumstances and in spirit, and it was generally supported that he was sinking for want of a patron, the late *Duke of Northumberland*, with becoming nobleness, invited the disconsolate artist to dine with him; and during the repast at Northumberland House, the discourse ran upon the distribution of the paintings around the room; among which was the inimitable effort, by *Titian*, of the Carnaro family. 'How, Mr Barry, do you approve of the placing of these pictures?' said his Grace. 'Oh, very well, my Lord Duke; but there is a capital place at the bottom there, in a side light, which is unoccupied.' 'I mean that vacancy to be filled by a production from your pencil, Sir; which I request you to finish as soon as possible. I wish the subject to be taken from the history of England; but shall leave the selection, the size, and the price, to be fixed by yourself; and have only this to add, that you will contrive to introduce a master of the Horse in the grouping, and draw my portrait in that character.' After this instruction the parties separated; and in the ensuing week his Grace called upon the artist repeatedly, who was uniformly denied. At length the Duke, fatigued by such caprice, sent him a letter by his servant, desiring to speak to him; when the inflated *James Barry* was pleased to express himself thus: 'Go to the Duke, your master, friend, and tell him from me, that if he wants his portrait painted, he may go to the fellow in Leicester-fields; for that office shall never be fulfilled by me.' This anecdote was told by *Mr Gabriel Stuart*, to whom the Duke related it; and though few persons may believe that such an instance of weakness ever occurred, it is assuredly a fact – poor man![3]

## NOTES

1    R.W. Lightbown, 'John Williams alias Anthony Pasquin', Introduction to facsimile reprint of *An Authentic History of Painting in Ireland*, London, Cornmarket Press, 1970, p. 20. See also Johannes Dobai, *Die Kunstliteratur des Klassizismus und der Romantik in England*, 4 vols., Berne, 1975, II, pp. 1167–8.

2    Apart from such well-known theorists as Leonardo (1452–1519), Giorgio Vasari

(1511–74) and Johann Joachim Winckelmann (1717–68), Pasquin is referring to Abbé Jean Baptiste de Bos, author of Reflexions critiques sur la poesie et sur la peinture, 1719; André Félibien des Avaux (1619–95), author of Entretiens sur les vies et les ouvrages des plus excellens peintres anciens et modernes, Paris, 1666–8 (translated into English, 1705); Francesco Algarotti (1712–64), whose Saggio sopra la pittura was published in Venice in 1784; Pierre-Francois Basan (1723–97), French engraver, print seller and dealer, author of Dictionnaire des graveurs, 3 vol., Paris, 1767. In saying that Basan mentions Ireland, Pasquin may be referring to the Frenchman's inclusion of such Irish-born engravers as James McArdell (c. 1728–1765) and Thomas Frye (1710–1762), see Basan, vol. 1, pp. 11–13 and 213.

3      Gilbert Stuart, American-born portrait painter (1755–1828). Pasquin also included a sketch on Barry in his *Memoirs of the Royal Academicians*, 1796, pp. 125–7, where he tells a story of Barry inviting Edmund Burke to dinner and making the states-man cook his own 'beef steaks'. In the mid-1780s, Barry did paint a portrait of the 1st Duke of Northumberland which shows him in his position as Master of the Horse, see William L. Pressly, *The Life and Art of James Barry*, New Haven and London, Yale University Press, 1981, pp. 110–11 and 240–1.

# — 16 —

# William Godwin, *The Looking Glass*, 1805

In the second quarter of the nineteenth century, William Mulready (1776–1863) was one of the most acclaimed genre painters in London. Earlier, in his late teens, this Irish-born artist, worked closely with the radical English author and philanthropist, William Godwin (1756–1836). In 1805, when Mulready was only nineteen years old, Godwin, under a pseudonym of Theophilius Marcliffe published an account of the early years of an artist 'calculated' he wrote on the title page, 'to awaken the emulation of Young Persons of both Sexes, in the pursuit of every laudable attainment: particularly in the cultivation of the fine arts'. By the end of Mulready's life it was as well accepted fact, among his intimates, that Godwin's artist was based on Mulready's childhood.[1] Included here is the whole of Chapter 1, entitled, 'Birth of our Artist in the Province of Munster in Ireland – Removed to Dublin – Indications of an early Propensity – Childish Attempts at Drawing.' *The Looking Glass* carried as its frontispiece, a supposed self-portrait of Mulready, drawn when nine years old (fig. 4) and was illustrated by further drawings by the child prodigy (figs. 5 and 6).

Source: William Godwin, *The Looking Glass: A True History of the Early Years of an Artist* . . . London, Thomas Hodges, 1805; Ch 1.[2] The original footnotes have been left out.

4    William Mulready, *Self-Portrait, c.* 1795, frontispiece to Theophilius Marcliffe's (pseudonym for William Godwin) *The Looking Glass*, 1805

The person whose history I am going to relate, was born in Ireland, a little to the north of the Shannon, in one of the principal towns of the county of Clare. His father and mother were Catholics; the father was by trade a leather-breeches maker, and had been for some years a private soldier in the volunteer army of Ireland: so that our young man derived no advantage from splendour of connection, or from wealth and refinement in either of his parents. They had however for sometime no child but him, that survived the hazards of infancy. The boy was tall and handsome, and both his parents were extremely fond of him.

When he was about a year and a half old, his father removed to Dublin, the capital of Ireland, distant one hundred and fifty miles from the place of his birth. The boy discovered a very early propensity for drawing; whether it were that he was endowed with an eye particularly adapted to catch the elements of this art, and a hand to execute them; or whether accident gave this bent to his genius. The old question between nature and fortune in this affair, can scarcely be satisfactorily decided in any single instance.

The earliest particular leading this way, which he has been able to recollect, is the hearing the name of one Corny [Cornelius] Gorman, who had probably been a fellow-soldier, or an associate leather-breeches maker, of his father. This man, whom he does not recollect ever to have seen, was much applauded by the boy's father for his skill in drawing tea-pots, dogs, and other matters upon paper, to which he gave suitable colouring. These things, tea-pots for example, are not to be supposed to have exhibited much grace of drawing, but they showed a truth of eye, and firmness of hand, which excited the admiration of Corny Gorman's companions. The boy's father emulated his friend at a modest distance. We are to suppose the leather-breeches maker's apartments not to have been very elegant; and their possessor amused himself with sketching hares and dogs, a sort of hunt, with chalk, on the vacant space of wainscot immediately over the chimney. He did this only once, and that for the diversion of his little boy, who during the performance was seated on his knee. This sort of pictorial composition, forcibly seized upon the boy's attention.

It was liable to accidents; the brush of the housewife might invade it; a careless visitor might sweep his coat against it; and thus part of the design unhappily become obscured or obliterated. The little boy, before he was three years old, would sit as before, upon his father's knee, with a bit of chalk in his hand, and endeavour to repair the depredations which time might have committed upon the outline. In Plate 1, figure 1 [fig. 5], you are presented with a tolerably accurate representation of the style in which he delineated a hare. At the same time he drew a man with chalk upon the wall (the discoloration of the smoke probably afforded him a ground dark enough to make his figure visible); the whole figure was whitened with the chalk, which was then rubbed off by him in spots, to represent eyes, nose, and mouth. He also drew in the same manner birds, and a sort of figure he was taught to call a grampus, but which I think was something more like a mermaid. This species of monster may be seen in Plate I, fig. 2 [fig. 5]. With the incoherence of fancy incident to his age, the birds and grampuses were represented as growing upon trees, and sometimes there was water below, into which the grampuses appeared to be falling. When he was four years of age, the whole of the hunting scene upon the chimneypiece was by some fatal accident obliterated at once, and the boy, taking his chalk, replaced it entirely with the efforts of his own hand.

It is difficult to distinguish at this age, how much of what was done was spontaneous, and how much encouragement. The father, perceiving the boy's propensity, took him out one day about this time, on purpose to show him the figure of an Indian, in feathers and gay attire, a sign which had just been fixed

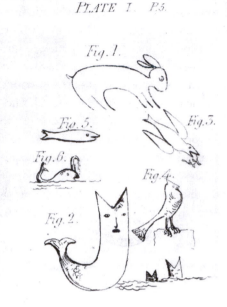

5        William Mulready, Plate I from *The Looking Glass*, 1805

up over the door of a teashop, near Trinity College. This was beyond the child's
age to imitate, but it was not lost upon him. He now took to designing flowers, with grapes and other fruit, upon the floor. The floor was an unfaithful
depository; and each morning probably destroyed the labours of the day before.
But the child did not mind; he worked for amusement, not for duration. It was
after this, that the object of his ambition became, to imitate the outline of a
twelve-penny loaf. I know not whether the twelve-penny loaf sat to him for
its portrait; but, if it did, he could not have chosen a more patient sitter. This
outline he corrected again and again; the dint made by the hand or finger of
the baker in the centre of the upper surface, particularly puzzled him. Men and
women were frequently portrayed by our lilliputian artist; but of men he could
exhibit only a front view; the legs puzzled him in any other situation: women
he represented in profile; the petticoat removed his difficulty in their case.

    Round his father's room there hung six views, one of them representing
St Paul's cathedral, the others different scenes. That of St Paul's he imitated.
He began at the cross, and descended to the dome, imitating the different
mouldings and projections as he descended. It is uncertain whether he ever
finished the cathedral, probably not. But, when he came over to England at
the age of five years and a half, and entered London, he immediately recognized St Paul's from the copy he had made.

The last circumstance I am enabled to relate of his history in Ireland, arose from the accident of a lame boy who lived near, and who supported his aged or infirm mother by little figures of soldiers, which he made of pasteboard or card, and having coloured, sold them to the children in the streets for a halfpenny or a penny a-piece. They were made with a little buttress behind, to enable them to stand upright. An exact representation of these figures, in frontview and in profile, is given in Plate II [fig. 6]. The amusement of the purchasers, when they had bought them, was to blow them up with gun-powder. Our young spark was very desirous to imitate their sport; but his father and mother refused him money to make the acquisition. Some of the more fortunate children would sometimes give him one or two of their sol-diers, when they had been partly maimed or disabled by the effects of the

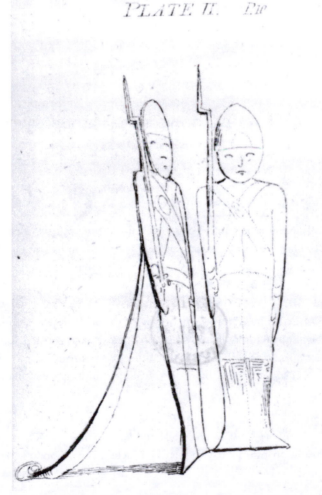

PLATE II. Fig

6    William Mulready, Plate II from *The Looking Glass*, 1805

gunpowder; he cut out, though not coloured, others for himself; and thus he too attained to his explosion.

Gentle reader, do not think these particulars trifling; for it was such beginnings, joined with persevering application, that this boy became, notwithstanding all external disadvantages, *an Artist*.

NOTES

1    See Marcia Pointon, *Mulready*, London, Victoria and Albert Museum, 1986, pp. 103–4.

2    A facsimile reprint was published by Benrose and Sons, London, in 1855 with an appendix by F. G. Stephens.

— 17 —

# Francis Sylvester Mahony, 'The Painter, Barry', 1835

The son of a Blarney wool mill owner, Mahony (1804–66) was ordained a priest in 1830. He went on to work as a journalist in London and authored the well-known song 'The Bells of Shandon'.[1] Originally published in the *Fraser's Magazine* in April 1835, the following satire on his fellow Corkman, the artist James Barry (1741–1806; see entries 5, 15, 28 and 53), is written in the form of a memoir by Mahony's fictitious Fr Prout, who is remembering his years as a priest in Rome. Mahony's lengthy fantasy is set in the late 1760s, when Barry was indeed in Rome, and mercilessly satirizes not only one of Ireland's most acclaimed artists but also the Jesuits and eighteenth-century papal politics.

Source: [Francis Sylvester Mahony], *The Reliques of Father Prout, later P.P. of Watergrasshill, in the County of Cork, Ireland*, collected and arranged by Oliver Yorke, Esq., with illustration by Alfred Croquis (D. Maclise, RA), London, Bell and Daldy, 1873, pp. 503–13.

In his visits to the Vatican, Barry had been noticed by the old custode who tenanted the *Torrione dei Venti* at the extreme end of the palace. Fabio Centurioni (such was the honoured name of this respectable veteran, the senior officer of the Vatican gallery) was in himself an object not unworthy of the antiquarian's attention. He belonged to a race distinct in character and feelings from the vulgar crowd who crawl through the streets of Rome. Of an old transtiberine family, he claimed with the *trasteverini* unconditionated pedigree, ascending through the vicissitudes of intervening barbarism to the ancient masters of the world. [. . .] But if solemn gait, gravity of deportment, absence of unnecessary speed in word or gesture, were of genealogical import, his descant on the great *Cunctator* was unquestionable. His affection for young Barry originated in a sort of fancied resemblance to the old Roman character which he thought he could discover in the foreign artist; and certainly, as far as energy, vigour, a proud and generous disposition, and an uncompromising dignity, were typical of the sons of Romulus, the Irish painter justified the old gentleman's discernment. He entertained for my friend a predilection he took every opportunity of exhibiting, being heard to declare Barry more of a Roman than the whole tribe of degenerate wretches who dwelt on the right bank of the river. But what set the seal to the custode's approbation, was the unbounded veneration both felt in common for the huge Torso at the extremity of the gallery – a colossal fragment, known throughout Europe from the many casts which have been taken therefrom, and which, in shape, size, and wonderful attributes, can only be compared to the Blarney stone; of which, to the vulgar, it appears an exact facsimile.[2] Fabio's eye glistened with delight as he watched our enthusiast sketching this glorious block, day after day, in every position and attitude. An invitation to his apartments in the palace was the result; thus Barry became acquainted with Marcella.

Pure, delightful, heavenly being! sixty years have passed over my head, and revolutions have swept over the face of Europe, and monarchies have passed away, and for more than half a century thy ashes have slept in the church of *Santa Cecilia in trastevere*; but thy image is now before me, lovely and animated as when thy smile cheered the wild Irish artist, whom thou didst unfeignedly love! In that church, near the tomb of the martyred saint (thy model and thy patroness), a marble tablet, carved by the hand of thy heart-broken father, may yet be seen, with the words, 'MARCELLA CENTURIONI, DI ANNI 18, VERGINE ROMANA, PACE, IMPLORA.' That peace is assuredly thine. Of too gentle a texture wert thou to endure the trials of life and the rude contact of adversity. Hence in mercy wert thou withdrawn from this boisterous world, and received into the harbour of rest. With grief I record thy early fate; but I sorrow not for thee! My mind loves to dwell on the probable destiny of my friend, had Heaven granted him a partner through life, adviser, help, tutelary deity, in her whom he had the misfortune to lose for ever. Of what avail are the fond speculations of friendship? Both are long since no more; and I myself must soon rejoin them in the mysterious region that stretches out beyond the grave.

[. . .]

The privilege of access to the gallery at hours when, by the established regulations, all others were excluded, was an advantage which Barry knew how to appreciate; and which I notice, because it gave occasion to an occurence I alone witnessed, and which I promised during his lifetime never to disclose. Since his death I have no motive for either publishing or con-cealing this anecdote; to tell the truth, I apprehended that its very singular-ity would perhaps, in the estimation of many, be a reason for refusing credence to the narrative; but in the eyes of the few, for whom I write [. . .] I hope the romantic nature of the transaction will not damage the statement, or prejudice my veracity; it being a trite saying, that matters more extraordi-nary occur in real life than are recorded in fiction.

Barry loved to study in the Vatican gallery by night; an indulgence the mildness of the season (it was now the close of May 1770)[3] would allow of. The custom of permitting foreigners to explore the museum by torchlight, on payment of fees, had not been established; James had no apprehension of intruders on the privacy of his studious hours. There, by the glare of a bronze lamp, he would sit while the city was hushed to repose; and while the glim-mering flame would cast a shadowy lustre on the contours of some antique group, he would sketch the forms of the mighty dead, drinking deep at the fount of Greek inspiration. I have before adverted to the notion he had imbibed, that the English artists at Rome were jealously watchful of his stud-ies; that they sought to appropriate the conceptions of his teeming fancy, and to rob him of his originality. Hence to Barry the consciousness of being unobserved constituted the charm of these nocturnal pursuits: none but I had been allowed access to his vigils in the gallery – a mark of friendship I have reason to remember. On the evening of the 20th of May we had both been staying up late with the old custode in the *Torrione*. Barry had been rather warmly engaged with his host in a controversy respecting the relative merits of the recumbent Cleopatra, and the reclining figure of a colossal river god, supposed to be the Nile. As I took some interest on behalf of his favourite the Cleopatra, he offered to accompany me thither, with the old custode's permission, and give me ocular demonstration of the correctness of his views. As by this time (it was near midnight) we had demolished not a few flasks of *gensano*, I felt nothing loath; so we folded our cloaks about us, and I bore the torch. I question whether Diomed and Ulysses, in their night excursion across the plain of Troy, experienced loftier emotions than did we, as with echoing tread we paced the solemn halls of the pontifical palace, between ranks of antique statues, confronting us in every possible variety of attitude – menace, grief, admiration, welcome, or terror. [. . .] Barry would pause before some marble favourite, introduce me to its individual merits, teach me to throw the light judiciously, delivering himself withal of some of those striking theories which I loved to trace in his subsequent printed lectures on the art he adored. But as we slowly approached the *sala de Cleopatra*, the term of our appointed pilgrimage, a sudden and unaccountable start on the part of my friend dashed the torch out of my hand – and 'I'll be hanged, Prout!' cried he, 'if the ruffi-ans don't listen to every word I utter: did you not see that scoundrel Nollekens lurking behind the Antinous?[4] – by G-d, 'tis he!' – 'For shame!' I rejoined; 'can't you keep from cursing at this hour of night, and in the very residence of the sovereign pontiff?' – 'Tis true, by hell!' cried out my infuri-ated friend, reckless of that stern reporter for the celestial press, the record-ing angel, who no doubt dropped a detersive tear on an oath the decided offspring of monomania; 'but I'll soon teach the rascal to exercise elsewhere his talents as eavesdropper, spy, and plagiarist!' – So saying, he rushed to the spot where he fancied he had seen his foe; and, in spite of the obscurity of the hall, on the floor of which lay the semi-extinguished torch, I could still perceive that he had in fact grappled not with a mere creation of his trou-bled fancy, but with a bona fide human shape, muffled in the ample folds of a long ecclesiastical robe, and yielding apparently without resistance to the rude energy of its assailant. Barry soon relaxed his grasp, when he had clearly ascertained that his prisoner was an old priest and an Italian; but muttered still, with indomitable wrath, 'You may thank your stars, my boy, that you weren't that blackguard Nollekens.' – '*Grazie tante!*' was the ejaculation of the venerable captive, when he had sufficiently recovered from his affright: 'your mistake had well nigh had consequences which none would regret more than yourselves. You are foreigners, and, if I may judge from your idiom, English; I am a resident of the palace. No doubt a love for the arts has occasioned your presence here at this unusual hour. 'Tis well. Follow me towards the *Sala di San Damaso.*' There was something authoritative, as well as conciliatory, in the tone of our new acquaintance; and as I shewed a disposition to accept the invitation of one whom I guessed to be a dignitary of the Papal court, Barry did not hesitate to accompany me.[5]

We paused not, we spoke not. Onwards we went through the different corridors and antechambers that separate the Vatican gallery from that por-tion of the palace which our guide had mentioned. Each *busola*, each door, seemed to recognise the passage of a master, flying open at his touch. At length we entered what appeared to be a study. The walls were hung with Flemish tapestry; and a bronze lamp of antique fashion, dependent from the gilt oak ceiling, faintly illumined the apartment. In the centre, a table inlaid with exquisite mosaic was strewed with various documents, seemingly of an official character; amongst which a single book, though torn and disfigured, quickly attracted my eye. I knew at a glance the familiar folio. It was a copy of the standard regulations of my old tutors, 'INSTITUTUM SOCIETATIS JESU'. We were seated at the Italian prelate's request. A servant in the papal livery was summoned by a rapid signal from an adjoining room; a brief order to bring wine and refreshments was delivered, and executed with magic promptitude. Meantime Barry kept his eye on me to ascertain what I thought of our singular position. Our host left no space for reflection, but pressed us with genuine hospitality to partake of what lay before us. Wine is the great dissolvent of distrust, and generator of cordiality. Never was this more forcibly exemplified than in my friend's case, who, totally oblivious of the late awkward scuffle between himself and the most reverend dignitary, launched out into a diversity of topics connected with the fine arts, of which our entertainer appeared to be a sincere and enlightened admirer.

Thinking it high time to mix in the conversation, 'I am happy to find,' said I, quaffing a glass of Malaga, 'that the Jesuits have a friend at the court of Ganganelli.'

'Speak you thus, *abbatino*?' rejoined our host. 'You are then an admirer of Loyola's institute. Are there many such in France, where it appears you have studied?'

I described the Gallican episcopal body as unanimously adverse to the proposed destruction of that society.

'The king of France, the kings of Spain and Portugal, think differently, young man,' said the prelate with some warmth, and with a tone that only served to kindle my zeal in defence of my old professors.

'The Duc de Choiseul and Madame de Pompadour may have persuaded the imbecile Louis XV to adopt the views of the writers in the *Encyclopédie* – the minister of his most Catholic Majesty of Spain may fancy the property of the Society, in the mother country, in South America, and in the East Indies, a fair object of plunder. Marquis de Pombal may entertain similar opinions at Lisbon; but surely the judgment of a knot of courtly conspirators, acting in unhallowed concert, should find its proper weight in the balance of the sanctuary. Catherine of Russia and the great Frederick of Prussia think differently of these men, and profess their readiness to offer them an asylum. But if it be true (as it is rumoured in the Piazza Colonna) that the restoration of Avignon, estreated by France during the late pontificate, is to be the reward of Ganganelli's subserviency to the court of Versailles, I must say, and I don't care who hears it, that a more flagrant case of simony and corruption never disgraced the annals of the Vatican. [. . .]

A dismal scowl passed over the brow of my interlocutor. 'Is it not the first duty of the supreme pastor,' he hastily observed, 'to conciliate the heads of the Christian flock? Your own country teaches a lesson on pontifical obstinacy. Had Clement VII shewn less rigour in refusing to your eighth Harry his demand, by insisting on the very doubtful canon law of the case, England would at this day be the most valuable ffeoff [fief] of St Peter's domain. In bygone days, the request of Philippe Le Bel, backed by the emperor, the kings of England and Spain, was deemed sufficient, in the teeth of evidence, to condemn the noble brotherhood of the Temple. These "*orders*" are of human institution: the Jesuits must be yielded up to the exigency of the times. To calm the effervescence of the moment, the Pope may safely dismiss his "Janissaries".'

'Yet the day may come,' I replied, 'when Christianity may want the aid of science and of literature – when the paltry defence of ignorant bigotry will be no longer of any avail – when all the motley host of remaining monks and friars, white, black, and grey, will find their inability to fill the space left void by the suppression of that intellectual and redeeming ORDER which once destroyed can only reappear in a feeble and inefficient imitation.'

Two hours had now elapsed since our midnight adventure and the warning chime of the palace belfry gave me an opportunity, in accordance with Barry's repeated signals, to take leave. The prelate, having carefully ascertained our names and address, placed us under the guidance of the attendant in waiting, who led us by the *cortile dei Suizzeri* to the *Scala regia*; and we finally stood in front of St Peter's Church. We paused there awhile, little dreaming that it was the last night we should pass in Rome. The moon was up, and the giant obelisk of Sesostris, that had measured the sands of Lybia with its shadow, now cast its gnomon to the very foot of that glorious portico. Gushing with perennial murmur, the two immense *jets d'eau* flung out their cataracts on each side of the sublime monument, and alone broke with monotonous sound the silence of the night.

Poor Marcella! those two hours had been a space of severe trial and sad suspense for thee; but we knew not till months had elapsed the fatal consequences that ensued. Barry, when he parted with her father, had promised to remain but a moment in the gallery; and old Centurioni bade his daughter wait up for his guests, while he himself sought his quiet pillow. Hours rolled on, and we came not. The idea of nocturnal assassination, unfortunately too familiar to the Roman mind, awakened by the non-appearance of the Irish artist, took rapid possession of her kindling imagination, as she watched in the *Torrione* in vain for his return. The transition from doubt to the certainty of some indefinable danger was the work of an instant. Yielding to the bold impulse of hereditary instinct, she seized the bronze lamp that burned on the mantelpiece, grasped a Damascus blade, the weapon of some crusader in olden time, and gliding with the speed of thought, was soon far advanced in her searching progress through the corridors and galleries of the palace. Had the statue of Lucretia leaped from its pedestal it might present a similar appearance in gesture and deportment. Alas, she was never to re-enter the parental dwelling! Ere the morning dawned the romantic girl was a prisoner in the Castle of St Angelo, under suspicion of being employed by the Jesuits to assassinate Ganganelli!

Strange whispers were current at break of day: 'An Irish painter and an Irish priest, both emissaries of "*the Society*", had been detected lurking in the Vatican: an assault had been committed on the sacred person of the pontiff: they had avowed all in a secret interview with his holiness, and had confessed that they were employed by Lawrence Ricci, the general of the order.' At the English coffee-house in the *Piazza di Spagna*, the morning's gossip was early circulated in Barry's hearing: the truth flashed on his mind at once. He ran to my apartments. I was thunderstruck.

Nothing had as yet transpired concerning Marcella's imprisonment; and we, unfortunately, resolved on a step which gave a colourable pretext to accusation. In the hurry of our alarm, we agreed on quitting Rome at once. Barry took the road to Bologna; and I was by noon in the Pontine marshes, on my way to Naples. Our friends thought us safely immured in those cells which the 'holy office' still keeps up at its head-quarters in the Dominican convent, called, ironically enough, '*La Minerva*'.

Old Centurioni was debarred the privilege of seeing his daughter; in silent anguish he mourned over his child, and bemoaned the fate of the young foreigners who, he doubted not, were equally in the hands of 'justice'. But the worst was to come. That angelic being, whose nature was too pure, and whose spirit was too lofty, to endure the disgrace and infamy imputed to her, remained haughtily and indignantly passive under the harsh and unmerited infliction. She gave no sign. An inflammatory fever, the combined result of her uncertainty concerning the fate of her lover, and irritation at the very thought of such heinous guilt thus laid to her charge, closed in less than a fortnight her earthly career. Her death set the seal to my friend's evil destiny.

## NOTES

1    For a reassessment of Mahony see Terry Eagleton's essay 'Cork and the Carnivalesque', in *Crazy John and the Bishop and Other Essays on Irish Culture*, Cork University Press, 1998, pp. 158–211.

2    Mahony is referring to the celebrated first century B.C. Greek sculpture, the *Torso Belvedere*, see Fintan Cullen, *Visual Politics*, pp. 26–40. Elsewhere in the *Reliques*, Prout supplies his own history of the Blarney Stone, see 'A Plea for Pilgrimages',

pp. 50–1, accompanied by Maclise's illustration of Prout and Walter Scott examining the Stone, opposite p. 54. Decades earlier, Anthony Pasquin had lampooned Barry in a never-performed farce entitled *The Royal Academicians* (1786) where he appears as Jemmy O'Blarney, see Cullen, pp. 38–9.

3    Barry had in fact left Rome a month earlier, see William L. Pressly, *The Life and Art of James Barry*, New Haven and London, Yale University Press, 1981, p. 15.

4    While in Rome, Barry was very friendly with the English sculptor, Joseph Nollekens (1737–1823), but he was under constant fear of assassination, see Pressly, op. cit., pp. 11–15.

5    The old Italian priest is in fact Giovanni Vincenzo Ganganelli, Pope Clement XIV (1769–74), who abolished the Jesuits in 1773. In other sections of the *Reliques*, Mahony attacks Clement's attitude to the Jesuits (Mahony had in fact been educated by the Jesuits at Clongowes Wood College, Co. Kildare). Clement also began the project of a Vatican Museum which later grew into the Museo Pio-Clementino.

# — 18 —

# W. Justin O'Driscoll, *A Memoir of Daniel Maclise,* 1871

Daniel Maclise (1806–70) was the subject of one of the great Irish artistic success stories of the nineteenth century, a status reflected by the publication of O'Driscoll's *Memoir* a year after the artist's death. Born in Cork, Maclise met Sir Walter Scott on his visit to Ireland in 1825 and soon left for London. He started exhibiting at the Royal Academy in 1829 and continued doing so for the next forty years. Declared a full Academician in 1840, he later went on to decorate the newly built Royal Gallery in the Palace of Westminster. A Cork-born lawyer, Maclise's biographer William Justin O'Driscoll seems to have acted for his long-time friend and to have been in the employment of the publishers Longmans, who brought out the *Memoirs* (as well as publishing Maclise's famous illustrations to Thomas Moore's *Irish Melodies*). O'Driscoll's highly laudatory *Memoir* is ostensibly a list of works and quotations from numerous letters. In the two extracts included here reference is made to Maclise's close friendship with Charles Dickens (1812–70).[1] The first tells of a painting purchased by the famous novelist and of Maclise's success as an illustrator to literary texts. O'Driscoll discusses illustrations to works by two Irish writers, Lady Morgan's *Life and Times of Salvator Rosa* (1848; fig. 7) and Moore's *Melodies* (1845, figs. 8 and 9). The second extract is an 1870 eulogy by Dickens

in honour of his recently deceased friend, delivered at a Royal Academy dinner; Dickens himself was to die shortly afterwards.

Source: W. Justin O'Driscoll, *A Memoir of Daniel Maclise, R.A.*, London, Longmans, Green and Co., 1871, pp. 122–27, 232–3. O'Driscoll's footnotes have been
omitted.

## A) ILLUSTRATING LADY MORGAN AND MOORE'S 'MELODIES'

Maclise produced within the same period (i.e., from the time when he exhibited his first picture in the Academy [1829] down to 1859) a prodigious number of works of every description – portraits of distinguished persons;
amongst others, Lord Lytton, Charles Dickens, Forster, Kean, Macready, &c.,
as well as illustrations of various works in prose and poetry, viz., 'The Pilgrims
of the Rhine', and other books by the same author; 'Keep-sake', &c., &c. He
also painted for his friend Dickens 'The Nymph of the Waterfall'. It represents
an Irish girl, with a pitcher of water, borne on her shoulder, which she has
just taken from a stream at the foot of a mountain, down the face of which
the torrent is rushing, intercepted in its descent by the projecting crags and
gnarled branches, which break it into a succession of falls. The features of the
nymph are inexpressibly sweet; her dress – that of a peasant girl – is simply
but tastefully arranged, falling in graceful folds, and disclosing the beautiful
symmetry and proportions of the figure. She stands on a stepping-stone
covered with moss and river verdure; the feet are bare, and her shoes are seen
on a rock, where she has left them to ford the stream. All the details – trees,
rocks, and water – are rendered with extraordinary minuteness and most picturesque effect. This work was engraved for the 'Art Journal', and was
distributed by the proprietors of their subscribers in 1848.[2] He produced
within the same period a singularly clever picture, 'Salvator Rosa offering one
of his Works for sale to a Jew Dealer' [fig. 7].[3] The subject was suggested by
the following passage in Lady Morgan's 'Life of Salvator Rosa':
    'In the earliest part of his career the far greater portion of his pictures were
painted on printed paper, his limited means not permitting him to purchase
canvas. These were sold to the Jew dealers, who kept stalls in the Strada della
Carita.'[4] The scene is represented in the boutique of an old Jew. The young
and graceful painter stands watching with anxious looks the face of the
Israelite, who, with his bony hand shading his eyes, is minutely scanning the
picture. In the background is a figure of a beautiful girl, the daughter, who is
reaching down the miser's money-box from the top of a 'buffet'; whilst thus
occupied she contrives to steal a sidelong glance at the handsome artist. The
principal figures are so disposed that the picture tells its own story. The

7     F. Jourbet after Daniel Maclise, 'Salvator and his Patron', *Art Journal*, 1848

background displays in exuberance the miscellaneous contents of the Jew's shop, disposed with the happiest effect. [. . .]

The eminent firm of Longmans & Co. commissioned him to execute the well-known illustrations of Moore's 'Melodies'.[5] To an artist less gifted with imaginative powers, facility of invention, and celerity of hand, these elegant compositions would nearly absorb a lifetime. The illustrious author of the Melodies – then in his sixty-sixth year – gave eloquent expression to the delight he felt at seeing these records of his genius enshrined in lineaments as beautiful and imperishable as the songs themselves.[6] The early associations of Maclise, his love of legendary literature and romance, the wonderful exuberance of his intellect, uniting at once versatility and depth of feeling; his genius assuming every form, and traversing every region of thought that could manifest its power, eminently qualified him for an undertaking which probably could not have been so felicitously achieved by any other living artist. The native airs of Ireland are so touchingly tender and sweet as the natural music of any other country in the world; but a wild irregularity pervades many of them, which obeys no rule of rhythm or counterpoint. Moore himself has said that he was compelled to exercise extraordinary ingenuity in effecting an harmonious union between the words and the music of his Melodies. Perhaps the same obsevation may be applicable – *mutatis mutandis* – to the difficulty of assigning to the pencil the task of interpreting the poetry. It is evident, however, that Maclise, in these illustrations, has proved himself the twin star of Moore, in one sense; and the artist must participate, to some extent, in the immortality of fame which the poet has won by lyrics of such original and surpassing beauty.

The volume enriched with these etchings is the most exquisite specimen of an illustrated work that has yet appeared in England.

It would be a difficult matter to endeavour to select, where all are so beautiful, the sketches which appear the most striking. A very charming one is the illustration of 'Erin, the tear and the smile in thine Eyes' [fig. 8].[7] The rays of a glowing sunset are falling on the figure of a female weeping over a harp; above her hangs the rainbow – the arch of peace – the blending of whose 'various tints' the poet yearns for as the advent of his country's happiness. The illustrations of 'Remember the glories of Brien the Brave' occupy three pages of the book. In the first 'the warrior king' is seen at the head of his martial host [fig. 9][8], leading them against the enemy; the second page represents a richly-ornamented shield, surmounted by a garland of trophies; and the third reveals the position of the archers in the act of discharging their arrows.

Erin, the tear and the smile in thine eyes,
Blend like the rainbow that hangs in thy skies!
Shining through sorrow's stream,
Saddening through pleasure's beam,
Thy suns with doubtful gleam,
Weep while they rise.

8      Charles G. Lewis after Daniel Maclise, 'Erin the Tear and Shine in Thine Eyes',
from Thomas Moore's *Irish Melodies*, 1845

## B) CHARLES DICKENS ON MACLISE, 1870

I cannot forbear, before I resume my seat, adverting to a sad theme to which
his Royal Highness the Prince of Wales made allusion, and to which the

9        Charles G. Lewis after Daniel Maclise, 'Remember the Glories of Brian the Brave',
             from Thomas Moore's *Irish Melodies*, 1845

President referred with eloquence of genuine feeling. Since I first entered the public lists, a very young man indeed, it has been my constant fortune to number among my nearest and dearest friends members of the Royal Academy who have been its grace and pride. They have so dropped from my side, one by one, that I already begin to feel like the Spanish monk of whom Wilkie tells, who had grown to believe that the only realities around him were the pictures which he loved, and that all the moving life he saw, or ever had seen, was a shadow and a dream. For many years I was one of the two most intimate friends and most constant companions of the late Mr Maclise. Of his genius in his chosen art I will venture to say nothing here, but of his prodigious fertility of mind, and wonderful wealth of intellect, I may confidently assert that they would have made him, if he had been so minded, at least as great a writer as he was a painter. The gentlest and most modest of men, the freest as to his generous appreciation of young aspirants, and the frankest and largest-hearted as to his peers, incapable of a sordid or ignoble thought, gallantly sustaining the true dignity of his vocation, without one grain of self-assertion, wholesomely natural at the last as at the first, 'in wit a man, in simplicity a child', no artist, of whatsoever denomination, I make so bold to say, ever went to his rest leaving a golden memory more pure from dross, or having devoted himself with a truer chivalry to the art-goddess whom he worshipped.

## NOTES

1   Maclise painted a much-celebrated portrait of Dickens in 1839, National Portrait Gallery, London, see Arts Council of Great Britain, *Daniel Maclise*, National Portrait Gallery, London and National Gallery of Ireland, Dublin, 1972, pp. 55–6.

2   *Waterfall at St Nighton's Keive, near Tintagel*, 1842, oil on canvas, purchased at sale of Dickens's paintings, 1870, by his friend and biographer John Forster, who bequeathed it to the Victoria and Albert Museum in 1876. See *Daniel Maclise*, p. 73. A number of letters from O'Driscoll to Forster, relating to the writing of O'Driscoll's *Memoir*, are deposited in the Victoria and Albert Museum Library, Forster MS, X, 78–98.

3   Painting is now lost; illustration here is from the *Art Journal*, 1848, see *Daniel Maclise*, pp. 60–2 and *Salvator Rosa*, London, Arts Council of Great Britain, 1973, plate 47.

4   These sentences are not a direct quotation from Lady Morgan's *The Life and Times of Salvator Rosa*, 2 vols., London, 1824, I, pp. 127–9. See also entry 6 in this *Reader*.

5   Thomas Moore's *Irish Melodies*, London, Longmans, 1845. In this instance the 1848 edition was consulted. See *Daniel Maclise*, pp. 79–80.

6   In the Preface to the *Melodies*, Moore wrote: 'I shall only add, that I deem it most fortunate for this new Edition that the rich, imaginative powers of Mr Maclise have been employed in the adornment; and that, to complete its national character, an Irish pencil has lent its aid to an Irish pen in rendering due honour and homage to our country's ancient harp.'

7   *Irish Melodies*, p. 5, etching by Charles G. Lewis. See also John Turpin, 'Maclise as a Book Illustrator', *Irish Arts Review*, 1985 2, 2, pp. 23–7.

8   *Irish Melodies*, p. 8, etching also by Lewis; the others mentioned, pp. 9–10, by F. P. Becker and L. Stocks. Moore supplied endnotes on the subject and references in the poem: 'Brian Borombe, the great monarch of Ireland, who was killed at the

battle of Clontarf, in the beginning of the 11th century, after having defeated the Danes in twenty-five engagements.' 'Mononia' refers to Munster and 'Kinkora', 'The palace of Brian', ibid., p. 251.

# — 19 —

# John Lavery, *The Life of a Painter*, 1940

Sir John Lavery (1856–1941) was a highly successful artist who, though born in humble circumstances in Belfast, rose to become portraitist to British high society from the Edwardian era through to the 1930s. Lavery produced a famous group portrait of George V and his family in 1913 (London, National Portrait Gallery) but in the 1920s, encouraged by his American wife, Hazel Martyn (1880–1935), he painted a series of portraits and subject pictures for the first Irish Free State government. In 1928 the artist used Lady Lavery as the model for his representation of 'Erin' on the new Irish banknotes. Lavery was one of the few Irish artists to produce an autobiography; not surprisingly, the book is full of uncritical anecdote (see also Paul Henry's autobiographical account of a decade later, entry 21). In the extract included here, Lavery recalls painting prominent Irishmen of the day, from Edward Carson (1854–1935) to Michael Collins (1890–1922).

Source: John Lavery, *The Life of a Painter*, London, Cassell and Company Ltd., 1940, pp. 207–9 and 212–17

Hazel, who was very keen on the Irish Question, said to me one day, 'John, why don't you do something for your country?' Now, an undeveloped sense of patriotism was my trouble. For years I did not seem to grasp what Ireland had suffered, and if I did the feeling was that possibly it served us right. But when the Great War came and the Black and Tans were given *carte blanche* to do their damnedest – which they did – the desire to fight stirred in my blood for the first time. Yet I very much doubt if it was patriotism and a love of country so much as a sense of justice. There was nothing much I could do. So when Hazel asked me why I did not do something for my country I replied, 'I cannot see that I can do anything without mixing myself with religion or pol-itics, and I have no time to differ with people.' 'Don't differ,' she replied. 'Just agree with them all, as you do anyway.' So it struck me that I might be some use in making my studio neutral ground where both sides might meet.

I started painting a triptych with Hazel as the Madonna, Eileen as Saint Brigid, and Alice as the boy Patrick, the swineherd, and presented it as an altar-piece to Saint Patrick's Church in Belfast, where I was baptized.[1] Then, to show the other side that I was not a bigot, I presented them with the original study for the Royal Portrait Group at the National Portrait Gallery.[2] Then I went south and entered the political arena by inviting Edward Carson and John Redmond to sit, on condition that they would allow me to present their portraits to the Dublin Gallery to be hung side by side. They both came and sat, and, as usual, they each thought the other's portrait was the better. Carson, knowing that I was a Catholic, although from Belfast, looking at the two portraits together, remarked, 'Ah, it's easy to see which side you're on.' Redmond did not criticize, he only said plain-tively, 'I have always had an idea that Carson and I might some day be hanged side by side in Dublin, and now it has come to pass.' When the Free State had been established I painted a second portrait of Carson, for Belfast. He looked at it for a long time and, as if speaking to himself, said, 'Well now, you can call that "Edward Carson after the Surrender".' I asked Lord D'Abernon for his opinion. 'My dear John, you have quite missed the char-acter. It is not like him, you haven't caught the criminal look. No, it's not good.' 'Well, his wife thinks it's the best portrait that has been done of him.' 'Yes of course, that damns it.'[3]

Hazel thought it a good beginning but she wanted something bigger done. Why not join together all the contending elements of my native city? It was rather a large order, but I started with a light heart. First of all two Archbishops, Cardinal Logue and Archbishop d'Arcy, then the Grand Master of the Orange Lodge, and Joe Devlin, Sir James Craig, Archbishop MacRory, and Bishop Grierson, with a judicious mingling of the others.

Hazel came with me to Armagh to paint the Cardinal, a little old man with round shoulders and his head shot forward, with beetling brows and a long upper lip, indicative, I believe, of humour.[4] Owing to the position of his head it was difficult to see his eyes. Towards the end of the last sitting I said, 'Your Eminence, I have not yet seen the colour of your eyes.' He looked up, and two piercing orbs were brought to bear on me. 'They are Irish grey, your Eminence.' 'No, they are black, or perhaps they have become grey with the years.' I doubt if he was pleased with the portrait, for after looking at it for some time he said, 'The last artist who painted me made me look like a mon-key in a bush.' I must admit there was something simian in what I had done.

He did not show any resentment, however, and when we were going away paid us both very charming compliments for coming to see a lonely old man. Hazel said, 'Your Eminence will forget all about us when we are gone.' He replied, 'Well, at any rate I'll remember the colour of your eyes.' [. . .]

Things in Dublin were getting pretty bad when an invitation came to Hazel to meet Lloyd George at dinner at Sir Philip Sassoon's.[5]

'Now is your chance,' said I to Hazel, 'to do something for Ireland.'

When she returned she said that he was a wizard right enough. He had made her feel so interested in herself that the Irish question was put in the background. She had never met anyone with greater charm, and she was sure of his sympathetic treatment of the Irish. Next morning she read in *The Times* that Lloyd George had the trouble well in hand, and that some thousand Black and Tans had landed and were driving all before them. 'Terrifying the rebels into submission and getting their own back.'

She was so disappointed that some time afterwards, when an official letter came stating that the Prime Minister desired to place my name before the King as one deserving recognition, she counselled declining the honour on the ground that 'Mr' was more distinguished than 'Sir'. But 'Lady Lavery' had a pleasing sound, so I accepted – men always blame their wives on such occasions. We both wondered who had been working to bring the distinction about, and it is only now that it occurs to me that it must have been the night at Philip Sassoon's.

England and Ireland were at war, Black and Tans and Republicans. I told Winston [Churchill] that I was going to Ireland to paint Michael Collins. 'Be careful, my dear John, our men are not all good shots.' But I was not able to go, and even if I had I didn't quite see how my sitter could have been expected to sit. At last the Treaty Negotiations were under way. Hazel got in touch with Collins's sister, and one morning he walked into my studio, a tall young Hercules with a pasty face, sparkling eyes, and a fascinating smile. I helped him off with a heavy overcoat to which he clung, excusing himself by saying casually, 'There is a gun in the pocket.'

He came over, as everyone knows, on a safe-conduct with Griffith, Gavan Duffy, Barton, Duggan, and Erskine Childers. De Valera had been over a week or two before but had failed to come to terms, and now sent these representatives in the hope that a treaty might result. De Valera came to sit for a couple of hours. I was naturally more interested in what he looked like than in what he said – something to the effect that the mass of the people were like sheep in that they run after each other. I cannot remember what called forth the remark, the statement was not new to me. My regret is that I had so little time to paint him.

I had more time with his delegates. Hazel was anxious that they should meet Englishmen of importance concerned with the Irish Question, and this resulted in many dinner parties and other functions. But there was one delegate who held out – Erskine Childers. I had him on the telephone once or twice, but he would not be induced to come, not even to a meal.

By many it was believed that had it not been for Hazel there would have been no Treaty – certainly not at the time it was signed. She had given up Erskine Childers as impossible to move, but she had overcome Arthur Griffith's objections. Michael Collins stood firm to the last minute. He seemed to have lost his temper. Even I, whose head was never really out of the paint-pot, could see that he who loses his temper in argument is lost, and told him so, but I failed to convince him. Eventually, after hours of persuasion, Hazel prevailed. She took him to Downing Street in her car that last evening, and he gave in. Yet he knew, knowing our queer race, that in signing he might well be signing his death-warrant. Neither friend nor foe ever accused this man of lacking courage.

One night at dinner Hazel had on one side of her Lord French[6] and on the other Michael Collins. Looking across at him, Lord French said. 'This is the first time I have had the pleasure of meeting you, Mr Collins.' 'It is not the first time I have seen your Lordship,' said Collins, 'for a couple of months ago you were by yourself near the Lodge and the boys surrounded you; but I called them off, I thought it so brave of you.' 'London,' said French, 'is the best place, after all, to meet people. For a considerable time I was on the heels of De Wet in South Africa and only caught up with him in London here, at dinner.'

Winston invited me with Collins to luncheon. He showed us some interesting things, among which was a copy of a South African poster which read: '£10 Reward for Winston Churchill, dead or alive.' 'We put a bigger price on you, Mr. Collins,' said Winston; 'I think it was £10,000.' 'Prices have gone up since your day, Mr Churchill.'

Collins was a patient sitter, but I noticed that he liked to sit facing the door. He was always on the alert. During the war in Ireland he was almost a wizard in the way he was never caught. He did not go into hiding, yet when the military came to some house they had seen him enter they never could find him, though there seemed no means of escape – in this and the capacity to disguise himself he bore a strong resemblance to Lenin, I am told. He told me that his mother died during the troubles, and that he insisted on going to her funeral. His friends implored him not to, for it would be putting himself into the hands of the military. But he went. And the military went. He stood in their midst. But they could not see him – so skilful was his make-up as a monk.

It was interesting to note how he and Lord Birkenhead[7] took to one another. Collins had a great admiration for the extraordinary facility of

Birkenhead's address, and the un-English directness of his phraseology on occasion. No one could be as successfully insulting to 'Noble Lords' as the 'Galloper'. Collins would have delighted in the occasion when, during the debate on the Treaty, the pale face of Lord Carson grew steadily paler as he listened to the heightening invective of Birkenhead, which reached at last to the words, 'The solution of this problem advanced by the Noble Lord would sound immature on the lips of an hysterical schoolgirl!' Many a morning before the Downing Street meetings Collins would be seen hurrying to meet Birkenhead. No one knows what transpired.

When the delegates returned to Dublin, Hazel and I also went over. We now learnt that Collins had 'sold his country'. Phrases are terrible things – why not hang every person who coins a dangerous one and impose a fine of £10 for a silly one? One day we lunched with Collins at the Gresham Hotel. On his way he was ordered to put his hands up by a youth with a gun. In putting them up he knocked the youth over and took the gun from him, telling him that he had stopped the wrong man, together with a few other points the youth had overlooked. They shook hands and parted friends, Michael keeping the gun.

One evening he came to dine with us at the Kingstown Hotel. I did not know till afterwards that Hazel had saved his life by sitting for half an hour between him and the window where a gunman had been placed. She was anxious that he should meet Horace Plunkett[8] and took him there the same evening alone. I was a little anxious, but for some reason did not go. Coming back they were waylaid and half a dozen shots were poured into the car. I examined it with an electric torch and it seemed a miracle that no one was hurt, for there were six people in the car, sitting close together. The bullets must have gone over their heads. Collins made light of it, but complained of a pain in his side that he thought might possibly be his appendix. After much persuasion he accepted my hot-water bottle, and placing it under his tunic he smilingly said that the pain had gone. With a 'God bless you both', he jumped into his car with Emmet Dalton and Joe Riley, dashing off into the night. That was the last I saw of him alive. [. . .]

[Collins's] body was brought to Dublin and placed in the mortuary chapel, where only relatives and closest friends were admitted. I was allowed to paint him in death.[9] Any grossness in his features, even the peculiar little dent near the point of his nose, had disappeared. He might have been Napoleon in marble as he lay in his uniform, covered by the Free State flag, with a crucifix on his breast. Four soldiers stood round the bier. The stillness was broken at long intervals by someone entering the chapel on tiptoe, kissing the brow, and then slipping to the door where I could hear a burst of suppressed grief. One woman kissed the dead lips, making it hard for me to continue my work.

## NOTES

1    *The Madonna of the Lakes*, originally St Patrick's Cathedral, Belfast, now, Ulster Museum, Belfast, exhibited at the Royal Academy in London, 1917, illustrated in *Sir John Lavery R.A., 1856–1941*, exhibition catalogue, The Ulster Museum, Belfast, and the Fine Arts Society, London, 1984, p. 77. Eileen Lavery was the artist's daughter, Alice Gwynn, his step-daughter.

2    Ibid., p. 73.

3    For an account of Lavery's Irish portraits see Kenneth McConkey, *Sir John Lavery*, Edinburgh, Canongate Press, 1993, chapter 9.

4    Michael Logue (1840–1924) became a cardinal in 1893; portrait of 1920 in the Ulster Museum, Belfast, illustrated in *Sir John Lavery*, exhibition catalogue, p. 94.

5    Sassoon (1888–1939) was a well-known political host, MP and connoisseur, see Sinéad McCoole, *Hazel: A Life of Lady Lavery*, Dublin, The Lilliput Press, 1996, P. 68 and passim.

6    John Denton Pinkstone French (1852–1925), first Earl of Ypres. In 1920, when he was viceroy of Ireland (1918–21), an attempt was made to assassinate him.

7    Frederick Edwin Smith, first Earl of Birkenhead, a British representative at the Anglo-Irish Treaty negotiations, 1921.

8    Sir Horace Plunkett, son of the sixth Lord Dunsany, had introduced co-operatives for farmers in the 1890s.

9    See McConkey, pp. 157–9; painting is in the Hugh Lane Municipal Gallery of Modern Art, Dublin, and is inscribed 'Love of Ireland'.

# — 20 —

# Ernie O'Malley, 'The Paintings of Jack Yeats,' 1945

Ernie O'Malley (1897–1957) is remembered as a republican fighter who later wrote one of the most eloquent accounts of the Irish Revolutionary period, *On Another Man's Wound*, first published in 1936. O'Malley lived in the United States of America from 1928 to 1935 where he befriended numerous artists and writers.[1] On returning to Ireland, he and his wife, the American sculptor Helen Hooker, began collecting contemporary art, including work by Jack Yeats (1871–1957). In 1942, Kenneth Clark, then director of the National Gallery, London, included two of Yeats's paintings from the O'Malley collection in a joint William Nicolson and Yeats exhibition. A few years later, in 1945, O'Malley contributed an essay to the catalogue of a one-man Yeats exhibition at the National College of Art in Dublin.[2] That essay is reproduced here in its entirety. It shows O'Malley's relaxed yet engaging style but also informs us as to what attracted an Irish republican intellectual to Yeats's romantic subject matter. O'Malley is entranced by Yeats's representation of the peasantry (fig. 10), who as he said himself, on another occasion, 'had more good blood in it than either middle or upper middle class'.[3]

Source: *Jack B. Yeats: A Centenary Gathering*, ed. Roger McHugh, Dublin, The Dolmen Press, 1971, pp. 64–70

Jack B. Yeats spent his boyhood in Sligo town, a small port on the Atlantic edge. Sligo is flanked in a half-circle by mountains which show a wild inland cliff scenery shaped to fantastic form; small lakes, then strong outbursts of rock carry the other flank to the sea. The sea brought the outside world to the doors of a small town in a casual mention of foreign cities, strange words and wild doings; it made for wonder and mystery later seen if only as a gloss on piracy. From the land side came the country people to shop, shy and awkward in the foreign life of a town, but fierce and intractable when following their realistic land calling at fairs and markets. Family life for them centred around the oldest of man's allegiances, the hearth, woven with memoried legend; their land work built as much on folklore as on the hard reality of uneconomic holdings.

The town presented a knowledge of character and incident, the vagaries of personalities with oddities even to the daft accepted as part of its world [fig. 10]. It would be an open book like any other Irish town, whose inhabitants are mainly interested in motive and intention of others, in knitting daily events in a conversational form to be related before evening as direct and indirect implication threaded by affection, malice or envy.

Here then in his native town he could see people who were not accepted in a conventional setting. They bore much the same relationship to the tightened security of bourgeois respectability, ringed by experience which it fears to enlarge, as the artist does to that life; and with them the unexpected was always in the offing. The sailor, a transitory form who came on shore for drink and company after the indifference of ocean, forgetful of hardship in his now remembrance of outland ways and customs, to light the imagination of stay-at-homes. Tinkers with the wildness of life in the open and their utterly untamed fierceness who fought after a feed of porter in a whoop of song. Countrymen, freed for a few days in the year from the greedy tyranny

10    Jack B. Yeats, *The Rogue*, 1903

of land, wander through their favourite pubs to meet neighbours and relations, ridding themselves of hard-earned money in a spacious generosity; at ease in gestured extravagance with a background of their own song. Outside in the street a ballad singer to relate past and present in a long string of verse, sure of heightened talk and soothing drink before the night came.

When the circus arrived its flamboyant posters exalted grace and beauty to ballet level, a band renowned for noise shook the side walls whilst brightly costumed performers wound through the streets. At night, clowns in their tragic way acted the scapegoat, slapped their fellows, made fun of themselves in simulated awkwardness, often to emerge from this chrysalis, as grace. The clown related his humour to the tragic scene of life inherent in his audience, though outsiders, as in the clown, might see only uncaring lightheartedness. Circus music, colour, baroque gesture, essentially sweep the mind, free the heart, but relate nomadic tent existence to settlement, leaving an aching sense of unfulfilment and nostalgia behind.

Jack Yeats would be moulded too by the physical nature of his province, Connacht. Great roaring winds sweep in from the Atlantic to drench the land with spray, soften the intention, weaken will and perseverance. Cloud forms drift slowly in threat or, when storm has ceased, model to a painter's delight land forms below. Sky bulks large to give a sense of infinite distance and mystery mixed with tragic desolation. This spaciousness of sky is the most noticeable feature of the Western scene; it is, at times, as if the land were a prelude to the atmosphere above. Swirling cloud makes for a Turneresque dramatic effect, difficult to register, shot as it is with daffodil, duck-egg green and improbable colour combinations. Land can become sogged with persistent rain; it is then more than ever a burden and a heart-breaking task to work, or to brood a melancholy in the mind. With shafted light after the rain comes a lyrical mood which tender greens vibrate in tones, whins crash with yellow glory and atmosphere is radiant.

The shifting scene is temperamental and induces mood. It is a hard country to paint as it presents problems of subtle unrelated colour which is not easily seen as pattern, but develops in a strange orchestration. This subtlety and its opposite, the strongly dramatic scene, must be the despair of academic painters whose minds have been trained to accept the conventional impression, but whose eye may fail to record the sudden unexpected impact. Memory must play its part, for painting hours are episodic, broken by rain or rebellious wind. The sense of man is present in enclosures of light-filigreed stone walls which map land hunger, or in unobtrusive cottages, dwarfed by mountain and hill to an almost tragic insignificance.

Beyond the Shannon in a train the West can be sensed: in a spate of talk, an expansion of interest which breaks down impersonal aloofness to introduce the co-operative sharing of a sense of life, an immediate hint of vitality and a degree of wonder which rounds a mediaeval quality of mind. People have charm, time is judged as a convenience not as a burden, talk is an expression in a form of entertainment which interests to free the imagination and give a sense of ease. Subtlety of mind, easily directed to cunning in land or business, is now judged as diplomatic adroitness. Above all is a sense of wildness and freedom, an untamed naturalness, the unexpected even in a phrase, a feeling of equality through an understanding of the natural dignity of man.

Jack Yeats experienced some such quality of life in Connacht and he has since interpreted it. With a hawk's swift eye he has seen this panorama as material, and his sensitive psychological understanding of it has fused its meaning in his spirit. The visual world has been absorbed, selected and recreated slowly with innocent freshness in terms of emotional colour. He can capture the intensity of his feeling which has viewed an aspect of as simple a pleasure of life as the interior of a circus tent. The circus is a boy's delight but also a man's, if his emotions have not been smothered by what is known as discretion, or by the death of the heart.

There is a genuine interest and affection in his work for the incidents portrayed. They grow out of love and a profound sensibility of what to some are outlandish ways with a certain colourful appeal. The outward form of life has changed since he has grown up but the fundamental attitude of mind remains. Practical people often find life in the West hard; as indeed it is when progress is viewed philosophically in relation to eternity; but artists whose energy is turned to observation see the relationship of people to each other, to events and to their environment.

In his earlier work he is a draughtsman who stresses illustrative content directing it in a *vital* sense of line to a personal idiom. Later, in water-colour he uses water-colour with this same illustrative content not as a medium but as flat colour tones to give vitality to his drawings. It was, I think, a lucky chance when he found a number of his early water-colours destroyed by damp. This accident made him think more in terms of oil and he began to experiment. Then continued a long period in which definition became gradually more colourful and his essential bent, that of a colourist, more emphatic. By the year 1921 he had reached the limits of his expression in this manner.

When the artist reaches his spiritual limit in any one method of expression he follows either of two ways. He continues to reproduce his impressions in a manner he has outgrown until the individual painting is no longer a problem for the sum total of what constitutes his being, but is related to hand and eye alone: or he experiments until he has created a new way of approach to his problem. Jack Yeats found his world in a greater feeling for the emotional use of paint, which slowly pushed back the limits of definition until paint, as it were, escaped its mould to become an end in itself. It is hard to explain a change in direction, but one of the factors may have been the heightened sensibility which could result from the tension of life during the struggle for freedom in Ireland then, and the new note of intensity felt by a sensitive observer.

As he enlarged his experience as a painter, he also enlarged his vision. His work no longer dealt with a perception of countrymen in relaxation or at ease in a folk-lore tradition. His figures now enter a subjective world in which they are related to the loneliness of the individual soul, the vague lack of pattern in living with its sense of inherent tragedy, brooding nostalgia, associated with time as well as variation on the freer moments as of old. Visionary worlds of Tir-na-nOg, California, palaces, are opened to us with persuasive paint, and all action is subordinated to thought. Aspects of Dublin workers are searched for inherent character or nobility. Anna Liffey gets its due tribute from one who has the Dubliner's realisation of its significance; reflective mood floods people and furniture in light-splashed rooms; or light itself is the subtly dramatic force. He had always a strong sense of man in relation to the impersonality of the Irish scene; isolated figures never dominate the landscape, but they are now more related to it in symbolical significance which increases their stature to bulk in the mind. One departure of his was completely new in Irish painting, the depiction of national events. The memory of the dead makes for a tragic understanding in Ireland. It evokes a feeling of dead generations who served or had died for a common cause, their struggle echoed in each generation. The Bachelor's Walk incident is shown as simple, but hieratic incident of a flower-girl who casts a flower outside a doorway where men have been shot down.[4] There is restrained dignity and grace in the movement of her hand and a tenderness that evokes a sense of pity.

He has used the funeral or burial as a symbol. The death of a man who has suffered in the national fight has often been one of the few public tributes that a people could give to one whom some of them recognised only by death. A sense of ceremonial, which had seemed to disappear from consciousness, would emerge and an impressive ordered intensity shows understanding and devotion. The memory of the dead has changed its meaning when seen as a political artifice, or has become outworn in verbal misuse, but in Jack Yeats's pictures it holds an eternal significance.

For over twenty years he has been painting in this new manner. For a time he worked in philosophic isolation amongst an indifferent audience who resent an artist's new direction in implementing his vision. This has always been the attitude of a world of punditry, which, becoming complacent, does not risk disturbance except in terms of what it regards as its own interpretation of creative work. A true artist's vision is directed by a keener mental and physical eye, trained selective capacity, contemplative detachment, and inventive technical sense, which is used to rebuild the microcosm architecturally, descriptively, or emotionally. Gradually, however, people came to recognise his genius and originality, his unusual colour sense and his absolute integrity. Of late he has himself been the major factor in the training of our eyes to understand what is indeed a school in itself, his quality of mind in paint.

In Ireland the visual sense is not strongly developed in terms of creative painting, but there is a fine feeling for colour, well expressed in small towns where white-wash is mixed with paint powder to give house fronts a fascinating texture of tender pastel shades. Irish atmosphere softens and blends the clash that might have ensued from the individuality of the owners in selection of colour. There is, as well, a peculiar unliterary affection of landscape, but the manner of looking at paint is too often determined, not by this corrective, based as it is on evasive colour and the inherent structural sense of line and form in bare mountain, but by thinking of other paintings. Due to the destruction of the arts by conquest there is but one continuous tradition, the literary tradition; we are inclined to see paint in a literary way as if the implied title should continue as a story on the canvas.

In Jack Yeats we have a painter who is as much concerned with what he has to say in paint as with his manner of saying it. He brings a fresh experience to each canvas he paints; his individual work can not be judged in terms of previous works but in the individual canvas one looks at. That demands alertness of mind and an unprejudiced, innocent eye. He is a romantic painter who through memory had made notes all his life of material which has stirred him by its emotional significance. Those notes may remain unused for years but they have been sifted in his consciousness. When he calls on them he can recollect his original impressions, organise his perceptions through an enlargement of that experience, and create a work of art.

With him colour is an emotional force and his method of using it varies in regard to its substance as pigment and as texture. He may create a homogeneous surface with his brush, improvise an absorbing study in chiaroscuro, or use the priming of the canvas to aid luminosity of light and shade. At times, impatient with the brush to communicate his feeling for the richness and charm of pigment and his sheer joy of expressive power, he employs the palette knife to give swiftness and vigour to the immediacy of his emotion. Seemingly unrelated colours directed by this urgency create an orchestration due to his unerring taste in colour harmony; and in a form of evocative magic, make a direct impact on the mind. Even a casual glance at a small collection of his work shows how inexhaustible is his colour invention. As he experiments in technique he reaches a point in mastery where his handling of knife or brush seems to be by instinct.

In this exhibition as his development is studied from his earlier stages to his more subjective and symbolical work, his steady growth can be seen. The new Ireland, still fluid politically and socially, has found in Jack Yeats a painter of major rank, whose vision is used to make us aware of inherent characteristics, psychological directives and eternal verities.

In return for this understanding of us it is pleasant to realise that Irish art lovers should, over the years, have made it possible to bring together a collection of his pictures that show his development in its completeness, and thus bring about the present tribute from the whole nation.

NOTES

1    See Richard English, *Ernie O'Malley: IRA Intellectual*, Oxford, Clarendon Press, 1998, chapter 1.
2    See Bruce Arnold, *Jack Yeats*, New Haven and London, Yale University Press, 1998, pp. 323–5.
3    Quoted in English, p. 78.
4    O'Malley is referring to Yeats's *Bachelor's Walk in Memory*, 1915, private collection; see Arnold, *Jack Yeats*, pp. 191–3.

— 21 —

# Paul Henry, *An Irish Portrait*, 1951

During the first three decades of independence, Paul Henry (1876–1958) was probably the most popular artist in Ireland. His nostalgic landscapes of the West of Ireland satisfied a country that viewed itself as still rooted in the soil, unaffected by the changes going on in other parts of Europe (see also entries 39 and 54). And yet, as a young man, Henry had trained for two years in Paris, where he came under the influence of Whistler and other moderns. While in Paris, Henry met the Scottish artist Grace Mitchell (1868–1953), and they married in 1903. The Henrys first visited Achill Island in 1910, the location of so much of Paul Henry's subsequent work. They lived full-time on Achill from about 1912 to 1919 and it is this period that was to be the subject of Henry's future autobiography. Amazingly, Grace is never mentioned. The portrait of the artist that comes across is thus a very distorted, highly romanticized image: one of an isolated figure, preoccupied with pursuing his art,

Gauguin-like in his fascination with the island and its life.[1] These two extracts from *An Irish Portrait* tell us why he went to Achill and of an encounter with a local boy who showed artistic talent.

Source: Paul Henry, *An Irish Portrait*, London, Batsford, 1951, pp. 50–51 and 62–66

The desire to live in Achill was a purely emotional one. I wanted to live there, not as a visitor but to identify myself with its life and to see it every day in all its moods, in wind, in rain, in storm, in summer and in winter, and by painting it in all these conditions to find out the driving force behind its attractiveness. I wanted to know the people, their intimate lives, the times of seedtime and harvest. Only after I had gained such knowledge would I be able to paint the country which I had adopted. I wanted to study them, I wanted to study the lives of the people and their surroundings as closely and as single-mindedly as the French naturalist Fabre studied the insects of his devotion in the stony fields and vineyards of Provence. Geographically Achill is an island, and it held all the islanders' susceptibilities to the outside world although only a few hundred yards separated it from the mainland, and its current of life was entirely traditional, which separated it still further. There were many folk who had never seen a train. All these things proved satisfying to me, and the habits and ways of this remote community surrounded by savage rocks and treacherous sea, provided me with all I require as a painter. But what attracted me above all these things was the wild beauty of the landscape, of the colour and variety of the cloud formations, one of the especial glories of the West of Ireland. [. . .]

It was not difficult to make friends on the island because everyone was so kind and helpful. They just came into my life naturally and unexpectedly. One day I met an old man who stopped me on the road and asked me if I would sell him some oil paints, as he had heard that I was an artist. I told him that I did not sell paints, that I used them for my own work. He seemed rather disappointed, so I asked him what he wanted them for and he replied that he wanted them for his son Anthony who wished to learn to paint. He said that he himself was a carpenter and had a certain amount of colour but that his son would like some more. I explained as tactfully as I could that paints were expensive things and that unless he was prepared to spend a certain amount of money for paints and brushes and the other incidental things that are necessary, his boy might find it difficult to get very far. But I was interested, and though I made no promises I thought I would talk to the boy himself, which I did later on.

After disposing of the matter of the paints Johnny and I drifted into a talk and so attracted was I by him and his talk as we sat by the roadside that I think we must have chatted for about an hour. Johnny was a MacNamara, one of a very numerous clan, and a family which carried very great weight in this part of Achill. Johnny MacNamara was the son of John MacNamara, the son of Tom MacNamara, the son of Owen MacNamara, 'Johnny Tom Owen MacNamara', known to the whole of the countryside as 'Johnny Tom Owen'. He was a short, thickset, but agile man of about sixty, a carpenter by trade but he could, like most Achill men, turn his hand to anything requiring ingenuity. He was extraordinarily shrewd and intelligent with the kindliest eyes I have ever seen in a human being and his good spirits were boundless. In time I came to know him very well indeed, and the more I saw of him the more I liked him. Johnny loved an out-of-door life and on that first talk with him on the roadside he told me that in his early youth he had worked as a cooper in the stockyards of Chicago but that he could not stand the life because he wanted to be near the sea or the mountains and that no other life would suit him. So he had given up America and come home to live in Ireland.

I did not know Anthony's appearance, but by making a few inquiries in the village I was able to locate the boy. I found him high up on the hillside above Corrymore where he was tending the few head of cattle belonging to his father. I have often been surprised to come upon so many of these friends of mine sitting alone on the hillside rapt in contemplation of the landscape, and I have wondered what they were thinking about in those silent hours far from anyone, a few sheep scattered over the hillside, an odd cow and nothing more but the remoteness of the landscape. Probably nothing at all was passing through their minds. But in the case of Anthony it was very different. He was tall and meagre with a beautiful adolescent figure and aloof and brooding eyes. We sat down on the grass and began to talk. We were looking out over the great expanse of Clew Bay and I said to him what a marvellous spot he had taken me to, how beautiful, and when I mentioned the landscape his face lighted up with a very attractive and pleased shyness and he began to tell me how he felt about the landscape surrounding him on all sides. He said how wonderful it must be to be an artist and transfer these things to canvas.

I am afraid I rather stressed the difficulties of the artistic life but he did not seem to understand what that meant. He told me he had one or two things that he had tried to do and that he would show them to me. He produced several sheets of ordinary cartridge paper, I think there were three or four sketches altogether, and showed me what he had done. I was prepared for crudity and an utter lack of knowledge, but as he unfolded his work I saw that the lack of knowledge was there but not the crudity, and it was obvious to me that the things were markedly mature with the maturity that comes from long brooding. I realised the many hours he must have spent with his father's cattle on that lonely spot absorbed and absorbing. He had borrowed his father's paints and great thick brushes. The only colours he had were a vile Prussian blue, an orange red, and black, but with these unpromising materials he had produced something that amazed me. He had not spent hours tending his father's cattle for nothing. His landscapes were savage in their intensity and made me think of Van Gogh. I imagine that Anthony must have been about fourteen, and I realised that I was in the presence of an instinctive artist.

In my time I have seen many different kinds of painting and different kinds of artists, but Anthony was unique in my experience. He didn't even know the names of the colours he was using, but in those lonely hillside hours he had been storing up a love of the landscape that was better than all the lore of the studios.

The cattle had strayed away and Anthony shyly reminded me that we must be moving on. So we followed the cattle a short distance and sat down again. I began to tell him about artists; how many were called and few were chosen, how it required courage and strength of endeavour to become even an ordinary artist – if there is such a thing! Anthony listened to it all but I knew that he was not taking in one word of what I said, that he had already made up his mind what he was going to be and do. The die had long ago been cast in that wayside village.

When I gave him back the sketches he handled them in the way that only an artist can handle his work, delicately and affectionately. I sat on that hillside with the cry of the curlews in my ears and the surge of the surf on Gubelennaun, and I thought of many things. And as I walked home I could not help thinking of Van Gogh with his tortured soul, who crucified himself in trying to express what was in his mind; and this youthful untrained mind who saw no difficulties in painting; he was too untrained for that, but he could convey what he wanted to express with unerring certainty because he felt so deeply and emotionally, and the fact that he did not know how to paint caused him no uneasiness. He painted as the birds sang and with as pure an emotion.

Later that day I went on up the hillside and lay above Corrymore in the heather. The interview with the boy Anthony had disturbed and unsettled me and I could not work. I was too engrossed with the thought of my own early life and the difficulties I had had to contend with, and my thoughts went back over the years to all the young painters I had known. These had all had some sort of preliminary training and did not come to their work with the utter unsophistication of Anthony, and I felt that I could not start him out and then leave him; better not to start out at all, it seemed to me the lesser of two evils. So I decided to do nothing for a little while. But all the same I could not get him out of my mind and thinking of him called up the ghosts of early memories. I had no illusions about the difficulties of the artist's life. My own experiences had taught me a great deal ... I had known hundreds of young artists, and recalling their names I was astonished to find how few of them had done anything worth talking about. Paris alone held thousands of them, but only a very small percentage would be heard of again after a few years.

## NOTES

1    See Catherine Nash, 'Landscape, Body and Nation: Cultural Geographies of Irish Identities', unpublished Ph.D. thesis, University of Nottingham, 1995, p. 89 (see also entry 54, below). For an account of Henry's career see Brian Kennedy, 'Paul Henry: An Irish Portrait', *Irish Arts Review*, Yearbook 1989–90, pp. 43–54. For an analysis of Henry's autobiography see Mary Cosgrove, 'Paul Henry and Achill Island', in *Landscape, Heritage and Identity: Case Studies in Irish Ethnography*, ed. Ullrich Kockel, Liverpool University Press, 1995, pp. 93–116.

# — 22 —

# Richard Kearney, *Transitions*, 1988

This extract from Richard Kearney's *Transitions: Narratives in Modern Irish Culture* focuses on one of Ireland's leading contemporary artists, Louis Le Brocquy (b. 1916). In turn Kearney is one of Ireland's major cultural commentators who is also a professor of philosophy at University College Dublin as well as teaching regularly at Boston College. The focus of his discussion of Le Brocquy is on the painter's position within an Irish tradition. Reference is made to the artist's well-known series of 'heads', which include examinations of James Joyce (fig. 11), W.B. Yeats and other prominent Irish writers.[1]

Source: Richard Kearney, *Transitions: Narratives in Modern Irish Culture*, Manchester University Press, 1988, pp. 199–202. Some of Kearney's notes have been retained but their numbering has been altered.

Le Brocquy's art could certainly not be described, by any stretch of the imag-ination, as an 'active intervention in the solution of society's problems'.[2] But his unflagging commitment to the exploration of visual *inwardness* may be seen as a disclosure of an aesthetic dimension which refuses the misery of exploitation and manipulation. By sustaining an irreducible distance, one might even say antagonism, between the interiority of art and the exterior-ity of the social universe, le Brocquy's work testifies to the fact that the pres-ent world of domination can never fully eliminate the potential world of freedom. The basic thesis that art must be a factor in changing the world, as Marcuse has observed, 'can easily turn into its opposite if the tension between art and radical praxis is flattened out so that art loses its own dimension for change [. . .] The flight into inwardness may well serve as a bulwark against a society which administers all dimensions of human existence. Inwardness and subjectivity may well become the inner and outer space for the subversion of experience, for the emergence of another universe.'[3]

Le Brocquy maintains that there is a deep connection between the aes-thetic dimensions of *inwardness* and *otherness*. As he explained in an interview with Harriet Cooke: 'I often think of painting as being a kind of personal archaeology. I feel one is digging for things and suddenly something turns up which seems to be remarkable; something apparently *outside* oneself, which one has found in fact *inside* oneself.'[4] By means of palpable paint, le Brocquy is groping towards an impalpable interiority of meaning, what he calls 'the inner reality of the human presence beyond its merely external appearance'. But when le Brocquy speaks thus of the primacy of subjective inwardness he is not for a moment advancing the romantic supremacy of the individual will or cogito (which typifies both Cartesian subjectivism and bourgeois individ-ualism). Le Brocquy has repeatedly affirmed that his painting is not prima-rily self-expression, but the exploration of an interior dimension of otherness which explodes our assured personal identity and suspends our controlling will. (It is what Beckett, in his Proust essay, called the revelation of involun-tary imagination.) Le Brocquy defines subjectivity accordingly as 'an interior invisible world', an 'autonomous disseminated consciousness surpassing indi-vidual personality'.[5] He believes that the painter must await the emergence of the image without imposing his own voluntary projections: 'When paint-ing I try not to impose myself. Discoveries are made – such as they are – while painting. The painting itself dictates and although the resultant image may seem rhetorical to some, it appears to me to be almost autonomous, hav-ing emerged under one's hands not because of them [. . .] *Invention* for me is *discovery.*'[6] By embracing the polyvalent stream of inwardness, the artist strives to overcome his centralizing cogito in order to 'discover, uncover and reveal'. Seamus Heaney has written perceptively of this aspect of le Brocquy's

archaeology of painting as an emergence of the *other* through the inner dis-
solution of the mastering *self*: 'Yet that hand does not seek to express its own
personality. It is obedient rather than dominant, subdued into process as it
awaits a discovery. What it comes up with will sometimes feel like something
come upon, a recognition. Like a turfcutter's spade coming upon the body in
the bog, the head of the Tollund Man, ghostly yet palpable, familiar and other,
a historical creature grown ahistorical, an image that has seized hold of the
eye and will not let it go.'[7]

How, if at all, does le Brocquy relate to his own culture or to those other
Irish authors and artists whose work we have been examining in the preceding chapters?[8] True to the paradox of the artistic consciousness as a
dialectic between sameness and otherness, le Brocquy maintains that, like
Joyce before him, it was only after his departure from Ireland and subsequent
encounter with 'foreign' cultures that he became deeply interested in his
native culture.

    'Although I was born in Dublin in the year of the Rebellion,' he writes,
'and brought up entirely in Ireland, I do not remember being conscious of
being particularly Irish [. . .] None seemed to me less manifestly Irish than
that small family whose name I bore. Then one day in my 21st year, I pre-
cipitously sailed from Dublin into a new life as a painter studying in the
museums of London, Paris, Venice and Geneva [. . .] Alone among the great
artists of the past, in these strange related cities, I became vividly aware for
the first time of my Irish identity to which I have remained attached all my
life.'[9] But le Brocquy strenuously resists the dangers of what he terms 'self-
conscious nationalism'. He believes that art betrays itself as soon as it sub-
scribes to cultural insularism. While admitting that the 'flowering of our
imagination is nourished by roots hidden in our native soil', le Brocquy
opposes the manipulative uses of a self-righteous national identity.

    The art critic, Dorothy Walker maintains that le Brocquy's preoccupation
with head images and cyclical structures is a distinct borrowing from the
Celtic heritage. This debt to Celtic visual motifs combines with le Brocquy's
modernist commitment to innovative forms of representation which run
counter to the Renaissance conventions of classical realism and centralized
linear perspective. Le Brocquy himself has argued that we are currently wit-
nessing a revolutionary transition from an essentially *perceptual* and outward-
looking art to a new de-centralized art which rediscovers the source of
meaning 'within the mind and within those *conceptual,* interiorised images of
a world transformed'. While the perceptual era, devoted to exterior surface
phenomena, held sway from the Renaissance up to the turn of this century,
in recent decades 'the painter has been insistently aware of those renewed

conceptual tendencies characteristic of painting in our time'. Le Brocquy suggests that it was Joyce's enthusiasm for this counter-Renaissance tendency that accounts for his profound interest in the Medieval and Celtic universes of nighttime consciousness (a suggestion confirmed by Arthur Power who was told by Joyce that 'the Renaissance and its return to classicism was a return to intellectual boyhood'[10]). We thus find le Brocquy surmising that the plural identity of his own images of Joyce 'may represent a more medieval or Celtic viewpoint, cyclic rather than linear, repetitive yet simultaneous and, above all, inconclusive'.

In his fragmented and polymorphous images of Joyce [fig. 11], le Brocquy succeeds in evoking the fundamental ambivalences of time, space and emotion which so typify the world of *Ulysses* and *Finnegans Wake*. The pluralizing interiority of consciousness tends to produce, le Brocquy notes, 'an ambiguity involving a dislocation of our individual conception of time (within which coming and going, beginning and end, are normally regarded) and confronts this *normal* view with an alternative, contrary sense of simultaneity or timelessness, switching the linear conceptions of time to which we are accustomed to a circular concept returning upon itself, as in *Finnegans Wake*'. And le Brocquy adds his conviction that this alternative mode of vision can be reproduced in a certain paratemporal dimension of painting, a dimension which manifests itself in a double role 'involving a transmogrification of the paint itself into the image and vice versa'. 'In my own small world of painting,' he writes, 'I myself have learned from the canvas that emergence and immergence – twin phenomena of time – are ambivalent: that one implies the other and that the state or matrix within which they coexist apparently dissolves the normal sense of time, producing a characteristic *stillness*.' This is certainly an accurate description of that enigmatic confluence of presencing and absencing which le Brocquy's studies of the head image embody. Indeed le Brocquy explicitly relates the visual paradoxes of his own paintings to the verbal paralogisms of Joyce's writing, simultaneously day-consciousness and night-consciousness, 'like Ulysses and Finnegan, or like a living human head, image of the whole in the part, the old synecdochism of the Celt'.

Is this, le Brocquy asks finally, 'the underlying ambivalence which we in Ireland tend to stress [. . .] the indivisibility of birth and funeral, spanning the apparent chasm between past and present, between consciousness and fact?' It may well be. But if it is, such a Celtic prototype offers le Brocquy and Joyce not the solidarity of some antiquarian repossession but the solitude of modern dispossession: less a Celtic Twilight than a Celtic darkness, an encounter with an inwardness that remains so irretrievably other that it abrogates any triumphalist tenure within a continuous tradition. When

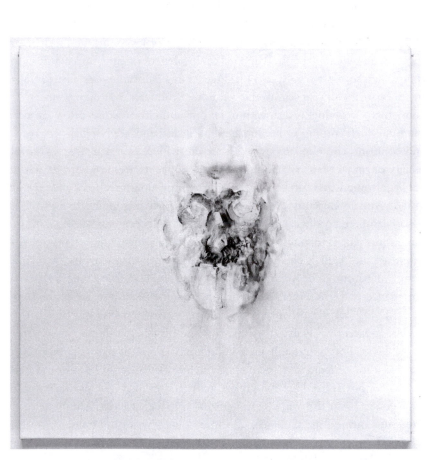

11    Louis Le Brocquy, *Study towards an Image of James Joyce*, 1977

Stephen Dedalus talked of forging the conscience of his race he significantly reminded us that it was still *uncreated*. Cultural identity, like national identity, is not something presupposed; it remains an open-ended task, an endless narrative to be reinterpreted by each artist in his own way. The time-space ambivalence of consciousness which manifests itself in le Brocquy's art is so different from our given modes of perception that it shatters rather than substantiates any centrist notion of identity. As another contemporary painter Patrick Collins remarked, one of the most consistent features of Irish art has been its propensity to erase any suspicion of a stable or unchanging tradition. In the best works of modern Irish art, Collins claims, the poet or painter brings himself 'to the point where he eliminates himself, and, by extension, the orthodox tradition from which he derives.'[11] So that if the Irish hero Finn becomes Finn-again in Joyce's writings, or the Irish writer Joyce becomes Joyce again in le Brocquy's paintings, it is only in both cases by becoming radically *other.*

Le Brocquy's dual fidelity to the *otherness* of both ancient Celtic and modern experimental art suggests that his work may be appropriately located in the tension between the revivalist and modernist impulses of contemporary Irish culture.

## NOTES

1   See *Louis Le Brocquy, Paintings, 1939–1996*, exhibition catalogue, Dublin, Irish Museum of Modern Art, 1996, nos. 62–97.

2   In the paragraph before this extract, Kearney had quoted Leonid Brezhnev, who in 1981 stated that 'The [communist] Party encourages ... art's active intervention in the solution of our society's problems,' Richard Kearney, *Transitions: Narratives in Modern Irish Culture*, Manchester University Press, 1988, p. 199.

3   Herbert Marcuse, *The Aesthetic Dimension,* Boston, Beacon Press, 1978, pp. 35, 39. [Orig. note.]

4   Le Brocquy, interview with Harriet Cooke in *The Irish Times*, quoted by Dorothy Walker, *Louis Le Brocquy*, Dublin, Ward River Press, 1981, p. 69. [Orig. note.]

5   Le Brocquy in ibid., p. 139. [Orig. note.]

6   Ibid., pp. 147-9. [Orig. note.]

7   Seamus Heaney, in ibid., p. 132. [Orig. note.]

8   Kearney discusses such writers as James Joyce, Sam Beckett, Flann O'Brien, Francis Stuart, John Banville, Seamus Heaney, Brian Friel, Tom Murphy and film maker Pat Murphy.

9   Louis Le Brocquy, 'A Painter's Notes on his Irishness', in *The Recorder*, vol. 42. [Orig. note.]

10   Quoted Vivian Mercier, 'James Joyce as Medieval Artist' in *The Crane Bag*, vol. 2, nos. 1 & 2, 1978, p. 11. [Orig. note.]

11   Patrick Collins, 'A Celtic Art?' Interview with Aidan Dunne in *The Crane Bag*, vol. 5, no. 2, 1981. [Orig. note.]

# − 23 −

# Fionna Barber, *Familiar: Alice Maher*, 1995

A leading contemporary Irish artist, Alice Maher (b. 1956) has, since the 1980s, been one of a number of women artists who offer an alternative voice to the previously dominant expressionism of such male painters as Patrick Graham (b. 1943), Brian Maguire (b. 1951) and others. In this essay the gender imagery inherent in Maher's work (fig. 12) is placed in context and the confrontational aspects of her art are discussed.[1] Fionna Barber teaches at Manchester Metropolitan University and has been a frequent contributor to *Circa Art Magazine*.

Source: Fionna Barber, 'Unfamiliar Distillations', from *Familiar: Alice Maher*, exhibition catalogue, Dublin, The Douglas Hyde Gallery, and Derry, the Orchard Gallery, 1995, pp. 11–18. The original notes have been retained.

The work of Alice Maher locates itself within the land of subversion and transformation; the menace of a child's dress bristling with unexpected bees [fig. 12], uncoiling tresses of fibrous hair, a regiment of turds encroaching upon two static feet. This is a place where mythologies are transmuted, shifting shape and meaning as they acquire concrete form; the flaxen hair of the fairytale heroine is turned into hair of flax. Instead of the goddess Venus rising resplendent from the sea an entire cohort of female heads emerges in the darkness and stillness.

This is work which draws upon memories of a rural childhood as much as mythology, but it is also informed by an engagement with the previous forms of representation found within art history. Such a concern has become a major feature of postmodernist practices, but Alice Maher's work tends to distance itself from the processes of irony and pastiche by which these are characterised. Her relationship to both postmodernism and modernism is something much more tangential, part of a practice which has also been informed by a knowledge of other earlier representational systems such as that of medievalism. From the perspective of radical tendencies within postmodernism, the preceding tenets of modernism have come to represent the last gasp of the authoritarian tradition of painting in place since the Renaissance.

12    Alice Maher, *Bee Dress*, 1994

In the practice of an artist like Alice Maher this progressive history of formalist innovation and technical autonomy becomes efficiently demoted. It subsides into a reservoir of imagery and memory where it becomes variously entwined with the pictorial strategies of medievalism, the narrative structure of mythology, and the logic of dreams. In some ways this is not so far removed from the figurative, anti-modernist tendency which took shape at the same time as the formalist innovations of the early 20th century; Maher's recent painting increasingly invokes de Chirico or Max Ernst in its distillation of imagery and emotional resonances of space. Without a degree of critical engagement this type of latter-day romanticism has a tendency to cause problems for women artists in anchoring them within highly restrictive identities. Despite its glorification, the sign of 'Woman' ultimately functioned as a catalyst for the emotional response of the male Surrealists, sublimated into an aesthetic programme which effectively contained and marginalised the position of women Surrealist practitioners.

This tendency towards a distillation and condensation of images represents a radical shift in Alice Maher's practice since her early work, and one which in turn needs to be located in a context of the relationship between gender and painting within Ireland. The formation of a feminist consciousness among many women artists in Ireland over the last two decades has also helped to problematise the practice of painting itself, and indeed by the mid-Eighties this had acquired particular gender-specific connotations in relation to the primacy of neo-Expressionism. One place where this was clearly articulated was within an essay written by Joan Fowler for the catalogue of the retrospective exhibitions assembled under the title 'A New Tradition: Irish Art of the Eighties' and held at the Douglas Hyde Gallery during 1990. As she convincingly argues, neo-Expressionism not only established a visible Irish art 'movement' within the public gaze, but it also helped to align Irish artists with international trends represented by German artists such as Anselm Kiefer.[2]

Throughout the twentieth century expressionist claims for the authenticity of the pictorial mark as a direct correspondence to the emotional or spiritual state of the artist have, however, been historically bound up with notions of masculinity; within the practice of American Abstract Expressionist painters such as Pollock or de Kooning, the privileged site of these representations became identified with gestural painting, the pictorial mark signifying the presence of the artist as a uniquely gifted individual. Perhaps unsurprisingly the rhetoric of expressionism has proved highly problematic for many women practitioners; the relative obscurity of Lee Krasner or Elaine de Kooning by comparison with their more famous partners demonstrates this clearly. However, the prioritising of neo-Expressionism within Irish art for much of the Eighties also had a clear effect on teaching in art colleges, in that it reasserted an already present tendency towards claims of authenticity attached to gestural practices and the production of large paintings as a vehicle for emotion or the exploration of formal relationships. For many women art students the gendered implications of expressionism thus became a key area for negotiation throughout their education.[3]

As a student during the mid-Eighties, Alice Maher's initial encounter with painting as part of college work proved to be frustrating and relatively unproductive for precisely these reasons. Painting for her became identified as a patriarchal discourse which served to marginalise the work of women, largely through the introduction of criteria of skill and proficiency which, despite their appearance of impartial judgements, were in practice bound up with issues of gender. Yet it is important to stress that the reaction to expressionism by many female practitioners in Ireland has not necessarily been in the form of an outright rejection, but of a negotiation. Although Maher's response during her early career was a tendency to reject key *physical* attributes of expressionism – such as gestural painting on a large scale – her drawings and collages maintained an engagement with expressionist pictorial *strategies* for the production of meaning, yet managed to subvert them at the same time. Within figurative modes of expressionism the insistence on a supposed authenticity of response tends to be predicated upon the representation of the female body as a catalyst for male heterosexual desire. The choice of these identifications is fairly predictable virgins, whores or vampires – and despite the claims to artistic radicalism its adoption serves only to reinforce the dominant representations of femininity which permeate Irish culture through the ideology of Catholicism. Despite the comic overtones of small collages such as 'Icon' (1987) with its reference to Piero della Francesca, Alice Maher's works on paper from the late Eighties are highly confrontational in their depiction of gender imagery, but operate as a means of doing violence to the stereotype and articulating an anger at its power. In their deconstruction of Catholic femininity they also could be seen as engaging with issues specific to the power of religious imagery in Irish culture; the small painting 'The Visit', for example, clearly evoked representations of the Annunciation.

The culmination of Maher's concern with these issues was within her 'Celebration Robes' (1988) which also represent a further shift in the artist's practice through the choice of materials used in the piece. The robes have as their basis a critique of images of the Virgin Mary, worked upon bedsheets bought at a secondhand market in Belfast. Sheets contain the detritus of people's lives, stained with the residues of experience; they are loved upon, cried upon, bled upon. Like the later installation 'Keep' (1992), which was made out of ropes of human hair they are materials which carry their own history, speaking of the body in profoundly anti–idealistic terms, in this case as an organism which both secretes and excretes. The canvas which traditionally forms the basis for big painting has been replaced by the soiled end products of domestic labour, as the drudgery of women's work in washing and maintaining the fittings of the home finally breaks down in the face of increasing resistance on the part of the material itself. What should be invisible becomes all too visible, witness to the impossibility of that work in attempting to service the ideal. On top of this Maher used her own bodyprint as a basis for further imagery. In this case the act of lying on a sheet, covered in paint, is perhaps more significant than it might appear; not only does it reconstruct this history of its staining, but it makes it conscious, literally fixing it within representation. Yet this work also proposes a radically gendered subversion, in terms of the role of the gestural mark on the pictorial surface as evidence of the corporeal presence of the artist. Here the sublimated trace becomes replaced by the sign of excess, the female body as inescapable, unregulated and uncontained.[4]

In 'Celebration Robes' or the subsequent installation 'Tryst' (1989), pictorial space teems with a cacophony of figures jostling for attention and coexisting in different hierarchies of scale and meaning. Consisting of four large tents suspended from the gallery ceiling, the painted walls of 'Tryst' surround the spectator, frustrating and fragmenting any attempts to view the surface from one single point and literally destabilising any attempts to construct a narrative. The title, imagery and processes of picture-making all invoke a self-conscious medievalism; in its retrospective usage by a late twentieth century artist this has the effect of subverting the narrative traditions set up by perspectival space of the Renaissance and predicated upon a submission to the surveying unitary gaze. A multiplicity of perspectives is opened up, some contradictory, others seemingly inconsequential, in effect offering a challenge to linear rationality also found in deconstructive tendencies of the early collage work. Yet medievalism also offers further insights into Maher's practice, and a discussion of marginality in medieval art by Michael Camille has proposed readings of some relevance here. For the medieval viewer the margins had a crucial significance as denoting the limits of a world which was both geographically circumscribed and largely rural; the edge of society was seen as a place which was both dangerous in that it was the place of exile for outlaws and the dispossessed, and powerful in that it represented a domain of transformation, the boundary between the worlds of visible and invisible populated by supernatural beings. Within a world whose morality was also determined by religion, sex was '*a further ineradicable trace of fleshly, fallen human nature*' also confined to the margins; consequently the edges of medieval manuscripts became the site of a fallen existence, signified by male and female bodies who in turn overflow their boundaries – copulating, excreting, gesturing.[5] The centrality of religion within medieval systems of representation can inform further readings for works such as Maher's 'Tryst'. Here the playfulness of humans and animals spills into the entirety of available space; the direct attack on religious definitions of femininity in her previous work now becomes more oblique, displaced onto an increasing celebration of the values of the liminal. An important space in the work has been opened up, and one with significant consequences for her future practice.

It is within the rural world and the spaces it contains that a key moment of transformation occurs in Alice Maher's work. In some of the nine drawings which made up 'The Thicket' (1990) a stillness begins to emerge in place of the barely contained chaos of the earlier work. It manifests itself through the representation of space. Although it still does not possess properties of containment, the space surrounding figures is not only increasingly acknowledged here; it begins to take on more of an active, defining role, engendering an increased focus on the actions of these girls. Some features of the previous depiction of figures will remain important, such as a distorted perspective or a sense of vertigo, but there is a sense in which the gaze is becoming increasingly introspective and subjective. The young girls playing in an undefined environment also inhabit the spaces of the artist's memory. Like the recollections of a dream, the representation is only fragmentary, providing a seemingly illogical focus on the unexplained acts whereby these girls acquire their knowledge of the world. Although suggestive of a rural background through the inclusion of strange fruits and ambivalent objects this is a space where memory and dream begin to fuse together. Soon they will be joined once more by the evocation of mythology, rising to the surface of the reservoir of imagery.

The layering and working of the surface of the drawings of 'The Thicket' also, paradoxically, place an emphasis on the act of scraping away so that previous imagery remains half glimpsed. Yet in retrospect it becomes clear that, for Alice Maher, this is a process of scratching into a space other than the fertile territory of pre-adolescence, into maturity, into '*the vastness of the space that lies within a woman's head*' – the site of representation. This should not be read, however, as implying a regression into the unconscious. Only incoherence would result from this, and although the Surrealists may have celebrated the babblings of the 'child-woman' such a state is of little value to the woman artist, actively involved in the production of culture.[6] This is clearly a different domain and one which actively works upon the terms of the unconscious – its dream-logic and production of disturbingly resonant imagery. The space of the unconscious is also that of mythical narrative, seemingly outside of history; yet it is also a place where things change constantly. According to the analysis proposed by Freud in 'The Interpretation of Dreams' the unconscious is not just a static pool of repressed knowledge, but dynamic, recreating its language through shifting currents of desire.[7] These come to the surface of waking consciousness in new forms and combinations through the memories of a dream, or erupt into speech through jokes and slips of the tongue. It is possible, therefore, that mythologies can shift and change their form in the moment of their enunciation. In one instance of Alice Maher's recent work this results in a radical reworking, with important consequences for a reading of the relationship of women to the production of culture.

What if Venus did not rise from the waves alone, the sole form of desire incarnate, but had been replaced by a multiplicity of figures? The key signifier of an idealised secular femininity would not have existed in painting from the Renaissance onwards, the perfection of her appearance masking the violence of her origins in one version of the myth: as the Greek goddess Aphrodite she is born from the foam which gushes from her father's genitals, torn off and cast into the water. Such subject matter would not have been out of place in Alice Maher's work of the mid-Eighties, but within this more recent work one aim is to subvert and reconstruct mythologies at their source. In 'Swimmers' an entire squadron of female heads waits in the waters, some looking out at the viewer, others perhaps not fully formed yet. Only the tops of these heads are visible, each with its own hair parting and wide eyes, emerging out of the indefinite space and time which characterises the mythological narrative. And yet like the sleeping heads in another painting in this series, these are also the inhabitants of the zone between worlds. Swimmers, moreover, have their own currency in post-Renaissance representation as the bathers within an Arcadian setting. These, however, are not the bodies deployed as spectacle for the viewer in the work of Cézanne, whose closeness to nature (albeit one that is highly stylised) removes them further from the domain of culture.[8] All we see of these swimmers is the top of their heads, cut off just below the eyes; the consequent emphasis on cerebrality is a far from usual characteristic of representations of female bathers. Above all, these are *thinking* swimmers, the mythical ancestors of the girls of 'The Thicket', absorbed in their tasks of measuring and weighing the world.

Apart from its radical significance here of the cerebrality of the feminine, the use of the head also has a precedent in different representational systems, which in turn provides further resonances for its meaning. On one level there is the Celtic belief in the power of the decapitated head, gifted with speech and prophecy and evidence of Maher's continual interest in Irish folklore and early history; yet the resting heads also evoke a significance as a fragment of a past civilisation. In some ways this is similar to the investigations of neo-classicism, where the work of Barry or Fuseli also frequently included parts of ancient unidentified statuary to dwarf the human figure at the same time as it was evidence of an increasing fascination with the classical past. The mid-eighteenth-century archaeological investigations of the civilisations of Rome and Greece were closely linked to the empiricism of the Enlightenment, and the desire to identify and record aspects of the historical past within a schema which could also inform the concerns of the present; and indeed certain aspects of Alice Maher's work could also be read as demonstrating a conscious concern with notions of empiricism. But despite the facility of such readings in the schematic categorisation of women's hairstyles in 'Folt' (1993) for Maher this process of documentation was one bound up with processes of memory and the recording of things seen.

The role of hair in the construction of female appearance also informs the making of the installation 'Keep'. Like the tents of 'Tryst' this also creates a space for the viewer to walk into, surrounded in this case by a material which

occupies a peculiar status between nature and culture; hair is an organic material, yet its significance is always perceived in cultural terms. 'Keep' shares this
property of dual marginality with other objects made by Alice Maher. Their
ambivalence is evidence of a constant oscillation of meaning between the two
domains of nature and culture, provoking continually contradictory readings.
The objects which accompany the recent large paintings are made of flax, a
natural 'soft' material which is used to construct forms evocative of Mini-
malist sculpture. Here the objects set up a relationship with the paintings in
which each actively works to open up, rather than close down, meanings for
the other; the elements of the 'Bee Dress' however have more disturbing
implications. The little girl's dress [fig. 12] could be read as a signifier of childhood femininity, echoing Maher's earlier concerns with the acquisition of
female subjectivity in works such as 'The Thicket'. But covered in dead bees
it becomes an object of authority far beyond that normally attributed to
children; the dress has become transformed into a mythical armour, both pro-
tective and powerful. Yet there is also a similarity to readings possible for
'Keep', with its evocations of the many tongues of the Medusa's hair. Like the
snakes, the bees speak from many places; a multiplicity of voices replaces the
child's faltering negotiation of language.

This degree of ambivalence obviously suggests the use of objects in the
work of the Surrealists, particularly Meret Oppenheim whose most famous
artefact 'Le Déjeuner en Fourrure' (1936) consisted of a cup, saucer and
spoon bought from a Parisian chain store and covered with Chinese gazelle
skin. A more specific area of reference might also be the photograph of a
bicycle seat covered with bees, found by Oppenheim in a Swiss magazine in
1952 and sent by her to André Breton, who subsequently republished it as
evidence of the Surrealist 'found object'. In some ways Oppenheim's practice can thus be seen as establishing a precedent for this work by Alice Maher,
in that its materials also suggest a location between nature and culture. However for male Surrealists the found (or fabricated) object functioned as a
highly fetishistic signifier of eroticism, situated within a circuit of male heterosexual desire; unsurprisingly this served also to marginalise the position of
women, who tended to be represented in much the same terms. For those
who continued to make Surrealist objects – such as Oppenheim this was
something which required negotiation; many of her subsequent pieces utilise
the signifiers of clothing to demonstrate an engagement with femininity as
actively constructed rather than as fetishised object of the male gaze.

The articulation of such precedents for Alice Maher's work is significant
in that it shifts it into yet a further context – a history of radical women
artists. And although its boundaries are continually shifting, this is finally a
location which can be given a definite name.

## NOTES

1    For a discussion of Barber's essay see Caoimhín Mac Giolla Léith, 'Strategic Representations: Notes on Irish Art Since the 1980s', in *When Time Began to Rant and Rage: Figurative Painting from Twentieth-Century Ireland*, ed. James Christian Steward, London, Merrell Holberton, 1998, pp. 117–18.

2    Joan Fowler, 'Speaking of Gender . . . Expressionism, Feminism and Sexuality', in *A New Tradition: Irish Art of the Eighties*, The Douglas Hyde Gallery, Dublin, 1990, p. 53. [Orig. note. An extract from Fowler's companion essay, 'Art and Politics in the '80s', appears as entry 52.]

3    This is somewhat different from the situation in Britain during the same period. A valuable account of the feminist rediscovery of painting is provided in Hosa Lee, 'Resisting Amnesia: Feminism, Painting and Postmodernism', *Feminist Review* 26, 1987, pp. 5–27. [Orig. note.]

4    See also Lynda Nead, *The Female Nude: Art, Obscenity and Sexuality*, London, Routledge, 1992, pp. 72–4, for a discussion of the use of bodyprints by Chila Kumari Burman. [Orig. note.]

5    Michael Camille, *Image on the Edge: The Margins of Medieval Art,* London, Reaktion Books, 1992, pp. 39–40. [Orig. note.]

6    See also Susan Rubin Suleiman's discussion of André Breton's Nadia in *Subversive Intent: Gender, Politics and the Avant Garde,* Cambridge, Harvard, 1990, pp. 107–10.

7    Sigmund Freud, *The Interpretation of Dreams* (1900), Harmondsworth, Penguin, 1980, Chapter 6, 'The Dreamwork'. [Orig. note.]

8    Tamar Garb, *Cézanne*, Open University television programme, *Modern Art: Practices and Debates*, 1993. [Orig. note.]

# SECTION II

## MAKING AND VIEWING

## INTRODUCTION

This section of the *Reader* deals with matter-of-fact issues: the availability of art, its patronage, the training of artists as well as the production and display of art from the eighteenth century to the present day.

## PATRONAGE AND EDUCATION

This subsection is made up of seventeen entries, the dominant issue being the provision and want of patronage. The establishment of the Dublin Society in 1731 and the subsequent creation of a series of schools for the training of artists and designers has been well charted by art historians. And yet, the still relatively unexplored writings of Samuel Madden (entry 24; fig. 13) and Thomas Campbell (entry 27) provide rich material for a fuller understanding of the biases and prejudices that accompanied Enlightenment. In calling for more public art in Ireland in 1739, Madden, for example, could not refrain from criticizing the excess expenditure of 'our good Catholicks' on indulgences which could be more appropriately spent on 'erecting Statues to all great and good Men'. Attention is also given in this section to private patronage and the compiler of the *Reader* will hopefully be forgiven for retelling the well-known story of Lord Charlemont's war of words with the great Venetian engraver Piranesi (entry 25). Piranesi's 1757 erasure of Charlemont's name and family crest from the dedication plate to *Le Antichità Romane* is not just a celebrated case of artistic defiance but also a comment on Ireland's precarious position in European visual culture during the *ancien régime*. A glance at the accompanying illustrations (figs. 14–15) makes this all too clear. The first shows Charlemont's name and declares his nationality, the second returns Hibernia to obscurity.

Combatting artistic isolationism is a constant in many of the entries included here. In 1802, Hugh Douglas Hamilton (entry 29) tells his friend the Italian sculptor Antonio Canova of Dublin's 'few men of talent' while half a century later the painter-poet Dante Gabriel Rossetti cannot take seriously a Belfast businessman with a taste for Pre-Raphaelite art (entry 33).

If the Charlemont–Piranesi débâcle is well known so too is the saga of the Lane pictures. Yet these controversies in Ireland's cultural history need periodic retelling. Hugh Lane features in a number of entries (nos. 36–38 and 45) largely because his attempt to introduce modern French painting to Ireland in the early years of the twentieth century raises important questions about the kind of modern nation that was then evolving. The specific Lane entries (nos. 38 and 45) highlight his endeavours but other entries, including

W.B.Yeats's devastating criticism of Irish philanthropists, inform us of the difficulties that Lane had to contend with (entries 36 and 37). As far back as the
mid-nineteenth century, R.R. Madden was complaining about a lack of
interest in Irish visual material (entry 34). Robert Elliott repeats the case in
1906 (entry 35), as does Tom Bodkin in 1932 (entry 39). More worryingly,
as recently as 1979 the Arts Council's report (entry 40) on *The Place of the Arts
in Irish Education* shows the lamentable degree of progress sixty years after
Independence.

DISPLAY

The focus here is on reactions to public exhibitions of art. The eighteenth
century hardly features except for some remarks by William Drennan written from Dublin in some private letters to his sister, Martha McTier, in Belfast
(entry 41). The other seven entries take us through the nineteenth and twentieth centuries. As Elizabeth Holt noted in her pioneering anthology of exhibition criticism and comment, 'The reviewers of the exhibitions kept a wide
public abreast of events and the stylistic tendencies in the art world. They
influenced the public's judgement, shaped its taste and could excite its curiosity.'[1] Ireland did not enjoy the rich exhibition culture of nineteenth and
twentieth century London or Paris, but as we move from the private views
of Drennan and his sister through published reviews in *The Nation* (entry 44)
to the satirical comments of Brian O'Nolan (Myles na gCopaleen) in *The
Irish Times* (entry 47), we can clearly establish, as did Holt, 'a connection
between art and the general intellectual interest of the epoch'.

NOTES

1    Elizabeth Gilmore Holt, *The Triumph of Art for the Public, 1785–1848: The Emerging
     Role of Exhibitions and Critics*, Princeton University Press, 1979, xxvii.

# Patronage and Education

## — 24 —

## Samuel Madden, *Reflections and Resolutions*, 1738

Founded in 1731, the Dublin Society, like many other comparable eight-eenth-century European institutions, was set up to improve commerce, agri-culture and the arts. A decade later an academy of arts was in place and one of the founding members, the Rev. Dr Samuel Madden (1686–1765), a County Fermanagh rector (fig. 13), has been described as 'the principal force behind the establishment of the Dublin Society's support for the drawing schools'.[1] The drawing schools were to become one of the great training grounds for artists in this island for the next hundred years (see fig. 18). Indi-vidually, Madden's main contribution was to originate the awarding of prizes in the art of drawing which gave the fledgling academy a professional status. The first awards were made in 1740, two years after he advocated such a scheme in his essay *Reflections and Resolutions*; he returned to the theme a year later in *A Letter to the Dublin-Society*. Excerpts from both pieces are included here. In 1746 the prize system was extended to include boys and girls under fifteen years of age. Future prize winners included George Barret, Hugh Douglas Hamilton and Thomas Roberts. In his will, Madden left twenty old master paintings to Trinity College Dublin.[2] For a contemporary account of the distribution of prizes see John O'Keeffe's memoirs (entry 30).

Sources: *Reflections and Resolutions proper for the Gentlemen of Ireland, as to their Conduct for the Service of their Country* . . . , Dublin, 1738, pp. 231–3, and *A Letter to the Dublin-Society, on Improving their Fund; and the Manufactures, Tillage, etc. in Ire-land*, Dublin, 1739, pp. 49–50

## A) *REFLECTIONS AND RESOLUTIONS*, 1738

Another Particular I shall mention as useful to make our People more Industrious is, by encouraging by proper Praemiums those politer Arts, which are in a Manner Strangers to our Country, I mean Sculpture, Painting, and Architecture. There are Nations in *Europe*, a great Part of whose Wealth consists in the vast Treasures left them by the illustrious Professors of these Arts in their Ways; and though we can hardly hope to rival them, we should, at least, aim so far to employ and enrich our People by them, as may both spur on their

13    Richard Purcell after Robert Hunter, *Portrait of Samuel Madden, c.* 1755

Industry, improve our Taste, and adorn our Country. Even Architecture alone, where Nations cultivate it, gives Business to a surprising Number of Trades; and it is impossible so many of our Nobility and Gentry cou'd be so meanly lodged as they are, if we had not so few Architects in Ireland, who are capable of directing or assisting them in their Buildings. 'Tis for want of good Houses of our own at Home, that we are apt to take up with Lodgings abroad with Foreigners, where we spend every Year what would build up lasting and beautiful Seats for our Families, and make our Lives delightful to ourselves, and useful to all around us. It is a plain Proof that a Nation flourishes, and its industry increases (and, indeed, a great Cause of it too) when its Buildings inlarge and improve, and as we see among the *Jews*, in their most thriving State, under *Solomon*, not only the great Temple of *Jerusalem*, but several Palaces for the King, and even Cities for the People were finish'd with immense Expence and Labour. So we find the Riches and Industry of the Nation, and all the Handicraft Arts, (and even Sculpture) flourish'd there, and, indeed ever will flourish in all Kingdoms thereby. And the same may be said of Painting and Sculpture, they wou'd create infinite Business for our Artists, and Amusement and Delight for our Gentry, if only they were cultivated and improv'd by due Encouragment among us; and, as they have still been consider'd by all the civiliz'd Nations as the greatest Elegancies and Ornaments of every Country, so that utter Neglect of them, which prevails in *Ireland*, will ever be a Proof against us of Barbarism and Gothick Ignorance, 'till we shake it off. [...]

Though our Country and Climate seems more cut out for Labour and Toil, and the Industry of the Manufacturer and Husbandmen, than the Pleasure and Delight of the softer Arts of the warmer and more delicate Regions on the Continent, yet certain it is, when the Necessities and Conveniencies of Nature are sufficiently provided for, the Arts of Delight and Amusement will constantly come in, and, if we don't bring them to us, we will be apt to go abroad to them. Since we must have Luxury, we shou'd encourage that kind of it which has the most of Pleasure, and nothing of Vice in it; which will give Bread and Industry to our Natives, and may be turn'd also to other useful Purposes; for, though possibly Painting and Sculpture may have hurt the Religion of the Continent, I am sure it might contribute, if well directed, to raise and enlarge the Virtue of our People here, since painted Histories of great Actions, and the Statues of great Men cannot possibly be beheld without warming the heart and enflaming the Mind to admire, emulate, and revere them.

At as low an Ebb as these Arts are in Ireland, I am confident, if reasonable Salaries were appointed by the Publick to two or three foreign Architects; or, if the Linen or Tillage Boards, or the Dublin-Society, had funds assign'd them to give Praemiums annually to the three best Pictures, and the three best Statues made here, or the Architects of the three best Houses built annually in this Kingdom, we should in Time see surprizing Improvements in them all among us.

## B) *A LETTER TO THE DUBLIN-SOCIETY*, 1739

Will you pardon me, Gentlemen, if I go yet further, and wish you would not only allow Praemiums to the best Inventors, but even assign annual ones to the best Picture, and the best Statue that shall be made in *Ireland*, and produ'd before you every year. If our People would consider how small a Fund would answer this expence, and of what credit and service it would be to our Country, to shew some marks of Genius this way, I hope the proposing such a design, will neither seem absurd or impracticable to any one. I am sure it would soon save us very large Sums, which the importing such things from abroad costs us, and would not only adorn our Houses and Gardens, and create a relish and emulation for those lovely Labours, in our Gentry and Artists here, but we might in time export them to others, and gain equal honour and profit, by encouraging them in Ireland. As therefore in both those views, they will highly deserve to have some favour shewn them, I hope those who are less acquainted with their usefulness and excellence will not continue to despise and neglect them, as to our reproach, we have been too long us'd to do. It is certain, they the fittest Arts for a poor Nation to encourage, as they only want Cloth and a Stone, and can set up with a Pencil and a Chizel, like a Surgeon with his Knife, without any other Expence. Painting has ever had the Eyes and the Hearts of all Mankind on its side, and has met with the fewest Enemies, and the most Admirers, even in the most barbarous Ages and Countries; and tho' Sculpture has not all that glare of Beauty which the other is set off with, yet as it has still flourish'd where-ever Arts and Learning thrive, we ought by all means to encourage it here. In one great national View, we should even prefer it to Painting, as that main Branch of it which is employ'd in Statuary, is actually one of the greatest sources of Virtue among Men, that can arise from proper incentives and spurs to Glory, by publick marks of due Praise and Honour paid to their Memories. I am sure as to *Ireland*, I may venture to say, had half the Money given by our good Catholicks to deliver their poor *Friends* from *Purgatory*, been laid out in erecting Statues to all great and good Men among them after their decease, this island had long since been as remarkable for producing Persons of the highest Characters, and the most distinguish'd Learning and Merit, as it is now for being a Nursery of lazy Bigots and Beggars, Fools and Fryars.

## NOTES

1    John Turpin, *A School of Art in Dublin since the Eighteenth Century: A History of the National College of Art and Design,* Dublin, Gill & Macmillan, 1995, p. 10.

2    A. Crookshank and D. Webb, *Paintings and Sculptures in Trinity College Dublin,* Trinity College Dublin Press, 1990, pp. 158–64.

# — 25 —

# John Parker, *Correspondence of the Earl of Charlemont,* 1755–8

In 1752, when only twenty-three years old, the Irish aristocrat James Caulfeild (1728–99), 4th Viscount (1763, the 1st Earl of) Charlemont, set up an academy in Rome for artists from Britain and Ireland, under the direction of John Parker (fl. 1740, d. 1765), an English history painter.[1] An incessant art buyer, Charlemont was Ireland's most important Grand Tourist of the eighteenth century (see also entry 26), his purchases ranging, as is clear from the first of the two letters printed here, from antique reliefs to a portrait of himself by the contemporary artist Pompeo Batoni.[2] Resident in Rome throughout the 1750s, Parker acted as Charlemont's agent, painting history pictures for his patron as well as purchasing old master paintings and antique marbles busts. Most importantly, Parker introduced Charlemont to the Venetian architect and engraver Giovanni Battista Piranesi (1720–78), thus initiating one of the most memorable acts of artistic patronage by an Irish Grand Tourist in the eighteenth century. Originally, Charlemont promised to sponsor Piranesi's single volume of etching, *Le Antichità Romane,* but in time, this grew into a spectacular series of four volumes of views of ancient Rome.[3] The set appeared in January 1756, dedicated to Charlemont, his name and coat of arms inscribed on an antique marble slab (fig. 14). The wording of the frontispiece to volume I, composed by either the Irish peer or his tutor, Edward Murphy (1707–77), proudly declares Charlemont's origins: 'Regni Hiberniae Patricio'; the oval family crest sits to the left, illusionistically embedded in the architectural framework amidst a wealth of antiquity.[4] As such, despite the ensuing saga of graphic defacement that the dedications were to undergo,

14    G.M. Piranesi, *Le Antichità Romane*, 1756, first frontispiece with
dedication to Charlemont

15    G.M. Piranesi, *Le Antichità Romane*, 1756, defaced frontispiece, third state,
dedicated to people of Rome

one must read this frontispiece as a clear case of the periphery penetrating the metropolitan centre. Unfortunately, the story did not end there. Piranesi's Irish patron failed to pay and did not answer the engraver's letters. In February 1758, as Parker describes in the second letter included here, written to Charlemont's tutor, Piranesi retaliated by producing a series of 'satirical' vignettes against both his erstwhile patron and the latter's three agents (Parker, Murphy and a Scottish priest, Abbé Peter Grant, 1708–84).[5] These vignettes and Piranesi's letters of justification appeared as the famous pamphlet *Lettere di Giustificazione scritte a Milord Charlemont e a' di lui agenti di Roma dal Signor Piranesi* . . . (Rome, 1757). But the story goes on. Piranesi furthered his attack on his 'unworthy' patron, as a recent scholar has labelled Charlemont, by suppressing the original frontispieces (fig. 14) to *Le Antichità Romane*, replacing them with the original dedications illusionistically chiselled away. The new frontispiece to volume 1 was reinscribed to the people of Rome (fig. 15) while, adding insult to injury, Piranesi represented Charlemont's coat of arms in a brutally smashed state.[6] In Rome, the fall-out of all of this was the forming of factions on each side. A group of Irish friars supported Charlemont, and eventually Monsignor Caprara, the Roman govenor of the day, got Piranesi to write a reluctant recantation which was sent to Charlemont.[7] The final outcome in favour of Charlemont indicates the reactionary Papal state's wish to maintain aristocratic power. By contrast, Piranesi scholars, rather naïvely, see the *Lettere* as transcending the 'tedious events of the affair' and celebrating 'the nobility of an artistic reputation, independent of a patron's whims, and the imperishable nature of art'.[8]

Source: *Historical Manuscripts Commission, 12th Report, Appendix, Part X: The MSS and Correspondence of James, 1st Earl of Charlemont*, vol. 1, London, 1891, letters no. 39 and 52, pp. 218–19, 245–8

## A) ROME, 26 JULY 1755 (PARKER TO CHARLEMONT)

By a letter from Mr Murphy, dated July 11th 1755, I have account of your lordship having been frightened about the case of medals, but that they were found, I hope in good condition, as I had taken particular care in packing them up.[9] With them is the French box which your lordship left and writ for from Florence. He sent me also list of things wanting, viz., all bronzetti, Gladiator, two Centaurs, Silenus, Antinöus, basso-relief Venus by Guglielmo della Porta. These I did not send, some not being in order, as the Venus that Virepoyl[10] was to bed in a frame (if your lordship remembers) and is not yet done, no more than the basso relief Antinöus (to bed also) nor the busts of Brutus, Pompey, and Cæsar in bronze, that he was to do, the busts too in red marble;

I have often recomended them to him, nor can I give them to others, he having your lordship's order to doe them; if yet not done [it is] no fault of mine. I suppose he will doe them when the Gladiator is finished, which, he says, is very forward. I have not seen it, as I am still unfortunately kept in bed with my wounds. The pictures I have bought for your lordship I had intended to have sent with Patche's and Pompeo's (to have had one expence only in the licence for them and bronzes), when done.[11] The first never let me know that he had finished, nor should I have known they were sent, but by the account of Belloni's of the mony paid etc., nor do I know his reason for sending them away unknown to me. Pompeo has not finished nor can I get the portraits out of his hands; he is paid the half of the great one. Mr Murphy desires a particular account of all those things sent as yet or to send. The first is impossible for me to do, as I had no inventory than of the books, the which I was obliged to leave for the license to send them away. I don't doubt but your lordship will find them all. They were packt up by me and Virepoyl in two large cases, one full of books only, the other, besides books, contained in a case at bottom your marble mosaick table the case of medals and the walnut-tree case with drawers for the medals. In other case the Farnese globe and under it the basso relief, Minerva teaching the use of olives, bedded in a frame, and other géssi of fasces, etc. belonging to Mr Murphy; other case, all the books of loose prints, views; and both your lordship's and Mr Murphy's other cases in one large one, the Etruscan vases, boxes of lava, etc. etc.; other cases containing Mr Murphy's clay heads and two bronze heads, Cæsar and Brutus. All your lordship's marble busts – viz., Swift, Homer, Brutus the elder and younger, antique faun, modern faun; girl's head from Alessandria, and Agrippina, each separate cases. These were all I sent and I have Peter Cassidy's letter of their safe arrival, not only at Livorno but at Dublin, for my satisfaction. Who or what ship or ships carried them, or to whom directed there, he never informed me, having, as he writ me word, Mr Murphy's orders, how to dispose of them, when he was there. [. . .]

## B) ROME, 5 APRIL 1758 (PARKER TO REV. EDWARD MURPHY)

Mr Grant and I having agreed to divide the affair between us, in relation to Piranesi's new insults, in order not to tire my lord or you by a long letter, the following is my part: Mr Grant writ in his last letter to his lordship, the order Piranesi had to not print or publish any more the scandalous letters sent to my lord, under great penalties. We thought the affair finished; but as Mr Grant nor monsignor Cenci[12] had not taken care of my character, by having my name also inserted in that order, I was informed that he continued selling the first two letters, annexed to the four volumes, as a justification of his having erased my lord's name out of the dedication [. . .]. I went to the governor's lieutenant criminel, to inform him of the proceeding; and as I had also notice, privately, he had reprinted the above two letters, with a third very scandalous against Messrs Grant and Murphy, and had engraved some and was engraving other satirical prints, as head and tail-pieces to the said letters, in order to publish them (in revenge of my lord's not satisfying his exorbitant demands, and his being obliged to refund the money received).[13] I desired the lieutenant to send and search his house for the copies and plates, the which, he told me, could not be done, unless I had a witness who would swear to have seen them. This was not to be done, as the gentleman who had seen them refused to appear as a spy on Piranesi; and in a few days after he published them. Now to the description of our new honours. The first print is an emblem of eternity, the serpent biting his tail, and a pen, porte–crayon, brush and compass forming a square, in the middle of which, he had writ the name of the person to whom he sent it. The second plate: ruins, and on an obelisk: 'Lettere di giustificazione scritte à milord Charlemont e à di lui agenti di Roma dal signor Piranesi, socio della real società degli Antiquari di Londra intorno la dedica della sua opera delle Antichità Rom: fatta allo stesso signore ed ultimamente soppressa. In Roma, 1757.'[14] [. . .]

[T]he rest are copper-plates, viz., the four dedication-plates to my lord; then, two other of the inscriptions you sent him; then another, with my lord's arms and name erased; this as he published the second time. The last print is his dedication to the public. In this he has broke my lord's arms to pieces, nothing remaining but the coronet. The inscriptions, in lieu of milord's, thus: 'Vrbis Aeternae vestigia e ruderibus temporumque iniuriis vindicata, aheneis tabulis incisa. J. B. Piranesius Venet. Romae Degens aevo suo Posteris et Vtilitati Publicae C.V.D.' [fig. 15]. This in the first volume. On the second inscription nothing; only rased my lord's name and title. [. . .] I have a copy; should you or my lord have the curiosity to see it, I can divide it in three letters. This book he sent, gratis, to all the cardinals, monsignori and other persons of quality, natives and foreigners. [. . .] He also sent copies to all the English painters, Italian, French and Germans, and where abroad God knows. [. . .] By the memorial the Irish friars gave in to cardinal Corsini,[15] they found the cardinal almost ignorant of the affront done my lord, [. . .] they at last made him see the injury he did my lord and me in protecting Piranesi, who had informed him falsely, and he gave them this precise answer: 'Send the printed letter to my lord, and let his lordship know that if he is not satisfied with it, that he has nothing to do but let me know, and that, on my word and honour, I will punish Piranesi as my lord shall think proper.' [. . .] I beg, sir, you would represent to my lord how sorry I am to have been the introductor of this fellow to his lordship, in the which I had no other intention than the glory of my lord's name. [. . .] I beg you would present my humble respects to his lordship, and remind his lordship that all his pictures, bronzes, etc., with the Miltons, have lain many months in Peter Cassidy's hands, and that I hope in a few weeks to forward him the Mercury of the Villa Medici, the which will be much better than the original, the which, in taking down from the fountain in the portico, to put it up in the gallery, fell down and split the body from the bottom to the top and one leg and arm broke, and has been so badly mended as to leave a rising of about a finger thick.[16] This in my lord's I had new modelled and moulded by signore Bracci, one of our best sculptors here, so that it is quite superior to the original. [. . .] I hope you have received your drawing and print of the Aldobrandini marriage from my father, and the 'Guerre civili degli case di York e Lancaster'[17] for my lord, as I supposed they arrived in the last fleet from Leghorn. My father will also, on the arrival of Sir William Stanhope's cases, give you the four vols. of Piranesi's work, with the dedication prints, the which I procured with the greatest difficulty, as he had destroyed what he had worked off. When I forward the bronze Mercury, I will send you the account of what I have as yet received and laid out on my lord's account, and draw as usual.

## Notes

1    For Charlemont see Maurice Craig, *The Volunteer Earl, Being the Life and Times of James Caulfeild, First Earl of Charlemont*, London, The Cresset Press, 1948, and Cynthia O'Connor, *The Pleasing Hours: James Caulfeild, First Earl of Charlemont, 1728–99: Traveller, Connoisseur and Patron of the Arts in Ireland*, Wilton, Cork, The Collins Press, 1999. For Parker, see John Ingamells, *A Dictionary of British and Irish Travellers in Italy, 1701–1800*, New Haven and London, Yale University Press, 1997, pp. 738–9.

2    Portrait in the Yale Center for British Art, see *Grand Tour: The Lure of Italy in the Eighteenth Century*, eds. A. Wilton and I. Bignamini, Tate Gallery, London, 1996, p. 61. Charlemont is shown with the Colosseum in the background. For Charlemont's collecton, see O'Connor, *The Pleasing Hours*, pp. 152–6.

3    For the Charlemont–Piranesi saga, see Jonathan Scott, *Piranesi*, London, Academy Editions, 1975, pp. 108–14, and O'Connor, *The Pleasing Hours*, pp. 157–72.

4    The stone slab reads: *Nobilisssimo Viro Utilitati Publicae Nato Iacobo Caulfield Vicecomiti De Charlemont Regni Hiberniae Patricio Quod Romae Dum Degeret Ingeniis Favebat Artes Promovebat Ioannes Baptista Piranesius Architectus Venetus . . .* (To that most noble gentleman, born to public service, James Caulfield, Lord Charlemont, nobleman of the Kingdom of Ireland, who, when in Rome, gave encouragement to the ingenious and promoted the arts, John Baptist Piranesi, Venetian architect . . . ), frontispiece to vol. I, G.B. Piranesi, *Le Antichità Romanae*, 1756.

5    For Grant and Murphy, see Ingamells, pp. 420–2 and 678–8.

6    See John Wilton-Ely, *Piranesi*, London, Arts Council of Great Britain, 1978, pp. 49, 58–9.

7    Dated 15 March 1758, see Craig, pp. 94–5, and *Historical Manuscripts Commission, 12th Report, Appendix, Part X: The MSS and Correspondence of James, 1st Earl of Charlemont*, vol. 1, London, 1891, pp. 244–5.

8    Wilton-Ely, p. 57.

9    See Ingamells, p. 198, for these purchases. Charlemont's collection was still intact in 1825, see G.N. Wright, *An Historical Guide to the City of Dublin*, 2nd ed., 1825, pp. 240–2.

10   Simon Vierpyl (*c.* 1725–1810), a London-born sculptor, who worked for Charlemont in Rome making copies from the antique and later came to Dublin to build Charlemont's Casino at Marino.

11   Two painters, Thomas Patch (1725–82), an Englishman who specialized in carica-tures, and Pompeo Batoni (1708–87), the Italian portraitist who, as this letter goes on to say, was then completing a portrait of Charlemont, see note 2 above.

12   An intermediary between the Charlemont camp of Grant, Parker and Murphy and the Roman authorities.

13   Illustrated in Scott, *Piranesi*

14   Wilton-Ely, nos. 139 and 140. Parker goes on to describe in detail the satirical vignettes that Piranesi had included in his published *Lettere di Giustificazione.*

15   Corsini was of the Piranesi party, see Scott, p. 114.

16   Parker is referring to two paintings of subjects from Milton that he had done for Charlemont in 1756 and a cast of the *Mercury* by Giambologna (1529–1608), see Ingamells, p. 739.

17   G.F. Biondi, *Storia delle guerre civili d'Inghilterra*, 3 vols., Venice, 1637–47.

# — 26 —

# The Earl of Charlemont, Letters to Hogarth, 1759–60

Today, the Earl of Charlemont (1728–99) is remembered as a politically active member of the 'patriot' party in the final decades of the eighteenth century. He is also celebrated for his important architectural patronage, most particu-larly the building of William Chambers's Casino outside Dublin. But as entry 25 shows, Charlemont was also a keen collector of art. He was by no means a wealthy Irish landlord however, his income having been estimated at less than £8,000 a year,[1] which given his occasional extravagances left him chron-ically short of cash. In 1759, a year after Piranesi's recantation (entry 25), Charlemont landed himself in yet more payment difficulties, this time with one of England's leading artists, William Hogarth (1697–1764). Initially,

Charlemont commissioned a portrait of himself, the subject of the first letter included here (fig. 16). It was left unfinished and shows 'only the face, a metaphor in effect, for [Hogarth's] relationship with Charlemont', as Ronald Paulson has remarked; 'the lips are too red, the smile too artificial, the face too idealized.'[2] That same year he also commissioned Hogarth to paint a subject picture, *Picquet, or Virtue in Danger (or, The Lady's Last Stake)*. In time, Charlemont purchased *The Gate of Calais* (Tate Gallery, London) and a large collection of Hogarth prints (Fitzwilliam Museum, Cambridge).[3] Charlemont's second letter to Hogarth uses flattery so as to delay the paying of a bill, in this case payment for *The Lady's Last Stake* (Albright–Knox Gallery, Buffalo, New York), which was eventually to hang in a bedroom in Charlemont House, Dublin.

Source: Charlemont's two letters to Hogarth are in the collection of the Department of Manuscripts, The British Library, Add MS 22394, f. 33 and f. 35.[4]

A) 19 AUGUST 1759

Dear Sir,

I have been so excessively busied with ten thousand troublesome Affairs, that I have not been able to wait upon you, according to my Promise, nor even to find time to sit for my Picture. As I am obliged to set out for Ireland tomorrow, we must defer that 'till my Return, which will be in the latter end of January, or in the Beginning of February at farthest. I am still your Debtor, more so indeed than I shall ever be able to pay, and did intend to have sent you before my Departure what trifling Recompence my Abilities permit me to make you. But the Truth is, having wrong calculated my expenses, I find myself unable for the present even to attempt paying you – However, if you be in any present need of Money, let me know it, and as soon as I get to Ireland, I will send you, not the Price of your Picture, for that is inestimable, but as much as I can afford to give for it. Sir, I am, with the most sincere Wishes for your Health and Happiness/Your most obedient Humble Servant/Charlemont.

B) 2 JANUARY 1760

Dear Sir

Enclosed I send you a Note upon Nesbitt for one hundred Pounds, and, considering the Name of the Author, and the surprising Merit of your Performance, I am really much ashamed to offer such a Trifle in recompence for the

16    William Hogarth, *Portrait of James Caulfeild, first Earl of Charlemont c.* 1759

Pains you have taken, and the Pleasure your Picture has afforded me. I beg you wou'd think that I by no means attempt to pay you according to your Merrit, but according to my own Abilities. Were I to pay your Deserts I fear I shou'd leave myself poor indeed. Imagine that you have made me a Present of the Picture, for litterally as such I take it, and that I have beg'd your Acceptance of the inclosed Trifle. As this is really the Case, with how much Reason do I subscribe myself/Your most obliged humble Servant/Charlemont.

NOTES

1    Maurice Craig, *The Volunteer Earl, Being the Life and Times of James Caulfeild, First Earl of Charlemont*, London, Cresset Press, 1948, p. 140.
2    Ronald Paulson, *Hogarth*, vol. 3, *Art and Politics, 1750–1764*, Cambridge, Lutterworth Press, 1993, p. 235, who goes on to say, 'Hogarth kept the portrait.'
3    For Charlemont's extensive correspondence concerning Hogarth, including letters from Jane Hogarth, the artist's widow, see *Historical Manuscripts Commission, 12th Report, Appendix, Part X: The MSS and Correspondence of James, 1st Earl of Charlemont*, vol. II, London, 1894, passim. See also Cynthia O'Connor, *The Pleasing Hours: James Caulfeild, First Earl of Charlemont, 1728–99: Traveller, Connoisseur and Patron of the Arts in Ireland*, Wilton, Cork, The Collins Press, 1999, pp. 195–205.
4    See also Paulson, vol. 3, pp. 233–4.

## — 27 —

# Thomas Campbell, *An Essay on Perfecting the Fine Arts*, 1767

Thomas Campbell (1733–95) was a clergyman who became chancellor of St Macartin's in Clogher, Co. Tyrone, in 1773 but is best known for his *Philosophical Survey of the South of Ireland*, published in 1778. He was a friend of Samuel Johnson and is frequently mentioned by Boswell.[1] In 1767 he was awarded the Dublin Society's first honorary silver medal for his pamphlet *An Essay on Perfecting the Fine Arts*. The *Essay* supported the teaching of drawing (see fig. 18) as being 'useful in the manufactures',[2] but, as shown in this extract, Campbell also called for the teaching of oil painting and the setting up of a permanent collection of works by the old masters.

Source: Thomas Campbell, *An Essay on Perfecting the Fine Arts in Great Britain and Ireland*, Dublin, William Sleater, 1767, pp. 35–40

If, then, reading the best books make these countries abound with judges of literary productions; and if of such a number of students, some arrive to be eminent *authors*, it may from parity of reason be inferred, that out of any given number of students in Design a proportionable number of masters would arise. But the fact is, we have not models sufficient to form the natural taste, nor students enough to be candidates for excellence.

Hence our Criticks and Poets are many and good; our Connoisseurs and Artists few and trifling. And this must necessarily be the case as long as things continue in their present state. Now we have no publick Statues, no publick galleries of Pictures, no academies for either Painting or Sculpture, nor will the great allow their pieces to be copied.

The case is very different wherever the arts have flourished abroad. You can never go into the *Vatican* or *Medicean* palace, the *Farnese* or *Luxemburg* gallery, but you will see a scaffold raised and an artist at work. One of the best collections in *Ireland* is entirely made up of copies, which the owner got painted during his stay at *Rome*. [. . .]

We have nothing like this. It should therefore be rather looked upon as a miracle than expected, that these islands should either breed masters, or have a taste. [. . .] Void of all true discernment, we prefer the daubings of Portraiture to Paintings in the highest style.

Accordingly, as the real virtues of Art are lost upon us, Portraiture is all that's thought of; and he that's happy in taking a likeness will thrive, while a *master* may perish. But we are in no danger of having *masters*; for our Painters study the antiques, or even the modern works, little more than is necessary to form their taste. Yet in them something more is necessary: It behoveth them to add judgement to taste, and execution to judgement. [. . .]

Now as we have no publick establishments for *Design*, either abroad or at home; and as few can bear the expence of travelling, our Painters get a slovenly manner, and yet, in spight of merit, is lucerative. The *learned eye* is wanting to distinguish excellence from mediocrity. [. . .] There should be, at least in the capital, one great collection of the masterpieces both of Painting and Sculpture, where there might be constant access under certain regulations. Here the *Publick* might view and form its *eye*: here the *Student* might copy and form his *hand*.

This would be bringing *Rome*, in some measure, home to us. This would at once create a style and a taste. This would rouse the fancy, and those blessed by *Minerva* might avail themselves of their genius.

Then if a few pensions were allowed the most distinguished proficients, to assist them in finishing their studies abroad, *England*, nay *Ireland*, might yet vie with *Italy*.

Nor let it be objected that the nature of our provincial government excludes excellence here, as it does in Literature. *Ireland* gave *England* the hint of a Drawing Academy. Some of the greatest artists have been bred here. In Landskips, we have no competitors. Mr *West* has sent out scholars of the greatest promise, now abroad [see fig. 18].[3] But, before that great Master presided in our Academy, we have had Painters the best in these islands at least. *Jervais* I would not mention, but that he is so celebrated by Mr *Pope*. *Reily*, the chief of *Dryden's* catalogue, was son of an *Irish* Painter. *Frye*, *Fisher*, *McArdel*, and many of the capital Engravers, were ours.[4]

Some of a Body, to whom the Arts in *Ireland* owe everything, complain of the success of their Academy, and lament that, notwithstanding all the expence they have been at in supporting it, and all the premiums they have given to encourage it, they have not produced one Painter, except the present ingenious Master.[5] But surely to have Painters from a mere Drawing-school, is to reap without sowing. If the SOCIETY would have Painters, there must be Schools for Painting.

The Academy has produced many excellent in Chalks, and more than this it could not do, for more it did not teach. To expect Painters from mere workers in Chalk, would be to expect Philosophers from a Grammar-school.

By giving children premiums for Drawing, you can only hope for merit in the first degree; and this in fact you always find. But Painting is a plant of slow growth, it must be reared by perseverance. Now by giving promiscuously, you frequently reward those who work for the amusement of the Art, and not the improvement of the profession; and besides, by gratifying the young student's vanity, you may damp his farther ambition to excel.

It should then be well weighed, whether premiums ought not to be almost confined to those who are to profess the Arts? And above all, whether such an ACADEMY FOR PAINTING, as we have described, be not a thing of absolute necessity to the perfection of the Fine Arts.

This is worthy of national attention, if the Arts of design were to be looked upon as merely *Mechanick*.* But when we reflect that the character of a people for politeness depends chiefly upon them, and that all civilized nations have ranked Painting among the *liberal Arts*, surely it can never be deemed unworthy of national encouragement, in countries so fam'd for publick Spirit.

* Silks, Tapestries, Velvets, Carpets, Carving, Gilding, Gardening, Architecture, owe the greatest part of their price to one branch or other of *design*. Nay it gives value even to toys. We see what sums the *French* extract for this article. Now tho' few would excel as liberal Artists, yet they might influence the form and fashion in some of the above works. He that might not rise to History, might yet paint a Landskip. And he that could not be a *Claude Lorrain* or a *Barret*, might yet paint coaches, or porcelain ware.[6] If the young Engraver could not be a *Strange* or a *Fry*,[7] he might grave Arms on Plate, and be excellent in chased Works.

**NOTES**

1    For Boswell see *The Ominous Years, 1774–1776*, eds. Charles Ryskamp and Freder-
     ick A. Pottle, London, Heinemann, 1963, passim. See also, S.C. Roberts's Introduc-
     tion to *Dr Campbell's Diary of a Visit to England in 1775*, James L. Clifford ed.,
     Cambridge, 1947.
2    For the background to Campbell's *Essay* see Anne Crookshank in *A New History
     of Ireland, IV, Eighteenth-Century Ireland*, ed. W.E. Vaughan, Oxford, Clarendon Press,
     1986, p. 518, and R. Raley, 'Beyond all Expectations: The Dublin Society's Draw-
     ing School in Dublin in the eighteenth Century', in *Academies of Art, Between
     Renaissance and Romanticism*, eds. Anton W.A. Boschloo et al., *Leids Kunsthistorisch
     Jaarboek* V–VI (1986–87), Sdu Uitgeverij, 'S-Gravenhage, 1989, p. 497.
3    Campbell is referring to Robert West (d. 1770), the founding headmaster of the
     Dublin Society's Schools, see Anne Crookshank and the Knight of Glin, *The Water-
     colours of Ireland*, London, Barrie and Jenkins, 1994, pp. 47–9. Campbell is making
     the point that Dublin had an Academy some decades before London; the Royal
     Academy of Arts dates from 1768; see John Turpin, *A School of Art in Dublin since
     the Eighteenth Century*, Dublin, Gill and Macmillan, 1995, p. 70.
4    Charles Jervas (*c.* 1675–1739), who painted various portraits of Alexander Pope, see
     Anne Crookshank and the Knight of Glin, *Irish Portraits, 1660–1860*, London, Paul
     Mellon Foundation for British Art, 1969, pp. 33–4; James Reily (d. 1780); Thomas
     Frye (1710–62); Jonathan Fisher (d. 1809) and James McArdell (1728/9–65). For
     Irish engravers in London see David Alexander, 'The Dublin Group: Irish Mezzo-
     tint Engravers in London, 1750–1775', *Quarterly Bulletin of the Irish Georgian Soci-
     ety*, vol. 16, no. 3, July–September 1973, pp. 73–93.
5    Robert West.
6    Campbell is referring to the French landscape painter Claude Gelée, called Lorraine
     (1600–82), and the Irish landscape artist George Barrett (1732–84).
7    Robert Strange (1725–96), one of the most prominent engravers in London in the
     second half of the eighteenth century. 'Fry' is presumably Thomas Frye, see above.

# – 28 –

# Edmund Burke, letters to James Barry, 1769 and 1774

Remembered as a statesman and a commentator on revolution, Edmund Burke
(1729–97) was also a philosopher (see entry 2) and a patron of artists. He spon-
sored James Barry (1741–1806) on a five-year study trip to France and Italy,
which lasted from 1765 to 1771. While Barry was in Italy, the correspondence

between patron and artist was warm and frequent. In his letters, Barry enthusiastically informed Burke of his views on Italian art, while the older man, writing from London, offered the painter advice, both in terms of social behaviour and artistic development. These issues characterize the first two letters included here. Of the first letter, dated 1769, the critic Richard Payne Knight (1750–1824), although not an admirer of Barry's, wrote, 'Better advice . . . was never given to a student, than that contained in Mr Edmund Burke's letter.'[1] On returning to London, the Burke–Barry correspondence became, understandably, less frequent and, as demonstrated by the third letter included here, dating from 1774, it also grew less intimate. The cooling of relations between patron and artist was due to the commissioning of a portrait of Burke in 1772 by Dr Richard Brocklesby (1722–97). Because of his busy political life, Burke found it difficult to keep his appointments with the painter and after two years of broken sittings, Barry was getting very angry.[2] The painter does not come out well from the correspondence.[3]

Sources: first letter: *The Works of James Barry, Esq. Historical Painter*, ed. Edward Fryer, 2 vols., London, 1809, vol. 1, pp. 86–8; second letter: *The Correspondence of Edmund Burke*, vol. 2, ed. Lucy S. Sutherland, Cambridge University Press, 1960, pp. 81–2; third letter: *The Correspondence of Edmund Burke*, vol. 3, ed. George H. Guttridge, Cambridge University Press, 1961, pp. 4–5

A) 1769

My dear Barry,

I am greatly in arrear to you on account of correspondence; but not, I assure you, on account of regard, esteem, and most sincere good wishes. My mind followed you to Paris, through your Alpine journey, and to Rome; you are an admirable painter with your pen as well as with your pencil; and every one to whom I shewed your letters, felt an interest in your little adventures, as well as a satisfaction in your description; because there is not only a taste, but a feeling in what you observe, something that shews you have an heart; and I would have you by all means keep it. I thank you for Alexander;[4] Reynolds sets an high esteem on it, he thinks it admirably drawn, and with great spirit. He had it at his house for some time, and returned it in a very fine frame; and it at present makes a capital ornament of our little dining room between the two doors. At Rome you are, I suppose, even still so much agitated by the profusion of fine things on every side of you, that you have hardly had time to sit down to methodical and regular study. When you do, you will certainly select the best parts of the best things, and attach yourself to them wholly. You, whose letters would be the best direction in the world to any other painter, want more yourself from me, who knows little of the matter. But, as you were always indulgent enough to bear my humour under the name of advice, you will permit me now, my dear Barry, once more to wish you in the beginning at least, to contract the circle of your studies. The extent and rapidity of your mind carries you to too great a diversity of things, and to the completion of a whole, before you are quite master of the parts, to a degree equal to the dignity of your ideas. This disposition arises from a generous impatience which is a fault almost characteristic of great genius. But it is a fact nevertheless, and one which I am sure you will correct, when you consider that there is a great deal of mechanic in your profession, in which, however, the distinctive part of the art consists, and without which the first ideas can only make a good critic, not a painter. I confess I am not much desirous of your composing many pieces for some time at least. Composition (though by some people placed foremost in the list of the ingredients of an art) I do not value near so highly.[5] I know none, who attempts, that does not succeed tolerably in that part: but that exquisite masterly drawing, which is the glory of the great school where you are, has fallen to the lot of very few, perhaps to none of the present age, in its highest perfection. If I were to indulge a conjecture, I should attribute all that is called greatness of style and manner of drawing, to this exact knowledge of the parts of the human body, of anatomy and perspective. For, by knowing exactly and habitually, without the labour of particular and occasional thinking, what was to be done in every figure they designed, they naturally attained a freedom and spirit of outline; because they could be daring without being absurd: whereas, ignorance, if it be cautious, is poor and timid; if bold, it is only blindly presumptuous. This minute and thorough knowledge of anatomy, and practical as well as theoretical perspective, by which I mean to include foreshortening, is all the effect of labour and use in *particular* studies, and not in general compositions. Notwithstanding your natural repugnance to handling of carcasses, you ought to make the knife go with the pencil, and study anatomy in real, and if you can, in frequent dissections. You know that a man who despises as you do, the minutiae of the art, is bound to be quite perfect in the noblest part of all; or he is nothing. Mediocrity is tolerable in middling things, but not at all in the great. In the course of the studies I speak of, it would not be amiss to paint portraits often and diligently. This I do not say as wishing you to turn your studies to portrait-painting, quite otherwise; but because many things in the human face will certainly escape you without some intermixture of that kind of study. Well, I think I have said enough to try your humility on this subject. But I am thus troublesome from a sincere anxiety for your success. I think you a man of honour and of genius, and I would not have your talents lost to yourself, your friends, or your country, by any means. You will then attribute my freedom to my solicitude about you, and my solicitude, to my friendship. Be so good to continue your letters and observations as usual. They are exceedingly grateful to us all, and we keep them by us. [. . .]

## B) 15 SEPTEMBER 1769

My dear Barry,

I am most exceedingly obliged to your friendship and partiality, which attributed a Silence very blameable on our parts to a favourable Cause; Let me add in some measure to its true Cause; a great deal of occupation of various sorts, and some of them disagreeable enough. As to any reports concerning your Conduct and Behaviour, you may be very sure, they could have no kind of influence here; For none of us are of such a make, as to trust to any ones report, of the Character of a person whom we ourselves know. Until very lately, I had never heard any thing of your proceedings from others; and when I did, it was much less than I had known from yourself – that you had been upon ill Terms with the Artists and Virtuosi in Rome, without much mention of Cause or consequence. If you have improved these unfortunate Quarrels to your advancement in your Art you have turned a very disagreeable Circumstance to a very Capital advantage. However you may have succeeded in this uncommon attempt, permit me to suggest to you, with that friendly Liberty which you have always had the goodness to bear from me, that you cannot possibly have always the same success, either with regard to your fortune or your Reputation. Depend upon it, that you will find the same competitions, the same jealousies, the same Arts and Cabals, the same emulations of interest and of Fame, and the same Agitations and passions here that you have experienced in Italy; and if they have the same effect on your Temper, they will have just the same Effects on your Interest; and be your merit what it will, you will never be employd to paint a picture. It will be the same at London as at Rome; and the same in Paris as in London; for the world is pretty nearly alike in all its parts. Nay though it would perhaps be a little inconvenient to me, I had a thousand times rather you should fix your Residence in Rome than here, as I should not then have the mortification of seeing with my own Eyes a Genius of the first Rank, lost to the world, himself, and his friends – as I certainly must; if you do not assume a manner of acting and thinking here totally different from what your Letters from Rome have described to me. That you have had just subjects of indignation always, and of anger often, I do no ways doubt; who can live in the world without some trials of his Patience? But believe me, my dear Barry, that the arms with which the ill dispositions of the world are to be combated and the qualitys by which it is to be reconciled to us, and we reconciled to it, are moderation, gentleness, a little indulgence to others, and a great deal of distrust of ourselves; which are not qualities of a mean Spirit, as some may possibly think them; but virtues of a great and noble kind, and such as dignifye our Nature, as much as they contribute to our repose and fortune; for nothing can be so unworthy of a well composed Soul, as to pass away Life in bickerings and Litigations: in snarling, and scuffling with every one about us. Again, and again, Dear Barry, we must be at peace with our Species; if not for their sakes, yet very much for [our] own. Think what my feelings must be, from my unfeigned regard to you, and from my wishes that your Talents might be of use, when I see what the inevitable consequences must be, of your persevering in what has hitherto been your Course ever since I knew you, and which you will permit me to trace out to you beforehand. You will come here; you will observe what the Artists are doing, and you will sometimes speak a disapprobation in plain words, and sometimes in a no less expressive Silence. By degrees you will produce some of your own works. They will be variously criticised; you will defend them; you will abuse those, who have attacked you; Expostulations, discussions, Letters, possibly challenges will go forward, you will shun your Brethren, they will shun you – In the mean time Gentlemen will avoid your friendship for fear of being engaged in your Quarrels, you will fall into distresses, which will only aggravate your disposition to further quarrels; you will be obliged for maintenance to do any thing for any body, your very Talents will depart for want of hope and encouragement and you will go out of the world fretted, disappointed, and ruined. Nothing but my real regard for you could induce me to set these considerations in this Light before you. Remember we are born to serve, or to adorn our Country and not to contend with our fellow Citizens: and that in particular, your Business is to paint and not to dispute. [. . .]

## c) 9 July 1774

Sir,

I ought to apologise to you for the liberty I have presumed to take of troubling you with what I find an unseasonable visit. I humbly beg your pardon for the intrusion. My apology is this: My worthy friend Dr Brocklesby, who has honoured me so much as to desire my picture, and wished to have it painted by you, complained to me yesterday, that he has been two years desiring it without effect. I should be very insensible of this mark of his attention, and very undeserving of it, if I had not endeavoured, as far as in me lay, to obey his obliging commands. I have therefore several times, almost in every week since he

first spoke to me (except about two months when I was wholly in the country, without coming to town at all), presented myself to you, that – if you were
not better engaged, I might sit to you. You have always been so much employed
that you have required a day's previous notice of my intention, and for that reason declined to paint the picture at the times which suited me. It has been very
unfortunate to me that my time too is so irregularly occupied, that I can never
with certainty tell beforehand when I shall be disengaged. No man can be more
sensible of the insignificance of my occupations, but to *me* they are of some
importance, and the times of them certainly very irregular. I came to town
upon very pressing business at four on Thursday evening; yesterday I had some
hours upon my hands; I waited upon you; but I found improperly. Contrary to
my expectation a gentleman who was to go out of town with me this morning, delays till half an hour after four o'clock; this gave me near five hours to
dispose of, and which I was willing to give to my friend's wishes. I waited on
you exactly at half an hour after eleven, and had the pleasure of finding you at
home; but as usual, so employed as not to permit you to undertake this disagreeable business. I have troubled you with this letter, as I think it necessary
to make an excuse for so frequent and importunate intrusions. Much as it
might flatter my vanity to be painted by so eminent an artist, I assure you that,
knowing I had no title to that honour, it was only in compliance with the desire
(often repeated) of our common friend, that I have been so troublesome. You,
who know the value of friendship, and the duties of it, I dare say, will have the
goodness to excuse me on that plea. On no other should I deserve it, for
intruding on you at other times than those you should please to order. Nobody,
I flatter myself, regards that time more; or pays, and has always paid, a more sincere (though a very unlearned) homage to your great talents and acquirements.
I must once more repeat my apology, hoping to obtain your pardon on the
usual plea of not committing the same fault again. [. . .]

## Notes

1    R. Payne Knight, *Edinburgh Review*, 16, August 1810, p. 295.
2    Another Burke letter is dated 13 July 1774, see George H. Guttridge, *The Corre-
     spondence of Edmund Burke*, vol. III, Cambridge University Press, 1961, pp. 7–9.
3    Barry's reply to Burke, dated 11 July 1774, is included in Guttridge, p. 6, and in
     Barry, *Works*, vol. I, pp. 231–8. The eventual Brocklesby portrait of Burke has not
     been located though a copy is in the National Gallery of Ireland, see William L.
     Pressly, *The Life and Art of James Barry*, New Haven and London, Yale University
     Press, 1981, pp. 69–73 and 238, nos. 46a and 46b.
4    A copy after Eustache Le Sueur (1616/17–55), *Alexander drinking the Potion*, now
     unlocated. Pressly suggests a date of *c.* 1766 as Barry would have seen the original
     painting in the Orleans collection in Paris, see *James Barry*, p. 242, no. 71.

5    Here Burke clearly disagrees with the views of Daniel Webb in *An Inquiry into the Beauties of Painting and into the Merits of the most Celebrated Painters Ancient and Modern*, 1760, Dialogue 7, 'On Composition', see entry 3.

# — 29 —

# Hugh Douglas Hamilton, letters to Canova, 1794–1802

The portrait painter Hugh Douglas Hamilton (1740–1808) lived in Italy from at least 1782 to 1792 where he became friendly with the Italian sculptor Antonio Canova (1757–1822). His acquaintance with Canova is celebrated in a splendid pastel dating from the late 1780s (fig. 17), and our knowledge of the Irish artist's international connections is furthered by the existence of various letters from Hamilton to his friend. Written after Hamilton's return to Dublin, the letters alternate between nostalgia and business

17    Hugh Douglas Hamilton, *Antonio Canova in his Studio with Henry Tresham and a Plaster Model for the 'Cupid and Psyche'*, 1789–90

news. They tell of the tiresome saga of a sculpture pedestal for a statue of an 'Amorino' or Cupid that a member of the wealthy Dublin banking family of La Touche had ordered from Canova, and also inform us of the low rating that the visual arts enjoyed in Dublin at the time.[1] The letters are among the few private documents we have from a late-eighteenth-century Irish artist which state personal feelings about art and indicate the local demand for portraiture and the paucity of alternative forms of patronage (for contemporary reactions to Hamilton's portraiture, see entries 41–3).

Source: Translated from the original Italian; Museo Biblioteca Archivio, Bassano del Grappa, Italy; Manoscritti Canoviani 3491, 1554–6[2]

## A) 20 FREDERICK STREET, DUBLIN, MAY 1794

With great shame I confess that it is a long time since I have had the pleasure of writing to my friend, Canova, but I am sure of receiving your pardon for various reasons, first of all, I must say that everyday I hope to receive an answer from you which would satisfy the young La Touche (the most indecisive and distracted man in the world)[3] of whom I have written to you and he speaks all the time of your pedestal which has been a long time in arriving. He wished to see all your letters (those which have been delivered to me by hand, for I see from some of yours that I have not received all) and in one of yours, dated 14 November 1792, you say, that Mr La Touche should pay me that money which I request, at least 100 scudi which is certainly not very much. He thought he had paid that amount on receipt of your last letter, dated 21 September 1793, when you included a letter for me in your letter to La Touche, which he forgot to deliver when he came to town. [. . .] I am sorry to go on about this affair as I do not want you to be put out and I hope that La Touche will go quickly to Rome as he has promised me, but I do not know, but I believe that he is somewhat restricted in his actions as he comes from a large family and his father is still alive; he has retired to the country after returning from England and I went to visit him at Marlay[4] so as to find out his plans regarding the pedestal, but he remains undecided, and I returned to town on foot so as to get some exercise for my health, but unfortunately the fatigue resulted in my suffering from a terrible attack of nerves, which resulted in my not being able to work, nor see anyone for some months; neither was I able to attend to my affairs or to yours – I am now a little better but I am not perfectly cured. [. . .]

It grieves me greatly to think that I have put you to such trouble over my crates, be assured that I would have settled this matter some time ago if it were not for this war because of which I cannot risk losing everything but if there was peace, I would return to view your campagna near Rome; I believe that it is the only place to visit for an artist who is anxious about his profession. I have finally given up executing pastels and I am now doing everything in oils, life size and in nature. I have painted a group of Cupid and Psyche, of which I believe you saw the sketch and appreciated it.[5] In this country, art has no direction while I spend my time improving my work prior to encountering the London critics. I would very much like to know what beautiful things you have made since I left. I would be very glad to know what good things have happened: write me a long letter with all the relevant facts of the latest happenings of your life and work, how other artists are flourishing and our friends in Rome. I hope your friend De Bonis[6] is well and still in Rome, I greatly revere him and would like it very much if he could make a copy of Titian's Venus in the Tribune of the Gallery at Florence. I would be grateful if you would ask him for me at what price he could do it, the price of the journey and whether he would start at 10 zechini and how much he would want for the painting. [. . .]

## B) 14 CLARE STREET, DUBLIN, 30 SEPTEMBER 1800

It is a long time since we have been privy to your news, who knows if you have received mine but your celebrity makes it impossible to escape your news.

The Honourable Mr Moor[7] who has left for Italy, wanted a letter of introduction because he did not want to miss out on making the acquaintance of such an esteemed friend and at the same time he wanted to present himself to you in order to give me the consolation that he has arrived and will excuse me for the illness which has prevented me and my daughter from communicating with you until now.

How time has flown since we last saw each other amidst the turbulence of war! How many times we have thought of you while reading and thinking of the misfortunes of Italy and especially of Rome. [. . .] The news today seems to imply hopes of Peace and tranquility for Europe. I hope that the arts can re-establish their position in Rome and we can have the consolation of returning, because I most certainly wish to return to live and die there.

With regards your affairs with Mr La Touche, I have written to you saying that I confronted him regarding his parting in haste with your money but the truth is that he has overspent and has not got the money. But if you would entrust me with this subject I will not fail to apply myself with all haste on your behalf to make him pay for the pedestal. [. . .] In this country at the moment we live quietly but between you and me, it is known that the French plan to invade in which case the rebellion will be renewed.

## c) 14 CLARE STREET, DUBLIN, 10 JUNE 1801

I am writing to you although I have not had the pleasure of receiving news from you and it is only today that I have learnt that you received a letter which I wrote a year ago for Mr Moor. [...] [H]ere in this end of the world one never hears news of anyone least of all the most famous, we were very pleased that we were able to place a letter with a lady who is leaving for a tour of Italy, and although not of our acquaintance, promises to deliver it. But Moor is most grateful to you for your kindness, he has written to his relations and today I have received a request for a letter of introduction to you from his uncle, the Earl of Moira,[8] a nobleman of the first rank (but one hears that he is a bit of a character) and a man of infinite superiority and of the most amiable spirit, the most gracious and in all the most considerate man in England. He leaves with young Mr William, his brother, who goes to study the architecture of Italy and he has asked me for a letter of introduction to you. I do not at all know the youth, but I do not doubt that he will be lacking in patronage. I know of your wish for leading a secluded life and he does not want to inconvenience you but you will understand that it is the least I can do.

Again we beg you to write, especially of your health and your work and of what art works you have produced amidst the confusion of war. I am painting in oils and have a lot of work, much of which I cannot finish because I suffer frequent attacks of nerves, but also the abundance of portraits impedes me from executing historical works, nor have I anyone with whom I can discuss art.

[...] I am not without hope of making another trip to Italy. [...] This country has been overwhelmed by rebellion, although it is apparently quiet at present, but I feel that a hostile enemy will create a situation of war even more horrible than before because the people here are full of revenge and it is very troubling to me that they seem incapable of forgetting. If peace comes, I wait not without hope of returning to Italy and perhaps even induce you to come to England; London, the capital, is truly something to be seen; the opulence and the commerce, the appearance of luxury and richness which is impossible to imagine anywhere else.[9]

## d) 14 CLARE STREET, DUBLIN, 8 NOVEMBER 1802

Although I have been late in replying, I am very grateful for the pleasure which your two letters gave me. Allow me to express my gratefulness in every way, especially for the expressions of benevolence and friendliness shown to me, as one who esteems you so highly particularly given the fame of your work and also your talents in many areas which is recognised and honourably renumerated, whatever the subject. In fact I wish I was in Rome, where I could see your works instead of only hearing about them, for the sole reason of renewing my spirit.

This country is almost like being in exile for one who truly loves art; here there are few men of talent that I have been overwhelmed by the infinity of portraits that I am forced to do and my health is not good anymore and the profession of portraits greatly tires me. All the same I get the occasional satisfaction from producing historical drawings, but there is not understanding nor appreciation for that kind of exercise here, thus I soon tire of trying.

The reason why I did not answer immediately to your first letter was because I was about to leave for London where I went with my daughter. [...] I saw Tresham in London,[10] who was angry with various Academicians of the Royal Academy because they were slow in officially thanking you for the magnificent offer you have made of your statue of Perseus. From what I was able to ascertain, their meeting was rowdy and they are jealous of any person who has merit. Altogether, of the arts in London, painting consists largely of portraits without style, without drawing and with unfocused colour (this is just between you and me). One must make an exception of the President,[11] who is a good history painter, and Tresham, but he, the poor man, has bad health and the climate does not agree with him. I saw Marchant who has considerable employment making gems and always makes beautiful things in his particular speciality. I will not talk of sculpture. I saw Flaxman,[12] whom like me you know, he has made many pieces which are composed with sentiment and simplicity.

If I am well enough and my affairs allow it, I will make a trip to Paris in the Spring and if things go well who knows but I may go on to have a look at Italy. [...]

## NOTES

1    Sergio Benedetti, *The La Touche Amorino, Canova and his Fashionable Irish Patrons*, Dublin, The National Gallery of Ireland, 1998, p. 25.

2    I am grateful to Sergio Benedetti and Gabriele Neher for assistance in translating these letters.

3    John La Touche (1772–1838), second son of the banker David La Touche, had been in Rome in the late 1780s and early 1790s where he commissioned a statue of an *Amorino* from Canova; Hamilton also painted his portrait (1790). The statue arrived in Dublin in August 1792. For this commission of an *Amorino* (now, National Gallery of Ireland) see Benedetti, *La Touche Amorino*, pp. 23–4 and p. 38.

4    Hamilton's writing is unclear at this point. The La Touche family owned the Marlay estate in Rathfarnham, Co. Dublin, as well as many other properties.

5      *Cupid and Psyche in the Nuptial Bower*, National Gallery of Ireland, see Fintan
       Cullen, 'Hugh Douglas Hamilton in Rome, 1779–1792', *Apollo*, CXV, February
       1982, pp. 86–91, and Fintan Cullen, 'The Oil Paintings of Hugh Douglas Hamil-
       ton', *Walpole Society*, L, 1984, p. 206.
6      Martino de Bonis, engraver and friend of Canova.
7      Possibly John Moore (b. 1771), second son of 1st Earl of Mount Cashell; see
       Catherine Wilmot, *An Irish Peer on the Continent (1801–1803) – Being a narrative of
       the tour of Stephen, 2nd Earl Mount Cashell, through France, Italy, etc.*, ed. Thomas U.
       Sadlier, London, 1920.
8      Francis Rawdon, 2nd Earl of Moira (1754–1826), leading Whig and friend of the
       future George IV. Hamilton had painted his portrait in 1797, see entries 41 and 42.
9      Canova did not visit London until 1815.
10     Henry Tresham, R.A. (1751–1814); although an Irish-born artist, Hamilton had
       befriended Tresham in Italy and included him in the pastel portrait of *Canova in his
       Studio with a Plaster Model for the 'Cupid and Psyche'* (fig. 17), see *Grand Tour: The Lure
       of Italy in the Eighteenth Century*, eds. A. Wilton and I. Bignamini, London, Tate
       Gallery, 1997, p. 72. See also Fintan Cullen, 'Who Owns Irish Art?', *Eire-Ireland*,
       Fall/Winter 1998 and Spring 1999, vol. 33, Nos. 3 and 4, vol. 34, No. 1 pp. 15–21.
11     Benjamin West (1738–1820).
12     Nathaniel Marchant (*c.* 1739–1816), a gem-engraver and John Flaxman
       (1755–1826), sculptor. Both had been friends of Hamilton's in Rome in the 1780s.

# — 30 —

# John O'Keeffe, *Recollections*, 1826

By 1826, when the Dublin-born John O'Keeffe (1747–1833) wrote a two-volumed autobiography, he had achieved fame in London as an actor and a dramatist, his most famous play being *Wild Oats* (1791), which is still performed today. Three-quarters of a century earlier, in the 1750s, he had trained as a painter in Dublin. He left this account of his training at the Dublin Society's drawing school run by Robert West (d. 1770; fig. 18).[1]

Source: John O'Keeffe, *The Recollections of John O'Keeffe*, 2 vols., London, Henry Colburn, 1826, vol. 1, pp. 1, 3, 12–16

I was designed by my parents and my own inclination for a painter, and not above six years of age when I was placed at Mr West's, the Royal Academy,

18    Matthew William Peters, *Self-Portrait with Robert West*, 1758

Shaw's Court, Dame Street, Dublin. West was a Waterford man, and took his painting studies in Paris, under Boucher, a disciple of Le Brun, distinguished for his painted series of Alexander's Battles. My drawing gave me an early taste for the Antique, and consequently set me reading. [. . .]

Whilst I was at West's academy, he took a very fine, highly finished drawing of me, in black and white chalks: I was then about eight years old: it is in the Guido style; and from this drawing the boys used to study. The late Mr Francis West, son, and successor to his father in the mastership of the academy, carefully preserved it, and it is still in being, as many of my friends had latterly told me they had seen it. [. . .]

In 1756, Hamilton (afterwards eminent in the first class of historical painters in England) was my fellow-student in the R.A. [*sic*] in Dublin: he might have been five years my elder; and was remarkable for choosing, when drawing the human figure, the most foreshortened view, consequently the most difficult.[2] [. . .] Our premiums were adjudged once a-year, in the House of Lords, Dublin: the drawings of the candidates were pinned round the walls to be examined as to their merits and classes. The boy wrote previously in chalk under his drawing 'from the life', if that was so; and 'from the round', if from a bust or statue. My brother Daniel, being one year one of the younger candidates, and all full of their gambols, got to plucking off the large scarlet tassels and bobbins from the benches, and pelting them at each other.[3] One of these struck Hamilton's drawing, which being in chalks was consequently much injured. He, enraged, thinking that poor Dan had done the mischief, gave him a most tremendous box on the ear. This accident, by the drawing being spoiled, lost Hamilton the premium. The names of those who obtained the premiums, and their different classes, were in the newspapers: this was the proudest stimulus to our emulation. I obtained many premiums in the different classes, and once the head premium for my drawing of Ariadne, the well known fine antique. We were early familiarized to the antique in sculpture, and in painting, to the style and manner of the great Italian and French masters. We also studied anatomy; and, indeed, the students there turned their minds to most of the sciences.

We had upon the large table in the Academy, a figure three feet high, called the anatomy figure; the skin off to show the muscles: on each muscle was a little paper with a figure of reference to a description of it, and its uses. We had also a living figure, to stand or sit: he was consequently a fine person; his pay was four shillings an hour. Mr West himself always *posed* the figure, as the phrase is, and the students took their views round the table where he was fixed. To make it certain that his attitude was the same each time we took our study, Mr West with a chalk marked upon the table the exact spot where his foot or his elbow or his hand came. We had a large round iron stove nearly in the centre of the school, but the fire was not seen; an iron tube conveyed the smoke through the wall. On the flat top of this stove, we used to lay our pencils of black and white chalk to harden them. The room was very lofty: it had only three windows; they were high up in the wall, and so contrived as to make the light descend: the centre window was arched, and near the top of the ceiling. At each end of this room was a row of presses with glass doors; in which were kept the statues cast from the real antique, each upon a pedestal about two feet high, and drawn out into the room as they were wanted to be studied from: but the busts were placed, when required, on the table. The stools we sat upon were square portable boxes, very strong and solid, with a hole in the form of a S on each side to put in the hand and move them. Each student had a mahogany drawing-board of his own: this was a square of three feet by four; at one end was a St Andrew's cross, fastened with hinges, which answered for a foot; and on the other end of the board, a ledge to lay our crayons upon. When we rose from our seats, we laid this board flat upon the ground, with the drawing we were doing upon it.

We had a clever civil little fellow for our porter, to run about and buy our oranges and apples, and pencils, and crayons, and move our busts and statues for us. He was a great favourite; and Mr West used every day to say to him, 'Master *Fling* (his real name was Flynn,) bring me a seedy *rowl*,' – and put a halfpenny in his hand. We had some students who studied statuary alone, and they modelled in clay. Cunningham (brother to the poet) invented the small basso-relievo portraits, in wax of the natural colours: they had oval frames, and convex crystal glasses and were in great fashion.[4] Berville, a most enthusiastic Frenchman, full of professional ardour, studied with us: and Van Nost, the celebrated statuary, often came amongst us: he did the fine pedestrian statue of Lord Blakeney, erected in Sackville-street.

The members of the Dublin Society, composed of the Lord Lieutenant and most of the nobility, and others, frequently visited our academy to see our goings on: and some of the lads were occasionally sent to Rome, to study the Italian masters. I was present (when about four years old) and saw the cases containing the casts from the antique brought from Rome, and opened; and from these in a very few years I studied.

## NOTES

1    For O'Keeffe see Anne Crookshank and the Knight of Glin, *The Watercolours of Ireland*, London, Barrie and Jenkins, 1994, p. 62.

2    Hugh Douglas Hamilton (1740–1808), see entry 29.

3    For Daniel O'Keeffe, see Crookshank and Glin, *Watercolours*, p. 111.

4    The sculptor Patrick Cunningham (d. 1774) went on to work with John Van Nost the Younger (d. 1787); his brother was the poet John Cunningham (1723–73).

— 31 —

# Benjamin Robert Haydon, *Diary*, 1841

The English artist Benjamin Robert Haydon (1786–1846) painted Daniel O'Connell (1775–1847) in London in 1841 and recorded the sitting in his diary for 9 February of that year. O'Connell was one of the most painted and caricatured Irishmen of the nineteenth century, but few of the many artists who sketched him wrote of their experiences in his company.[1] Haydon visited O'Connell for a sitting in preparation for a canvas celebrating the Anti-Slavery Society Convention which had taken place in London in June of 1840. Haydon made sketches from the life of the leading delegates and kept a detailed account of his sittings in his diary. The huge if not wholly success-ful painting was eventually exhibited in the Egyptian Hall, Piccadilly, and is now in the collection of the National Portrait Gallery, London.[2]

Source: *The Diary of Benjamin Robert Haydon*, ed. W.B. Pope, 5 vols., Cambridge, Mass., Harvard University Press, 1963, vol. 5, pp. 31–2

## 9 FEBRUARY, 1841

Sketched O'Connell. I came at *ten* & he was *asleep*. I came at eleven & he came out as usual – rolling & good Natured – & I went up to his breakfast room; as he read his letters I sketched him. He then sat regularly, and when I said I was sorry to keep him so long, he said, 'I have used you so *ill* by lying a bed, my conscience obliges me to give you a good sitting!' We talked of the Catholics & Protestants. He said, 'If you apply to a Man's *reason*, you only apply to *half* of him, & the *smallest* half.'

He said the Puseyites had adopted the great proportion of the Catholics doctrines (I did not know).[3] He said the Whigs would go out, but the Queen would not let them.

There is in O'Connell a keen, lynx look, and a great good nature, but cun-ning & trick[y]. He said when Mary persecuted the Protestants there was great connection between Bristol & Dublin, that the Irish afforded protec-tion to the Bristol Protestants till the persecution was over. He said the Irish *never persecuted* the Protestants – I thought of the Rebellion of 1797![4]

'You English,' said he, 'don't know what is going on in Ireland. Repeal will triumph.' He is got older, considerably, but there is in his look inexpressible good nature. He told me he sat to Wilkie for his Portrait, at the same time as the Duke, & said such was the Duke's determination to be in proper cos-tume, he used to come for the Queen's Picture of Her being first in Coun-cil at Kensington, in the coldest Weather, in White duck trowsers.[5]

O'Connell swore the Duke was wounded in his bum in Spain. It is not true. He replied, 'One of his Aide-camps told me so.' This was a bit of O'Con-nell's spite, but seeing I didn't relish it, he ceased.

All these Men are surrounded by Toadies who hope to share something of the immortality of their Leader.

When I went away, he said, 'I am so pleased I'll give you an hour at your House.' He thought it very like, & so it is.

I reminded him of many things during the Whig Picture,[6] at which we laughed. I said, 'Don't you think the Whigs have acted with great Spirit in Syria?' 'Yes,' said O'Connell, with great brogue, 'and it is the only spirit they have shewn.' We talked of Tyburn, near where I live. He said Dr Nugent was hung there, the last of Titus Oates' plot, & his heart & bowels taken out long before he was dead.

We then talked of the Miraculous conception. O'Connell said some Women were burnt for saying the nature of Christ came through the Virgin's Womb, like Water out of a Pipe! As he said this, he looked superstitious & catholic.

The curious thing of Catholics, they talk of things mere traditions as if facts − of history.

I took my leave, having been much gratified & amused, except at what he said about the Duke − I could have put my fist in his face.

NOTES

1    See Fintan Cullen, *Visual Politics*, pp. 90–101. For O'Connell iconography see Richard Ormond, *Early Victorian Portraits*, 2 vols., London, HMSO, 1973, I, pp. 347–9.

2    Ibid., I, pp. 538–44: II, plates 1035–9; painting measures 297.2 x 383.6 cm.

3    Edward Bouverie Pusey, parliamentarian in favour of a curtailment of Anglican privileges.

4    Haydon means 1798.

5    Referring to the Duke of Wellington; O'Connell sat for Wilkie, 1836–8, Royal Bank of Scotland Art Collection, see Cullen, *Visual Politics*, plate 41. O'Connell is also referring to Wilkie's *The First Council of Queen Victoria*, 1838, Royal Collection, Windsor Castle.

6    Haydon had previously sketched O'Connell in 1834, see John Jolliffe, *Neglected Genius: The Diaries of Benjamin Robert Haydon, 1808–1846*, London, Hutchinson, 1990, pp. 151–2.

# − 32 −

# Stewart Blacker, *Irish Art and Irish Artists*, 1845

A barrister by training and a native of Co. Armagh, Stewart Blacker (1813–81) was instrumental in founding the Royal Irish Art Union − or the Society for the Encouragement of Fine Arts in Ireland, by the Purchase and Diffusion of the Works of Living Artists. This extract from his 1845 essay on Irish art is part of an address delivered on 18 December 1844 to the pupils

of the Royal Dublin Society Schools of Design. His theme was 'the forma-
tion of a really good and flourishing Native School of Art'. In his preamble,
Blacker asks, 'Are there any Irish artists?, What have they done?, and What are
they doing?' The format of his speech is to respond with a resounding 'Yes'
to the first question and through anecdote and detail to answer the other two.
His address is thus largely an account of various early-nineteenth-century
Irish artists such as George Petrie, William Cuming, William Mulready and
Thomas Kirk. In the excerpts included here the focus is on the painters Martin Cregan (1788–1870) and Martin Archer Shee (1769-1850) and the sculptor John Henry Foley (1818–74). Although invited in 1844 to address the
students of the RDS, Blacker was not adverse to criticizing that institution
for 'continuing incompetence', an accusation levelled in a pamphlet published
a few months later.[1] He was also active in setting out early proposals for the
establishment of a National Gallery of Ireland.[2]

Source: Stewart Blacker, *Irish Art and Irish Artists*, Dublin, Gunn & Cameron,
1845, pp. 10, 20

Happy as I am to see the aristocracy of rank and birth honoured, and the
aristocracy of the industrious wealth respected, yet it gives me redoubled
pleasure that we live at a time and in a country where the aristocracy of
genius and of talent is becoming every day more and more appreciated. [. . .]

My Lord, at the head of the R[oyal] H[ibernian] A[cademy], as President
is Mr Martin Cregan, formerly a diligent student in these schools. Mr Cregan deservedly holds the first rank in this country as a portrait painter. He
was a favourite pupil of our eminent countryman Sir Martin Archer Shee,
also a student in these schools: and it is a remarkable and gratifying coinci-
dence to see the master and pupil each filling the presidential chair in the
respective academies of England and Ireland, with the esteem and respect of
the profession and the public. [. . .]

I happened one summer to spend a short time in the Isle of Guernsey, and
at the home of a newly made acquaintance saw a portrait which rivetted my
attention as a highly creditable production of modern art. It was admirable for
unexaggerated expression and fine tone of colour, and evidently painted some
time ago. I asked the name of the painter; my friend had forgotten it, but said
that if I mentioned some as likely to have painted it, he might hit on the name;
I named some of the leading portrait painters of the day, Sir M. Shee, Phillips,
and Jackson, in England, and Sir Henry Raeburn, of Scotland, fully expecting
each time to be called to a halt, when my host said 'No; it is neither England
nor Scotland. My father was in Ireland, most probably you will find the artist's

name.' I did so, and found to the infinite gratification of my national and local feelings, the name at full length of Martin Creagan. [. . .]

Look to the venerable Sir Martin Shee – the eminent artist – the finished poet – the eloquent speaker – the accomplished scholar – and the perfect gentleman – arriving, by his talent, perseverance, and rectitude of conduct, at the summit of his profession, and inverted with the honourable position of being the medium of communication with his Sovereign and that profession. Then turn to young Foley, who has not very long left the ranks of this institution, and contemplate the high position in art which he has already acquired for himself. Without influential friends, or interested patrons in the vast metropolis of this great empire – with nothing but his own genius and his own exertions to rely upon, he sends in his works to the national competition, and is at once called forth and placed in the pathway of honour and emolument by that noble commission, of which his Royal Highness Prince Albert is the very efficient head.[3] Here you have two striking instances out of many that might be produced of those who once occupied the position you now hold – the one in honoured and advanced life, the other in the opening of (it is to be hoped) an equally successful career.

Let each and all of you, therefore, say to yourselves, we also will use our best exertions to obtain a name for ourselves, and do credit to our country and to this institution.

## Notes

1    Stewart Blacker, *A Suggestion on the Present Election and that of Future Masters of the Schools of Design of the R.D.S.*, Dublin, 1845, see John Turpin, *A School of Art in Dublin since the Eighteenth Century: A History of the National College of Art and Design*, Dublin, Gill & Macmillan, 1995, p. 91.

2    See Eileen Black, 'Practical Patriots and True Irishmen: The Royal Irish Art Union 1839-59', *Irish Arts Review Yearbook*, vol. 14, 1998, pp. 140–6.

3    Blacker is referring to Foley's success in a commission to execute statues for the new Houses of Parliament at Westminster, see Walter Strickland, *A Dictionary of Irish Artists*, 2 vols., Dublin, 1913, I, pp. 357–8. For Shee, see Fintan Cullen, *Visual Politics*, pp. 41–3.

## — 33 —

## Dante Gabriel Rossetti, 'McCracken', 1853

Dante Gabriel Rossetti (1828–82), along with a number of other English Pre-Raphaelite artists, benefited from the patronage of the Belfast cotton spinner Francis McCracken (1802–63). By no means wealthy, McCracken paid for his purchases in instalments. Between 1851 and 1853 he bought paintings by William Holman Hunt, Ford Madox Brown and John Everett Millais (*Ophelia*, 1851–2, Tate Gallery, London) as well as Rossetti's now well-known representation of the Annunciation, *Ecce Ancilla Domini!* (1849–50, Tate Gallery, London).[1] He does not seem to have been interested in buying Irish paintings. McCracken's eccentric way of paying for his pictures, together with his endless letter-writing to the artists concerned, caused them great annoyance. Rossetti voiced his attitude to his patron, whom he referred to as 'an Irish maniac' by means of a parody of Tennyson's sonnet 'The Kraken', a poem about a sea monster.[2] Rossetti sent the parody to his sister Christina Rossetti in a letter dated 8 November 1853, saying that the poem was 'perhaps rather a stern view of the character'.

Source: *Letters of Dante Gabriel Rossetti*, eds. Oswald Doughty and John Robert Wahl, vol. I, Oxford, Clarendon Press, 1965, pp. 164–5

McCracken

Getting his pictures, like his supper, cheap,
    Far far away in Belfast by the sea,
His watchful one-eyed uninvaded sleep
    McCracken sleepeth. While the P.R.B.
Must keep the shady side, he walks a swell
    Through spungings of perennial growth and height:
    And far away in Belfast out of sight,
By many an open do and secret sell,
Fresh daubers he makes shift to scarify,
    And fleece with pliant shears the slumbering 'green'.[3]
There he has lied, though aged, and will lie,
Fattening on ill-got pictures in his sleep,
Till some Praeraphael prove for him too deep.
    Then, once by Hunt and Ruskin to be seen,
Insolvent he will turn, and in the Queen's Bench die.

NOTES

1    Dianne Sachko Macleod, *Art and the Victorian Middle Class: Money and the Making of Cultural Identity*, Cambridge University Press, 1996, pp. 160–2, 447–8.

2    Martyn Anglesea, 'A Pre-Raphaelite Enigma in Belfast', *Irish Art Review*, vol. 1, no. 2, Summer 1984, pp. 40–5.

3    This may refer to McCracken's refusal of Ford Madox Brown's *The Pretty Baa-Lambs* (Birmingham City Museum and Art Gallery) because he did not like the fact that the grass was more blue than green, see *The Pre-Raphaelites*, ed. Leslie Parris, London, Tate Gallery, 1984, p. 94.

# — 34 —

# Richard Robert Madden, *The United Irishmen*, 1858

Born in Ireland, Madden (1798–1886) trained as a surgeon and led a peripatetic life in different parts of the world: as a campaigner against slavery in Jamaica and as a Colonial Secretary in Western Australia. He was also a prolific author who, on returning to Ireland, published his major work, *The United Irishmen: Their Lives and Times*, which originally appeared between 1842 and 1846 but had many subsequent editions and revisions. Madden gathered detailed documentation on the United Irishmen, all of which is dressed in a highly hagiographic tone.[1] At the end of a long account of the career of Lord Edward FitzGerald (1763–98), Madden lists a number of material objects that added to the cult of the United Irishman. The largest and potentially most interesting piece of Geraldine memorabilia was a now lost oil painting of 'The Arrest of FitzGerald' painted by James Dowling Herbert (1762/3–1837), a Dublin painter/actor who later gained some reputation by the publication of his memoirs, *Irish Varieties for the Last Fifty Years* (London, 1836). The composition of Herbert's lost oil is known to us now only by means of a crude woodcut that appeared in Watty Cox's *The Irish Magazine* in 1810 (fig. 19).

Source: R.R. Madden, *The United Irishmen: Their Lives and Times*, second series, second edition, Dublin, 1858, pp. 472–3.

Arrest of Lord Edw.ᵈ FitzGerald
18ᵗʰ May 1798

19      After J.D. Herbert, *The Arrest of Lord Edward FitzGerald*, 1810

This picture was painted a few years after the event of which it is a faithful representation, by an artist of some merit, of the name of Dowling, who deemed it prudent in 1798, or subsequent to the rebellion, to change his name to Herbert. He was an eccentric man of some genius. He published a volume of his reminiscences, now rarely to be met with, and died, I believe, in poverty. He devoted his pen and pencil to the wrong cause for patronage. This highly interesting picture of Herbert's is now in the possession of Mr O'Connor, a chandler, of Thomas Street. A few years ago I had the pleasure of accompanying to O'Connor's to see this picture the sister of Lord Edward's biographer,[2] to whose memory I beg to pay this poor tribute of my respect for her unaffected, unobtrusive worth and goodness, and that warm interest in her country's honour and attachment to it, which seem to be hereditary in her family.

The picture was painted for engraving. John Hervey, Nicholas Murphy, and a few others subscribed five guineas each for this object. Hervey paid the artist for it. It was in his possession for some time, then passed into the hands of one Thomas Hurst, a master bricklayer, and finally into O'Connor's. It is to be noted that all of these persons were in the middle rank of life. Not one 'gentleman' of the United Irish leaders subscribed for it, or seems to have taken the slightest interest in it, and yet it is a picture that is of the highest value for the fidelity of the likeness of the different actors in the scene which is represented. The subject is the capture of Lord Edward, who has just risen from his bed, and is represented grappling with Major Swan and attempting to stab him; the amateur assistant of the latter, Ryan, is lying on the floor, mortally wounded by his lordship; while Major Sirr is seen cautiously taking aim at Lord Edward, and in the act of firing at him. A soldier is represented seizing Nicholas Murphy by the collar, and some other military men in the act of rushing up the stairs. The picture wants cleaning; it has evidently been 'hidden away' in some damp place for a long time, and is now hung up in a dark room in a very bad light.

The likenesses, as I have before observed, are admirable. Is there no public body in Ireland that has sufficient patriotism to secure this representation of the mortal conflict wherein the noblest being that Ireland ever produced received his death wound?

Walter Cox, with all his faults [...], had some feelings of a generous nature. He established his Irish Magazine with the avowed purpose of rescuing the memories of the men of 1798 of the stamp of FitzGerald from oblivion and more than oblivion – from obloquy and injustice. The intended engraving of Herbert's picture of Lord Edward FitzGerald's capture, which the original subscribers for the latter had in view, was never made. Cox, however, had a very spirited woodcut representation of the capture made for his magazine from the picture, in which the four principal figures only were introduced. It is an excellent illustration of that memorable scene [fig. 19].[3]

I visited with Miss Moore, in 1842, the house formerly of Nicholas Murphy, in which Lord Edward was last sheltered, and the small room in which he was captured on the third floor. There was then the stain of a spurt of blood on the wall. It will be remembered that Lord Edward was shot in the shoulder, and that a violent struggle ensued, during which he may have kept his assailant at bay for some time with his back to the wall.

## NOTES

1    See Kevin Whelan, *The Tree of Liberty: Radicalism, Catholicism and the Construction of Irish Identity, 1760–1830*, Cork University Press, 1996, pp. 167–8.

2    Ellen (Nell) Moore (d. 1846), sister of the poet Thomas Moore (1779–1852) author
     of *The Life and Death of Lord Edward FitzGerald*, 2 vols., London, 1831.

3    See Fintan Cullen, 'Lord Edward FitzGerald: The Creation of an Icon', *History Ire-
     land*, vol. 6, no. 4, Winter 1998, pp. 17–20. The woodcut appeared in *The Irish Mag-
     azine*, vol. 3, 1810, opposite p. 387.

# — 35 —

# Robert Elliott, *Art and Ireland*, 1906 (d. 1910)

The Dublin painter/art-critic Robert Elliott (d. 1910) was an 'incessant voice'
in early-twentieth-century Ireland against imported ecclesiastical art work.[1]
In 1906 he collected a number of his previous articles from such journals as
*The Rosary* and *The Leader* into book form and called for the support of native
Irish art. The dramatist and art patron Edward Martyn (1859–1923) contributed a preface to Elliott's book, claiming that he and the author were anxious in 'saving . . . modern church design and ornament from the crude paw
of the tradesman and their restoration, as in olden time, to the delicate hand
of the artist'.[2] Elliott claimed that 'this book has been written in the interests
of these – of Catholic and Ireland-loving Irishmen wherever they may be
found caring just one iota for art'.[3] The frontispiece to the book carries a
photograph of John Hughes's altar relief (1902–5) representing Jesus as 'The
Man of Sorrows' in St Brendan's Cathedral, Loughrea, Co. Galway, which, to
this day, displays some of the best examples of Celtic Revival church decoration in Ireland.

Source: Robert Elliott, *Art and Ireland*, Dublin, Sealy, Bryers & Walker, 1906,
Introduction, xi–xviii

'What is the good of talking art to Ireland now?' asked a writer in a weekly
journal – *The Leader* – three years ago. He doubtlessly voiced the opinion of
a very large section of Irishmen; a questionable opinion it was – and the article in which it appeared elaborated that opinion – and it meant that it was
no use 'talking art' to Ireland at all. She was to become commercially pros-
perous first. That article by a well-known writer, who assumes the *nom de*

*guerre* of 'Pat' I noticed at the time. I have not noticed my reply, or rather my criticism of his standpoint, in the selected essays published in the following book; but as this book has for one object the setting before Irishmen some of the reasons why it is still necessary to talk art to Ireland, and to condemn a very great deal of what has already been talked to her, I shall here summarise some of that article in this short introduction to the selected and revised essays incorporated in the book.

Without art we cannot be said to live, except as machines live. Many men remain machines all their lives. If a country were to become a vast aggregation of human and other machines, though the millennium of the ultra utilitarians would have arrived, something else would have arrived to qualify that state of machine-made bliss – utter disgust at life and a loathing of it. Men live not by bread alone (as it is now tritely said) but they live truly by religion of some kind, by faith of some kind in something outside of themselves, the attributes of which 'something' must be made palpable to the senses by art of some kind. Such has been the true life of the world. [. . .] It is true that when a country decays its arts decay, when it flourishes its art flourishes; or perhaps it would be more exact to say that when a country decays its artists leave it for another that is not decaying, and when it marches toward importance, art accompanies, refines, and purifies that procession.

Everything of value that is done well is done with a knowledge of that art which alone can make it beautiful. Preaching, singing, tailoring, soap-making, saint-making, and especially writing when directed against the arts themselves. The production of certain very useful things for the bodily health and comfort of the Irish people, for the satisfaction of its pleasures and for the assuaging of its pains, is increasing daily. But in the producing of anything necessary to the life of the body, the production pure and simple becomes insignificant beside the artistic concomitants; and the many productions that are not classible in the category of art, are yet through some friendly art made stimulative of the spiritual life without which man is lower than the beasts of the field.

So much as a summary of what I said three years ago. But despite the continued existence of an Academy of Art, of Art Schools, and Art Masters and Art Inspectors, the influence of the art of the *artist* in the land – and especially in the church – is almost as languid as it was then. Commercialism trading under the usurped title of 'Art' seems to be as vigorous as ever. To condemn what has been 'talked to Ireland' in the name of this spurious art is of small importance compared to the condemning of what has been *done*; for the talking or writing of a pander to the enterprising exploiter of skilled labour advertising his wares as regally as any other usurper his services to the commerce of men – such, after all, may not have a fraction of the influence that the advertisement of the doer himself has with possible patrons.

These possible patrons to-day, actual ones tomorrow, still do not seemingly appreciate that God has not created two worlds alike, nor two countries alike, nor two souls alike, nor two flowers alike. A similarity of form and purpose in certain groups of things may be at the foundation of our ideas of order and harmony; but harmony is not monotony, and the human duplicating machine that has so largely superseded the old creative hand that studied God's creation so well and wisely, is patronised by the Church, and in the haunts of villadom; and thus is enabled to go on monotonously adding like to like with callous and mathematical regularity. That duplicating machine is, in many an art, the hand that from its youth up is cramped in the vice of an exploitive trademan's will; and evidence of this lamentable tabefaction of the art impulse in the individual is to be found in almost every church in Ireland that the writer has seen himself, or heard from reliable witnesses.

## NOTES

1    Paul Larmour, *The Arts and Crafts Movement in Ireland*, Belfast, Friar's Bush Press, 1992, p. 130.
2    Edward Martyn, in R. Elliott, *Art and Ireland*, Dublin, 1906, vii.
3    Ibid., xviii.


## — 36 —

# W.B. Yeats, 'The Gift', 1913

This Yeats poem relates directly to the calls for a modern art gallery for Dublin in the early decades of the twentieth century. It is one of the poet's great public poems but also shows how art was, potentially, the preserve of an anti-Catholic, avant-garde élite. Yeats (1865–1939) wrote a number of poems relating to Hugh Lane's campaign for a gallery, the others being 'September 1913', 'To a Friend whose Work has come to Nothing', 'Paudeen' and 'To a Shade'. The campaign had begun when Lane promised to present Dublin with paintings by such artists as Manet (see fig. 21), Degas and Renoir on condition that Dublin build a suitable home for these modern works (see also entries 37–8 and 45). The drama reached a peak in 1912 and 1913 with the drawing up of plans by the architect Edwin Lutyens (1869–1944) to design a gallery spanning the Liffey. The major obstacle was the raising of money and much pressure was put on Dublin benefactors to exhibit public philanthropy. One such benefactor was the Guinness peer, Lord Ardilaun (1840–1915), who had refused to permit St Stephen's Green as a possible site for the gallery.[1] To Yeats, Ardilaun was the antithesis of the noble patronage that had made the Italian Renaissance. In January 1913, he published the following poem in *The Irish Times*, where it was accompanied by an account of the latest meeting of the Municipal Art Gallery Building Fund Committee. The version here is that which appeared in the newspaper; Yeats slightly altered the title and some lines when he published it along with the other Lane poems in *Responsibilities* in 1914.[2]

Source: *The Irish Times*, 11 January 1913

*The Gift (To a friend who promises a bigger subscription than his first to the Dublin Municipal Gallery if the amount collected proves that there is a considerable 'popular demand' for the pictures)*

> You gave, but will not give again
> Until enough of Paudeen's pence
> By Biddy's halfpennies have lain
> To be 'some sort of evidence',
> Before you'll put your guineas down,
> That things it were a pride to give
> Are what the blind and ignorant town
> Imagines best to make it thrive.
>
> What cared Duke Ercole, that bid
> His mummers to the market-place,
> What th'onion-sellers thought or did
> So that his Plutarch set the pace
> For the Italian comedies?
> And Guidobaldo, when he made
> That grammar school of courtesies
> Where wit and beauty learned their trade,
> Upon Urbino's windy hill,
> Had sent no runners to and fro
> That he might learn the shepherd's will.
>
> And when they drove out Cosimo,
> Indifferent how the rancour ran,
> He gave the hours they had set free

To Michelozzo's latest plan
For the San Marco Library,
Whence turbulent Italy should draw
Delight in Art whose end is peace,
In logic and in natural law
By sucking at the dugs of Greece.

Your open hand but shows our loss,
For he knew better how to live.
Leave Paudeens to their pitch and toss,
Look up in the sun's eye and give
What the exultant heart calls good
That some new day may breed the best
Because you gave, not what they would,
But the right twigs for an eagle's nest.

## NOTES

1    See R.F. Foster, *W.B. Yeats: A Life: Vol. 1, The Apprentice Mage, 1865–1914*, Oxford University Press, 1997, pp. 479–81.
2    'To a Wealthy Man who promised a second subscription to the Dublin Municipal Gallery if it were proved the people wanted pictures', see *The Collected Poems of W.B. Yeats*, ed. Richard J. Finneran, London, Macmillan, 1983, pp. 107–8.

# — 37 —

# George Moore, *Vale*, 1914

*Vale*, the final volume in George Moore's autobiographical trilogy *Hail and Farewell!*, was published in 1914 and gives an often scurrilous account of the author's acquaintance with Dublin leading figures in the literary revival of the early twentieth century. The scion of a wealthy, landowning, Catholic family in Co. Mayo, Moore (1852–1933) had turned his back on both his estate and his father's horses to settle in Paris and become an artist. In Paris, he befriended many of the avant-garde artists of the day, including Édouard Manet who painted Moore on at least three occasions (fig. 20).[1] On realizing his limitations

20     Édouard Manet, *George Moore (au Café)*, 1878/9

as an artist, Moore turned to art criticism and moved to London. In time, he became a celebrated novelist, finally returning to Ireland in 1903 where he set up house in Ely Place, Dublin, which he decorated with his fine collection of paintings. Given his past association with many notable painters, Moore was not surprisingly swept up in the campaign led by Hugh Lane (1875–1915) to establish a modern art gallery in Dublin (see entries 38 and 45). In this extract from *Vale*, Moore tells of Lane visiting his house in 1904, in an attempt to encourage Moore's support. The writer clearly admired Lane's dealing skills, as evidenced by his discussion of the dealer's recent acquisition of Manet's *Éva Gonzalès*, now one of the still controversial 'Lane pictures' (fig. 21). Yet Moore also caricatures Lane and supplies an anecdote on the connoisseur's penchant for cross-dressing. Offended by such references to him in *Vale*, Lane attempted to have the book suppressed but failed.[2]

Source: George Moore, *Vale*, Uniform Edition, London, Heinemann, 1933, pp. 92–8

Just then the servant opened the door to ask me if I were at home to Mr Hugh Lane.

Yes.

And a moment after there came into the room a tall, thin young man, talking so fast that I gathered with difficulty that there must be a great many pictures in Irish country houses which he would like to exhibit in Dublin.

If anybody cares for pictures, I contrived to interject, and he sat twisting and untwisting his legs, linking and unlinking his hands, his talk beginning to bore me a little, for I could not detect any aestheticism in him, only a nervous desire to run a show. Your brother, I said, called here a few days ago to prepare me for your visit. He said that you were going to revive Irish painting. I came here to revive the Irish language; it existed once upon a time, but Irish painting –

Lane interrupted me, admitting that the men who had painted in Ireland at the end of the eighteenth century were merely reflections of Sir Joshua and Romney.[3]

But your brother –

Without noticing my interruption he continued telling me that, for the last fortnight, he had been travelling through Ireland, visiting all the country houses, and had obtained promises from many people to lend their pictures.

Now, your name among the list of patrons at the exhibition –

But why are you giving yourself all this trouble? What is your object?

Well, you see, I am Lady Gregory's nephew, and must be doing something for Ireland.

Striking a blow, I said.

A bewildered look, quickly repressed, however, revealed to me that he did not understand my remark. You don't speak with a brogue. Your brother said you didn't. How is that?

He produced his little hysterical laugh, and without stopping to explain why it was that he had no brogue, looked round the room in search of pictures worth borrowing, and having decided upon two, a portrait of Rachel by Couture and a small Constable, he said he hoped I would try to influence Sir Thornley Stoker[4] in his favour; he would like to print Sir Thornley's name among the patrons of the forthcoming exhibition, an exhibition designed for the advancement of Art In Ireland. I gave Lane my promise that he should be invited to the palace, our nickname for Sir Thornley's house, so full was it of beautiful things. But Sir Thornley could not be persuaded, and my affection for him was strained to the uttermost by his persistent speaking of Lane as a London picture-dealer who had come to Ireland to see what he could pick up.

Or perhaps he's on the look-out for a post in the Museum.

I have told you, Sir Thornley, that he is Lady Gregory's nephew, and would like to do something for Ireland. That should be sufficient. He growled and muttered that Lane might tell us he was a great expert, but what proof had we of it? And the old doctor grew as grumpy as if I had been speaking of a bone-setter. My dear Thornley, we do not learn anything that we did not know before; and I sketched out the life-history of a chef who before discovering his vocation had wandered from one trade to another, trying all, until one night in the kitchen two ducks were roasting before the fire, the gravy running out of their backsides, and deeply moved, he had stood immersed in a great joy.

But what has that got to do with Lane?

Lane is Lady Gregory's nephew.

You have told me that before; you have said that before.

Of course, if you interrupt me. I was going to tell you that Lady Gregory told me herself that the family had thought of all kinds of professions suitable for Hugh, but his heart was not in any of them, and they were beginning to feel a little anxious, when one day, as they were sitting down to lunch –

Was there a duck for luncheon?

No. He caught sight of the fold of Lady Gregory's dress, a tailor-made from Paris; it is always a pleasure to a woman to hear her gown admired; but there was a seriousness in Hugh's appreciation of the hang of the skirt, and a studied regard in his eyes which caused her a moment's perplexity, and when they rose from table he stood watching her as she crossed the room. Of course, the skirt fitted rather nicely, but . . . In the same afternoon she had occasion to go to her bedroom, and to her surprise found her wardrobe open and Hugh trying on her skirts before the glass. Hugh! Doesn't it seem to you, Aunt Augusta, that this skirt is a little too full? During the evening he spoke of some premises in Conduit Street; but tailoring was only a passing thought, and the next thing they heard of Hugh was that he had gone into Colnaghi's shop to learn the business of picture-dealing.

Nature is always unexpected, Thornley, bounding about like a monkey, and it may be that Lane sprang from tailor-mades right into Salvator Rosa, and up again to Giorgione and Titian. But if I had to choose Lane as the hero of a novel or play, I should proceed more regularly, a transition would be necessary, a little shop in St James's, down some court long ago swept away by an enterprising builder. In my novel there certainly would be a little shop with a window full of old fans and bits of silver, just the kind of shop that you would hang about every afternoon when you came back from the hospital, and I should place Lane in a little den out of which he would come to show you some paste – old paste. I have it, Thornley; cameos and old paste would be the steps whereby Lane mounted from tailor-mades to Salvator Rosa and then on to – whom did I say, Thornley?

Giorgione, the old doctor muttered, laughing in his beard. Two years is long enough. I was five years walking the hospitals.

It was long enough for Lane. When he left Colnaghi's shop and took a lodging in Bury Street, he was able to buy and sell pictures so successfully that in two years he had put together, I think he told me, ten thousand pounds.

Yet you say he is not a dealer; and the old doctor continued to growl by the fireside.

He is a collector who weeds out his collection. Let us call him a weeder; and let us never speak of the lavatory but of the cloak-room or the toilet-room. [. . .]

If you would only meet him you would be converted. [. . .] He has got such pretty ways. When you ask him if he is going to sell a picture he will say: Don't talk to me about selling; I can't bear to part with my pictures. One of these days I shall have a house and shall want pictures; and immediately the conversation will slide away, and you'll find yourself listening to a long tale of a collection of pictures which he intends to present at cost price to some provincial gallery. He is all for Art, and you, who have been talking Art and buying beautiful things all your life, now repudiate the one man who comes to Ireland to revive the art of painting.

It never existed in Ireland.

Never mind. It will be revived all the same.

He's a dealer. He has made, according to you, ten thousand pounds in two years, and a dealer never will miss the chance of picking up something, and you'll find that he will pick up something.

There's no use talking any more. I've spent a very pleasant evening. Good night, Thornley, good night.

Well, you'll see, were his last words, and he was very sarcastic when it became known that Lane had bought a large Lancret from Sir Algernon Coote[5] at the close of the exhibition, and whenever I went in to smoke a cigar with him he referred to this deal with extraordinary bitterness. I could not see what ground of complaint he had against Lane. Sir Algernon Coote, I often said, was glad to get seven or eight hundred, perhaps a thousand for his picture. What concern is it of yours the price the picture fetches afterwards? He growled in his armchair, averring that Lane had no right to ask Sir Algernon Coote to lend him a picture and then to buy it from him. A most extraordinary proposition, I said. If nobody is to make a profit, there can be no buying or selling. Yourself made a profit upon your sale of Wedgwood.

Sir Thornley did not think that this was quite the same thing, and I said, Pooh, pooh.

We had just begun to forget Lane when we heard that he had run across a Tiepolo at Ostend, and had picked up another picture in Antwerp, and for these pictures and Sir Algernon Coote's Lancret he had been paid seventeen thousand pounds by Durand Ruel. He had not taken it all out in cash; Lane's genius lies in swopping. It is a bold man that dares to swop with Durand Ruel, but Lane dares everything, and he got Manet's portrait of Mademoiselle Gonzales [fig. 21] probably cheaper than a private buyer could have gotten it, on the plea that it was going into a permanent exhibition.[6] It came over with a number of Impressionist pictures, lent by different people – Monet, Pissarro, Renoir, Sisley, Berthe Morisot – all the Impressionist school.

And for what object? Sir Thornley cried.

To found a Gallery of Modern Art. Again I set myself to explain Lane to Sir Thornley, without arriving at any results whatever. He would not, or he could not, understand that though it is Lane's instinct to make money it is also his instinct to spend the money that he makes upon Art. Nobody that I have ever met, Thornley, desires Art as purely as Lane. I have known many people who make money out of Art, but it is generally spent on motorcars, women, cooks, and valets. But Lane spends hardly anything upon himself. His whole life is absorbed in Art, and he would not be able to gratify his passion if he did not make money. Why will you not be reconciled to him? Why will you not accept him for what he is? I said again and again. But he remained grumpy, doggedly refusing to become a member of the committee, consenting, however, to visit the exhibition, not being able to resist my description of the portrait of Mademoiselle Gonzales, the *Itinerant Musician* and the other pictures.[7]

A wonderful exhibition it was, organised by Lane, who rushed about Dublin from one end to the other, begging of everybody to come to his exhibition, gathering up the ladies into groups, giving them all something to do, telling one that she must collect subscriptions to buy a certain picture, another one that she must play the piano for him another would oblige him by playing, or trying to play, it did not matter which, a violin solo, the *Kreutzer Sonata*, or anything else she liked. He discovered a young gentleman who sang comic songs very well; for the sake of Art he was asked to sing. Anybody who could write at all was asked to write letters to the papers. Everybody in Dublin was swept into the exhibition, and as soon as the receipts began to decline Lane was again devising some new method whereby they might be revived. So far I had resisted him, and he came one evening to ask me to write an article.

No, ten thousand times no.

Lane laughed, and suggested a lecture.

I am the only one in Dublin who knew Manet, Monet, Sisley, Renoir, Pissarro – I knew them all at the Nouvelle Athènes. Lane, you tempt me.

When will you be able to give the lecture?

A terror came upon me, and I stuttered, When? One has to speak for an

21    Édouard Manet, *Éva Gonzalès*, 1870

hour, an hour and ten minutes, an hour and fifteen minutes. That would make two fortnightly articles at the very least. Oh, Lane!

I'll begin to advertise the lecture to-morrow. You'll have four days to prepare it.

Four days!

And Lane, who is always in a hurry, bade me good night abruptly.

## NOTES

1    For an account of Moore's interest in the visual arts and his time in Paris see Julian Campbell, *The Irish Impressionists*, Dublin, National Gallery of Ireland, 1984, pp. 50–5. For Manet's 1878–9 sketches in oil and pastel of Moore see *Manet, 1832–1883*, New York, The Metropolitan Museum of Art, 1983, nos. 175–6, pp. 424–29.

2    Thomas Bodkin, *Hugh Lane and his Pictures*, Dublin, The Arts Council, 1956, p. 76.

3    Reference is to the British eighteenth-century portraitists Sir Joshua Reynolds (1723–92) and George Romney (1734–1802).

4    Sir William Thornley Stoker (1845–1912), surgeon to Swift's (St Patrick's) Hospital, Dublin, governor of the National Gallery of Ireland and brother of Bram Stoker, the author of *Dracula*. Moore is referring to the *Exhibition of Pictures presented to the City of Dublin to form the nucleus of a Gallery of Modern Art, also pictures lent by the executors of the late Mr J Staats Forbes and others*, which opened in November 1904 in the galleries of the Royal Hibernian Academy, Dublin. See S. B. Kennedy, *Irish Art and Modernism, 1880–1950*, The Institute of Irish Studies at The Queen's University of Belfast, 1991, p. 9, and Lady Gregory, *Sir Hugh Lane, His Life and Legacy*, Gerrards Cross, Colin Smythe, 1973, pp. 58–70.

5    Sir Algernon Coote (1847–1920), Premier Baronet of Ireland, of Ballyfin, Co. Laois.

6    See Martin Davies, *National Gallery Catalogue:.French School*, London, 1970, p. 90; also Kenneth McConkey, 'Some Men and a Picture', in *When Time Began to Rant and Rage: Figurative Painting from Twentieth-Century Ireland*, ed. James Christen Steward, London, Merrell Holberton, 1998, pp. 29–39.

7    Now known as *The Old Musicians*, 1862, National Gallery of Art, Washington, D.C., Chester Dale Collection, see D. Rouart and D. Wildenstein, *Édouard Manet*, Paris, 1975, vol. I, no. 52, p. 62.

# — 38 —

# Hugh Lane, Codicil to his Will, 1915

The Lane Pictures are a group of thirty-nine, largely French nineteenth-century paintings that the Irish connoisseur and dealer Hugh Lane (1875–1915) purchased in the early years of the twentieth century (see also entries 37 and 45). The collection consists of such well-known canvases as Édouard Manet's *Le Concert aux Tuileries* (1862), his portrait of Éva Gonzalès (1870, fig. 21; see also entry 37) and Pierre Renoir's *Les Parapluies* (1881–6), all of which were on show in the Dublin Municipal Gallery of Modern Art from 1908 to 1913. Lane had hoped to bequeath these paintings to Dublin, along with canvases by Gustave Courbet, Berthe Morisot, Edgar Degas and many others, on the condition that the city build a suitable modern art gallery. Owing to a range of petty objections, this was not to be (see entry 36) and in frustration, in late 1913, Lane gave the paintings to the London National Gallery. Although happy to exhibit some of the thirty-nine pictures, London was as hesitant as Dublin in displaying modern French paintings. Angered by this turn of events, Lane attempted to reverse his will and bequeath the paintings back to Dublin. He duly changed the will but failed to have it witnessed. He was drowned on 5 May 1915 when the *Lusitania* was torpedoed during World War I. The result was that London's National Gallery kept the paintings. Many cases were made to return the pictures to Ireland, the initial request being led by Lane's aunt Lady Augusta Gregory (1859–1932), W.B.Yeats and Thomas Bodkin (see entry 39). Over the years, a variety of agreements were reached which allowed the paintings to be seen in both capitals. By the 1980s the situation had become intolerable, leading to the comment that the paintings were being 'shuttled from one [gallery] to the other like children of divorced parents'.[1] Finally, in 1993 a more satisfactory arrangement was made allowing for certain paintings to stay in each city for a lengthy period of time.[2]

Source: Thomas Bodkin, *Hugh Lane and His Pictures,* Dublin, The Arts Council, 1956, p. 43

### 3RD FEBRUARY, 1915

This is a codicil to my last will to the effect that the group of pictures now at the London National Gallery, which I had bequeathed to that Institution, I now bequeath to the City of Dublin, providing that a suitable building is provided for them within five years of my death. The group of pictures I have lent to Belfast I give to the Municipal Gallery in Harcourt Street. If a building is provided within five years, the whole collection will be housed together. The sole Trustee in this question is to be my aunt, Lady Gregory. She is to appoint any additional Trustees she may think fit. I also wish that the pictures now on loan at this (National Gallery of Ireland) Gallery remain as my gift.

Hugh Lane.

I would like my friend Tom Bodkin to be asked to help in the obtaining of this new Gallery of Modern Art for Dublin.

If within five years a Gallery is not forthcoming, then the group of pictures (at the London National Gallery) are to be sold, and the proceeds go to fulfil the purpose of my will.

Hugh Lane.
3rd February, 1915

## NOTES

1    'Editorial', *The Burlington Magazine*, CXXVI, March 1984, p. 131. The author of this comment, Neil McGregor, is presently Director of the National Gallery, London.

2    For details see Barbara Dawson, 'Hugh Lane and the Origins of the Collection', in Hugh Lane Municipal Gallery of Modern Art, *Images and Insights*, Dublin, 1993, p. 30.

— 39 —

# Thomas Bodkin, *Irish Free State,*<br>*Official Handbook,* 1932

An art historian and museum director, Thomas Bodkin (1887–1961), played a leading role in trying to achieve the return of the Hugh Lane pictures to Ireland and wrote an official government publication on the issue.[1] Director of the National Gallery of Ireland from 1927 to 1935, he went on to become founding director of the Barber Institute for Fine Arts, University of Birmingham. While at the National Gallery, Bodkin contributed a section on 'Modern Irish Art' to the *Irish Free State, Official Handbook,* a publication described by the newly elected President of the Executive Council, Eamon de Valera (1882–1975), as a 'spendid specimen of Irish printing and Irish production'. The editor of the *Handbook* stated confidently in his introduction that it provided 'an account of the Irish Free State as it is to-day'.[2] Throughout, the book conveys a highly traditionalist view of Ireland, the frontispiece carrying Paul Henry's landscape of *Errigal,* a forbidding quartzite cone in

Co. Donegal, while the interior of the book is decorated with a range of woodcuts and drawings showing dolmens, medieval churches and great eighteenth-century houses.

Source: Saorstát Eireann/*Irish Free State, Official Handbook*, Dublin, The Talbot Press, 1932, pp. 239–44

The arts of painting and sculpture only flourish in communities that enjoy peace and prosperity. The Free State has not yet been established for a sufficient time to redeem the promise of those Irish artists who, in the eighth century, won for their country a pre-eminence in illuminated manuscripts and precious metal work over all the other nations of Europe. The intervening dark ages of turmoil and misery effectively prevented the development of a distinctively Irish School of Fine Art.[3] [. . .]

Signs are not wanting to show that the Irish people recognise their backwardness in these respects and are resolved to advance. The Royal D[ublin] S[ociety] has recently decided to offer substantial encouragement to designers. The Haverty Bequest provides attractive prizes for Irish painters working in Ireland. The example of foreign countries, such as Sweden, in successfully applying art to industry, is not lost upon Irish intelligence. Many of us have asked ourselves how it is that the Swedish firm which a few decades ago manufactured nothing but a small supply of coarse glass bottles, can now turn out glass ware in enormous quantities, which are eagerly sought for, at high prices, by connoisseurs everywhere, and has made the name of Orrefors famous. We realise that the Ringsend Bottle Factory collapsed while the Orrefors Bottle Factory flourished, because the latter appreciated the prime importance of good design.

There are well-equipped Schools of Art under Government control in Dublin, Cork, Limerick and Galway; but they still suffer from a lack of public encouragement, and have great difficulty in recruiting pupils with sufficient preliminary training. Drawing is not yet systematically taught in many Irish schools. Neither of the two Universities in the Irish Free State has fully awakened to the necessity of devoting serious attention to the study of art history or aesthetics. We have had so many vital problems to deal with in the last few years that we may well be excused for having allowed the problem of art to bide awhile; and the Government can claim that public opinion has hitherto been turned towards what we have too often supposed to be more urgent realities.

We are now, at last, ready to deal with the situation; and it is not an idle dream to hope that within a few years travellers will seek, confidently, poplins in Dublin as beautiful as the silk tissues of Lyons, porcelain figures in Belleek as elegant as those of Copenhagen, and carpets in Donegal as rich and lasting as those of Persia; and that this nation, once so distinguished in the practice of the arts, will recreate a national art of its own, not based on out-worn styles and lost endeavours, but reflecting the energetic aspirations and enthusiasms of a reborn race.

## NOTES

1    See Thomas Bodkin, *Hugh Lane and His Pictures*, Dublin, The Arts Council, 1956.
2    Bulmer Hobson, Introduction, Saorstát Eireann/Irish Free State, *Official Handbook*, Dublin, The Talbot Press, 1932, p. 15. De Valera quoted by Brian P. Kennedy in 'The Irish Free State, 1922–49: A Visual Perspective', *Ireland: Art into History*, eds. R. Gillespie and B.P. Kennedy, Dublin, Town House, 1994, p. 145.
3    Bodkin goes on to list various Irish artists from the eighteenth century onwards as well as discuss the foundation of the National Gallery of Ireland and the saga of the Lane pictures.

# — 40 —

# Ciarán Benson, *The Place of the Arts in Irish Education*, 1979

Ciarán Benson, former Chair of *An Chomhairle Ealaíon*, The Arts Council, is also Professor of Psychology at University College Dublin. In 1979, as Education Officer for the Arts Council, he produced a seminal report on *The Place of the Arts in Irish Education*, which was published by the Council. He had requested submissions from the public and interested parties and conducted a wide range of interviews. The publication was the end product of the Arts Council's Working Party on the Arts in Education, which met under the direction of Professor Seán Ó Tuama, Professor of Modern Irish at University College Cork. The report was accepted by the Arts Council in December 1978. Benson traces the history of the place of the arts in Irish education, the focus of the excerpt included here; he then goes on to outline training and facilities for the arts and concludes by offering some ten

pages of recommendations for change. Blame for neglect of the arts in education is specifically levelled at the Department of Education.

Source: The Arts Council, *The Place of the Arts in Irish Education*, Dublin, 1979, sections 1.8 to 1.33, pp. 16–26. Benson's notes have been retained; the text was originally presented in outline numbered paragraphs, which have been removed.

### The Historical Place of the Arts in Irish Education

In recent centuries the arts have not occupied a central position in Irish school
curricula. In the era of mass-education during the nineteenth century, the
thrust of policy for the national school system was towards the development of
literacy in the English language and the attainment of a certain level of numer-
acy. With the introduction of the payment-by-results policy in 1872, considerable improvements in these areas were recorded but on the basis of a narrow
3R type curriculum and through teaching and inspection procedures which
tended to be rigid, formal and uninspiring. The provision of a basic minimum
education for everybody was the aim, and quantity (rather than quality) was
uppermost in the minds of the policymakers. The year 1900 saw a radically different programme introduced for national schools, based on a more child-cen-
tred approach. This was a wide-ranging programme which made singing,
drawing and physical education obligatory subjects in the national school.
Many factors, however, impeded the full implementation of this programme.

With the establishment of the Irish Free State a radical change again
occurred, which resulted in a narrowing of the programme, including the
dropping of drawing and physical education as obligatory subjects. The main
concern of curricular policy following independence was the restoration of
the Irish language and great emphasis was placed on the school's role in
bringing this about. One of the beneficial results of the new state policy was
that literature in the Irish language got a level of attention which had not
been facilitated or encouraged under the previous administration. Ireland had
a very large number of national schools (for a declining population) many of
which were very small and many of which suffered from inadequate fund-
ing, resources and maintenance. The tradition of school attendance was poor
though improvements followed the rather belated legislation of 1926 on
compulsory school attendance.

The curriculum for national schools devised in the early years of the Irish
Free State remained in being, with only minor alterations, until the new curriculum of 1971 was introduced. The programme tended to be narrow, with
Irish, English, arithmetic and singing forming the main core, while some history, geography and algebra was taught in senior classes. The introduction of

a compulsory primary certificate in 1943, involving written examinations in the three subjects Irish, English and arithmetic, tended to narrow the focus of the programme. Scholarship examinations, though including a wider subject range, acted as further pressure to edge out artistic or aesthetic subjects in national schools.

The new curriculum of 1971, accompanied by other developments, has changed considerably the philosophy, approach and atmosphere of primary education. The inclusion of imaginative programmes in music, art & craft, drama and mime activities, physical education and dance, as integral parts of the curriculum, heralded a new era in Irish national education. The equipping of many schools with tape-recorders, record-players, slide and film projectors, TV sets, school libraries etc., as well as improved school design, may have a revolutionary effect on the schools when contrasted with the experience of former generations in Irish society. The potential for great advance is there. [ . . . ]

Until quite recently in Irish society, experience of post-primary education, particularly in any extended sense, was confined to a small minority of the population. The intermediate schools, established and run by private individuals and religious societies in the nineteenth century, largely followed the humanist curriculum of the Renaissance tradition, with its emphasis on the classics and literary studies. When, through the Intermediate Education Act of 1878, the state intervened to give some financial support to intermediate education, this trend was further endorsed. The marks and fees allotted, as well as the mode of examination, were all unfavourable to the study of artistic subjects.

For almost half a century, until 1924, the dead hand of the payment-by-results system hung over intermediate education. While science benefited from changes introduced after 1900, arts subjects continued to be under-emphasised if not seriously neglected. Certainly if aesthetic education is regarded as integral to a balanced education then the characterisation of the system as 'the murder machine' was all too true.

When, in 1924, the results system was abolished and replaced by the Intermediate and Leaving Certificate examinations, new programmes were introduced which allowed more elasticity in courses and more scope for teachers in the selection of texts. Yet the basic pattern of curricular imbalance continued with art and music on the periphery of secondary schooling. Even as late as 1962/63 the weak position of these subjects emerged strikingly from the analyses carried out by the Investment in Education team, whose conclusion was: 'The curriculum in a great many schools is limited and is of a classical grammar school type. Small schools, in particular, appear to have difficulty in providing a varied course.'[1]

The establishment of the Department of Agriculture and Technical Instruction in 1899 provided an authority sympathetic to the development of agricultural and technical training. Under its auspices, forms of technical education and crafts were given a new support and importance. However, while it was the educational rather than the utility aspect of such crafts which was stressed, the Department was more directed to technical training rather than cultivation of art as such. The Vocational Education Act of 1930 led to a reorganisation and expansion of vocational and technical education and helped to equip many young people with craft skills as well as some general education.

This brief historical review paints a rather bleak picture of the position the arts have occupied in the formal school system in Ireland. Such a picture, however, does not do justice to the often heroic and inspirational work of many individuals within the system, who helped young people to an appreciation of the arts and fostered their creativity. It is also true that by means of various extra-curricular activities some pupils were encouraged to participate in the arts.

Educational systems are closely interlocked with wider political, economic, social and moral elements of the society at large, and at certain stages of development school systems can only achieve limited goals, and the place occupied by artistic subjects in the scale of priorities may not be high.

Many circumstances conspired to keep the artistic subjects off the centre of the stage in Irish education, an important one being the harsh economic conditions which prevailed for much of the time and which manifested themselves in many ways.

The majority of Irish post-primary schools were very small. In its survey of secondary schools which admitted day pupils, the Investment in Education report showed that 63% of them had under 150 pupils while 73% of vocational day schools had less than 150 pupils. Thus the size, equipment, facilities and staff qualifications of many schools were a further severe hindrance to the introduction of a balanced post-primary curriculum in which the arts might play a significant rôle.

The many significant initiatives and developments which have taken place in Irish post-primary education in recent years combine to reflect, as is the case in the primary system, a much changed and more favourable framework for the proper cultivation of aesthetic education as part of the pupil's general education. Many of the secondary and vocational schools have been expanded and, in some instances, amalgamated. New forms of post-primary school, such as comprehensive and community schools, have appeared on the scene. The massive expansion in pupil enrolment and consequent increase in the teaching force have made a wide curriculum much

more viable in many schools. Indeed the concept of comprehensive education which was officially espoused, lays great stress on the availability of a
wide curriculum allowing scope for the varied talents and abilities of the
student body. The concept of the community school further enlarges the
traditional view of the school to encompass wide-ranging inter-relation-
ships between the school and community at large. The provision of radically improved facilities in the form of auditoria, libraries, leisure facilities,
gymnasia and audio–visual equipment is seen as an investment not just for
the school-going population but for the benefit of the wider community
also. The influence of changed thinking is not, of course, confined to the
purpose-built community schools, but has its effects on all schools. It is,
however, true to say that no magic wand has changed the structure of the
majority of our schools, many of which still suffer from over-crowding, pre-
fabricated buildings, poor equipment etc. Yet in general, there are many
hopeful signs that Irish post-primary education is on the verge of an interesting and exciting era.

Specialist training in the arts at third level has also suffered from neglect.
It was not until the publication in 1961 of the Scandinavian report, *Design in
Ireland*, that the seriousness of the neglect of design was fully realised – a real-
isation which eventually led to constructive change. Student unrest in the
National College of Art, in 1968, and the accompanying public focus on the
College, led subsequently to a restructuring of the College in 1971.[2] The last
decade saw more development in art and design education in Ireland than did
the previous half century. The establishment of the Art and Design Board of
Studies by the National Council for Educational Awards was of major significance and has been an integral part of this development. [. . .]

## AN ARGUMENT FOR CHANGE

Regrettably, there is a particular stereotype of the arts in many Irish schools.
The arts are seen as more suitable for girls than for boys, and for the less intelligent rather than for the more intelligent pupils. They are often judged to be
more interesting than useful, and their most significant contribution is frequently conceived of as a pleasant means of passing time. It is no accident that
Friday afternoon is such a popular time for art and craft in the primary
school. This stereotype, though commonly held, is the result of a self-fulfill-
ing prophecy. A set of subjects regarded and treated as unimportant will
become peripheral in the curriculum. It is not sufficient, however, simply to
assert that the arts should assume a more central position in the curriculum.
Good arguments are needed for any field of study before it receives even part

of the money and resources that its proponents feel it deserves. Educational-ists and policy-makers must be urgently persuaded that the arts have a seri-ous and unique contribution to make to education.

As a social instrument it is the task of education to introduce the young to the general culture of their society and to prepare them for a place in it. In our society it is accepted that everyone should have access to education, at least up to the age of 15, and that it is the responsibility of the state to pro-vide it. Every child should have adequate educational access to the artistic heritage both of his own society and of mankind in general. The state must strive to provide this access for young people and support other agencies which are trying to provide facilities and opportunities. To the extent that the state fails to do this it is failing in its responsibility to the young.

The arts in education have richly benefited from the development of tech-nology. Fifty years ago, access to works of art was limited to those who could visit them in person. Technology has not only assisted existing art forms but has created many new ones such as film. An increasing use of technology by present and coming generations of artists will be one of the most important features of future artistic developments. There is now enormous democratic access to the arts in the form of slides and prints, of records and cassettes, of films, radio, television and video systems. These have made the arts available to greater numbers of people than ever before.

This has very important implications for education. Teachers now have great opportunities to introduce young people to the arts. But education must prepare young people to cope critically with the vast range of art now accessible to them. The instantaneous availability of images and sounds means that teaching methods and even the conception of the arts as 'subjects' must be re-examined. The integration of different art forms, as occurs for exam-ple in film, will become more common.

This revolutionary change means that schools must prepare critical audi-ences for the arts and regard this objective as vitally important. In general, this change, which has only begun to be felt in Irish society in the last twenty years, presents an unavoidable challenge to education, a challenge which if well met could bring the arts to a level of popular appreciation undreamed of before. Alternatively, if the education system does not make every effort to develop critical perspectives in the young, then Ireland may be faced with a future public which, far from fruitfully exploiting the opportunities available to it, may be characterised by a uniform mediocrity of taste controlled by commercial interests. The best, because less popular and more difficult to appreciate, will become less available and a major cultural opportunity will have been lost. As yet, there is little evidence of a recognition of this process within the education system, and official policy has not come to grips with the significance of the changed circumstances. No serious initiatives have been taken to ensure that the education system is in a position to draw maximum advantage from the opportunities available. There is a need for greater vision in the design of policy, and a greater commitment from many sides of the education system to the importance of the arts in our society.

The arts have a major educational contribution to make in enabling young people, and indeed adults, to learn how to cope with the rapid advance in communications. This is because the skills required to understand what a work of art is 'communicating' are of a different type to those needed for most other subjects in the curriculum.[3]

The content of most subjects in the curriculum can be well communicated by a teacher because this content is capable of being logically included in and organised by words or numbers. The position is essentially different, however, when a painter or a sculptor or a musician makes something. The visual artist or the musician does not seek to communicate in the modes that are most familiar to children i.e., words or perhaps numbers. The child looking at, listening to or even reading a work of art needs to develop the necessary sensitivities to derive the meanings and intentions of the artist. An education in the arts can provide one of the best opportunities for training in the skills needed to interpret the complex situations so frequently presented or re-presented by today's forms of mass-communication. This is an obviously valuable skill, and particularly so in a culture which is increasingly dependent for communication on audio–visual media. When it is realised that there is no image, be it photograph or film, that is not by the very nature of the process a construction or a fabrication then the full implications of the need for such skills in an educated public becomes apparent.

The educational value of the arts is often conceived of in terms of the 'well-rounded education'. This view tends to regard the pupil in a rather fragmented way as having intellectual, affective, physical, social and moral needs. Subjects such as mathematics and science, languages and history are seen to develop his intellectual potential while the arts are conceived as 'rounding off' in the affective areas. This conception of the pupil as being largely composed of separate areas each of which can be dealt with more or less separately by different sets of subjects is a gross over-simplification which can have damaging implications. Science and art are often conceived of in opposition: sport and art are rarely associated in the popular imagination. It is increasingly recognised in educational practice that thinking and feeling, personal interests and achievements etc. are all intimately linked and must be considered as such when developing educational programmes. This is a key aspect of the child–centred movement in education.

In this context the arts are seen as contributing as much to a person's education as any other curricular area. Their contribution can be as great to intellectual development as to the development of feeling and of sensory and manual skills. A proper aesthetic judgement is a very high-level achievement. Consequently the arts can make a wider contribution to the education of persons than is often imagined: a contribution whose importance has increased rather than diminished with the advances of science and technology.

As well as contributing to the personal development of young people, the arts can play (and often have played) a key rôle in imaginative and flexible educational programmes. For example, any attempt to deal with the history of man and his development (especially before the advent of photography and film) inevitably turns to art for its images and for clues to the past, whether these be carvings, pictures, poems, music, dances or buildings. Art is a repository of the myriad expressions of recurring themes in human thought, feeling and action. The greatest works of art, together with those of science, philosophy or religion, represent man's highest reaches of imagination and creativity. The arts provide a unique resource that can greatly enhance the teaching of subjects in other curricular areas. In a more general way art can assist in the making of an aesthetically alert educational environment by contributing to book design and illustration, the design of buildings, furniture and equipment etc.

In the wider perspective of adult and community education the arts can provide opportunities for social and personal development as well as those benefits gained by becoming proficient in a particular art form.

Anything which increases an individual's ability to make sense of and order his experience, and anything that enables an individual to communicate the subtleties of his experience to another person is desirable. The arts can provide images, symbols and themes for the expression of personal experience which might well lie beyond the ability of most individuals to create for themselves. In this sense a familiarity with the arts can provide a form of language which can assist communication across the divisions of class, religion and nationality.

The arts can enrich individual lives in yet another related sense. Because life is short and limited in opportunities for experience, a well-grounded sympathetic understanding of the lives of other people in different circumstances, times or places is difficult to achieve. Yet in a period of world history such as the present, demanding a greater mutual trust between peoples and communities, this understanding is essential. The arts can valuably assist the growth of this understanding. They can provide an individual with vicarious experiences (through writings and films, music and paintings etc.) of a vast range of lives and circumstances beyond the scope of any one person to experience for himself, and in this way they can provide a uniquely rich and relevant basis for understanding. This is particularly so when we recall that art is a means of understanding society and of presenting to it an interpretation of specific aspects of itself.

Within a community the presence of a creative artist can have a very enhancing effect. The artist can provide new eyes for a community to look at itself. The works of a creative artist in any situation, however drab, dismal or depressing, can provide a sense of value and pride in a community which might not otherwise have felt it. The result can be that whole landscapes come to be seen through the eyes of a single writer or painter. The interpretative rôle of the artist is evident here as well as the capacity of the arts to heighten our sensitivity to aspects of environment which are obscured by familiarity.

One of the strongest and most frequently voiced arguments for a greater inclusion of the arts at all levels of education is that a preparation must be given to people for the coming age of increasing leisure. The arts are seen here as providing one valuable way in which people can occupy their leisure time. There is a danger here, however, that the present peripheral rôle of the arts will be confirmed by its association with the present widely accepted idea of leisure.[4] Basically, 'leisure' is that time not occupied by 'work'. Leisure is a time to be 'enjoyed' and is therefore less serious and less valuable than work. Indeed leisure is often interpreted to mean 'lazing around'. Work is thought of as being in some way morally superior to leisure. Through their historical association with the leisure of the nobility and the wealthy, the arts have also tended to acquire the connotation of being rather self-indulgent. This distinction between work and leisure is a very damaging one when used as the basis for planning a curriculum and for dividing it into 'work-subjects' and 'leisure-subjects'.

Any argument that proposes a more central rôle for the arts in the education of the community, both young and adult, must, because of the problems presented by increased leisure time in society, take account of the implications above. What is really needed is a concept of leisure as something valuable in itself and not as something contrasted with work. Leisure time must be seen as being capable of employing a person's full range of talents and energies in a manner that is as productive in its own way as work. In that sense the arts can make the valuable contribution claimed for them.

In a small, developing country such as Ireland, the economic viability of the arts is very important and any investment which helps the arts to pay for themselves is a sound use of money and resources. Investment in the arts in education means investing in the audiences of the future. Without such audiences national theatres, dance companies, orchestras and other state-aided arts groups would find their professional existence precarious. If, as it does, the state considers the arts a valuable part of society deserving of state support, then it must also ensure that it is providing the necessary education to create critical and appreciative audiences. The interaction of all appreciative public with the arts provides the vital basis for high standards as well as for the economic development of the arts. It means also that state-supported enterprises in, for example, the crafts area, could look forward to a more receptive home market.

Those convinced of their value will need no arguments as to why the arts deserve a more central position in education. For them, the most forceful reason is the simplest one. Participation in or appreciation of the arts can be a most enjoyable and stimulating experience which adds a new dimension to life. If the development of the arts in education means adding a new quality of excitement, involvement and growth to the lives of young people and adults then that is justification enough for any curricular area.

## CONCLUSION

This chapter has briefly reviewed the rôle of art in society and in Irish society in particular. It has suggested that art is a means whereby a society can reflect on itself, on its traditions and directions of development: that it also plays a central rôle in enabling members of a society to transcend mundane life. Art in Irish society has played both rôles, but often in the service of two different traditions (frequently indifferent to each other) i.e. the native Irish and the Anglo-Irish traditions. Because of the political, economic and social factors in Irish history, the various art forms tend to be viewed differently within the country today. The visual arts, classical music, opera and ballet carry with them associations of exclusiveness which are not so characteristic of literature, or traditional music and dance. Within the Irish system of education, the arts, apart perhaps from literature, have traditionally been a neglected area. Our education system is best considered as one more typical of a developing post-colonial nation than of a wealthy western European nation. The historical difficulties confronting the developing school system have for long prevented the arts from playing a significant part in Irish education. However, many changes have occurred within the education system which would now seem to allow a much more favourable environment in which the arts might flourish and assume their rightful place as a central concern of our educational process.

## NOTES

1    *Investment in Education: Report*, Dublin, Stationery Office, 1965, p. 280, par. 10.26. [Orig. note.]

2    For *Design in Ireland* report of the 1961 and the 1968 student unrest see John Turpin, *A School of Art in Dublin since the Eighteenth Century*, Dublin, Gill and Macmillan, 1995, Chapter 24 and 27–28.

3    L.R. Perry, 'Education in the Arts', in D. Field and J. Newick (eds.) *The Study of Education and Art*, London, Routledge & Kegan Paul, 1973. [Orig. note.]

4    See Perry [ibid.] [Orig. note.]

*Display*

# — 41 —

## William Drennan and Martha McTier Letters, 1797–1807

The United Irishman Dr William Drennan (1754–1820) and his equally rad-
icalized sister, Martha McTier (1742–1837), maintained a copious correspondence between 1776 and 1819. Both were born in Belfast, the children
of a Presbyterian minister.[1] Drennan studied medicine in Scotland and spent
many years practising in Newry and Dublin. McTier stayed in Belfast and
married a local merchant. Because of his involvement in radical politics,
Drennan was tried for sedition in 1794 but went on to write on reform and
later penned the well-known poem *The Wake of William Orr*. In Dublin,
Drennan knew everyone, and his letters and those of his sister offer a fascinating account of intellectual and radical life in Dublin and Belfast during a
politically active time. Portraiture, both private and public, is occasionally discussed in their correspondence. Three extracts from the letters are included
here; the first two, from Drennan to his sister, date from 1797–8 while the
third, from McTier to her brother, dates from 1807. In the first letter (a),
Drennan describes a visit to the studio of Dublin's leading portraitist, Hugh
Douglas Hamilton (1740–1808), where he views a large painting in progress
of the celebrated charity preacher Walter Blake Kirwan (1754–1805; fig. 22;
see also entries 29 and 42).[2] In the second letter (b), Drennan discusses portraiture in general while in the third letter (c), McTier tells of a visit to the

Belfast studio of the artist Thomas Robinson (d. 1810), who wished to include Drennan in a large historical painting.

Source: The Drennan–McTier Letters are in the Public Record Office of Northern Ireland, Belfast (D/591); the extracts from the three letters quoted here are numbers 716, 727 and 1347 in *The Drennan-McTier Letters*, 3 vols., ed. Jean Agnew, gen. ed. Maria Luddy, Dublin, The Women's History Project and Irish Manuscripts Commission, 1998–9. Some contemporary contractions have been expanded.

### A) DR WILLIAM DRENNAN, DUBLIN, TO MRS MARTHA MCTIER, BELFAST

*20 November 1797*

[McTier had sent her brother a description of Dean Walter Blake Kirwan] I think you need not have sent the description of Kirwan – it is stiff. His portrait is taken here by Hamilton at full length in attitude of invocation for the poor children some of whom are at his feet [fig. 22], one sleeping. The tears glisten in his eyes, his lips are touched with fire – yet he resembles his picture as much as it does him – He is painted and it is so – The last sermon I heard from him was a hypocritical adulation of Castle politics.[3] His picture is to cost 100 guineas, to be placed in the Orphan School, and is paid for by some of the Latouche family – You would like to see these pictures. *Three* of Lord Moira – all very like, and all very like Don Quixote – I never saw his Lordship – O'Connor – Lord Edward very spirited – his lady twice, in one likeness, or rather, sketch (think of it), as a Medusa, with snakes round her head and falling on her bosom[4]– I think it ill-judged, though Medusa was a fair Lady – Perhaps it was a vagary of the painters – I have attended her child who has had the whooping cough. Her manner is very natural. The last of the visits I paid, she came from a place they reside at near the Rock to Leinster House, now vacant, the Duchess being at Bristol – She came in a foggy Morning with the nurse and child, *in one of the common 'Rock cars'* which she would get for three sixpences – The daughter of the Duke of Orleans[5], worth £150,000 a year, and whom a gentleman with me by chance at the time, while she passed by assured me he saw in a coach and six surrounded by servants, and saluted by all the *gardes du corps* in Paris, as she passed along their line. Her father, unhappy man, rode once in a cart, and when the mob cried is that the Duke of Orleans? – Yes – said he – the very man – I do firmly believe his daughter and her Lord are poorer than I am – of the very first families in France and Ireland. Why should I complain?

22    William Ward after Hugh Douglas Hamilton, *Rev. Walter Blake Kirwan Pleading the Cause of the Destitute Orphans of Dublin*, 1806 (after the original oil of 1797)

## B) Dr William Drennan, Dame St, Dublin, to Mrs Martha McTier, Belfast

*13 February 1798*
These portraitures always flatter, as for example, I saw yesterday in Allen's print shop, a reduced likeness taken lately from the original picture in Belfast. It was handsome, a fine mahogany, manly complexion, eyes penetrating, hair sportively scattered on the forehead and temples – and through this disguise, I instantly recognised *my* old friend Waddell Cunningham, for *David* was

yours. Allen told me that he himself (not the heir, nor even yet the widow), but he himself had sent down a person to make a copy from the original taken by Home, in order to get an engraving made from it in London, and thus coin Cunningham's countenance for the pleasure of his friends – and his own profit.[6] He said he was sure it would sell, certainly, said I with one of my cynical smiles, as *you* have christened them, and I then began to think that one posthumous fame is much like another and that fame itself is little else than the oyster shell in my picture which reveals the deep mystery of this my meditation, so long the puzzle of your little public and my learned friend the Doctor.[7] And thence I might put the question, and say to my sister whether would you rather (as children speak it), whether would you rather have me sink down quietly into public insignificance rising into somewhat of domestic enjoyment, or be devoted on the public stage (of what kind of materials that stage may be made, being extremely uncertain) by giving free scope to those powers I certainly do in some degree possess and more so than lately you seemed inclined to give me credit for.

### c) MRS MCTIER, BELFAST, TO DR WILLIAM DRENNAN, 33 MARLBOROUGH STREET, DUBLIN

*1 March 1807*
Mrs Bruce[8] delivered a message to me from Robinson, the painter, requesting as a particular favour, that I would allow him to copy Home's picture of you and place it in that he is doing of the review in Belfast of the yeomanry by Lord Hardwicke, and she added, 'there is a *poet's* corner for the Doctor.'[9] I gave no answer, but, as numbers were going daily to see the picture, I went the next day at an early hour and found Robinson alone. He gave me the history of the picture, which he said, arose from the talk and puffing of that taste for the fine arts which was said to have arisen here; that his plan had been mentioned to the Donegalls, who appeared so pleased with it that he had little doubt they would be the purchasers. *That* was now over; it had cost him much time and trouble, and he had told William Sinclaire he believed he would not finish it. S[inclaire] desired him to do it and that *he* would take care he should not be a loser, probably meaning to be himself the purchaser. *This* also was over, and I believe his only hope is that somehow it will be bought for the Exchange Room.

He is an interesting, sensible man, of great simplicity, and *very poor*, befriended by Bruce, Joy, Williamson, etc.[10] He told me he had long wished to know *you*, & for this purpose had gone twice to Dr B[ruce]s [. . .] He told me Dr B[ruce], Joy, and many others wished much to have you in the picture

– but *Joy* said he *feared* Mrs McTier w[oul]d not consent. And *why* said I, did Joy think I wanted roses and lilies – or – is it possible he suspected I w[oul]d not place you with lilies yeo[manry]. R[obinson] declared he did not *know*, and I said I wished to learn only as Joy was a *wise* man he might suggest a *proper* reason. R[obinson] begg[e]d I might not mention this. I ask[e]d him where he meant to place you. – 'Why – there is room here'– pointing to Drummond Armstrong with Romney leaning on him, Stewart on Love, and Dr *McDonnell*. 'and why not Bruce here' I said – he did not like it, saying it w[oul]d seem *vain*, exactly my opinion, *I* w[oul]d not have my friend *there*. 'Here there is room for a head in this group of Dr B[ruce], Mrs N[arcissus], Batt, Miss Lyle and John Sinclair[e], I will write and ask my Brothers leave.' No, he is a modest man and may deny it, let me do it and if he does not approve of it I promise to brush it away. He has got the picture. B[ruce] was there and desires it may not be made so dark.[11]

## NOTES

1    See Maria Luddy, 'Martha McTier and William Drennan: A 'Domestic' History', in *The Drennan–McTier Letters*, ed. Jean Agnew, gen. ed. Maria Luddy, Dublin, The Women's History Project and Irish Manuscripts Commission, 1998–9, 3 vols., vol. I, xxix–li.

2    The oil painting was destroyed in London during World War II and is now known only by means of William Ward's mezzotint published in 1806; see Fintan Cullen, '"The Cloak of Charity": The politics of representation in late eighteenth-century Ireland', *The Irish Review*, No. 21, 1997, pp. 66–64.

3    The letters make many references to Kirwan, see *The Drennan-McTier Letters*, I, pp. 529–30, where McTier describes attending one of Kirwan's sermons.

4    The portraits of the liberal Lord Moira and the United Irishmen, Lord Edward FitzGerald and Arthur O'Connor have survived, while the one of Lady Pamela FitzGerald has not been traced, see Fintan Cullen, 'The Oil Paintings of Hugh Douglas Hamilton', *The Walpole Society*, 50, 1984, pp. 187–8, 195–7, and his essay 'Radicals and Reactionaries: Portraits of the 1790s in Ireland', in *Revolution, Counter Revolution and Union: Ireland in the 1790s*, ed. Jim Smyth, Cambridge University Press (forthcoming).

5    The FitzGeralds lived at Frascati House, Blackrock, Co. Dublin. Pamela FitzGerald (1773–1831) was the adopted daughter of Philippe 'Égalité' (1747–93), cousin of Louis XVI.

6    A liberal, Waddell Cunningham (*c.* 1729–97) was a successful Belfast businessman who in 1784 challenged Lord Donegall's political hold on the city. Drennan is refer-ring to William Ward's engraving after Robert Home's painting, a version of which with the sitter in a Volunteer's uniform appears in *Up in Arms: The 1798 Rebellion in Ireland: A Bicentenary Exhibition*, Belfast, Ulster Museum, 1998, p. 54; see also Eileen Black, *Irish Oil Paintings, 1572–c. 1830*, Belfast, Ulster Museum, 1991, pp. 35–7, and *The Drennan–McTier Letters*, vol. I, illustrated, p. 80, and reference, p. 259. Robert Home (d. 1836?) was an English portrait painter active in Ireland in the 1780s.

7    An oyster shell inscribed in Greek appears in the foreground of Robert Home's portrait of Drennan (painted in December 1786), now in the Ulster Museum, reproduced in *Up in Arms*, Ulster Museum, 1998, p. 89; see also *The Drennan–McTier Letters*, vol. I, p. 259. The 'Doctor' is Alexander Haliday (1728–1802), a leading Belfast physician.

8    Susanna Bruce, wife of Rev. William Bruce, a Belfast Presbyterian minister.

9    Thomas Robinson is particularly remembered for his large painting of the *Battle of Ballynahinch* (1798, Office of Public Works, Ireland, on loan to Malahide Castle, Dublin). The painting being referred to here is his *Review of the Belfast Yeomanry by the Lord Lieutenant, the Earl of Hardwicke, 27 August 1804*, later renamed *A Military Procession in Belfast in Honour of Lord Nelson* (1804–7, Belfast Harbour Commissioners), see Eileen Black, *Paintings, Sculptures and Bronzes in the Collection of The Belfast Harbour Commissioners*, Belfast, 1983, pp. 37–8, a key is reproduced on p. 97; see also Anne Crookshank and the Knight of Glin, *The Painters of Ireland, c. 1660-1920*, London, Barrie and Jenkins, 1978, pp. 166–9. Drennan's portrait seems to have been painted out at a later date.

10    The 2nd Marquess (and Marchioness) of Donegall, one of Ireland's great landowners (George Augustus Chicester, 1769–1844). Donegall's estates included the whole town of Belfast; his family had built the Exchange, referred to in the letter, and other distinguished buildings. William Sinclaire (1758–1807) was a local merchant but had died a month earlier. Robinson never found a buyer for the painting and it was presented to the Belfast Harbour Commissioners by the artist's son in 1852. Other references are to the Rev. Dr William Bruce (1757–1841; see also note 8), once a close friend of Drennan's and possibly Henry Joy (1754–1835), proprietor of the *Belfast News-letter*.

11    Drennan's reaction to being included was not favourable: 'I don't care not even the value of my old slipper about it, or how you will think proper to dispose of my exaggerated likeness, but I fancy you will find it awkwardly done and out of place' (5 March 1807, *The Drennan–McTier Letters*, vol. 3, p. 581, a detail from Robinson's painting is on p. 580).

# — 42 —

# *Dublin Evening Post*, 1800–4

Public art exhibition in Dublin began in 1765 under the auspices of the Society of Artists with a display at Napper's Room, George's Lane. Exhibitions continued almost annually until 1780. After a twenty-year lapse, in 1800, the renamed Society of Artists of Ireland organized a series of annual exhibitions, but Dublin was now a changed place: parliamentary Union was in the air, a rebellion had been recently crushed and the city was altogether a more muted capital. The exhibitions, mounted in Allen's print shop at 32 Dame Street, attracted journalistic attention, examples of which are included below. The concentration here is on paintings exhibited by Hugh Douglas Hamilton (1740–1808) in the years 1800 and 1804. As Dublin's leading portrait painter, Hamilton satisfied all shades of opinion. He enjoyed commissions from the United Irishman Lord Edward FitzGerald and other liberal aristocrats such as the Earl of Moira (see also entry 41), as well as members of the Dublin Castle executive, most notably the Earl of Clare, Lord Chancellor of Ireland, and Lord Kilwarden, the ill-fated Chief Justice of Ireland (for more on Hamilton, see entry 29).[1]

Sources: *Dublin Evening Post*, 1800 and 1804

### A) Thursday 12 June 1800, 'Exhibition of the Arts'

This day commenced the public exhibition of the works of the Artists in this city, which we understand they mean to continue annually should they meet with that protection and encouragement which so spirited an effort to revive the Arts in this Kingdom so deservedly merits. We are happy to hear that his Excellency, in imitation of his Majesty's example honoured it with his presence yesterday, in consequence of the promise made by his excellency to a deputaton from the Artists, who waited on him for that purpose.

### B) Tuesday 17 June, 1800

The crowds of visitors have increased daily, which is a convincing proof of the merits of the performances, and a just criticism of the improved taste of the nation – and we sincerely hope and trust that this auspicious dawn of the Arts in Ireland, will meet with increased success, till they rise to meridian splendour. We want not talent, we want not genius, to any other nation under Heaven in any of the arts, we want the grand incentive – Encouragement! Let, then, the men of rank and spirit ably step forward and put the Arts upon a permanent foundation. That accomplished there cannot be a doubt, but that the Irish would soon equal the Flemish or Italian Schools. It would act as a stimulus to genius, and prevent men of merit from pining in obscurity, or seeking in a foreign country, the reward of those talents, which to the disgrace of his own, it had denied him.

In the present exhibition there are many artists that would not disgrace the first cabinet in Europe. In historical portrait painting, Hamilton, Cummins and Chinnery, stand in the foremost rank and really a credit to their country. [. . .]

['The Rev. Dean Kirwan Pleading the Cause of the Destitute Orphans of Dublin' by Hamilton, fig. 22]: the subject is interesting [. . .] well conceived, and admirably executed. The figures are well grouped, and happily dispersed, particularly the children around the foot of the pulpit, and have a very pleasing effect. [. . .] In short we consider it equal to any production we have seen of the modern school and a chef d'oeuvre of that most excellent artist.[2]

## c) 7 AUGUST 1804, 'EXHIBITION OF ARTS'

Although the exhibition of this year is not as numerously supplied with pictures as those which have preceded it – and that, from what cause we know not, the opportunities of public observation and of public praise seem to have narrowed and depressed instead of extending and encouraging the emulation of our artists, the present exhibition, nevertheless merits the attention of the public, and the just admiration of the connoisseur. [. . .] In the department of oils, indisputable, and we may suppose, an unreluctant, superiority must be yielded to Mr Hamilton's veteran pencil, the production of which occupy a principal, if not the principal part of the room.

Portrait of the late Lord Kilwarden,[3] the loyalist and the patriot – the Christian and the moralist, the man of legislative thought, cannot look upon this picture without an interest arising out of those characters, and which must merge the narrow office of the connoisseur in the stronger feelings of the man. He beholds less the magic of the pencil in producing an exquisite likeness, than the shade of a just and constitutional judge, rising to reproach his country – of a man the victim of popular fury, and who, when expiring in cruel torture, was only anxious that the law should survive and live in that constitutional vigour which he, himself, had always endeavoured to maintain. Considered, however, as a mere picture, this is not the best in the room.

The Portrait of the Rt. Hon. David LaTouche,[4] if we err not through ignorance, is the best in the exhibition. The likeness is not only such as almost to equal the mirror's reflection, but in all other respects it is a picture of the very first order. The colouring and harmony of the parts cannot be exceeded. The drawing is intimately just, the foreshortening exquisitely fine, and altogether, it is a picture calculated to advance the fame of the artist and the art.

## d) 9 AUGUST 1804

The Earl of Moira [by Hugh Douglas Hamilton] – the eye and the heart of every Irishman, not recreant to his country and his King, must receive pleasure from the portraiture of this gallant and illustrious countryman, to whom, with the chivalric spirit and soul of honour, which animated a Bayard, may be applied the same character: a Knight, *Without fear and without reproach.* The likeness is very close, and the costume military. The noble earl is represented in his study – a situation not affected in the foppery of the painter, or the subject, for in the original is represented the best fruits of study. [. . .] Not content with the tinsel of adventitious rank, the illustrious Moira has vindicated and confirmed the nobility of birth by the earnest acquisition of knowledge and the practice of virtue. A brave soldier, he is not less ambitious of legislative character – and though even among the foremost to draw his honest and unsullied sword in defence of the state, the bias of such a sword must be to advance the interests of his sovereign and country by civil services, and the application of legislative wisdom.[5]

NOTES

1    See Fintan Cullen, 'Radicals and Reactionaries: Portraits of the 1790s in Ireland', in *Revolution, Counter Revolution and Union: Ireland in the 1790s*, ed. Jim Smyth, Cambridge University Press, (forthcoming).

2    Picture now destroyed and known only by a mezzotint of 1806, see also entry 41 and Fintan Cullen, '"The Cloak of Charity": the politics of representation in late eighteenth-century Ireland', *The Irish Review*, No. 21, Autumn/Winter 1997, pp. 66–74. The other painters referred to are William Cuming (1769–1852) and George Chinnery (1774–1852).

3    National Gallery of Ireland, see Fintan Cullen, 'The Oil Paintings of Hugh Douglas Hamilton,' *Walpole Society*, 50, 1984, p. 191, fig. 84.

4    Collection of the Bank of Ireland; see Sergio Benedetti, *The La Touche Amorino*, Dublin, The National Gallery of Ireland, 1998, p. 34.

5    See Cullen, *Walpole Society*, pp. 195–6, fig. 93.

# – 43 –

# Anonymous Diarist, Dublin exhibitions, 1801

A private diary kept by an anonymous Dublin connoisseur and amateur artist (possibly a member of the Tighe family from County Wicklow) is one of the few written accounts of serious art viewing in Dublin *c.* 1800.[1] In these extracts, the author writes of attending two exhibitions, the first being the 1801 annual exhibition of the Society of Artists of Ireland which was held in the recently vacated Parliament House on College Green. In the second extract, the writer views the popular exhibition of a panorama of the recent British capture of Mysore (fig. 23). Elsewhere in the diary, the writer visits Ellis's print shop and has his portrait painted by the miniaturist Henry Kirch-hoffer (1781–1860). The report on the exhibition of Irish artists is largely descriptive but reveals an opinionated mind and a noticeable romantic sensibility. The diarist is also concerned with the development of an indigenous art world in Ireland, yet he (a presumption based on the diarist's references to business interests) is unhesitant in his enthusiasm for the display of a blatantly imperialist panorama by the London artist Robert Ker Porter (1777–1842) detailing David Baird's defeat of Tipú Sultán at Seringapatam in 1799 (fig. 23). The huge panorama had previously been exhibited in London and Edinburgh and its display in Dublin (it was also shown in Cork and Belfast) in the very year that the Union of the parliaments had come into effect gives us an indication of how the Irish capital was turning into an important venue on the imperial propaganda circuit.[2]

Source: MS 24K14, Dublin, Royal Irish Academy, pp. 244–58 and 273–78

**May 14 1801:** Long much for the opening of the Exhibition. It is to be this year on a grander scale and proper apartments are fitting for it in the *ci-devant* Parliament House. Kirchhoffer, who exhibits for the first time, tells me there is much emulation amongst the painters.

   **June 2 1801:** [. . .] as an exhibition of fine arts in London is always viewed by the Royal Family, before it is exposed to vulgar eyes, His excellency proceeded in State to the Parliament House, for the same purpose, and tomorrow the public are to be admitted.

   **June 3 1801:** [. . .] a busy morning, but achieved afterwards to spare an hour to the exhibition – as I intend to make it several visits, the present was merely to satisfy curiosity by a general view, and it was indeed highly gratified – my own performances insignificant as they are here given me a much greater pleasure in the examination of paintings – exclusive of the general effect of design and colouring; the folds of a drapery, the shading of a button, or the most minute part of the composition is a separate source of amusement, and I hope from a critical observation of each, to convert something to my own use. The exhibition of last year was a little better than a closet, the present is in a palace – you pass thro' a magnificent colonnade and Hall into a couple of noble apartments, arched ceilings and lighting at top – the walls hung with green cloth, shew both the paintings and the superb frames which surround them, to the greatest advantage. The first room is appropriated to miniatures, sketches, drawings, elevations, etc. The second to the paintings, the catalogue contains in the whole, 200 pieces.

**July 6 1801:** Monday. Rose at 8 to my pencil — breakfast — the office — &&& — a day of violent and incessant rain. Experienced the usual fate of a piece of procrastination, a disappointment. I had intended a very minute examination of the paintings of the exhibition, laziness deferred it from day to day, and the rooms are at length closed, without having effected it — Three weeks ago, I should have been able to give some account of the pieces, but the impression is now much faded.

As usual in an infant exhibition, that of this year, consists in the figure line almost entirely of portraits, in fact had the artists practising in Ireland, inclination, ability and sale for composition, portraiture is at present so much the rage, that they have *not leisure for any* other branch of study. In his present exhibitions, Cuming is I think by no means entitled to the same superiority, as in those of last year.[3] The following are the most remarkable of his pieces —

A large picture containing 5 full length portraits, a Lady of quality, and her four children; it has the disadvantage of being unfinished but can never I should think be an agreeable picture. The mother is seated full in front, an attitude necessarily stiff. The children placed round her – the arms of the whole group linked together in a variety of forms, affording an opportunity to the artist of displaying his scientific knowledge, but it would be so difficult to meet with similar situations in nature, that you see the painter at work, harnessing to his canvas the arrangement which he has made for the purpose.

[. . .] Portrait of Mrs Cresswell of the Theatre Royal – an half length sitting – front view – the dress simple – a black lace cloak thrown over one shoulder with a good effect, the hair curled over the forehead, [. . .] the portrait is a likeness, & of course handsome, but coarsely finished; the drapery shaded with an uncommon tint of a yellowish green – it was accused of total want of animation from a deficiency of white in the eye ball, but this defect might easily be remedied. [. . .]

A number of fine pieces by *H. Hamilton*, decidedly the best exhibitor of this year – some however are criticized with severity — to begin with the worst —

A large piece containing whole length of a Lady of Quality and her son.[4] The mother in the dress of a barefooted peasant carries the child stark naked on her back; the figure leans forward as about to step a stream, which rims at her feet, but the attitude has an appearance of falling. The Drapery which is white is very coarsely executed, a number of long parallel folds, stiff as possible, and shaded in a cold grey tint, the landscape gloomy and the whole unpleasing — I have since seen an engraving from a portrait of Mrs Sheridan and her son, by a London artist, the design of which though executed with much more freedom is so similar to the above that I should almost think it had served for a copy.[5]

Portrait of a Nobleman, half length, an ugly subject rendered more so by the dress in which he is painted, he is buried to the chin in his scarlet robes which entirely conceal the figure & over a pair of high shoulders convey the idea of concealed deformity.[6] The story of the young king in the Arabian Nights whose closed robe covered his lamentable metamorphosis occurred to me while viewing it.

A very large piece. A full length portrait of a lady standing & tuning a pedal harp.[7] The countenance animated and beautiful. The white Drapery finely shaded with a rich warm tint. The folds natural and well imagined. The harp with the rich ornaments which are now lavished on that instrument capitally relieved. The only fault which I conceive this picture to possess, is a kind of glare or excessive cleanness, which gives the columns in the background the appearance of having just come from the chisel — was this effect supposed to arise from strong light, the shades should I think be deeper, and the glare more partially disposed.

Portrait of Mrs Tighe, a full length.[8] The design of this painting is uncommonly pleasing; she is seated on a garden chair amidst rural scenery; the attitude is nearly a front one, but the face being inclined over her work, at once prevents the fault of appearing to look out of the picture & affords the artist an opportunity of shewing much ability in foreshortening — the fault which I have imagined in the last picture is in this completely obviated; everything is natural, you do not look at a picture, you imagine yourself standing amongst the opposite trees. In the minutest parts of the drapery, an anxiety to prevent anything of stiffness is discernible, even a red shoe which peeps but a couple of inches from under the petticoat exhibits some creases, lest a new one should have too formal an appearance. The projection of the muslin, which she is embroidering with gold thread, from that of the robe, struck me as particularly natural. [. . .]

Portrait of the late Colonel St George, a picture highly esteemed. I had several years ago seen and admired it at the house of Mr Hamilton.[9] The Colonel is in his light horse uniform, his helmet on the ground; he is drawn leaning against his wife's tomb – the expression of the countenance is admirably delineated, it is that of a man versed in misfortune, whose accounts with this world are closed & who cares not how soon he should be removed to another. This, with the solemn scenery in which he is placed & the recollection of the late shocking termination of his existence by the hands of assassins, combine to fill one while gazing on it, with the most melancholy sensations. [. . .]

*V. Waldré:* an enormous piece of 16 or 18 feet by about 12. The subject, 'Saint Patrick converting the Druids'. It is a compartment of the ceiling from Saint Patricks Hall in Dublin Castle, but it is of a displeasing proportion for a picture.[10] Of this piece I have at present but an imperfect recollection, farther than that the figures are placed too much on a line like the characters in the last scene of a theatrical representation & that their colouring from its paleness and want of strength conveys the idea that you view the back scenery of a picture, the foremost figures of which have not yet been delineated — If however the future exhibitions of Mr Waldré excel each other in the same degree as the present does that of the year before, his merit will soon be unquestionable. [. . .]

*W. Ashford.* Decidedly the first landscape painter; his productions are large and very numerous, yet finished with the most minute exactness. They are really beautiful – the principal are 5 very fine views in Charleville Forest, the seat of Lord Viscount Charleville.[11] There is here abundant scope for an exertion of the artist's genius in the delineation of foliage. The articulation is perfect and the colouring so beautifully rich, and various, that I could with pleasure have spent hours in viewing them. Some beautiful pieces of composition in the style of Claude – & a view of the Bay of Dublin from the Lighthouse, etc.

**21 July 1801:** I spent a couple of hours with very great pleasure at a Panorama, which at present engages the attention of everyone here, and has been honored with the highest approbation of the Royal Academy and the most celebrated artists and judges. The subject which is the storming of Seringapatam [fig. 23], is most admirably delineated on the immense surface of 2550 square feet of canvas. It is painted by Robert Ker Porter[12] and is indeed most justly entitled to universal applause. The design and colouring throughout discovers the hand of a master and with so much truth even in the minutiae, that few of its visitors can avoid expressing their surprise at so perfect an imitation of nature. The centre object is General Baird on the ascent to the breach surrounded by his staff, and calling his men to follow Sargent Graham on the Forlorn Hope*, who having obtd. the colours from the Ensign planted them on the Breach and as he gave the 3rd shout of victory, an Indian with a pistol shot him through the heart. At the foot of the Bastion is a party of Tippoo's soldiers, who are repulsed by the grenadiers of the 74th. Lieutenant Prendergast appears mortally wounded and Lieutenant Shaw lies among the slain. A little to the right is Captain McLeod, who at the onset was wounded through the lungs, led off by a Sergeant. [. . .] You are placed as it were in the middle of the battle before the ramparts and without the danger view precisely as in reality, the whole tumult of such a scene. [. . .] The artist will observe in it, the finest specimen of shading, perspective, foreshortening, etc. It contains

23    John Vendramini after Robert Ker Porter, *The Storming of Seringapatam*
(centre portion) 1802

beside the innumerable small ones, several hundreds of figures of which those
in the foreground are large as life, and those of all the officers, and the most distinguished subalterns, much esteemed portraits. The rich and fanciful dresses
of the East, the curious and magnificent architecture of their Mosques and
Zenanas, and other novelties in European eyes contribute to render this noble
picture more interesting. [. . .]

There are at present in forwardness, three superb engravings from the
painting which are to cost 2000 Guineas, and deposits are already made for
almost every impression at 6Gs. per set. The East India Company, as might be
expected affording the most liberal patronage.[13]

*The Forlorn Hope – the appellation given to the party who first mount the
breach, as they have hardly hope of escaping the swords of the enemy. [. . .]

NOTES

1    The journal was presented to the Royal Irish Academy by Mr James Tighe in 1861.
2    The panorama was subsequently destroyed, see Ralph Hyde, *Panoramania! The Art
and Entertainment of the 'All Embracing' View*, London, Barbican Art Gallery, 1988, p.
65 and Stephen Oettermann, *The Panorama: History of a Mass Medium*, New York,

Zone Books, 1997, pp. 115–17 and also Fintan Cullen, 'Union and Display in the Nineteenth Century,' in *Was Ireland a Colour*, eds. Terry McDonough, Tom Boylan and Tadhg Foley, forthcoming.

3    William Cuming (1769–1852), later President of the Royal Hibernian Academy.

4    Hugh Douglas Hamilton (1740–1808), *Portrait of Viscountess Mount Charles (Lady Conyngham) and her son*, Slane Castle, Co. Meath, see Fintan Cullen, 'The Oil Paintings of Hugh Douglas Hamilton', *Walpole Society*, 50, 1984, no. 87, p. 196. For further references to Hamilton in this reader see entries 29, 41 and 42.

5    A perceptive observation; the similarity between the Hamilton and Hoppner's *Mrs Richard Brinsley Sheridan and her child* (*c.* 1797–8) is very close, though Hamilton's composition is a reverse of the earlier canvas. The Hoppner is now in the Metropolitan Museum of Art, New York, see Cullen, *Walpole Society*, plates 86 and 87 and p. 173.

6    Similar to portrait of Viscount Mount Charles, Slane Castle, and husband to the subject of the previous painting, see ibid., no. 86, p. 196.

7    Untraced.

8    Marianne Tighe (d. 1853), wife of William Tighe of Woodstock, Co. Kilkenny, see ibid., p. 201, plate 90.

9    See Fintan Cullen, *Visual Politics: The Representation of Ireland, 1750–1930*, Cork University Press, 1997, pp. 104–15, and entry 4 of this volume.

10   For a discussion of Waldré's Dublin Castle ceiling paintings, see Cullen, *Visual Politics*, chapter 2.

11   See Anne Crookshank, 'A Life Devoted to Landscape Painting: William Ashford', *Irish Arts Review*, Yearbook 1995, p. 128, plates 10 and 11.

12   For more on Porter and his panoramas see Oettermann, *The Panorama*, pp. 115–18.

13   The diarist's knowledge on who was who in the panorama is based on information in the *Descriptive Sketch* which carried a key, see *Narrative Sketches of the Conquest of Mysore*, Edinburgh, 1801. Giodanni Vendramini's engravings after the panorama appeared in 1802–03, see Mildred Archer, *India and British Portraiture 1770–1825*, London, Sotheby Parke Bernet and Oxford University Press, 1979, pp. 427–9.

# – 44 –

## *The Nation*, 1843–4

These two mid-nineteenth-century articles on the visual arts in Ireland are taken from *The Nation*, a newspaper founded by Thomas Davis (1814–45; see also entry 8), and some fellow Young Irelanders in 1842. The articles were not signed although their authorship is known through the assiduous inscriptions of the newspaper's editor George Gavan Duffy (1816–1903), whose annotated editions of *The Nation* are in the Library of the Royal Irish Academy. The first extract is a review of the 1843 Royal Hibernian Academy annual exhibition, mounted in their premises in Dublin's Lower Abbey Street. It calls for the establishment of an Irish school of art, the author being Denny Lane (1818–1895), a Cork barrister, poet and prominent member of the Young Ireland movement. A close friend of Davis, he contributed regularly to *The Nation*. The second piece, by Davis himself, dates from a year later and is a discussion of an illustration (fig. 24) for a book of Irish ballads and songs published in 1845. Entitled *The Spirit of the Nation*, the book and the drawing were regarded by Davis 'as a symbol of renascent nationalism in Ireland.'[1] Drawn by his friend William Frederick Burton (1816–1900), the illustration is read by Davis in highly optimistic terms. In the end, Davis's views were to have little effect. Burton's ambitions lay elsewhere, he eventually became Director of the National Gallery in London, while Davis himself was to die within a year.

Sources: *The Nation*, May 27, 1843, p. 522 and July 27,1844, p. 667

## A) ROYAL HIBERNIAN ACADEMY EXHIBITION, 1843

The day is gone by – and glad we are that it is so – when men, looking only to the money value of everything, contemned [*sic*] the Fine Arts as idle amusements, and valued pictures only as producing so many pounds, shillings and pence, in the market. Political economists, knowing the imports of the works of art in these countries to be greater than the exports, justly discouraged a taste which would produce a 'balance of trade' in favour of foreign nations. Happily, we live in a country where such opinions could never gain much ground, and where the natural love of the people for the arts, and music in particular, enabled them to appreciate justly, though unphilosophically, the true value of those agents in civilization.

   A number of circumstances have occurred at the present time to give an increased impetus to the progression of the arts. The genius of our fellow-countrymen for music has been abundantly developed since the foundation of Temperance Societies; and the establishment of Art-Unions, by transferring the patronage and support of art from the very wealthy to the middle classes, has produced the same beneficial effect, by nearly the same means that the invention of printing had upon literature. The reward of the artist's labours being now given by the many, and not the few, the painter or sculptor does not endeavour to please the erringancy [*sic*] of some

individual patron, but, in the true democracy of art, seeks to win the suf-
frages of mankind by following out those principles of immutable and universal truth by which alone he can hope to gain the voices and the hearts
of the many.

Although this country has already produced many great artists, it has not as
yet given birth to a distinct school of art. As many holy individuals may live,
according to divines, without forming a church, so, many painters of the greatest talent may be produced by a country without forming a school. Most of
our greatest painters have been included in the English school, and have not
made a separate class from it. Many of our friends – and amongst them several
whose opinion is entitled to the greatest respect – think that the exhibition of
the Royal Hibernian Academy should be confined to the works of Irish artists
only, wishing to give to it an exclusively national character, and believing that,
by the admission of the paintings of other artists, the Irish members of the profession are subjected to an unequal competition with our more advanced
neighbours. With respect to the latter objection, we have the opinion of Irish
genius that we believe, with fair opportunities, it need not fear the rivalry of
any other nation; and feeling, as we do, that our artists are as yet only in progress,
and by no means advanced to that position which we are sure they will one
day attain, instead of rejecting, we welcome every good English production that
may become either a source of beneficial instruction, or an object of honourable rivalry. If our artists are superior, they have nothing to fear from the
competition; if inferior, they have much to learn from the labours of others.

The great object of any true lover of the fine arts in this country should
be, the foundation of a national school – in fact, of any school; for the genius
of the Irish nation would soon make it Irish in its character. [. . .]

We are firmly convinced that there never was a country that contained
within itself more of the elements of a great school of art than our own. We
do not say this out of any overweening national vanity. [. . .] First of all, none
can deny to the Irish people that poetical spirit which is equally and essentially necessary in all the arts, no matter what be the instrument by means of
which it holds communion with the world. [. . .] This we see equally in the
written poetry of Goldsmith and of Moore – in the spoken poetry of Grattan and O'Connell – in the painted poetry of Maclise and Burton – in the
chiselled poetry of Hogan and M'Dowell.[2] It sighs in the strains of our
ancient music, and smiles from the canvas of our modern art. It is the same
in all its developments. One of our ablest sculptors, we know, when model-
ling an Irish subject, works at his statue with the sound of music in his ears,
and catches from the old melody the character of his design.[3]

## B) 'THE SPIRIT OF THE NATION', 1844

We have lying before us a proof of the design for the title-page and cover of *The Spirit of the Nation* [fig. 24].[4] It is not the work or thought of any one connected with *The Nation*; it was the gift of friendship from one differing in many things from us, and we may speak freely of it.

Look at it, reader, as we run over the design. Like everything thoroughly good, its beauty will grow on you; you will have lookd often ere you have seen it all, and you will return to it with fresh pleasure. In the centre of it, the name is inscribed on a pillar-stone. Over it an Irish eagle is soaring from a serpent, vast, wounded, and hissing – the bird is safe – need we translate the allegory?

But we come to the main design – it is simple in its means, great in its design and perfect in its execution. On one side of the picture is a young bard, harp-bearing. The hills of Ireland are behind him, he has come down full of strength, and wisdom, and faith. He played with the fair hair of the cataract till his ears grew filled with its roarings – he has toiled up the mountain till his sinews stiffened and his breath deserted him, for he was full of passion and resolve – he has grown strange among the tombs, and, perchance, has softened, too, in the hazel glen; but he has another, or rather his one great mission, the dream of his childhood before him, and he moves along through the land. There are Laurels on his brow, he has no sense of their touch – he has awakened the slumbers of ages, and he treads on a broken chain, yet he has no eye nor hand for these tokens of fame, he is full of his great thought, abstracted from all else, even from his own echoes.

An old bard, vast, patriarchal, rigid with years (for he might have harped at the landing of Owen Roe), sat tranced and clutching his harp of broken chords. The singing of the minstrel of the Nation has broken the old harper's spell, and his hand is rising, and there is life coming into his huge rocky face. Two young brothers in arms (friends and patriots) are looking wildly at the passing bard, and as his song swells louder, there is fierce daring in their eyes and limbs. They are in old Irish costume, barred, cloak, and trews; one wears the gold torque of an Irish knight, the other grasps a yet sheathed sword – it will be drawn.

Disconnected from this immediate group (and sunk in the corner of the structure, beneath whose antique arch the minstrel has past) are figures of the four provinces. Leinster sits gazing in historic grief at the shield bearing England's leopards. Under that shield is a skull, the emblem of Dermod's fatal treason. But Leinster, that holds Dublin, and Tara, and Clontarf, and Wexford (the last adventurer for liberty), may forgive our friend for telling the treason of her king, and the more so, as a fairer being never made sorrow sweet. To Munster – exuberant Munster, a child is leading lambs, and he totters under

24    Carolyn Millar after Frederick William Burton, *Spirit of the Nation, c.* 1844

the rich sheaf. Ulster is seated among the basalt rocks of the Causeway. She
has hope and anxiety in her face and action; and she proudly shows the red
hand of O Neil on her shield. And Connaught sits on the shore, the waves
comes a wild subject to her fair feet, and dreamily she looks where the sun
sinks behind the western waters. Nothing can surpass the grace of form, the
simple force of thought, the noble disposition of limb and drapery, and the
masterly lightness of touch in all these figures.

We feel hearty pleasure in speaking of this most beautiful design, the most original and thoughtful that we have ever seen in this country. Resch never surpassed it, and the only alloy to our pleasure is a little envy, lest every one should say, as we did when we saw the design, that there was more poetry in it than any poem in the volume.

We again repeat our hope that this is but the beginning of a series of national designs to which every Irish artist of ability may contribute. We cannot yet arrange the frescoes of our Parliament House; but the panels of the Conciliation Hall are yet to be filled, and the prizes by the Association for historical pictures to be given.

## NOTES

1    Harry White, *The Keeper's Recital: Musical and Cultural History in Ireland, 1770–1970*, Cork University Press, 1998, p. 57.

2    Daniel Maclise (1806–70), Frederick William Burton, John Hogan (1800–58) and Patrick MacDowell (1799–1870).

3    The author then goes on the discuss the merits of Irish draughtsmanship in such figures as James Barry and Maclise, as well as mentioning the importance of the Cork collection of casts, for which see Peter Murray, *Illustrated Summary Catalogue of the Crawford Municipal Art Gallery*, Cork, 1991, pp. 196–8.

4    *The Spirit of the Nation: Ballads and Songs by the Writers of 'The Nation' with original and ancient music arranged for the voice and piano-forte*, Dublin, 1845. See also Jeanne Sheehy, *The Rediscovery of Ireland's Past: The Celtic Revival, 1830–1920*, London, Thames and Hudson, 1980, pp. 6-7, 41, and Harry White, *The Keeper's Recital*, 57–60. Davis's essay also appears in D.J. Donoghue, ed., *Essays, Literary and Historical by Thomas Davis*, Dundalk, Dundalgan Press, 1914, pp. 164–6.

# — 45 —

# Hugh Lane, Municipal Gallery of Modern Art, 1908

Hugh Lane (1875–1915) was the principal instigator in the founding of a gallery for modern art in Dublin (see also entries 36 and 37). When it eventually opened in January 1908, Lane wrote a 'Prefatory Note' to the *Illustrated*

*Catalogue*. The first home of the collection was 17 Harcourt Street, where it stayed until 1933 when Charlemont House in Parnell Square was given to the city. The collection was arranged in distinct sections, Irish Painters, British Schools, French Barbizon and French Impressionist. The paintings on display included Lane's recently acquired *Éva Gonzalès* by Manet (fig. 21) and Renoir's *Les Parapluies*, which were on conditional loan and later became the famous contested 'Lane Pictures' (see entry 38). Other exhibits included unconditional Lane gifts: works by Irish and British artists such as Frank O'Meara, Walter Osborne, Charles Shannon, Whistler, Albert Moore, George Frederic Watts and Wilson Steer as well as the gift of some Constables and Corots from the Prince (later George V) and Princess of Wales. On the staircase, Lane hung a selection of portraits, mainly by John Butler Yeats and William Orpen, of 'Contemporary Irishmen and Women'. There was also a small collection of prints and drawings and sculpture, the latter section dominated by Lane's gift of a cast of Rodin's *Age of Bronze*, which also graced the cover of the catalogue. This cover was in green with all headings in both Irish and English.[1]

Source: Municipal Gallery of Modern Art, *Illustrated Catalogue*, Dublin, Dollard, 1908, vii–ix. Reprinted by the Friends of the National Collection of Ireland and the Hugh Lane Municipal Gallery of Modern Art, Dublin, 1984.

The project of founding a Gallery of Modern Art in Dublin is no longer an idea, it is now an accomplished fact. Till to-day Ireland was the only country in Europe that had no Gallery of Modern Art. There is not even a single accessible private collection of Modern Pictures in this country. That reproach is now removed.

The National Gallery of Ireland has a fine collection of works by the old masters, yet Sir Walter Armstrong himself says: – 'I would place the importance of a modern Gallery even before that of a National Gallery.' To those actively engaged in Art this must be so, as it is his contemporaries that teach the student most, their successes that inspire him, for their problems are akin.

The necessity of such a collection was realised six years ago, when the first of the series of winter exhibitions aroused a wide interest in pictures, and after the exhibition of works by Irish artists at the Guildhall, London, in 1904, where so many distinguished artists were at last recognised as Irishmen, the idea took definite form, and many of these artists construed to promise a picture to form the nucleus for a Gallery. This showed their practical interest in the project.

The executors of the late Mr J. Staats Forbes having arranged that if any portion of this well-known collection were sold for a public Gallery the price would be below the actual market value, it was decided to make a selection of the pictures most suitable, and have them exhibited in Dublin that winter (1904–5). Owing to the generous enthusiasm of Colonel Hutcheson Poë, Mr W.P. Geoghegan, Mrs Fry, Lord and Lady Drogheda, Lord Mayo, Lady Ardilaun, and many others, and the practical sympathy of Lord and Lady Dudley, twenty-five pictures were acquired for Dublin, and Their Royal Highnesses the Prince and Princess of Wales presented five more on the occasion of His Royal Highness's first visit to Dublin as Prince of Wales. This practical interest was widespread, a fund having been opened in Montreal by Mr Buckley, which was generously responded to, and President Roosevelt, in sending a subscription, expressed his cordial sympathy, writing that 'the realisation of this project would be an important step toward giving Dublin the position it by right should have'.

These, with the pictures already given or promised by artists and collectors, were so substantial an instalment that in February, 1905, the Municipal Council authorised the Estates and Finance Committee 'to provide the sum of £500 per annum to maintain a Gallery in which the valuable collection of pictures offered to the City by Mr Lane and others might be housed'; and at a meeting held on 11th June, 1906, the Council adopted the following resolution: – 'That with a view to retaining for the benefit of the citizens the valuable paintings which have been offered to the City by Mr Lane and others, the Estates and Finance Committee is authorised to hire and maintain temporary premises in which these valuable Works of Art can be preserved and exhibited pending the erection of a permanent building in a suitable locality, the annual cost involved not to exceed the sum already authorised by the Council. And that the Estates and Finance Committee be first empowered to obtain expert opinion respecting the various pictures and report thereon.'

On the 6th September, 1907, the Report of the Public Libraries Committee, recommending the acquisition of the premises No. 17 Harcourt Street for the purposes of a temporary Art Gallery, was adopted by the Council with but one dissenting voice.

The project also has received warm encouragment from Art lovers both here and in England, and I would take this opportunity of thanking the Art critics who have so generously seconded our efforts, headed by Mr D.S. M'Coll, who has steadily and earnestly supported the scheme from its inception, 'as the first real attempt at a representative collection of Modern Art to be found in the British Isles'.

I must also record the encouragement I received from the enthusiasm awakened in Belfast in the Spring of 1906 by an Exhibition of Pictures, which included many of those I now give to this Gallery.

Part of the opposition that we had to contend with was, no doubt, due to the fear that the Gallery would be managed, as many other Municipal Galleries are, by people with no practical experience in Art matters. But the Dublin Municipal Authorities have enabled the Libraries Committee to avail itself of the advice of such experienced persons as will effectually remove this danger. This Committee has invited the co-operation of two representatives of the National Gallery, two members of the Royal Hibernian Academy, and four of the original Art Gallery Committee, and has asked me to be their Honorary Director.

I now hand over my collection of pictures and drawings of the British Schools (70), and Rodin's masterpiece, 'L'Age d'Airain'. I also present the group of portraits of contemporary Irishmen and women (which will be added to as time goes on). These are to be ceded to the National Portrait Gallery when the usual time limit has elapsed.

I hope that this Gallery will always fulfil the object for which it is intended, and – by ceding to the National Gallery those pictures which, having stood the test of time, are no longer modern – make room for good examples of the movements of the day. The National Gallery can encourage this desire on my part by depositing in this Gallery the few modern pictures which it has (recently) acquired.

I have also deposited here my collection of pictures by Continental artists, and intend to present the most of them, provided that the promised permanent building is erected on a suitable site within the next few years. This collection includes a selection of the Forbes and Durand Ruel pictures, bought by me after the Royal Hibernian Academy Winter Exhibition, and some important examples of Manet, Renoir, Mancini, etc., which I have purchased to make this Gallery widely representative of the greatest painters of the nineteenth century.

The Gallery is open free from 10 a.m. to 10 p.m. on every weekday, and from 3 to 6 p.m. on Sundays. Its influence must of necessity show itself in the next generation of artists, and of their critics. The opponents of the Gallery have been those who have not had the advantage of the study of these modern classics abroad, and who naturally cannot accept a standard so different from that which they have hitherto recognised.

NOTES

1    See Barbara Dawson, 'Hugh Lane and the Origins of the Collection', in *Images and Insights*, Dublin, Hugh Lane Municipal Gallery of Modern Art, 1993, pp. 13–32. Also, John Hutchinson, 'From the Edge to the Centre', in *Inheritance and Transformation*, Dublin, The Irish Museum of Modern Art, 1991, pp. 7–11.

# — 46 —

# Thomas MacGreevy, 'Picasso, Maimie [sic] Jellett and Dublin Criticism', 1923

Thomas MacGreevy (1893–1967) is mainly remembered today as a poet who wrote in a modernist, experimental idiom, but he was also an art historian who in time became Director of the National Gallery of Ireland.[1] After serving in the British army and being wounded at the Somme, he attended Trinity College Dublin and soon became an early supporter of Irish modernist art as can be seen from this article written for the short-lived, Dublin-based, international quarterly, *Klaxon*, which was 'concerned with the activities of all nations in matters of Art, Music and Literature'. In this essay, MacGreevy champions the abstract paintings of Mainie Jellett (1897–1944), whose name he mis-spells in the title (for Jellett see entry 12), placing her within a Celtic, non-figurative tradition. But MacGreevy goes further and, as in his poems of the 1920s, he displays a Catholic sensibility which merges with a nationalist bias.[2] His support for modernism is at the expense of old master painting and its tired subject-matter, a well-rehearsed argument by the early 1920s, but he concludes by blaming England for an unenlightened artistic inheritance that goes back to the eighteenth century.[3] MacGreevy pursued his nationalist agenda in later art criticism, most notably in his monograph on Jack Yeats (1945), where he claimed that Yeats painted 'the Ireland that matters'.[4]

Source: *Klaxon*, 1923–4, pp. 23–7

I once heard an Irish man of letters say that for many years he had arranged with his publishers, a London firm, that his books were not to be sent for review to Irish papers, because none of them took criticism seriously as a branch of the art of writing. I think our literary criticism has improved of recent years, but our desolate condition in the matter of serious art criticism was brought out by the reception that Miss Jellett's two pictures at the Dublin Painters' Exhibition got from the Dublin critics. One did not mind the criticism that could see in Mr Harry Clarke's work only the mannerisms of Aubrey Beardsley. That sort of thing is probably no more than the showing off of his knowledge of great names by a very young, very ingenuous, very provincial journalist. Mr Clarke may have been influenced by Beardsley, but unless a Clarke drawing could be mistaken for a Beardsley by a knowledge-able person, there must be some essential quality that differentiates them, as there is some essential quality that differentiates say, a Raphael from a Perug-ino. It is this quality that constitutes a 'Clarke' an original work and that makes the influence in it a matter of minor importance. But the angry per-plexity of older critics before Miss Jellett's work, though, no doubt, flattering to Miss Jellett, was not at all flattering to the standard of our education in modern art.

It is ten years and more since Mrs Duncan, the late Curator of the Munic-ipal Art Gallery, organised two representative exhibitions of work by the lead-ing French Post-Impressionists in Dublin, and one would have thought that by this time our young artists would have taken up, and got over, cubism, and our critics be familiar with cubism and every other kind of Post-Impressionist *ism*. But not they. Miss Jellett is the first resident artist to exhibit a cubist pic-ture in Dublin, and our critics are as hopelessly at sea in front of her work as her benighted predecessors were about Picasso and Othon Frieze [*sic*] and Matisse in 1912.[5]

There is less excuse for the critics to-day, apart from the time they have had to get used to Post-Impressionist idioms, for where Picasso, with his wicked Catalan sense of humour, called his coloured patterns 'Portrait of André Salmon', 'Miss Gertrude Stein Reading', and so on, and drove our humourless great into a gratuitous frenzy thereby, Miss Jellett calls her pic-tures simply 'Oil Painting', and 'Tempera Painting', so no sense of humour on the part of the critic was called for. And yet in front of her very pleasant piece of Byzantine decoration the Dublin world of criticism gaped and asked 'What does it mean? what does it symbolise?' And when you told them that it meant nothing, symbolised nothing, they could only say 'Why exhibit it then?' You might as well ask the reason why people have Adams ceilings in their houses. They mean nothing. Neither do the Book of Kells illumi-nations, neither does an Italian Renaissance doorway, or a 'Hicks' chair. There is pattern in all these things, and it is either beautiful pattern or it is not. The pattern in your mantelpiece may be carried out in coloured mar-ble, the colours may be beautifully harmonised or they may not; if you are able to perceive whether they are or not, then you will be able to perceive what Miss Jellett is trying to do.

Of course, Miss Jellett herself may like to believe that a geometric arrange-ment symbolises some purely human idea. But the experienced critic should be the last person to be impressed by an artist's views on the significance of his own work. Symbolism is neither here nor there in a work of art. Gauguin, in one of his letters, says, apropos of some Parisian artist's work, 'Symbolism is only another name for sentimentality.' Wagner meant 'Die Meistersinger' to symbolise his attitude to the academic musicians of his day. Much anyone listening to it cares what it symbolises. It is magnificent drama and magnificent music if we never knew even the names of Wagner or his enemies. Music is one of the of mediums of expression of human emotion. It is not an instrument of thought, and neither is any other art. The fact that Mr Yeats uses beautiful English to express his thought does not affect the value of his thought. We do not accept the moral outlook of Plato or Machiavelli merely because they were great literary artists. In so far as we care for the art of writing, we read for the sake of words and phrases, in so far as we care for thought, we read for the ideas that words and phrases convey.

As for Miss Jellett, her words and phrases, her colours and her relating of them to each other that is to say, produced, it seemed to me, a pleasing harmonic effect. That the freedom from subject, from painted psychology, from symbolism, has heightened the aesthetic value of her work is not, I think, to be doubted by anyone who has seen the pictures she has exhibited in Dublin at intervals during the past four or five years. She is now beginning to understand what painting means, painting, that is, apart from literature or 'message', or any other kind of illustration. Not, however, that she discovered it for herself. There are a dozen first-rate painters in Paris to-day (there is only one in Dublin, and there is none in London, as usual), and the study of their work at first-hand is bound to be a revelation to the intelligent art student. Miss Jellett is decidedly an intelligent art student. Whether she should be acclaimed as an artist time will tell.

To say that her recent work shows understanding of the function of painting does not at all mean that she ought, or that she is in the least likely, to confine herself to painting geometrical patterns, cross-sections of fiddles, or clay pipes, or easels or newspapers. Picasso paints very beautiful naturalistic portraits nowadays, and only the aesthetically thick-skinned see in his return to figure painting a confession of the error of his recent ways. All his early work is overburdened with subject matter. He reproduced, with his pencil and his brush, the features that made human beings interesting to the humanist, not those which made them interesting to the visual artist. It is one of the characteristics that emphasise his affinity to Velasquez and Morales and Goya, that make him, Catalan though he be, more of a Spaniard than a Frenchman. His 'Lame Man' is interesting because it reproduces the essential quality of lameness just as Velasquez's 'Enfant de Vallecas' reproduces the essential quality of dwarfishness. But Velasquez never settled down in Parnassien Paris as Picasso has done, and he was never made to realise acutely how unaesthetic a complication so-called 'human interest' in a work of art may be. As I imagine it, Picasso, living in Paris, was made to realise this, and, desiring to be recognised as an artist rather than an illustrator, he decided to get rid of human interest altogether. For some years, therefore, he painted only still life; a fragment of a box, a palette, anything sufficed; it was arranged into some design, some harmony or discord that pleased his eye, and painted. With this elimination of subject matter that had intrinsic unaesthetic interest of its own, he had either to prove to himself that he could paint beautifully or admit himself an illustrator rather than an artist. He proved (to the world as well as to himself, though it is a matter of less importance) that he could paint beautifully – more beautifully often than Chardin who also eliminated subject matter from his work. (The sober Chardin never achieved such shimmering beauty of colour as Picasso at his best has done; Picasso's yellows and blues and burnt reds can be miraculous.) Now, Picasso is painting women's portraits with superb confidence in the artistic quality of his work. And they are finer portraits than those he painted before he schooled himself in cubism. Psychology has been subordinated to aesthetic in them. The Picasso intellect does not obtrude itself. He has readjusted the balance between it and his visual sense.

And having succeeded in doing that he has learned all that France can teach him. The degree of mastery with which he can express what, in the light of his learning, he wants to express, is a question of his natural capacity. Mastery cannot be taught. That is why Miss Jellett does not need to go back to Paris. She, too, has learned all that France can teach her, and her future depends upon herself. So far as the aesthetic value of her work is concerned, it is of no consequence whether it is done in Paris, in Dublin, or in Ballydehob.

Whether she could have got through all that schools are able to teach an art student as quickly if she had remained in Dublin is doubtful. Our art teachers are in the grip of the English tradition – the worst of all traditions in painting, not excluding the German. For all Lord Lee of Fareham's efforts to prove the contrary, the English have never been painters.[6] Think of the artist that Gainsborough would have been if he had lived in France or Italy. That old Whig humbug, Sir Joshua Reynolds, imposed himself and his ideas so effectively on his artistically insensitive countrymen that even Gainsborough was compelled to make concessions to his influence. That is why Gainsborough wasted time, energy and space covering acres of good canvas with meaningless paint, as in that full length portrait that hangs in the National Gallery beside the small portrait of his brother John, a picture that is almost worthy of sixteenth century Venice.[7]

That Gainsborough could make such concessions is a sign of the curious inability of the Englishman ever to be more than half an artist. Spencer,

Marlowe, Dryden, Landor, and Keats are perhaps the only exceptions; and Webster, who may have been an Irishman. Practically all the others are moralising snobs as much as they are artists, Chaucer and Shakespeare and Shelley and Reynolds as well as G.F. Watts and Mr John Galsworthy and the detestable Doctor Johnson. There is no artistic conscience in the country whose greatest genius could write both 'King Lear' and 'King Henry V'. That Ireland, in spite of Anglo-Irish provincialism, can produce a consistently artistic, unmoralising, ungenteel genius, even in modern times, is, I believe, clear, in the light of the literary achievements of Mr Yeats, Mr Joyce and Mr George Fitzmaurice. James Barry and John Hogan had already proved for those with eyes to see. Look at the fine seriousness of Barry's portrait of Edmund Burke in the National Portrait Gallery.[8] It is worth all the Reynoldses we have, with their portentousness and their playfulness, and their woolliness. Or look at Hogan's 'Dead Christ' in Clarendon Street Church, or his 'Davis' at Mount Jerome. They are worth all the materalistic gentility of Foley.[9] Hogan and Barry both studied in Italy, and it is not impossible that our young artists will have to go to Paris before they learn to tear away the layers of English humbug that lie between us and clear artistic vision. They could, of course arrive at it by going back upon our own artistic past in an inquiring and critical spirit, but the opportunities of doing so are few. Painting in oils has been practised in Ireland for well over two hundred years – Murphy and Jervas were both painting in the seventeenth century – but the handful of pictures, mostly bad pictures, in the Irish room at the National Gallery, and a few portraits in the National Portrait Gallery are all that the student has to study at present. (Hone and John Butler Yeats and Duffy all three of them represented in the Municipal Gallery, now count as our artistic past too, of course.) I think the National Gallery might well give up one of the three Milltown rooms at present occupied by English pictures, and purchase and hang in it a sufficiently large number of pictures by such men as Barry and young George Barrett, to give the Irish art student some idea of their real achievement.[10]

We have quite enough representations of lower middle-class Dutch and upper middle-class English interiors to go on with. The National Gallery has never been a favourite haunt of Dublin people, except for an odd pair of lovers who discover what a delightfully lonely retreat it is. The Municipal Gallery has from its earliest days been popular with students as well as with the general public. For we are all – except our newspaper critics – interested in pictures by Irish artists and French artists. We are not interested in dead Dutch boors and dead English gentlemen. They only tell us about boorishness and gentility. They tell us nothing about art.

# NOTES

1    For recent assessments of MacGreevy see the essays by Tim Armstrong and J.C.C. Mays in *Modernism and Ireland: The Poetry of the 1930s*, eds. Patricia Coughlan and Alex Davis, Cork University Press, 1995, chapters 2 and 4.

2    See Susan Schreibman, *Collected Poems of Thomas MacGreevy: An Annotated Edition*, Dublin, Anna Livia Press, Washington, D.C., Catholic University of America Press, 1991, and the Thomas MacGreevy Archive, http://www.ucd.ie/~cosei.

3    For a discussion of MacGreevy's essay, see Tim Armstrong, 'Muting the Klaxon: Poetry, History and Irish Modernism', in Armstrong and Mays, *Modernism and Ireland*, pp. 43-4.

4    *Jack B. Yeats: An Appreciation and An Interpretation*, Dublin, Victor Waddington and Colm O'Lochlainn, 1945, p. 5. MacGreevy's friend Sam Beckett reviewed the Yeats book in *The Irish Times* but disagreed with its thesis; see Bruce Arnold, *Jack Yeats*, New Haven and London, Yale University Press, 1998, pp. 326–7.

5    Othon Friesz (1879–1949) was a French Fauve artist.

6    Arthur Lee, Viscount Lee of Fareham (1868–1947), statesman, benefactor and patron of the arts. In 1917 he presented his home and estate at Chequers, Buckinghamshire, to the State and a few years later bequeathed art works to the Courtauld Galleries, University of London.

7    MacGreevy is referring to two Thomas Gainsborough portraits in the National Gallery of Ireland, a full-length of *General James Johnston*, bequeathed by Hugh Lane in 1918 (cat. no. 794) and a head and shoulder portrait of *John Gainsborough*, presented by Lane in 1914 (cat. no. 675).

8    For Barry's portrait of Burke in the National Gallery of Ireland, see entry 28 and William L. Pressly, *The Life and Art of James Barry*, New Haven and London, Yale University Press, 1981, pp. 72–3.

9    Although both were Irish-born, the neoclassical sculptor John Hogan (1800–58), returned to Ireland after many years in Italy while John Henry Foley (1818–74) enjoyed great success in London. The two Hogan statues are *The Dead Christ*, 1829, Carmelite Friary, Clarendon Street, Dublin, and *Thomas Davis*, 1853, formerly Mount Jerome Cemetery, Dublin, now City Hall, Dublin. MacGreevy later wrote enthusiastically on Hogan, 'Some statues by John Hogan', *Father Mathew Record*, August 1943, reprinted in *The Capuchin Annual*, 1946-7, p. 422.

10   MacGreevy is referring to the artists Garret Morphey (fl. 1680–1716) and Charles Jervas (c. 1675–1739); Nathaniel Hone the Younger (1831–1917), John Butler Yeats (1839–1922) and Patrick Vincent O'Duffy (1832–1909), as well as the landscape painter George Barret (1732–84).

# — 47 —

# Brian O'Nolan, *The Irish Times*, 1942

The writer Brian O'Nolan (1912–66) used two pseudonyms, Myles na gCopaleen for his satirical columns in *The Irish Times*, and Flann O'Brien for his novels and plays. He is particularly remembered for his novel *At Swim Two Birds*, 1939. Starting in 1940, O'Nolan's 'Cruiskeen Lawn' column appeared in *The Irish Times* for 25 years, the best pieces dating from the 1940s. The extract included here lampoons a 1942 furore over the rejection by Dublin Corporation's Art Advisory Committee of the painting *Christ in His Passion* (fig. 25) by the French artist Georges Rouault (1871–1958).[1] Subsequently given on loan to Maynooth College, the Rouault, dating from 1930, was eventually accepted by Dublin's Municipal Gallery (now Hugh Lane Municipal Gallery of Modern Art) in 1956. O'Nolan used his newspaper column to address a wide range of contemporary issues, including Ireland's wartime cultural isolationism, bourgeois provincialism and the role of élitism and social class in the discussion of art.[2]

Source: This piece originally appeared in *The Irish Times*, but is here taken from *The Best of Myles*, ed. Kevin O'Nolan, London, Hart-Davis, MacGibbon, 1975, pp. 235–7

Since the controversy over the Rouault picture raises important issues in the sphere of aesthetics and public morality, I know that many readers will look to me for an authoritative pronouncement.

The picture was bought for £400 by the Friends of the National Collections and offered as a gift to the Municipal Gallery. (Here let me digress to reiterate once more my demand that that narrow thoroughfare in Parnell Square where the Gallery stands should be re-named Hugh Lane.) The Board of the Gallery, presumably composed of members of the Corporation, rejected the picture. The ex-Lord Mayor, Mrs Clarke, is quoted as having said that the picture is 'a travesty' and 'offensive to Christian sentiment'. Mr Keating says it is 'childish, naive and unintelligible'. On the other hand, a foreign nobleman is cited as praising the work.[3] M. Rouault himself preserves silence.

The picture is executed in the modern manner, and could not be expected to please persons whose knowledge of sacred art is derived from the shiny

25    Georges Rouault, *Christ in His Passion* (or *Christ and the Soldier*), 1930

chromo-lithograph bon-dieuiserie of the Boulevard Saint Sulpice, examples of which are to be found in every decent Irishman's bedroom. Such persons, however, never enter picture galleries, and there is no obvious reason why their opinion should be considered at all. What is important is the attitude of the 'intelligent' person. Many forms of modern art are devoid of rules. The artist makes his own. However formless or chaotic the manifestation, it is art if it expresses something, possibly something bad and negative. Even our own pathetic and untidy advance guards who have never learnt to draw are artists because they express artistically (and convincingly) the fact that they can't draw. But inasmuch as the modern artist makes his own rules, the onlooker must also be permitted to fix his own standards of appraisal. In other words, the faculty of appreciating a 'modern' painting is just as personal and individual as that exercised by the artist. A 'representational' portrait of a bishop (such as is carried out so embarrassingly often) can be assessed by merely mechanical standards. The best judge of such a picture would be a child of three who could say authoritatively whether 'it is like him'. But what different dual parts of a garment is the 'modern' picture?

Pair of sleeves.

It is safe to say that, while the bishop's portrait strikes everybody in the same simple way, it is scarcely possible that the reaction of any two individuals to Rouault's work could be identical. Indeed, how divergent they may be has been demonstrated. His picture has been stated to be 'blasphemous' and 'charged with deep religious significance'.

It will be seen, then, that the charm and value of such work lies in the diversity of the communications achieved by the artist. The attitude of each individual to the picture is personal, and is not necessarily related to any conventional artistic criteria. For that reason it is an impertinence for Mr Keating to say that the picture is 'childish'. Nobody wants to be bothered with Mr Keating's opinion. We can form our own. Equally inadmissible is the attitude of other commentators who have assured us that Rouault was taken a high view of by the stained-glass man Healy,[4] and that a bunch of Frenchmen (who alone in the world understand good taste) thought so much of him that they devoted a whole room to a display of his work. What has that got to do with it? Must we 'like' whatever some individual or coterie has pronounced to be good?

Impertinent as the expression of individual opinions must be in such a situation, it is a gross outrage that this Board of the Municipal Gallery, having apparently formed opinions desperate and dark of hue, should decide that the citizens of Ireland should not be permitted to form any opinion at all. By what authority does this bunch take custody of the community's aesthetic conscience?

The members of the Corporation are elected to discharge somewhat more physical tasks, such as arranging for slum clearance and the disposal of sewage. Here there is scope for valuable public service, a vast field of opportunity confronts the eye. Why must the members trespass in other spheres where their intellectual equipment cannot be other than inadequate?

## NOTES

1    Also known as *Christ and the Soldier*, see Hugh Lane Municipal Gallery of Modern Art, *Images and Insights*, Dublin, 1993, pp. 236–7, and Bruce Arnold, *Mainie Jellett and the Modern Movement in Ireland*, New Haven and London, Yale University Press, 1991, pp. 187–92.
2    See Steven Curran, "'No, This is not from *The Bell*": Brian O'Nolan's 1943 *Cruiskeen Lawn* Anthology,' *Éire–Ireland*, 32, 2 & 3, Summer–Fall 1997, p. 81.
3    The references are to Kathleen Clarke, widow of the executed 1916 patriot, Tom Clarke, the academic painter Sean Keating (1889-1977), and Count Michael de la Bedoyère, editor of the *Catholic Herald*.
4    Michael Joseph Healy (1873–1941), stained glass artist.

# — 48 —

# Michael Scott and James Johnson Sweeney, *Rosc*, 1967

The six Rosc exhibitions held between 1967 and 1988 have had a great impact on the Irish art scene. Primarily they brought contemporary foreign avant-garde art to Dublin, frequently with the artists in tow. They also stirred debate, and the large-scale nature of so much of the art displayed introduced 'modern art' to a large number of Irish people for the first time. The brain child of Irish modernist architect Michael Scott (1905–89) and the Irish-American James Johnson Sweeney (1900–86), formerly of the Museum of Modern Art and the Guggenheim Museum, New York, the first Rosc exhibition took place at the Royal Dublin Society in November/December 1967. The jury was chaired by Sweeney and included a Dutchman, Dr Willem Sandberg, Chairman of the Israel Museum, Jerusalem, and a French critic, Jean Leymarie.[1] Their agenda was uncompromisingly modernist: historical and contextualized detail were sidelined to the advantage of form. At the same time, as their introductory remarks to the catalogue demonstrate, Scott and Sweeney use the past to legitimize the present. Both men draw visual connections between 1960's abstraction and pre-twelfth-century Irish stone carvings, thus indulging in the then-current fashion for relating the modern to Ireland's Celtic past (see also entries 13 and 50). This ahistorical connection was re-emphasized in visual terms on the cover of the exhibition catalogue by the use of Patrick Scott's abstract design, derived from a Celtic precedent.[2]

Source: *Rosc*, exhibition catalogue, Dublin, 1967, pp. 8–9, 14–15

## INTRODUCTION BY THE CHAIRMAN OF THE COMMITTEE [MICHAEL SCOTT]

The name Rosc, an old Irish word, was chosen to express the ideals of this exhibition. Rosc means the poetry of vision.

The uniqueness of this exhibition lies in the form of selection; three art experts of the highest international repute were asked to choose 50 painters of the international scene, and from these to select from 2 to 5 paintings executed in the last four years. The jury do not suggest that these paintings are the best in the world. The guarantee, however, for the quality of the agreed selection is the reputation of the internationally recognized panel of jurors, whose knowledge and integrity is beyond question.

During the preliminary discussions, the jury and committee came to the conclusion that a contrast of the modern paintings with some of the great objects of our ancient culture would be of the greatest aesthetic interest both nationally and internationally. Accordingly, the jury made a selection of examples of our pagan art, and that of the early Christian period up to the 12th century. These are being specially displayed in the National Museum in Dublin. Stone sculptures from these periods are shown integrally with the contemporary paintings in order to exemplify the close relationship between the art of the past and that of today.

The freedom and range of modern art has increased our understanding and appreciation of the arts of the past. The confrontation of early Irish works and modern ones will further illuminate and augment the appreciation of the ancient art of Ireland. [. . .] Cultural forces have united Ireland in the past, and it is hoped that future Rosc exhibitions, to be held every four years, will further enhance Ireland's cultural unity.

This recurrent exhibition should form a part of the effort leading toward the establishment of a world cultural heritage, and thereby to the unity of nations.

FOREWORD BY JAMES JOHNSON SWEENEY

As poetry comes before prose in the literature of any primitive people because it can be readily memorized, the early visual art of any people, by the same token, looks primarily to the production of striking and memorable organizations of shapes and colours, rather than towards a simulation of natural forms. In this character a work of primitive art – and most of the fresh expressions of painting and sculpture of the past seventy-five years – bear a close analogy to the fly of the salmon fisherman. The sportsman accepts without demur the fact that a 'Black Doctor', a 'Jock Scott', or a 'Red Torrish' are not copies of actual insects but organizations of shapes and colours for the visual appeal they exert through the tensions and intensities of their relationships. The fly-tier does not provide a simile as a lure to his game, but a metaphor. His creation does not depend for its efficacy on its resemblance to a living insect, but on its own attactiveness. It does not copy a 'Black Doctor', a 'Jock Scott', or a 'Red Torrish'; it is a 'Black Doctor', a 'Jock Scott', or a 'Red Torrish'.

The beginnings of all great art traditions have been metaphorical in this sense. This is evident in the early art of Ireland, whether in the decorated stones of the great neolithic tombs near Slane in Co. Meath – Knowth, Dowth and Newgrange; in the massive gold ornaments from the Bronze Age; in the two-faced and three-faced heads from Woodlands, Co. Donegal, and Corleck in Cavan; or in the early Christian art of the Carndonagh monuments, the Moone Abbey cross, or its most elegant distillation in the pages of the Book of Durrow.

It is of course true that all forms in sculpture and painting, no matter how arbitrary, formalized, or schematic, are derived from visual experiences of nature just as are the individual elements of the salmon fisherman's fly. And because these shapes and colours are found in nature the temptation to the artist is to try to copy in his medium the natural source-form rather than to face the more difficult task for the imagination, that of organizing a new form from these factors. Naturalistic representation is an outgrowth of virtuosity in the employment of copying techniques which, once they get out of hand, tend to bury the essential form – to hide it under distractions. The ideal in painting and sculpture is an objective reality which is the product of an artist's personal selection of natural shapes and colours, their abstraction from nature and reconstitution into an individualized form which can be admired for itself, that is to say for the order it embodies.

West European art during the past seventy-five years, in turning from its temptations to copy nature and the production of something that was primarily interesting for its resemblance to something else rather than for its own sake, has made a major advance in re-seeing and in the intensification of expression. We see this notably illustrated in the painting of the past four years. In poetry the sinew of expression is metaphor. And the power of the metaphoric approach in contrast to that of the simile toward an achievement of the intense and memorable in the visual arts is clear from the great art of pre-twelfth-century Ireland.

## NOTES

1    For a recent assessment of Rosc's contribution to the Irish art scene, see Dorothy Walker, *Modern Art in Ireland*, Dublin, The Lilliput Press, 1997, pp. 111–38. See also *Michael Scott: Architect In (casual) Conversation with Dorothy Walker*, Kinsale, Gandon Editions, 1995, passim.
2    See Walker, *Modern Art in Ireland*, p. 110.

# SECTION III

## CREATING HISTORIES

## INTRODUCTION

As any close reader of this anthology will acknowledge, the densely argued investigation into romantic nationalism that Luke Gibbons applies to the art of James Barry (entry 53; fig. 29) creates new agendas for Irish art historiography that a reading of the comments by Anthony Pasquin (entry 15) or Francis Sylvester Mahony (entry 17) on the same artist could not conceivably suggest. This final section of the volume concentrates on how the visualization of Ireland has been discussed by contemporary critics and historians. The six entries are taken from the last third of the twentieth century and by calling this section Creating Histories, the aim is to chart the analytical confidence that has, at last, entered the discussion of Irish visual material.

Brian O'Doherty (entry 49) together with Anne Crookshank and Desmond FitzGerald, the Knight of Glin (entry 51) offer us carefully constructed histories but ones that do not allow for much debate. Both texts impose fixed views on what defines the Irish visual experience. Focusing on the 1960s, O'Doherty examines the works of artists such as Nano Reid and Louis Le Brocquy in terms of a 'Native Heritage', the dominant feature being 'an atmospheric mode'. In the extract from their pioneering survey, *The Painters of Ireland*, Crookshank and FitzGerald inform us on the career of the eighteenth–century landscape painter Thomas Roberts (fig. 26). After identifying Roberts's individual style we are told that his works 'were the most important advertisement of the splendours of the Irish landscape.' What we are not asked to do is to place these works in some sort of cultural context. Despite its wide sweep, Cyril Barrett's important essay of 1975 (entry 50) does ask a key question, did Ireland produce a 'nationalistic' art and if not, why not?

Finally, the more recent contributions of Joan Fowler and Catherine Nash (entries 52 and 54) together with Gibbons's piece on Barry (entry 53) indicate the closer role that art historical investigations must now play in the burgeoning field of Irish Studies. Issues to do with the representation of gender in Irish society as well as the legacy of colonialism need urgent analysis. It is hoped that this reader will reveal some of the histories that still need to be written.

— 49 —

# Brian O'Doherty, *The Irish Imagination*, 1971

Brian O'Doherty (b. 1934) is an Irish-born critic who has lived most of his adult life in the United States; he is also well known as the conceptual artist Patrick Ireland.[1] A former editor of *Art in America,* O'Doherty is the author of *Inside the White Cube: The Ideology of the Gallery Space* (1986). As part of the second Rosc exhibition in 1971 (see entry 48 for Rosc 1967), O'Doherty organized an associated exhibition of Irish art entitled *The Irish Imagination, 1959–1971.* He also contributed a number of short essays to the catalogue, one of which is included here along with his Introduction. In these short pieces, O'Doherty takes a firmly modernist line in defining Irish art, mystification and 'an atmospheric mode' being the dominant characteristics. For a discussion of O'Doherty and other Irish critics of the 1970s and 1980s, see entry 13.

Source: *The Irish Imagination, 1959–1971,* Dublin, Municipal Gallery of Modern Art, 1971, pp. 10–11, 20

## INTRODUCTION

No colour field, no op, no art and technology weddings, no environmental machinery, very little pop, hard edge or minimalism are to be seen here. Yet local translations of international modes are *de rigueur* from Taiwan to Buenos Aires, signifying if not membership in the avant-garde club, at least a desire to belong. Why has Ireland, handily situated between Paris, London and New York not displayed these international symptoms?

   That avant-garde ideas could themselves be quietly examined and rejected without any great fuss, simply because they didn't prove useful, is unthinkable. But this, I suggest, is the explanation for the works here. In my experience seeing local exhibitions can be a bit of a chore. Their ventriloquism of the latest modes extracts a pity that tends to bring out the worst in one. The absence of such doppelganger provincialism made this a refreshing exhibition to select, as did its attractively modest cultivation of a position neither sycophantic nor truculent. The results have a consistency that requires some explanation. The reasons go back to the second world war which forced Ireland into some of its dullest isolation, when the probity of the literary magazine, *The Bell*, revealed by contrast the brackish intellectual climate in which self-indulgent apologies were the order of the day.[2] The spiritual powers of tradition and the secular power of the Church were equally oppressive, and food and intelligence were both rationed. Yet for painting the war proved fortunate in the most unexpected way. Before the war cut off the trickle of ideas a few important ones were introduced. The ensuing isolation allowed them to be examined, related to local temperaments and developed within a context of local needs. An artificial situation – deprivation – was, by accident, turned into one of natural and leisurely assimilation.

The person most responsible for this was Mainie Jellett, a pupil and later colleague of Gleizes. Her example and enthusiasm led to the founding of the Irish Exhibition of Living Art in 1943, a kind of *kunsthalle* without portfolio.[3] After the war, its annual exhibitions made modest but telling liaison with advanced art abroad. Distinguished modernist work was shown side by side with native art, providing standards and challenges, and renewing, in assimilable amounts, the flow of ideas. The invited art indicated the taste of the artists who made up the Living Art committee. Though there was an excessive regard for such second generation cubists as André L'Hote, the taste was fairly good – far more related to local needs than to international reputations. Victor Waddington's gallery in South Anne Street augmented the effect of the Living Art, gave focus to the local scene and assembled the first stable of Irish artists: Thurloe Connolly, Neville Johnson, Gerald Dillon, Colin Middleton and [Louis] Le Brocquy.[4] But Waddington's most important contribution was to create for these artists an audience which he educated with a series of small-scale international shows. This audience developed collectors who still surprise me with their knowledge and connoisseurship of the Irish artists. When these collectors began to buy avant-garde art abroad a kind of modern 'museum' developed, distributed through the many houses the artists visited. They could not see advanced art anywhere else. [. . .]

All this took place outside the official Dublin art world, represented by the pleasant body of men who make up the Royal Hibernian Academy. The Academy controlled the only art school, the National College of Art, where the teaching was and is splendidly irrelevant to its students' needs.[5] The floating complex of dealers (Waddington was joined by the Dawson Gallery in 1944 and by the Hendriks Gallery in 1956), artists and collectors thus had no access to the institutions. This explains the peculiar lack of influence by many of the best artists, such as Patrick Scott – they never got the opportunity to teach. One would have expected Jellett's demanding ideas to affect some of the younger artists, but the only painter who shared her tough-mindedness was Thurloe Connolly. His loss – he abandoned painting for design and went to live in England – further testifies to the lack of response to anti-romantic ideas in Irish art. Jellett's failure to give Irish art a firm cubist underpinning (apart from the work of Nano Reid) is easily understood. A suggestive form of painting with a particular atmospheric complexion, a product of the interaction of the artists and the audience created by and for their art in the forties and fifties, gathered force. Owing to the war, something 'local' in the best sense had the opportunity to develop. To call it a national quality could be an exaggeration, though all the paradoxes and misunderstanding of that idea were in operation.

The new audience discovered their souls, as it were, at the same time the artists discovered theirs. This audience had enough education and social pride to want an art of their own, and enough money to buy it. The art that appeared gives a clear idea of what the artists and their audience considered to be Irish not in the sense of presenting it to foreign eyes, but to themselves. A genuine transaction had taken place. Rumours of this got around and the *London Magazine* sent an emissary to look into it, who understandably failed to recognise what was going on.

The major figures who evolved this atmospheric mode were – and are – Nano Reid, an underrated artist of considerable pictorial intelligence, and Patrick Collins, whose work was highly influential. Hosts of Irish painters, including Camille Souter, Anna Ritchie, Noel Sheridan, helped evolve this 'poetic' genre.[6] The landscape and the Irish light – with its long twilights – affected this art deeply. Its atmosphere is characterized by a mythical rather than historical sense, an uneasy and restless fix on the unimportant, and a reluctance to disclose anything about what is painted, let alone make a positive statement about it. Its evasiveness summarises a whole defensive and infinitely discursive mode of existence in Ireland in the forties and fifties. In its way, it could be considered a last examination and confrontation of a certain minority or subject mentality that never responds to anything directly. Undoubtedly it is connected to a national self-image as explicated by a small community of artists and audience – not consciously or as a program, but as a natural outgrowth of an isolation that encouraged introspection.

This atmosphere became the dominant force in the 'look' of Irish painting well into the sixties. It caused the rejection of everything that didn't apply – not to Irish art *but to the Irish experience*. Pop, for instance, could only be an irrelevant joke in a country still dominated by rural manners. The perceptual confrontation tactics of op were anathema to Irish artists. Technological rhetoric was hardly convincing in a country where technology frequently demonstrated its lack of infallibility. Since that atmosphere required painterly illusionism, anything that interfered with the pictures' surface got short shrift. Rauschenberg, the most influential artist of the sixties, had no influence in Ireland at all.

Three other artists should be mentioned here, each related to this atmospheric painterliness in their own way. Le Brocquy used that atmospheric *donnée* to surround and amplify his points of single focus. Cecil King fairly recently transferred the atmospheric energies into exquisite works that quietly engage the problems of hard-edge painting. And Patrick Scott, more than any other Irish artist, responded to international ideas while producing the most consistently excellent body of work of any Irish artist; hints of atmospheric graces abound in his work in which impeccable taste is used not only for self-preservation but as a discreet weapon.[7]

The atmospheric mode was breached in the mid-sixties by Micheal Farrell whose work, while it indulges some romantic feeling, is aggressive and intellectually hard, giving a lead to a group of confident younger men such as Bulfin, Brian King, Ballagh and Henderson, all untroubled by the self-inquiries of the older generation. This second generation gives to painting in Dublin a diversity and energy it did not have before, and most of them show an acute political awareness. [. . .]


## THE NATIVE HERITAGE

With the decline of modernism, local art looks better. New York and Paris were hardly cities to the local artist; they were the Eye as Super-Ego. What local artists were accommodating, one discovers, was the *expectation* of the hostile eye – setting the stage for those comedies of misunderstanding that local art often plays out. There are some classic roles: dressing local themes in modernist styles; adapting a local motif for permutation; borrowing a persona from the hot centre to put down the yokels. In Ireland one is spared this doppleganger provincialism (the *Irish* Warhol, the *Irish* Rauschenberg) so prevalent in more visually sophisticated cities. Dublin still preserves a somewhat rural mentality within its urban Pale. A jeering suspicion makes short work of modernism's more exotic hybrids. Both the artist and his audience discourage formal impoliteness or radical gestures. Modernism is kept at a distance by what modernism eventually rid itself of – taste. Most Irish art since 1959 is very tasteful. But after this genuflection to modishness, it pursues its real concerns which, one way or another, revolve around the local artist's identity crisis: Can art be made here? If so, what kind? And by what kind of artist? In Ireland, where the past always had a big future, artists have a lot to choose from in seeking answers. Irish artists have recycled so much of the past that one sometimes has the impression that memory is recalling itself – that this is the Irish artist's idea of process. What do Irish artists, from the admittedly limited evidence in this exhibition, choose to remember? This falls naturally enough into categories, each of which bespeak a state of mind: *Pre-Christian art* which provides entry to the timeless compounds of myth through stone forts, Dolmens, tumuli, gold, burial chambers, decorated stones etc. Its timelessness makes it more imaginatively accessible than historical periods. Examples: [Anne] Madden's Standing Stones; [Nano] Reid's, [Patrick] Collins's and at times [Louis] Le Brocquy's atmosphere.

*Early Christian art* which in its linear intricacies is purported to image the Irish mind. Its manuscripts, metalwork and sculpture have been duly studied. Examples: Le Brocquy's *Clonfert: Four heads evoked* is part of this artist's thorough meditation on all aspects of what is visually usable in Irish culture; [Micheal] Farrell's brusque quotations of Celtic motifs are so formally convincing that his work has an attractive arrogance, as if the past had been invented just to suit *him*; Oisin Kelly's work has devoted itself to learning from Irish Romanesque sculpture.

*The Folk Tradition* is a rich resource that has been tapped consistently by only one painter of any stature, Gerard Dillon, whose early work had a wit and humour otherwise absent from Irish painting. *The Landscape*, annotated with ruins, earthworks, etc. can be seen as a repository of projected moods. As in very old countries with strong oral traditions, it is alive with memories. These graces civilize the Irishman's savage appetite for land. They also define aspects of the landscape as precisely as Catholic ritual used to be codified, so that they assume the force of a national icon – like the flag; for instance, the white-houses-dotting-the-patchwork-landscape cliché. This cliché is rescued by the most intelligent of the Academicians, Maurice McGonigal.[8] But more than specific configurations, atmosphere and light, however disguised, are a major theme in Irish painting. The main exhibition provides numerous examples. This atmosphere returns one to the first category above. Conspicuously missing is any reference to *previous* painting in Ireland – either through ignorance or some primitive wish continually to begin again. But an Anglo-Irish tradition in painting has existed in this country since the seventeenth century [. . .] Though this tradition has its own definite if muted glories, contemporary Irish artists have not been influenced by it – partly, one imagines, because the Royal Hibernian Academy [. . .] was seen as this tradition's curator (indeed, embalmer).

The complicated strategies of the local (as distinct from the provincial) artist raise questions that this small exhibition cannot possibly answer. But the best works here have an independence that is not obtuse, avoiding the provincialism of the right (nationalism) and the provincialism of the left (modernism). They show that the successful local artist has to be as intelligent as any modernist, and perhaps even more self-conscious, since he has more to think about.

Notes

1     See Dorothy Walker, *Modern Art in Ireland*, Dublin, The Lilliput Press, 1997, pp. 86–8, 91, 98–100.
2     For *The Bell* see Terence Brown, *Ireland: A Social and Cultural History, 1922–79*, Glasgow, Fontana, pp. 199–206 and passim.
3     For Jellett, see entry 12.
4     For all these artists and Waddington see Walker, *Modern Art in Ireland*, passim; for Le Brocquy see also entry 22.
5     See John Turpin, *A School of Art in Dublin since the Eighteenth Century: A History of the National College of Art and Design*, Dublin, Gill & Macmillan, 1995.
6     See Walker, passim.
7     Cecil King (1921–86) and Patrick Scott (b. 1921), see ibid., passim.
8     MacGonigal (1900–1979), President of the Royal Hibernian Academy from 1962–68.

— 50 —

# Cyril Barrett, 'Irish Nationalism and Art', 1975

Barrett is a Jesuit priest, a philosopher and an art historian who taught at the University of Warwick for many years. In 1971 he curated the exhibition *Irish Art in the Nineteenth Century* at the Crawford Municipal School of Art, Cork, which was mounted to coincide with the contemporary Rosc exhibition in Dublin (see also entry 49). Barrett has also written on kinetic and op art. His article on 'Irish Nationalism and Art 1800–1921' influenced at least one major reassessment of nineteenth-century Irish art production,[1] while its wide sweep of ideas and observations suggest many other areas in need of exploration.

Source: *Studies*, Winter 1975, pp. 393–409. The original article was not footnoted and has been severely edited; the two accompanying illustrations of Frederick W. Burton's *The Aran Fisherman's Drowned Child* (1841, Dublin, National Gallery of Ireland) and John Hogan's *Erin and Brian Boru* (1855, Cork, Crawford Municipal Art Gallery) have not been reproduced.

## NATIONALISTIC ART

It is impossible to discuss nationalism and art without making a number of tedious distinctions.

First, one must distinguish between national or regional art and nationalistic art. This distinction is slippery. What may count as merely national according to one definition of nationalism may count as nationalistic according to another. We shall meet these difficulties in due course, but first it would be useful to make some broad distinctions. By *national art* I mean art which is distinctive of a particular nation (or region). One would speak of Flemish medieval or Dutch seventeenth-century art as national. By *nationalistic art* I mean works which are either (a) designed to arouse or (b) capable of arousing national sentiments. [. . .]

There were at least three forms of nationalism in Ireland and a possible fourth which may have a doubtful claim to the title. First, there was what I will call *extreme nationalism* which involved both republicanism and separatism. This was the form of nationalism advocated by the United Irishmen, the Fenians and Sinn Féin. Secondly, there was what I shall call *mitigated nationalism*, that is, separatism without republicanism. This might take the form of establishing an Irishman (an O'Conor) or foreigner (Leopold of the Belgians) to rule over an independent Ireland. No particular party advocated this view, but a number of moderate nationalists toyed with it. Thirdly, *moderate nationalism*, by which I mean all those proposals which advocated some form of repeal of the Union without severing all links with Britain; in other words, not exactly republican nor completely separatist. O'Connell, the Young Irelanders and the Home Rulers were moderate nationalists in this sense. Finally, there were what I call the *patriotic Irish* or a mild form of moderate nationalism. This may be a controversial term, since each of the other groups would consider that they alone were patriots. However, I wish to identify a group who were either opposed to or indifferent to republicanism and separatism, and yet considered themselves first and foremost Irish. In a sense they owed a double allegiance: to Ireland and to the British crown. They were the sort of people who in Ireland might be regarded as pro-British in varying degrees but in Britain were regarded and regarded themselves as Irish. They have to be distinguished from the *loyalists* whose sole loyalty (and patriotism) was to the British crown; those who might be described as the British in Ireland, the British raj of the Western World.

Applying these distinctions to the period, it can, I think, safely be said that there was no body of art in support of mitigated nationalism, that is of a king of an independent Ireland. It can also be said, though with less confidence, that before 1921 there was no body of art which could be described as unequivocally supporting extreme nationalism. The portrait of John O'Leary, the Fenian, by John Butler Yeats and the bust of him by Oliver Sheppard hardly amount to a body of art, and in any event are as much tributes to O'Leary the man as to O'Leary the Fenian. It is, therefore, in the area of moderate nationalism and Irish patriotism (in the broad sense) that we are to look for a nationalistic Irish art. This brings me to the last preliminary question – and it is a large one – namely, what constitutes nationalistic art?[2] [. . .]

It should not be assumed [. . .] that every historical painting with a national subject is a nationalistic painting nor that every portrait, statue or bust of a national hero is nationalistic. A contemporary artist may merely wish to record an event such as an eviction, the potato blight, or emigrants, without wishing to stir up nationalistic sentiment. However, if, in the context of a nationalistic movement, an artist choses to paint national heroes or events of national significance, then this must be regarded as nationalistic art.

In a way one is on surer ground where the subject is symbolical: a subject such as Erin or Caitlín Ní Ullacháin (alias Cathleen Ni Houlihan) with her wolfhounds and round tower.

Another category of nationalistic art might involve satire and ridicule the opponents of national aspirations.

Finally, and this is much more tricky, subjects such as landscape, genre and even still-life, in certain contexts, can count as nationalistic. One would hardly call the landscapes of Constable, Turner or the Impressionists nationalistic, nor the studies of peasants by Millet and Courbet (though these might be described as socialist, but that is another matter), nor a vase of flowers by Fantin-Latour. But when we come to a Connemara landscape or the ruins at Glendalough or a study of Aran fishermen or a table covered with potatoes lying on a tattered copy of *The Nation*, then the case for calling them nationalistic in some sense of that word is strong. Of course an artist may choose to paint Connemara out of nothing more than an interest in its visual qualities: its barren mountains, spectacular clouds, its colour and light; he might paint Glendalough out of purely antiquarian interest, as he would Baalbek or the Campagna; he might paint fishermen in Aran because he found them picturesque – they could as well be in Bergen as on Aran. One has to take the context of production into account: who painted the picture, how does it fit into his *œuvre*, for what kind of public was it intended? And there is one other consideration. It seems to me that in all nationalistic painting there must be some element of symbolization. This is obvious in the case of the still-life described above, but it is equally true of the fishermen, Glendalough and even the Connemara landscape. These subjects not only arouse national and patriotic sentiment but also define it. It is all very fine to depict patriots in the battlefield or on the barricades or haranguing their fellows, but, if this is not to be the total extent of nationalism, some glimpse must be given of what these people are striving for, what values they wish to preserve, what kind of life they wish to bring into being, and the landscapes and genre symbolize this.

In the light of these general considerations, crying out as they are for modification, I now wish to study in a rather summary fashion (for the topic is vast) the extent to which Irish artists of the period from the Union to Independence evolved an art which could, by any stretching of that term, be called nationalistic.

## THE ABSENCE OF IRISH NATIONALISTIC ART

No one can doubt that throughout the nineteenth century, and indeed back into the eighteenth, some form of nationalism was passionately held in Ireland. To what extent it affected the community is another matter, but there were times – O'Connell's repeal campaign was one of them – when it manifestly gripped the vast majority. Ireland ranked with Poland, Hungary, and Italy as one of the most nationalistic countries in Europe. And yet when one comes to examine the art of the period, far from there being anything which could be described as a nationalistic art in any strict sense, it seems that there is hardly any art which could be described as nationalistic in any sense.

Hogan, the sculptor, who spent most of his life in Rome, comes nearest to being a nationalistic artist. He did statues of Davis, O'Connell and Father Mathew, and studies for Erin, and Erin and Brian Boru. Yet, in his total output, national themes form a small part in comparison with religious and mythological subjects.[3]

The only nationalist event which was treated extensively by artists of any merit was the literary revival. But, then, these artists were associated with that movement one way or another. AE's painting was a visual extension of his writing. John Butler Yeats's portraits of Standish O'Grady, Douglas Hyde, Synge, Lady Gregory and, of course, his own sons, may fairly be regarded as nationalistic in a broad sense: they could be used to arouse feelings towards a movement which was at least complementary to the political movements of the time. There is also the case of the two portraits of O'Leary, who was a political nationalist, but this case is isolated.[4]

Some people may be inclined to regard Jack B. Yeats as a nationalistic artist. He was certainly much concerned with political events during the period between 1915 and 1925 when he painted those oblique hints at these events – 'Bachelor's Walk, for remembrance', 'The funeral of Harry Boland', 'Talking to political prisoners'. It is arguable that these were the finest things that nationalistic art has produced in Ireland, but they might not have been very effective in arousing national sentiments; they were too subtle for that. As for the rest of Yeats's painting, it might be said that he was nationalistic in so far as he portrayed the life of the ordinary people. Thomas McGreevy, in his book on Yeats, wrote: 'Jack Yeats fulfilled a need that had become immediate in Ireland for the first time in three hundred years, the need of the people to feel that their own life was being expressed in art'.[5] We have the jarvey, the bargee, the jockey, the boatman, the ganger, the circus-man and the couple on a trip to Malahide. This is 'Irish patriotism', to be sure, and in some sense it might be described as nationalistic; but it is significant that these people, though poor and poorly dressed, are never suffering. There are no unemployed loafers, no down-and-outs, no struggling small farmers, no women and children in urban or rural hovels suffering from malnutrition or prematurely aged. What we have is the humorous and picturesque side of Irish life among the poor classes: Sommerville and Ross country for the most part, though Yeats, to be fair, penetrated a little deeper. There are also the Cuala Press, the Dun Elimir[6] Guild and his *A Broadsheet* and *A Broadside*. In these Yeats, often in collaboration with his brother William and his sisters, Lotty and Letty, employed the symbolism and mythology of Irish nationalism, and to that extent, if somewhat remotely, he might be regarded as intermittently a nationalistic artist.

Besides Yeats there is no one who could be regarded as even a candidate for the title of a nationalistic artist. Hugh Douglas Hamilton painted contemporary portraits of Lord Edward Fitzgerald and John Philpot Curran. John Comerford did a miniature of Robert Emmet, said to have been based on a sketch taken while Emmet was in the dock. Hogan, Foley, Turnerelli and others made statues, busts and portraits of O'Connell (it is said that 10,000 plaster copies of Turnerelli's bust were sold). There were occasional pictures such as the somewhat crude 'An Irish family discovering a blight in their store' (1847) by Daniel MacDonald or McDaniell or MacDonnell.[7] But, over a period of 120 years these are isolated instances. The best studies of the famine, eviction, destitution and emigration were made by a Scotsman, Erskine Nicol, who studied and worked in Ireland from 1845 till 1850 and returned many times subsequently. But Nicol's work could hardly be called nationalistic: it was sympathetic reporting. If one wants a picture of the events of the period one turns to *The Illustrated London News* or *Punch*, neither of which could be accused of having Irish nationalistic tendencies, and to what broadsheets have survived, and, later, photographs. A potential nationalistic cartoonist was lost to the nation when John Doyle emigrated to England in 1821. He did not begin his *900 Political Sketches* until 1829 and, though many referred to Ireland, not many were complimentary.

It might be possible to collect a sufficient number of works together in an exhibition and give the impression that there was unquestionable nationalistic art during the period. But this would be a false impression, as can be shown by consulting the catalogues of exhibitions which actually took place.

Taking first the great exhibitions between the Cork exhibition of 1852 (inspired by the Great Exhibition in London in 1851) and the Dublin exhibition of 1907, we find very few pictures or sculptures which can certainly be called nationalistic.[8] There were plenty of Irish landscapes and Irish ruins and Irish peasants, but these, as we have seen, are not necessarily nationalistic. Moreover, they were more than balanced by scenes from Britain, France, Italy and other places. In the Cork exhibition of 1852 there was nothing. The Dublin exhibition of 1853 had 'O'Connell addressing the Great Cliften meeting' (1385) and 'Father Mathew giving the pledge' (1488) by Martin Haverty. The Dublin exhibition of 1861 had nothing. The Dublin exhibition of 1865 had 'Departure of Irish emigrants' by W. Brocas (British section 83) – Irish art at this time was regarded as British – yet a whole gallery was devoted to soldiers who had won the Victoria Cross in the Crimea, India and elsewhere. The Dublin exhibition of 1872 had nothing, though there were thirty sketches of the Franco-Prussian War. But in the Dublin exhibition of 1882 there were busts of O'Connell (1680) by J.E. Jones, of Isaac Butt (1687) by James Cahill and 'Erin' (1681) by John Farrell, the sculptor. By 1900 Irish art was no longer classified as British, but there was nothing in the exhibition of Irish art organized by Hugh Lane in 1902, and in the Cork exhibition of that year there were only maquettes for statues of Tom Moore and Thomas Davis by Hogan. Finally, the Dublin exhibition of 1907 contained only Sheppard's bust of O'Leary (467) and his 'Oisin and Niam' (61), 'The spirit of Celtic art' (64) and 'The fate of the children of Lir' (79) by the same artist. [. . .]

Throughout its history *The Nation* had exhorted Irish artists to produce an Irish art, and it looked in particular to the RHA. Some years its hopes were raised only to be dashed the next.[9] [. . .]

The bitterest disappointment for the authors of *The Nation* was Frederick (later Sir Frederick) William Burton. They pinned great hopes on him. His qualities as an artist are unquestionable, even if many of his pictures are somewhat lacking in fluency and grace. He had learnt drawing from the Brocases and had acquired an interest in antiquarian and ethnographical subjects through his friendship with George Petrie.[10] His painting of Patrick Coneely (Connolly), the blind piper of Galway (now in the National Gallery), or his 'Aran fisherman's drowned child', encouraged the view that he might well become the leader of a new Irish nationalistic artistic movement. According to a contemporary, Stewart B[lacker] [. . .] he was the foremost Irish painter living in Ireland in the mid 1840s.[11] [. . .] of his contribution to th[e] 1846 RHA exhibition, a portrait of Lord Chancellor Sugden, 'an English

Cockney', [*The Nation*] can only say that it is not 'worthy of his Irish feeling – worthy of his Irish name worthy of himself'. In my opinion the Young Irelanders completely misunderstood Burton. I do not think he had any 'Irish feeling'. His interest in the Aran fisherman or the blind piper of Galway was purely ethnographical and detached, as were his studies of Franconian peasants. In 1844 he had been sent to Bavaria to copy (in watercolours) the great masters for the Duke of Bavaria. In 1851 he settled in Germany, and when he left there in 1856 he settled in London, where he eventually became director of the National Gallery, and earned his knighthood. [. . .]

## THE SIGNIFICANCE OF THE ABSENCE OF NATIONALISTIC ART

It is no answer to say that, with the possible exception of Poland, no European nation produced art which was both nationalistic and art. The question still remains: why not? [. . .]

There cannot have been much demand among the gallery-going public before Independence for nationalistic art. If what artists provide is not always to the public's liking they seldom fail to satisfy the public's known wishes. Clearly nationalistic art was not in demand. (Nor, it must be said, if the catalogues are anything to go by, was religious art.) We seem, therefore, to be left with two alternative conclusions: either the national events made no impact on the cultured section of the community or art is no index of national sentiment.

Now it is quite clear that the Lord Lieutenant and his entourage or, indeed, what is loosely called 'the ascendancy' would not like to find the walls of the RHA crowded with pictures of Wolfe Tone, Mitchell, famine victims, the eviction of tenants, the boycott of Captain Boycott, Fenians drilling, and other nationalistic subjects. But apparently a much wider public was uninterested in such subjects also. I do not know what the adult population of the ascendancy was but it would seem to be less than the art-going public. It is unlikely, for instance, that the 128,650 visitors to the National Gallery in 1867 (its maximum until 1968) or even the 64,342 who attended in 1895 (the lowest for the nineteenth century), were entirely made up of the ascendancy. I suspect that, whatever the number of that body was, it was as interested in grouse and pheasant and rough shooting, and fishing as in art, so it is unlikely that the visitors to the National Gallery or the 35,848 people, *excluding season ticket holders*, who attended the RHA exhibition in 1880, were all of the ascendancy. It would seem, then, that the apathy towards a nationalistic art was not confined either to the administration or to those who implacably considered themselves British. This view seems to be confirmed by the fact that

*The Nation* offered not only comment on the absence of nationalistic art but also reviews of RHA exhibitions at some length and without bias, and *The Nation* was certainly not directing its artistic criticism to members of the ascendancy. The *Freeman's Journal* and the *Irish Daily Independent* also reviewed the exhibitions. Moreover, there were special penny admissions to the exhibitions to encourage a wide public to visit them.

What, then, were the subjects with which Irish artists and their public were concerned? For the most part these were seascapes or landscapes, and not always what one would call national landscapes. Following the Continental fashion towards the end of the century (and many of the Irish artists of the period, who were later content to settle down in Ireland, studied on the Continent), many of these landscapes, though Irish in setting, such as Nathaniel Hone's *Cattle at Malahide*, could have been painted elsewhere. The same may be said of genre pictures such as Walter Osborne's *Tea in the Garden* and his *Lustre Jug*. They have the intimacy of pictures by Renoir and Vuillard and give no hint of the national passions which were eating out the hearts of some of their fellow-countrymen. Even when Osborne paints a Galway fair or an urchin in a Dublin street his preoccupation is not with the nationalistic significance of such scenes but with the visual qualities as seen through the eyes of a realist painter. As for the rest, the subjects were mostly genre pictures, often, it is true, with Irish subjects; illustrations of the classics, in which Shakespeare, and other English authors, dominated such Irish authors as Goldsmith; and mythological subjects, particularly in sculpture. Historical subjects were most likely to be scenes from British history: the Crimean War, Cromwell, Nelson, Wellington. Daniel Maclise's great 'Irish' picture is about the wedding of Strongbow and Eva![12] [. . .]

## NOTES

1    Jeanne Sheehy acknowledged the influence of this article on her book, *The Rediscovery of Ireland's Past: The Celtic Revival, 1830–1920*, London, Thames & Hudson, 1980, p. 195, n. 30.

2    Here Barrett goes on to discuss Thomas Davis's 'Hints for Historical Paintings', see entry 8, b.

3    For Hogan see John Turpin, *John Hogan: Irish Neoclassical Sculptor in Rome*, Dublin, Irish Academic Press, 1982.

4    On John B. Yeats's art see William M. Murphy, *Prodigal Father: The Life of John Butler Yeats (1839–1922)*, Ithaca and London, Cornell University Press, 1978, and Fintan Cullen, *The Drawings of John Butler Yeats*, Albany Institute of History & Art, 1987.

5    Thomas MacGreevy, *Jack B. Yeats: An Appreciation and An Interpretation*, Dublin, Victor Waddington and Colm O'Lochlainn, 1945. The most recent reassessment of Yeats is Bruce Arnold, *Jack Yeats*, New Haven and London, Yale University Press, 1998. See also entry 20.

6       Barrett is referring to the Dun Emer Guild. See Hilary Pyle, *The Different Worlds of Jack B. Years. His Cartoons and Illustrations*, Dublin, Irish Academic Press, 1994, pp. 283–90.

7       See *Folk Tradition in Irish Art, An Exhibition of Paintings from the collection of the Department of Irish Folklore*, University Collge Dublin, 1993, pp. 27–8 and 49. For Hamilton's portraits of FitzGerald see Fintan Cullen, 'Lord Edward FitzGerald: the creation of an icon,' *History Ireland*, vol. 6, no. 4, Winter 1998, pp. 17–20.

8       See also the two chapters by Cyril Barrett and Jeanne Sheehy on the 'Visual Arts and Society, 1850–1921', in *A New History of Ireland, VI, Ireland Under the Union, II, 1870-1921*, ed. W.E. Vaughan, Oxford, Clarendon Press, 1996, pp. 436–99.

9       For extracts from *The Nation*, see entry 44.

10      For Burton see Marie Bourke, 'Rural Life in pre-Famine Connacht: A Visual Document', in *Ireland: Art into History*, eds., Raymond Gillespie & Brian P. Kennedy, Dublin, Town House, 1994, pp. 61–74; for the Brocas family see Patricia Butler, *The Brocas Collection*, Dublin, The National Library of Ireland, 1997; for Petrie see entry 9.

11      For Blacker, see entry 32.

12      Daniel Maclise, *The Marriage of Strongbow and Eva*, 1854, National Gallery of Ireland, see Fintan Cullen, *Visual Politics: The Representation of Ireland 1750–1930*, Cork University Press, 1997, pp. 47–9 and Jeanne Sheehy, 'Irish Art and Natural Identity', *Oxford Art Journal*, 22, 2, 1999, p. 139.

# — 51 —

# Anne Crookshank and the Knight of Glin, *The Painters of Ireland*, 1978

When it appeared in 1978, *The Painters of Ireland* was the first illustrated comprehensive survey of Irish painting.[1] The book is, as the authors themselves say, 'a simple chronological account of the history and development of Irish painting'. The focus is invariably on the artist, and the establishment of a verifiable corpus of works lies behind nearly every individual discussion. The section chosen for inclusion here tells of the eighteenth-century landscapist Thomas Roberts (fig. 26), whose *œuvre* has also been the subject of investigation by staff at the National Gallery of Ireland. Between them, the authors of *The Painters of Ireland* and curators at the National Gallery have defined, over the past quarter of a century, the most important artists and developments in Irish visual history from the seventeenth century to the early twentieth century. Anne Crookshank and Desmond FitzGerald have

established a canon which had only been tentatively suggested by such pre-
cursors as Anthony Pasquin (see entry 15) and Walter Strickland. Crookshank
is Professor Emeritus of the History of Art at Trinity College Dublin as well
as a founding member of the Rosc committee. FitzGerald is a former curator at the Victoria and Albert Museum, London, and is at present Irish representative for Christie's, the international art dealers.

Source: Anne Crookshank and the Knight of Glin, *The Painters of Ireland, c.
1660–1920*, London, Barrie and Jenkins, 1978, pp. 127–33. Some of the original
notes have been kept but abbreviated, while illustrations have been left out. Fig.
26 has been added.

Irish painting in the eighteenth century reached its high point in the landscapes of Thomas Roberts and William Ashford which were to a large extent
exhibited at the Society of Artists in William Street, Dublin, from 1765 to
1780. Their quality was underlined by the condescending traveller Richard
Twiss, who remarked about the exhibition of 1775, 'I saw an exhibition of
pictures in Dublin, by Irish artists; excepting those (chiefly landscapes) by Mr
Roberts and Mr Ashford, almost all the rest were detestable.'[2]

Thomas Roberts (1748–78), the most brilliant and shortest-lived Irish
landscape painter of the second half of the eighteenth century, was connected
with Mannin, Mullins and Butts as he was taught by all three.[3] He entered
the Dublin Society Schools as a boy in 1763, in which year he also obtained
a prize. Presumably he later went on to Mullins as an apprentice. Pasquin only
states that while he studied under Mullins, he acquired his pocket money '. . .
by painting the black eyes of those persons who had been fighting and bruis-
ing each other in his master's tap-room on the preceding evening'. Pasquin
adds that 'he was improved by Butts', though no details are given and he
thought that he 'gained more reputation as a landscape painter than any other
Irishman'.

By 1766, Roberts was exhibiting at the Society of Artists and seems to have
made a name almost at once. Between 1766 and 1773 he exhibited some fifty-
six works and continued to exhibit until 1777. His earliest surviving works,
exhibited in the 1770 and 1771 exhibitions, include views of Ballyshannon
and Belleek, which are topographical townscapes and do not altogether suit
his talents. However, in the same exhibitions, he showed a number of pure
landscapes, where his main interest lies. He clearly looked at Dutch pictures
and at Vernet, for one of the exhibited works, *A Sea-Storm*, is entirely in the
Vernet manner. In these same years he showed two horse paintings: in 1771
no. 48 is described as *A landscape from nature, in which is introduced the portrait of*

*a Mare. &.* and in 1772 he showed the *Portrait of bold Sir William, (a Barb) an East Indian black, and French dog, in the possession of Gerald Fitzgerald Esq.* The latter has recently been identified[4] as the painting from the Carton collection which has been called from the label on the frame, Lord Edward FitzGerald's negro servant, *Tony and his white pony.* If the latter subject was correct then the picture would have to date from after Roberts's death and it has therefore been given to his brother Thomas Sautell Roberts. The attribution to Thomas Roberts seems most likely because of the high quality of the work both in landscape and in the treatment of the horse which is close to that in other certain pictures by the elder brother. It indicates that he must have been a very fine horse painter. It is not possible from the existing known works, roughly thirty in number, to deduce any stylistic development though some of his works have a hazier or lighter touch, perhaps due to over-cleaning. Roberts's paint surface is incredibly delicate and agrees with the description of his character given by Pasquin, when he says 'there was an elegance and a gentleness in the manners of Mr Roberts'. He also tells us that Roberts had 'a pulmonary complaint' as a result of what is commonly termed 'good fellow-ship'. In 1778, he went to Lisbon for his health and died there in the same year.

His patrons included the Duke of Leinster, Viscount Powerscourt, Viscount Cremorne, the Earl of Ross and Earl Harcourt when he was Viceroy between 1772 and 1777. Roberts frequently painted series of views, such as the brilliant set of Carton Park, the lake at Dartry and Upper Lough Erne at Bellisle. Two paintings commissioned by Harcourt, which are of exceptional quality, still belong to one of his descendants and the Earl may have introduced Roberts to English patronage. Certainly, in 1775 Roberts was paid by Sir Watkin Williams Wynn for two pictures, for the staircase of his new Adam house in St James' Square. The pictures are still there, inset into upright panels. He was paid £52 10s. 0d. for the pair and described in the bill as 'Mr Roberts of Dublin'. However, he might as easily have been introduced by Mullins who, having painted round Wynnstay, presumably knew Sir Watkin Williams Wynn. One of these two uprights, an unusual form for Roberts, include the ruined abbey of Castle Dermot with a ruined church and an Irish round tower in the background, which is also a feature of one of the Harcourt pictures. The other shows a waterfall on a windy day, with a man walking up the hill clapping his hand to his tricorne hat, which is typical of Roberts's lively observation of his figures. A rather similar picture with a windblown tree and waterfall falls into the category of a Roberts which might have been completed after his death by his brother, Thomas Sautell Roberts. In contrast to these stormy scenes, most of his views have an idyllic pastoral atmosphere of long, sunny summer days, boating expeditions set in ordered nature, but with limitless romantic scenery to be discovered and no doubt described with all the enthusiasm of *The Post Chaise*

*Companion.* The Dartry, Carton and Bellisle views are typical of the admiration evoked by the Irish landscape garden. Roberts's appreciation of the blue distances, the soft changing light and tree-begirt castles and mountains of Ireland, together with the now fashionable antiquarianism of the period, make his paintings some of the most nostalgic and evocative ever painted of the country. The Harcourt pictures admirably sum up these moods, as does the large landscape in the N[ational] G[allery] [of] I[reland]. The minute, crisp technique which he employs for his foliage is aptly described by Sarsfield Taylor, who says 'He pencilled in his foliage beautifully'[5] and it contrasts with the softer warmth of his rocks. His water varies from the serenity of pellucid lakes to the tumult of waterfalls and this water, in a very marked degree, gives to his pictures the vaporous atmosphere typical of Ireland.

Roberts was engraved by [Thomas] Milton, who used two of his pictures in his *Collection of Select Views from the Different Seats of the Nobility and Gentry in the Kingdom of Ireland.* Milton came to Ireland in 1783 and, between then and his departure for London in 1786, he issued a number of plates. The remainder date from 1786 to 1793 and were issued in London on his return. William Bell Scott in his *Autobiographical Notes* says that 'Milton had a unique power for distinguishing the foliage of trees and the texture of all bodies, especially water, as it never had been done before, and never will be done again'. A glance at his engraving of Roberts's *View of Beauparc from the River Boyne* [fig. 26] illustrates his remarkable ability to maintain the character of an artist's works. These plates were the most important advertisement of the splendours of the Irish landscape and not only propagated the knowledge of a number of Irish artists, but also immortalised Francis Wheatley's stay in this country.

NOTES

1    Ten years earlier, Bruce Arnold had produced *A Concise History of Irish Art*, London, Thames and Hudson, 1968. Prior to *The Painters of Ireland*, the most comprehensive account of Irish art in the modern era had been Walter Strickland's *A Dictionary of Irish Artists*, 2 vols., Dublin, 1913.

2    Richard Twiss, *A Tour of Ireland in 1775*, 1776, p. 52. [Orig. note.]

3    James Mannin (d. 1779), French/Italian teacher of ornament and landscape at the Dublin Society Drawing Schools; George Mullins (fl. 1763–75), landscape painter; John Butts (*c.* 1728-64), landscape painter, faker and first teacher of James Barry.

4    See Michael Wynne, 'Thomas Roberts, 1748-1778: Some reflections on the bicentenary of his death', *Studies*, Winter 1977, pp. 299–308, and *Thomas Roberts, 1748–1778*, exhibition catalogue, Dublin, National Gallery of Ireland, 1978. [Orig. note.]

5    William B. Sarsfield Taylor, *The Origin, Progress and Present Condition of the Fine Arts in Great Britain and Ireland*, 2 vols., London, 1841, vol. II, p. 283. [Orig. note.]

BEAU · PARC .
Most Humbly Inscribed to Charles Lambart Esq.ʳ by Thos. Milton .

26     Thomas Milton after Thomas Roberts, *View of Beauparc from the River Boyne,* from
*Collection of Select Views from the Different Seats of the Nobility and Gentry in the King-
dom of Ireland*, 1785

# — 52 —

## Joan Fowler, 'Art and Politics in the Eighties', 1990

Between September 1990 and March 1991 the Douglas Hyde Gallery, an
exhibition space for contemporary art attached to Trinity College, Dublin,
mounted five exhibitions under the general title of *A New Tradition: Irish Art
of the Eighties*. Each one had a different focus, 'Nature and Culture',
'Sexuality', 'Politics', etc. Works by more than thirty artists were shown. Joan
Fowler, a lecturer at the National College of Art and Design in Dublin, wrote
two of the seven catalogue essays. The following is an edited section from one
of these essays, 'Locating The Context – Art and Politics in the Eighties'.
Fowler sets out to discuss what she believes to be 'the more significant themes
in visual art in the 1980s'. Taking a cue from W.B. Yeats, she concentrates on
two forms which identify Irish expression in opposition to the colonial

presence, a sense of Place and Ireland as Woman; the focus of this extract is in the 'politics of place'.[1]

Source: *A New Tradition: Irish Art of the Eighties*, Dublin, The Douglas Hyde Gallery, 1990, pp. 117–18, 122–3. Some of the original notes have been kept but are abbreviated or contracted. The original illustrations have been omitted except for Willie Doherty (fig. 28), while Richard Hamilton's *The Citizen* (fig. 27) has been added.

The opening line of a 1985 essay on Northern Irish poetry by Edna Longley reads, 'Poetry and politics, like Church and State, should be separated.'[2] On the face of it, the comparison between Church and State, poetry and politics is a strange one: if in theory, there is a measure of separation between Church and State in Ireland, everyone knows that in practice the edges are very blurred, and yet no-one has even suggested that poetry assume a relationship with politics as Church with State. No, Edna Longley is talking about a principle, a principle she clearly feels she should be forthright about because she detects occasional leanings towards political viewpoints among Northern poets, but perhaps more particularly because she opposes positions assumed in contemporary intellectual organs such as *Field Day* and *The Crane Bag*.[3] She agrees with Conor Cruise O'Brien's forebodings about 'an unhealthy intersection', and is in disagreement with the tone established by Richard Kearney in the first sentence in the first article of *The Crane Bag* journal back in 1977 when he wrote 'Politics is far too grave a matter for the politician. Art is far too potent a medium for artist.'[4] Longley points to examples where political affiliation has restricted the poet's ability to represent different subject positions, thus limiting his or her art. Moreover she believes certain literary critics and theorists encourage a political reading of poetry.

Despite the opposition expressed in these rhetorical flourishes, Longley and Kearney are not so distantly removed from one another in their views about art. Both believe that art is autonomous but that it can also serve in some way as a corrective to politics. Their differences seem more to do with their understanding of what politics is, or should be. Kearney believes that imagination is vital to politics, whereas Longley believes that politics is too fixed and intransigent for imaginative recreation. Kearney, it seems, has greater faith in the possibility of artistic vision being projected to the forefront of the political stage.

While Edna Longley's essay is specifically about poetry and Richard Kearney uses the term 'art' in the broadest sense, it is possible, I think, to find echoes of such arguments throughout the arts in Ireland in the 1980s. If *The*

*Crane Bag* was the most consistent, intellectual and sometimes portentous forum for debates on art, culture and politics in its life-span from 1977 to 1985, it should take some credit for maintaining an interdisciplinary policy in which politics and the arts rubbed shoulders. In turn *The Crane Bag* was responding to currents in critical theory, to Postmodernism, and of course to events in the north of Ireland, all of which have contributed to a considerable number of visual artists producing work which, in the mid-1980s, was less isolated and more concerted in using certain political themes. This immediately begs the question, what is political art? It may be necessary to address the question if only because it was made into an issue in the only book to be published on Irish visual arts and politics, that is, Brian McAvera's *Art, Politics and Ireland*,[5] in which the definition of 'politics' is the subject of the first chapter. McAvera is correct to the extent that he sees a preponderance of art criticism in Ireland concerning itself with the medium rather than the content of art, but he is wrong to pigeon-hole art into degrees of social-political statement. The question, 'what is political art?', is the same kind of misnomer as the older question, 'what is art?', because it attempts a catch-all definition instead of looking to the practices and production of artists and how these interconnect with social/political/cultural practices and ideologies. The question is 'how?' not 'what?'.

But if a priori categorisation blots out possibilities, the issue can be over-simplified in other ways. In 1984 the American art writer Lucy Lippard made a crucial visit to Ireland to select contemporary Irish art for a touring American exhibition. Lippard was particularly interested in finding political and 'activist' art in Ireland and she was asked to submit her views in an article for *Circa*, an extended and slightly different version of which was published in the same year in the United States.[6] In the later essay she writes: 'For present purposes, I'd describe a political artist as someone whose subject and sometimes contexts reflect social issues, usually in the form of ironic criticism . . . political art tends to be socially *concerned* and "activist" art tends to be socially *involved* not a value judgement so much as a personal choice.' While Lippard argues that defining roles and mediums for artists 'is a classic way of keeping everybody in their places', her description that political artists '*reflect* social issues' at worst suggests passive retrospection by the artist. In fairness to Lippard, she is someone who believes in accessing art on as broad a base as possible, and 'reflect' conveys the artist's subject in simple terms. However it does little to explain the complexity of art's production and reception [. . .]

First let us return to the 'unhealthy intersection'. It should be noted when Edna Longley and Richard Kearney talk about art and politics, whatever their differences of opinion, they both assume an important role for art in the directions of the society – Church and State, art (or poetry) and politics are presented as though in the same order of magnitude. Neither writer is crude enough to say that art's role is pedagogic, neither writer has lowered their sights to a discussion of the formal qualities of artwork which effectively, in the case of the visual arts, consigns art's social role to adornment or enhancement of public or private spaces. Longley's concern is that art and politics ultimately lead to art as propaganda. This indeed has been a source of much consternation in the visual arts. In her 1984 visit to Ireland, Lucy Lippard found little which was, in her terms, political or 'activist': 'The complexity of Irish political life appears to be paralleled by the layered, contradictory images that I often found tantalizingly indirect.' Her comments prompted a reply from John Kindness who, in a letter to *Circa* said, 'To engage in the sort of activism she describes from her American experience the artist needs to be committed, s/he needs to take sides, to make choices; this is the choice that most artists find impossible to make in the Irish situation.'[7]

In these statements neither Lippard nor Kindness acknowledges partition and although there was nothing new in the idea that Irish art is indirect (i.e. *The Delighted Eye* exhibition, London, 1980[8]) it did seem to have a particular import coming from Lucy Lippard. Her visit became part of a process in a general shift in thinking towards political content among several young Northern artists. Even so, when this culminated in the *Directions Out* exhibition in the Douglas Hyde Gallery in 1987 as a showcase for 'political art' from the North, the curator, Brian McAvera, decided to make a virtue of indirectness.[9] Here, as in the Irish landscape exhibition, *The Delighted Eye*, the supposed avoidance of direct statement or 'the oblique approach' was made into an Irish personality trait, thereby realigning art with nature instead of art with politics. John Kindness, however, is suggesting that the Irish situation is different to the American and in Ireland one cannot make an absolute choice. An obvious example of Kindness's difficulty is in the North where an individual may feel obliged to be either Nationalist or Unionist because there is no substantive political ground in between. But in no sense does this prevent the artist from broadening the narrow definitions of Nationalism and Unionism, or from creating provisional solutions to a particular set of problematics. Whatever the status quo of the ballot box, the artist can, in artistic terms, deal with the inadequacies of his or her society, or even be pedagogic in suggesting a different society and be at the same time consistent in using electoral politics. There are no more irrevocable choices in politics than in art, even if Unionist and to some extent Nationalist interests have polarised the situation in such a way that the democratic right to choose is very limited.

The sub-text here, as with McAvera and Longley, is that politics leads art down the road to being used for propaganda purposes. In this respect, Brian

27    Richard Hamilton, *The Citizen,* detail, 1982–3

McAvera is partly right when he criticises *The Citizen*, 1982–3, the painting by English artist Richard Hamilton [fig. 27], when he says, 'The blanket-draped figure exposing (the hunger-striker's) chest and thus his crucifix, presents a neat propaganda image of the equation: Hunger-Striker = Christ = catholic church support for the Provisional IRA, an image perfectly attuned to the republican wall murals.' While Hamilton claimed that his painting was a response to media representation of the prison protest for political status by Republican prisoners during 1980 and 1981, McAvera along with a number of artists and critics in the North, saw it as a naive replication of the symbolism of martyrdom which had appeared in Nationalist areas at the time. In other words, *The Citizen* fell short as 'art' because, for the more sophisticated art audience who also knew something of the background to the North's crisis, the painting's explicitness was unpalatable as it echoed the 'religious pictures' of a Catholic tradition rather than a modern or modernist art and society. In this sense Hamilton's painting raises historical and ideological questions about art, firstly because *The Citizen* was directly 'readable' in such a way that it was down-graded alongside Nationalist street images, and secondly, because form and content were in crucial respects non-modernist, the painting did not construct the kinds of meanings that might allow it to be read as 'art' about a contemporary issue in Irish society and politics.

*The Citizen*, then, is an object lesson in how 'art' is predicated on structures of representation which are not reducible to a purely propagandistic message. The art context is involved, and it is through this that particular artworks are interpreted. This is not to say that art is necessarily difficult, obtuse

28    Willie Doherty, *Closed Circuit, Sinn Féin Advice Centre – Short Strand, Belfast,* 1989

and for the art-initiated only, it is only to say that *The Citizen* offended sensibilities in the North because it was a crude reminder of religious devotionalism as much as anything else. If we compare *The Citizen* with Willie Doherty's *Closed Circuit* (1989) [fig. 28], we may note that the sub-title of the latter gives vital information which helps to identify the location: 'Sinn Fein Advice Centre, Short Strand, Belfast 1989'. The photograph shows a scene in which partitions dominate, and below, across a road, the artist has printed, 'Closed Circuits'. It is useful to know that Sinn Fein is a target, and more, that the recent censorship legislation leaves the Party without direct access to the media. *Closed Circuit* is, I think, accessible while at the same time it avoids the standard and sensationalist media images of Northern Ireland. Moreover, in terms of art, it uses an interplay of image and text to create meaning, whereas *The Citizen* reproduces a redundant iconic image in which there is no apparent self-conscious comment on its own redundancy. [. . .]

Since the claim is made that what is emerging in the visual arts in the mid-eighties is somehow related to a general body of theory, more demonstration is required. Art, theory and The National Question winds inexorably back to the figure of W.B. Yeats, regarded as one of the major poets in modern English literature, and a member of the Senate in the early years of the Irish Free State. Yeats's vision of an Ireland free of British oppression assumes two forms which have since been pursued by artists and intellectuals. One is the metaphoric use of the land as the Nation, the other is the metaphoric use of Ireland as Woman. [. . .]

In an analysis of Yeats, Edward Said[10] argues that there are two phases of a nationalist liberation movement. The first is a period of nationalist anti-imperialism in which 'there is a pressing need for the recovery of land which, because of the presence of the colonizing outsider, is recoverable at first only through the imagination. Now if there is anything that radically distinguishes the imagination of anti-imperialism it is the primacy of the geographical in it.' The second phase, according to Said, is when liberation becomes more realizable: 'With the new territorality there comes a whole set of further assertions, recoveries and identifications, all of them quite literally grounded on this poetically projected base. The search for authenticity for a more congenial national origin than that provided by colonial history, for a new pantheon of heroes, myths, and religions, these too are enabled by the land.' A crude interpretation of Said would be that the first and second phases of the Nationalist movement correspond with Yeats's career, in the latter stages of which the vision becomes increasingly pedagogic and idealized.

If the land issue was fundamentally important in the agrarian struggles of the nineteenth century and in the subsequent development of Nationalism, is it of any contemporary consequence when, in the South, scarcely lip-service, usually symbolic, is paid to the territorial claims on the North? The answer is surely that the legacies of the land issue survive in a real sense where, in the North, Catholics still hold the poorer land, lower paid jobs and higher unemployment, and in the South, where the advent of the Free State and later the Republic brought little by way of radical land reform. The tenaciousness of land issues [were] such during the 1986 Divorce Campaign [that] there was a successful deflection from divorce to land inheritance rights by the anti-divorce lobby. Such issues have certainly emerged in theoretical studies. In Art History, for example, there has been a move from seeing landscape as scenery, to seeing landscape as property and territory. Following John Berger's widely disseminated *Ways of Seeing*, of the early seventies, there are now several substantial texts examining the historical relationships between landscape painting and land ownership, and these have been to some extent applied to colonialism in Ireland by John Hutchinson and Mary Cosgrove.[11]

In 1982, Deirdre O'Connell made an installation in the Art and Research Exchange Gallery in Belfast entitled, *The Palatine's Daughter*. The exhibition space was defined by two lines of fragile white plaster forms, each of which was propped (almost) upright by cords attached to the gallery floor. The installation was accompanied by an artist's statement which was a series of words: Territory, Barrier, Obstacle, Zone, Enclosure, etc. In Belfast, Catholic and Protestant communities had mentally defined their own areas but the British army intervention of 1969 had set up physical barriers between the communities and in the process had got it wrong. O'Connell's installation takes into account the 'no-man's land' created by the partitioning of sections of a city and the disturbance or removal of community identity. It is as much about a psychological condition as a physical deprivation. In about 1985 Willie Doherty began his photo-text work and, in the same year, he produced *Fog/Ice* and *Last Hours of Daylight*. The ostensible subject of both is the Bogside in Derry. In *Fog/Ice* the mist, descending from the hills around, is 'Shrouding/Pervading' and, in *Last Hours of Daylight*, the Bogside is 'Stifling' and 'Surveillance' is hidden but present. The security forces watch over the Bogside but beyond the security forces lie the unknown, shrouded hills of Ireland.

If these works by O'Connell and Doherty are about a psychological state of play, land and territory also have important material consequences. In the South, Mick O'Kelly combines urban and rural locations. As part of a series of photographs with text entitled *Allegories of Geography* (1987), he shows two photographs, one of a worked bog, the other of an open hillside. Centred under the photograph of the bog is the word 'Soil', beside which are words such as 'Territory, Displacement, and Domain'. Centred under the other photograph is 'Property', and beside it are words such as, 'Divide, Boundary and Map'. These are the politics of economics versus ecology.

Said's arguments on Nationalism have a particular resonance today for the North where there has been a growing body of opinion in favour of what has been called the 'politics of place'. This is a move to assert the identity or identities of the North, subsumed as these were by British culture. It is a presentation of the vernacular and the locality of the North in art, and to that extent, the features of the 'politics of place' are very similar to the Nationalism of the late nineteenth and early twentieth centuries: the Celtic Revival, Synge and Yeats. The development of Place in the visual arts is signposted by the establishment of the Orchard Gallery in Derry and the appointment of Declan McGonagle as its Director in 1978, and the Art and Research Exchange in Belfast in the late '70s with its offshoot, *Circa Art Magazine*, in 1981. In the first issue of *Circa*, the poet Tom Paulin suggested that while many Irish writers have established Ireland on the international literary map, this was not the case with the visual arts. He goes on to describe several images, specific to the North, which he believed the artists could well utilize.[12] In fact one of Paulin's examples, the black taxi, appeared in the Artpages of *Circa* in 1989, (no. 45), in a piece by Anthony Davies, but in the intervening years the amount of visual work from the North that could be described under the politics of place would incorporate many of the younger artists established in the North, including Willie Doherty and, in some aspects, Deirdre O'Connell and Micky Donnelly.

Much of this work records the actualities of sectarian life in the North, for example, the Orange parades (Anthony Davies), the Protestant community in Belfast (Rita Duffy), but while the specificities were important in establishing identity and confidence for Northern artists, there is a sense in which the very particularity of representation was a closure rather than an opening for political art. However, the work of these artists, and those included in the *Directions Out* exhibition, is informed and informing in ways in which *The Citizen* is not and is a considerable achievement in representing the locality in ways it had not been represented before. But it is notable that most of these artists have not continued to restrict their subjects to Northern Irish material. Dermot Seymour has moved from the 'realism' of *All the Queen's Horses* (c. 1983), to the enigmatic *Do you ever think of Daniel Ortega?* (1986), to a position in the late 1980s in which humans are replaced by animals and the meaning for human life is veiled. This is to say that Seymour has latterly begun to make more demands of his viewer in finding context and meaning which is a cut 'above' the raw realities of repression and sectarianism. In Seymour's paintings there is, therefore, an intimation of ideological existence beyond the barricades, and if Seymour is approaching a more universal language, then Willie Doherty has sustained the broader issues in his photo-texts on Derry between 1985 and 1988. His two-part *Stone upon*

*Stone* (1986) is eloquent testimony to the internalised aspirations of Nationalism (west bank of the Foyle), and Unionism (right bank of the Foyle), as well as a telling juxtaposition of the territorial reality.


NOTES

1       For an assessment of *A New Tradition*, see Caoimhín Mac Giolla Léith, 'Strategic Representations: Notes on Irish Art since the 1980s', in *When Time Began to Rant and Rage: Figurative Painting from Twentieth-Century Ireland*, ed. James Christen Steward, London, Merrell Holberton, 1998, pp. 112–17.

2       Edna Longley, 'Poetry and Politics in Northern Ireland', *The Crane Bag*, vol. 9, no. 1, 1985, p. 26. [Orig. note.]

3       See Field Day Co., *Ireland's Field Day*, London, Hutchinson, 1985, and Seamus Deane, gen. ed., *The Field Day Anthology of Irish Writing*, 3 vols., Derry, Field Day, 1991; *The Crane Bag Book of Irish Studies*, eds. Mark Patrick Hederman and Richard Kearney, Dublin, Blackwater Press, 1982.

4       Richard Kearney, 'Beyond Art and Politics', *The Crane Bag*, vol. 1 (1977–81), p. 13. [Orig. note; see also entry 22].

5       Brian McAvera, *Art, Politcs and Ireland*, Dublin, Open Air, 1989 [Orig. note.]

6       Lucy Lippard, *Circa*, no. 17, July/August 1984, pp. 11–17, and 'Trojan Horse: Activist Art and Power', in *Art After Modernism: Rethinking Representation*, ed. B. Wallis, New York, The New Museum of Contemporary Art, 1984. [Orig. note.]

7       John Kindness, *Circa*, no. 18, September/October 1984, p. 25. [Orig. note.]

8       For comments on the exhibition *The Delighted Eye: Irish Painting and Sculpture of the Seventies*, London, 1980, see Tom Duddy in entry 13.

9       Brian McAvera, *Directions Out: An Investigation into a Selection of Artists whose Work has been Formed by the Post-1969 Situation in Northern Ireland*, Dublin, The Douglas Hyde Gallery, 1987.

10      Edward Said, *Nationalism, Colonialism and Literature: Yeats and Decolonisation*, Derry, Field Day Pamphlet, no. 15, 1988. [Orig. note.]

11      John Hutchinson, *James Arthur O'Connor*, Dublin, National Gallery of Ireland, 1985, and Mary Cosgrove, 'Paul Henry and Achill Island', in *Landscape, Heritage and Identity: Case Studies in Irish Ethnography*, ed. Ullrich Kockel, Liverpool University Press, 1995, pp. 93–116.

12      Tom Paulin, 'Where are the Images?', *Circa*, no. 1, November/December 1981, pp. 16–17. [Orig. note.]

# — 53 —

# Luke Gibbons, 'A Shadowy Narrator', 1991

Originally read as a paper at the 1989 Irish Conference of Historians gathering in Trinity College Dublin, this essay highlights the vital inter-connections that exist between the visual representation of Ireland and a wide range of cultural and political concerns. Luke Gibbons, who teaches at the School of Communications, Dublin City University, is a major contemporary voice in discussions on culture and Irish identity. In this piece, he focuses on the eighteenth-century painter James Barry (1741–1806), who is the subject of a number of entries in this volume (nos. 5, 15, 17, 28).[1] Compared with many other commentators on Irish art, Gibbons strives to find meanings for Barry's art while at the same time he suggests a previously unacknowledged Irish contribution to European Romanticism.

Source: '"A Shadowy Narrator": History, Art and Romantic Nationalism in Ireland, 1750–1850', in *Ideology and the Historians*, ed. Ciaran Brady, Dublin, The Lilliput Press, 1991, pp. 99–127. The edited extract included here is from pp. 108–19. Because of their quantity, the original endnotes have been reduced in number while only two illustrations have been retained, figs. 1 and 29.

As Tom Dunne has observed, it has become a commonplace to link the social conservatism of cultural nationalism in Ireland to Edmund Burke's formulation of a theory of community and tradition based on custom and the inherited wisdom of the ages.[2] What is interesting from the point of view of visual arts, however, is that the full weight of Burke's formidable critique of the Enlightenment made its presence felt in England rather than in Ireland, and, in fact, met its most sustained opposition at a cultural level from an Irish painter and one-time protégé of Burke, James Barry. The vehicle for shifting the theoretical basis of English painting from universal reason to local and national custom was the later lectures of Joshua Reynolds's *Discourses on Art*; but if, to adapt an aphorism from a later era, the voice was that of Joshua Reynolds, the mind was certainly that of Edmund Burke. Burke was Reynolds's intellectual mentor and closest friend – so close, in fact, that he was at Reynolds's bedside on the artist's death in 1792, and was entrusted with making his funeral arrangements and acting as executor of his will. Reynolds regularly sent his lectures to Burke for examination and revision before delivery, and indeed to Irish readers, the affinities between Burke's and Reynolds's critical opinions seemed so strong that as late as 1810, the *Hibernian Magazine* was still claiming that Burke actually wrote the *Discourses*.

Be that as it may, the discernible shift in Reynolds's *Discourses* after 1776 from the universalism of civic humanism to a language of custom and natural sentiments was prompted, as John Barrell has suggested, by the appearance on both sides of the Atlantic of a spectre that was to haunt the Whig imagination: the outbreak of revolution in America and, more particularly, in France.[3] By 1790, when history painting had met its nemesis in the Oath of the Tennis Court, Reynolds was in a position to exonerate himself from the charge that his own creative investment in portraiture did not live up to the high ideals enunciated in the early *Discourses*. In his final lecture (1790), he pointed out that the universal rhetoric of the grand style, and by extension republicanism, was simply not suited 'to my abilities, and to the taste of the times in which I live' – the best of times for republican Paris being the worst of times for London, at least where history painting was concerned. Reynolds was, in fact, able to disengage himself from the more radical implications of civic humanism without any great loss of face, for even in his most explicit pronouncements on the ideal of universalism, there was always a latent commitment to custom and tradition. This was because of his resolutely empiricist approach to 'abstraction' and 'general ideas'. In keeping with Hume's celebrated attack on causality, Reynolds held that the 'essence' or 'general form' of any object was not immanent in nature, but was simply what most people from habit and experience had agreed to be the case. What we perceive as general or universal is the residue of custom and accepted practice. The tenuous connection between this idea of universality and local custom was sufficient to permit Reynolds to argue that in certain cases local interests merge with the common good of humanity. [...]

What was good for general humanity apparently was also good for the empire. The hidden premise here was the assumption that custom in its political guise – the unwritten constitution and the tradition of common law – bequeathed the proud legacy of the freeborn Englishman. The recourse to tradition which was dismissed as an outcrop of Catholic superstition in Ireland was thus reclaimed in England under the pretext of liberty. It was this traducing of both republican ideals and Irish history which galvanized the Irish émigré James Barry into an unremitting – and, in terms of his own self-advancement, very costly – attack on the British art establishment that led ultimately to his expulsion from the Royal Academy in 1799: the only painter to enjoy that dubious honour.

Barry's strategy was simple if audacious: it was to deny that England had any right to be regarded as the custodian of liberty, and to propose instead that the very features of Irish society which English rule had systematically repressed were the true inheritors of the spirit of freedom. The idea that the torch of liberty had passed from England to Ireland was familiar enough in Volunteer rhetoric of the 1780s, but Barry took this a stage further by arguing provocatively that *Catholic* Ireland was the true repository of the kind of freedom and virtue enshrined in republican discourse. Presented with an Irish society based on tradition and community, it would have been easy for Barry to relapse into Burkean homilies on 'the little platoon', and to counterpose the merits of local custom to English pretensions to universal liberty. But this was not his approach: he distanced himself explicitly from the kind of parochialism which, as he put it, on 'being made acquainted with the domestic detail of one neighbourhood', states 'we shall profit very little by extending our enquiries to another'.[4] With this in mind, Barry sought to rehabilitate the native Irish for the cause of progress and to bring about a fusion — a highly combustible one, as it turned out — between the forces of Catholicism and republicanism in Irish culture.

In 1776 Barry published a striking print entitled *The Phoenix or Resurrection of Freedom* [fig. 29], which was intended to mark the flight of liberty from England to a new home in an America still basking in the light of independence. The dramatis personae gathered in the foreground around the bier of Britannia were stock figures in the annals of republicanism — Algernon Sidney, John Milton, Andrew Marvell, John Locke and, not a little presumptously, Barry himself. At the left-hand side, Father Time pays homage to the cradles of classical republicanism — Athens and Rome — but more important for Barry's ideological project is the barely perceptible trace in the midground of Florence, the birthplace of modern republicanism. It was in Florence, and more generally in Renaissance Italy, that the discourse of civic humanism and 'virtue' was revived[5], and not least of the factors promoting its rebirth in Barry's eyes, and facilitating the extraordinary flowering of the visual arts in this period, was the presiding influence of the Catholic Church. Barry had no hesitation in delineating the unacceptable face of Catholicism, and in his great painting *Elysium and Tartarus or the State of Final Retribution* he took some pleasure in placing the visage of what he called 'a political pope', along with a monarch and a wretch holding the sectarian 'Solemn League and Covenant', in the depths of Tartarus, his vision of eternal damnation. But he took particular exception to the imputation in the writings of thinkers such as Montesquieu that Catholicism was incompatible with the sense of public spirit fostered by republicanism.[6] For Barry, the break-up in the whole idea of public life, what a modern critic has referred to as the fall

29    James Barry, *The Phoenix or the Resurrection of Freedom*, 1776

of public man[7], began with the rise of individualism and unbridled self-interest during the Reformation.

The extent to which the Protestant ethic brought about the collapse of the public sphere was a complex and controversial question, but in one area there was a measure of agreement among Barry and his contemporaries that the Reformation had led to a deterioration in the quality of civic life. This was in the decline of a public role for the visual arts, particularly the disappearance of the kind of church art practised by Michelangelo and others during the Renaissance which raised painting to new levels of moral grandeur. It was fashionable to lament the baneful influence of puritanism on the visual arts – even Reynolds saw fit to condemn this modern form of iconoclasm – but Barry considered this as having disastrous consequences not just for art's relationship with the public but also for its relationship to time and history. In place of the sweep of narrative painting, pictorial styles had degenerated, he maintained, into 'portraits of ourselves, of our horses, our dogs, and country seats'.[8] It was fitting that this type of painting should lend itself to the depiction of inanimate objects, for it involved an attempt to step outside the remorseless flow of time into the private repose of the still-life. Soon after his death, a critic sought to disparage Barry's greatest works by comparing them to the narratives of stained glass[9], but this would have been welcomed as fulsome praise by Barry himself. He lauded the arrangement of pictures in Italian churches as 'serving at once for books, intelligible to the unlettered'[10], in a word, for having a democratic mode of address. It was for this reason that the abject failure of an ambitious scheme in 1773 to decorate St Paul's Cathedral with an extensive series of history paintings proved a turning-point in Barry's life. Barry, Reynolds and Benjamin West were among the six distinguished painters chosen to carry out the project, but its ignominious collapse due to lack of interest and patronage convinced Barry that the republic of taste was a lost cause where Britain was concerned.

Partly out of desperation to execute a series of history paintings on a grand scale, Barry offered in 1777 to decorate the Great Room at the Adelphi, the new headquarters for the Society for the Encouragement of the Arts, at no cost to the Society save his own expenses. This monumental project, which one way or another consumed Barry for the rest of his life, required the completion of six epic paintings charting the progress of the arts in western civilization, culminating in a vast sprawling canvas, over 42 feet long, entitled *Elysium and Tartarus or the State of Final Retribution*. This provided him with an opportunity to fasten the links between republicanism, liberty and Catholicism that underlie so much of his work. As he expressed it himself: 'It was my wish to bring together in Elysium, those great and good men of all ages and nations, who were cultivators and benefactors of mankind; it forms a kind of apotheosis, or more properly a beatification of those useful qualities which were pursued through the whole work.'[11]

It might be expected that such a cosmic vision would be prepared to fix its gaze only on the everlasting things, or the most dignified expressions of human nature, and indeed as the eye traverses the canvas it encounters many of the notable historical figures who devoted their lives to liberty: for example, Junius Brutus, Cato the Younger, Shaftesbury and his adviser, Locke. The centrepiece is provided by William Penn, the founder of American liberty, who is imparting his code of laws to other great legislators, such as Numa, Solon and Lycurgus, and towards the right of the painting overlooking the precipice of Tartarus, the assembly of the faithful is comprised of the greatest writers and artists who have graced human history: Apelles, Homer, Shakespeare, Milton, Michelangelo, Raphael, and so on. As we look beyond the familiar figures, however, it transpires that not only has Barry given a Catholic tincture to the entire panorama – in the form of various popes, monks, Jesuits, and Catholic monarchs such as Francis I – but there is also a distinctive Irish sub-text running through it. Situated at the very apex of the painting is Ossian, or rather Barry's intervention in the Macpherson controversy, for having gone to some lengths to consult those authorities who argued in favour of Ossian's Irishness, he equips him with a historically accurate Irish harp.[12] Further down the painting, behind Junius Brutus and facing the group of legislators, is William Molyneux, complete with his *Case of Ireland Stated,* the first systematic presentation of the case for Irish legislative independence. The emblematic harp on the cover of Molyneux's book calls attention to Ossian's harp at the top of the picture, as if the claim to legislative independence is bound up with a vindication of ancient Irish civilization.[13]

Molyneux, or for that matter William Penn, did not quite fit in with the Catholic contribution to liberty and progress, but in 1792–3, in the first flush of the concessions made by the government to the Catholic Committee in Ireland, Barry amended the original centrepiece in an engraving. Penn was forced to give pride of place to a nobleman with an Irish title, the Catholic Lord Baltimore [fig. 1], who as early as 1649 had anticipated the eminent Quaker by passing the Maryland Act of Toleration, which established a pioneering legal framework for human rights and civic harmony between Catholics and Protestants. In the top left hand corner, as if benefiting from the passing of the Act, one of the most unlikely groups ever assembled in a history painting is taking part in a convivial discussion: Benjamin Franklin, Pope Adrian, Bishop Berkeley, the Jesuit Mariana and Cardinal Reginald Pole, the arch-opponent of Henry VIII's break with Rome.

The choice of figures in this engraving may seem idiosyncratic but in fact it was keenly attuned to the thinking of some of the most prominent supporters of the Catholic Committee in Ireland. Berkeley, for example, had provided a model for Charles O'Conor's observations on the Popery laws, and in a letter to Joseph Cooper Walker in 1787, O'Conor mentions how, on seeing a portrait of Reginald Pole, he found his praises of the Catholic prelate reciprocated by Lady Moira.[14] Even more to the point, William and Edmund Burke had given the spirit of toleration in Maryland their imprimatur by citing it as an early example of the American pursuit of liberty, and this was seized on by Charles O'Conor in 1777 as an alternative to some of the republican excesses in the American Revolution. As George Sigerson was later to point out, the importance of the example of Maryland for Catholic apologists was that it had offered a haven to both Catholics and Protestant dissenters escaping persecution in Ireland – thus forging a common interest between them in the face of English oppression.[15] The idea that Catholics had prepared the ground for Protestant conceptions of liberty and national independence proved immensely attractive to Barry, and it was with this in mind that he included Molyneux in the corner of the Baltimore engraving. [. . .]

It is possible [. . .] to see in this vast work a series of oblique but politically charged comments on the state of Ireland, as if only the breadth of vision furnished by history painting could show the way out of the impasse presented by British rule in Ireland. Barry himself admitted that this was the motivating principle in the work: 'I have no small satisfaction in reflecting', he wrote, 'that the business transacted in the group of legislators in the Elysium, goes all the length of the remedy for the disorders of Ireland, the application of which remedy has been so long desired, prayed for, and hoped for.' [...]

Barry's tendency to let the surge of the narrative overpower the visual cohesion of his paintings was an affront to the neoclassical sense of order and decorum, and featured regularly in negative appraisals of his work. But it did not simply challenge the rule of order: it also prevented a painting from achieving the kind of spatial unity which allowed it to arrest the flow of time, and hence to disengage itself from history. It was a central tenet of neoclassical aesthetics that a painting be taken in by a single act of perception: if the apprehension of work required the passage of time this meant that time itself, in the form of contingency, had entered the frame. Part of [Jacques-Louis] David's appeal to republican ideology was that by foreshortening time into space, he released classical republican themes from the flux of history, and converted them into abstract moral exemplars. But this option was not available to an Irish painter. Classical antiquity may have been dead and gone, but the appeal of ancient Ireland to nationalist historiography lay in the belief that it was part of a lived historical experience, a product of an embattled collective memory.

## NOTES

1    For Barry see William L. Pressly, *The Life and Art of James Barry*, New Haven and London, Yale University Press, 1981.
2    Tom Dunne, 'Haunted by History: Irish Romantic Writing 1800–50' in R. Porter and M. Teich, eds., *Romanticism in National Context*, Cambridge Universtiy Press, 1988, p. 72. [Orig. note.]
3    John Barrell, *The Political Theory Painting from Reynolds to Hazlitt*, New Haven and London, Yale University Press, 1986, pp. 158–62. [Orig.note.]
4    *The Works of James Barry Esq., Historical Painter*, ed., Dr Edward Fryer, 2 vols., London, 1809, vol. 2, p. 445. [Orig. note.]
5    Ibid., vol. 1, p. 374 ff. [Orig. note.]
6    Ibid., vol. 2, p. 457 ff. [Orig. note.]
7    Richard Sennett, *The Fall of Public Man*, Cambridge University Press, 1977. [Orig. note.]
8    Barry, *Works*, vol. 2, p. 246. [Orig. note.]
9    'James Barry' in Richard Ryan, *Biographia Hibernica*, London, I, 1819–21, p. 68. [Orig. note.]
10    Barry, *Works*, vol. 1, p. 372. [Orig. note.]
11    Ibid., vol. 2, p. 361. [Orig. note.]
12    Ibid., vol. 2, p. 371. [Orig. note.]
13    See entry 5b for Barry's 1793 account of these inclusions.

14    *The Letters of Charles O'Conor of Belanagare,* Catherine Coogan Ward and Robert Ward, eds., Michigan, Ann Arbor, 1980, vol. 1, pp. 283, 284, 286, 294 and vol. 2, p. 264. [Orig. note.]

15    George Sigerson, *The Last Independent Parliament of Ireland,* Dublin, 1919, pp. xxv–xxvi. [Orig. note.]

# − 54 −

# Catherine Nash, 'Gender and Landscape in Ireland', 1993

Catherine Nash teaches cultural geography and Irish Studies at Royal Holloway College, University of London. In her essay 'Remapping and renaming: New Cartographies of Identity, Gender and Landscape in Ireland', she examines the work of the contemporary Irish artist Kathy Prendergast (b. 1958), while also reflecting on 'gender, nation and landscape in early twentieth-century Ireland'. When discussing the latter, Nash refers to the paintings of Paul Henry (1876–1958), an extract from whose autobiography appears as entry 21.

Source: Catherine Nash, 'Re-mapping and Re-naming: New Cartographies of Identity, Gender and Landscape in Ireland', *Feminist Review,* no. 44, Summer 1993, pp. 39–57; this extract, pp. 40–9. The original references have been greatly shortened. Only one of four drawings by Prendergast examined by Nash has been retained (fig. 30), while the illustrations of paintings by Henry have been left out.

## GEOGRAPHY AND GENDER

Issues of geography and gender arise in the work of Kathy Prendergast, one of the younger generation of Irish artists who have adopted a critical, ironic and sometimes humorous approach to traditional Irish landscape art. In using the map motif, her work raises connexions between landscape and the female body, between the political control of landscape and territory and the control of female sexuality. Prendergast rejects the interpretation of her images as feminist statements and describes the work as a representation of a 'personal geography'. The work can, however, be discussed as an instance where the tension between this 'personal geography' of the body and the space of the national landscape is manifest. In a series of drawings of 1983, as in other work by Kathy Prendergast, accepted scales are confused, references to other artistic conventions are employed. She uses a device of creative interplay between words and image, of detailed cross-sections and plans of a female body. In 'Enclosed Worlds in Open Spaces' the drawing of a truncated female body evokes cartographic conventions of grid lines, compass point and ships on the sea surrounding the body/land. The style of geomorphological, surveying or civil-engineering diagrams and plans is used in 'To Control a Landscape – Irrigation', 'To Control a Landscape – Oasis' and 'To Alter a Landscape' [fig. 30]. These conventions are conflated with the styles of anatomical and gynaecological diagrams. In the drawings, operations of control, manipulation and alteration are in process on and within the passive land/body. In their dissection of the female body they evoke anatomical drawings of female organs which functioned in the medico-moral politics of the late nineteenth century. The quietness of the images in their carefully drawn style, their reference to yellowed historical maps and navigational charts, make the violence of the subject-matter more powerful. In using several registers of representation such as the cartographic, geological and medical, the drawings are complex multi-layered texts which do not provide a sealed and completed set of meanings to be consumed but engage the viewer in the making of meanings. The images draw us in as explorers, navigators, engineers, in search of fullness, wholeness and simplicity of meaning, only to disrupt the process of reasoning and understanding in their ambiguity, 'the un-naming power of ambiguity'.[1] The familiarity of the connexion between colonial control of other lands and the control of female sexuality and the use of gender in the discourse of discovery and territorial expansion, is displaced by the powerful subtlety of these images.

Kathy Prendergast draws on traditions of representation of women in order to deconstruct their supposed neutrality. It is her ironic position as a female artist in relation to these traditions that gives Prendergast's reinscriptions their counterstrategic power. The artist's use of the idea of land and landscape and its relationship to control of the feminine is understandable in the historical context of colonial efforts to control 'an essentially feminine race' and post-independence attempts to employ notions of femininity, rural life and landscape in the construction of Irishness and the subordination of Irish women. Issues of gender and national identity intersect in multiple ways; in the gendering of the concept of the nation, in the idea of the national landscape as feminine, in the concern with issues of race, place, and the national population and the delimiting of gender roles in the idealization and representation of rural life. The symbolism of Ireland as female derives from the sovereignty

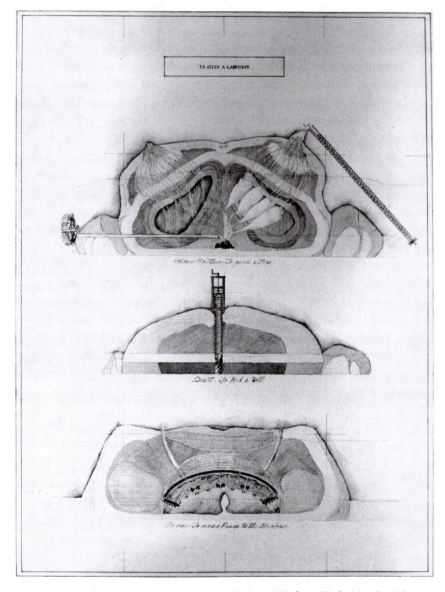

30    Kathy Prendergast, *To Alter a Landscape*, 1983, from 'Body Map Series'

goddess figure of early Irish tradition, the personification of this goddess in the figures of Irish medieval literature and the allegorization of Ireland as woman in the eighteenth-century classical poetic genre, the aisling, following colonial censorship of the expression of direct political. It also relates to the colonial feminization of Ireland and the Irish which was adopted, adapted and contested within nationalist. The continued use of the notion of Ireland as female, against which male poets assert both personal and national identity, endorses and strengthens the signifying use of women in Ireland, their erosion from Irish history and contemporary silencing. Traditional landscape representations in Ireland are imbued with conceptions of both national and gender identity, most significantly in the imagery of the West of Ireland.

## 'WOMEN OF THE WEST': GENDER, NATION AND LANDSCAPE IN EARLY-TWENTIETH-CENTURY IRELAND

In the construction of the image of the West of Ireland in the first decades of the twentieth century, many of these intersections of gender, landscape and nation are manifest. The image of the West stands at the centre of a web of discourses of racial and cultural identity, femininity, sexuality and landscape which were being used in attempts to secure cultural identity and political freedom. The construction of the West must be seen both in the context of Irish history and culture, and within the broader context of the anti-modernism and romantic primitivism of the period, of European discourses concerning racial degeneration, eugenics, evolution and environmentalism, spiritualism and rural regeneration, and the particular context of Irish nationalist attempts to revitalize and revivify the nation. These discourses intersected with the idea of national identity and gravitated around notions of place and landscape. Images of the peasant women of the West in travel writing and photography, literature and painting, were one set of several versions of femininity being contested at the time, as part of a set of discourses which participated in the negotiation and inscription of ideas of femininity and, through femininity, the future ideal form of Irish society. The Irish suffrage movement was at this time posing questions about the role of women in political life and within the independent state, as were the women's military nationalist organizations. This threat to the male monopoly of political power by politically active women intensified the drive to fix the role, position and the very nature of womanhood. These issues overlapped with concerns of cultural purity and preservation, centred on the image of the West of Ireland as an Irish cultural region, whose physical landscape provided the greatest contrast to the landscape of Englishness.[2] Onto the body of the peasant woman were focused concerns over racial, sexual and cultural purity and the social and moral organization of a future independent Ireland.

The visual iconography of the West as an archetypal Irish landscape was largely based on the paintings of Paul Henry, whose work was part of a tradition of European early modernist cultural primitivism which sought spirituality, stability and authenticity in a move to the Celtic fringes. Henry's work was also indebted to the Anglo-Irish search for a sense of community and natural spirituality in the West. In line with both traditions, the women in Henry's painting became part of the visual iconography of the West and acted as emblems of an idea of femininity based on a supposedly natural identification with nature and the landscape.

While primitivism afforded a limited, positive evaluation of the Irish West as a source of cohesion, simplicity, instinctiveness and an organic relationship between lifestyle and environment, the primitive was ultimately considered lower in a hierarchy of civilization. As constructions of the imperial centre, both art history and anthropology contributed to the production of primitivism as a discriminatory discourse which posits the 'other' as both an object for the artist's gaze and for analytic scrutiny. The discourses which primitivized women and the colony were fused in the representation of the female colonial subject. Yet, as a result of nationalist anti-urbanism and anti-imperialism, this primitivizing continued in nationalist accounts of the West. The idea of the primitive was appropriated but positively evaluated against the urban, industrial, colonial power. This primitivization of the West and of women, which had as a strong element the supposed unsuppressed instinctiveness, sexuality and unselfconscious sensuality of the primitive, had to be reconciled with the use of women by cultural nationalists as signifiers of moral purity and sexual innocence.

While convergences can be noted between the colonial appropriation of the landscape of the colony and the production of the subject woman, the codes of representation of both the peasant woman and the West as landscapes of desire were re-employed in nationalist writing. In the shift from emphasis on Celtic to Gaelic, the feminine was rejected as epitomizing the national character. Instead, ideas of anti-urbanism, nationalism, concern about the body, health and physique, were projected on to the woman's body, and against England as urban, industrial and debased. The emphasis on dress in the description of the people of the West corresponds to the importance of dress as a marker of national identity, constructed from elements of race, class and geography. Its importance was testified to in the concern over national costume in the Gaelic revival movement, which amounted to a 'national dress debate' in the 1910s. In that movement, an emphasis on the red skirts of women was tied to the symbolism of the colour as an indication of vitality, to the belief in the national love of colour evident from ancient costume, and to the rejection of modern fashion, which was considered to restrict the female biological functions. The concern over dress can be understood in the context of the cultural and biological role which was afforded to women within Irish Nationalism. The celebration of the women of the West intersects with issues of concern with degeneration, anti-urbanism and the moral economy of the body, and the sexual politics of representation.

In later painting and travel photography, by contrast, the image of the young woman was usually absent, reflecting both the demographic structure of Irish rural society in the context of large-scale rural depopulation and also the problematic nature of representation of young women. In the context of the construction of femininity by cultural nationalists and later, Church and State, which denied women an autonomous sexuality in their idealization of asexual motherhood, the visual representation of the idealized country woman rested uneasily with the history of eroticized images of women in Western art. The young woman was replaced by the depiction of the old peasant women who could represent the successful outcome of a life lived in accordance with the demands of motherhood, as well as being emblematic of the traditions, folklore, language and way of life extolled in the state. Alternatively, the depiction of the peasant woman was replaced by the portrayal of Western men, who epitomized the Gaelic masculine ideal. Thus nationalist writers of the Irish Ireland movement, in reaction to the nineteenth-century construction of the Celtic as feminine, asserted masculinity as the essential characteristic of the 'Gael'. While the idea of 'woman' remained the embodiment of the national spirit and the allegorical figure for the land of Ireland, this land now became the domain of the overtly masculine. The West was redefined as Gaelic, masculine, wholesome, pragmatic and Catholic in contrast to the femininity and natural spirituality of the Celtic. This denial of the female was also linked to the control of sexuality by Catholicism. This moral code supported the economic and social system of family farming, which demanded the regulation of sexuality for the control of inheritance. With the perceived threat of an autonomous female sexuality to this social order, the counterpart of the Gaelic male had to be the desexualized mother figure.

The cottage in the landscape came to carry the cultural weight of the idealization of traditional rural, family life and its fixed morality and gender roles. It became a surrogate for the depiction of the rural Irish woman and the values of motherhood, tradition and stability. The cottage as 'cradle of the race' evoked the idea of women as preservers of the race, active only as nurturers and reproducers of the masculine Gael. The homosocial bonding of Irish nationalism depended upon the exclusion of women from the body politic, while its conception of the landscape as female facilitated a masculinist relationship to place. The discourses which confined women within the domestic sphere simultaneously conferred on them the responsibility of maintaining the national population. Women's function was to reproduce the bodies of the 'body politic', represented as masculine. The conflation of body and nation in Irish national discourse (which found more explicit expression in the contemporaneous British eugenics movement) provided a vehicle for the systematic expression of concern over this 'body politics' – the nation and the national population. Concerns over the national population were closely linked to ideas of landscape. The idea of an organic link between environment and people was utilized in discourses which employed scientific conceptions of current climatology and anthrogeography to discourage emigration. Fears of loss of population were made more urgent by the associated loss of Irish-language speakers, cultural bearers and vigorous genetic stock from the West of Ireland. Concern over emigration fused issues of gender and race, as it was felt that loss of those who 'would have made the best mothers and wives' leaves 'at home the timid, the stupid, and the dull to help in the deterioration of the race and to breed sons as sluggish as themselves'.[3] Both ideas of racial pride and racial fears were thus projected on to the body of the woman.

The cottage as an 'Irish citadel' stood for a preservation and reproduction of Irish language, tradition and folklore, for which women were considered to have paramount responsibility in their capacity as childcarers. This of course echoes the role accorded to women within other nationalist movements. The cottage was also considered as the basic unit of a distinctive Irish settlement pattern and therefore symbolic of Irish social organization in opposition to English culture. Thus the isolated rural cottage represented the realization, both in the physical fabric of the landscape and in the moral and spiritual domain, of the ideal form of Irish society. Its depiction in Irish landscape painting participated in the construction of Irish identity and the gender identities upon which it relied. Representation of landscape in early twentieth-century Ireland was coded with meaning in terms of both national and gender identity.

NOTES

1    Chris Prentice, 'Rewriting their stories, renaming themselves: post-colonialism and feminism in the fictions of Kerri Hulme and Audrey Thomas', *SPAN: Journal of the South Pacific Association for Commonwealth Literature and Language Studies*, 1986, vol. 23, p. 70. [Orig. note.]

2    Catherine Nash, 'Embodying the nation – The West of Ireland, landscape and national identity', in Michael Cronin and Barbara O'Connor, eds., *Tourism and Ireland: A Critical Analysis*, Cork University Press, 1993. [Orig. note.]

3    George Russell, *Co-operation and Nationality*, Dublin, Maunsel, 1912, pp. 67–8. [Orig. note.]

# COPYRIGHT ACKNOWLEDGEMENTS

The publishers gratefully acknowledge the following copyright holders for permission to quote from previously published works:

George Berkeley from 'First Journal in Italy', courtesy of Clarendon Press, Oxford; Edmund Burke from *A Philosophical Enquiry* courtesy of Professor J.T. Boulton and Laurence Pollinger Ltd., London; W.B. Yeats 'Art and Ideas' courtesy of Macmillan, London; Mainie Jellett 'My Voyage of Discovery' courtesy of Dundalgan Press Ltd., Dundalk; Tom Duddy 'Irish Art Criticism – A Provincialism of the Right' courtesy *Circa Art Magazine*; Declan McGonagle 'Looking Beyond Regionalism' courtesy of Declan McGonagle and *Circa Art Magazine*; John Lavery from *The Life of a Painter* courtesy of Cassell & Co., London; Ernie O'Malley, 'The Paintings of Jack B. Yeats' courtesy of Clarendon Press, Oxford; Richard Kearney, from *Transitions* courtesy of the author; Fionna Barber from *Familiar: Alice Maher*, courtesy of the author; Earl of Charlemont, Letters to Hogarth 1759–60 courtesy of The British Library, London; Benjamin Robert Haydon from *Diary* 1841 of Harvard University Press, Cambridge, Mass.; Dante Gabriel Rossetti, 'McCracken', courtesy of Clarendon Press, Oxford; W.B. Yeats 'The Gift' courtesy of A.P. Watt Ltd., London; George Moore from *Vale* 1914 by permission of Colin Smythe Ltd. on behalf of the Estate of C.D. Medley; Hugh Lane, Codicil to his Will, courtesy of The Arts Council of Ireland; Ciarán Benson from *The Place of the Arts in Irish Education*, courtesy of The Arts Council of Ireland; William Drennan and Martha McTier from *The Drennan–McTier Letters 1797–1807*, courtesy of The Women's History Project and Irish Manuscripts Commission, Dublin; Extract from *Illustrated Catalogue 1908* courtesy of The Hugh Lane Municipal Gallery of Modern Art; Brian O'Nolan / Myles na gCopaleen courtesy of *The Irish Times*; Michael Scott / James Johnson Sweeney from *Rosc* courtesy of Scott Tallon Walker Architects, Dublin; Brian O'Doherty from *The Irish Imagination* courtesy of the author;

Cyril Barrett from 'Irish Nationalism and Art' courtesy of *Studies*, Dublin; Anne Crookshank and the Knight of Glin from *Painters of Ireland* courtesy of Desmond FitzGerald; Joan Fowler from 'Art and Politics in the Eighties', courtesy of the author; Luke Gibbons from "*Shadowy Narrator*": *History, Art and Romantic Nationalism, 1750–1850* reproduced courtesy of Luke Gibbons and The Lilliput Press, Dublin; Catherine Nash from 'Gender and Landscape' courtesy of *The Feminist Review*, London

We would also like to thank copyright holders of the artworks featured in this anthology (full details are given in the List of Illustrations).

Every effort has been made to trace the copyright holders of the works quoted herein. If there are any omissions Cork University Press will correct them in reprints or future editions of the book.

# SELECT BIBLIOGRAPHY

This bibliography is not a comprehensive guide to readings on Irish art but rather an aid to written sources on the subject. Reference is made to most of the sources used in this volume with the exception of manuscript material in entries 4, 29, 43. Reference to other relevant works by some of the writers quoted is also given. A list of additional source material not used in the volume is supplied together with a select bibliography of published catalogues of permanent holdings of Irish visual material. It is hoped that this last category will lead students to explore the Irish collections in a range of public institutions. The bibliography is divided into the following sections:

- Works by and/or related to the writers cited in the volume
- Additional source material for Irish art
- Permanent holdings of Irish art

## WORKS BY AND/OR RELATED TO THE WRITERS CITED IN THE VOLUME

Barber, Fionna, *Relocating History. An Exhibition of Work by 7 Irish Women Artists*, Belfast, The Fenderesky Gallery and Derry, The Orchard Gallery, 1993
——— *Familiar. Alice Maher*, Dublin, Douglas Hyde Gallery, 1995
Barrett, Cyril, 'Irish Nationalism and Art, *Studies,* Winter 1975, pp. 393–409
——— and Jeanne Sheehy, 'Visual Arts and Society 1850–1921,' in *A New History of Ireland, VI, Ireland Under the Union, II, 1870–1921*, ed. W.E. Vaughan, Oxford, Clarendon Press, 1996, pp. 436–499
Barry, James, *The Works of James Barry, Esq., Historical Painter*, ed., Edward Fryer, 2 vols., London, Cadell & Davies, 1809
Benson, Ciarán, *The Place of the Arts in Irish Education*, Dublin, Arts Council of Ireland, 1979
Berkeley, George, *The Works of George Berkeley*, eds. A.A. Luce and T.E. Jessop, 9 vols., London, Thomas Nelson & Sons, 1948–57
Blacker, Stewart, *Irish Art and Irish Artists*, Dublin, Gunn & Cameron, 1845

Bodkin, Thomas, *Hugh Lane and His Pictures,* Dublin, The Stationery Office, 1956

———— *Four Irish Landscape Painters,* 1920 (reprinted Dublin, Irish Academic Press, 1987)

———— *Report on the Arts in Ireland,* Dublin, The Stationery Office, 1949

Burke, Edmund, *The Correspondence of Edmund Burke,* vols. 1–3, eds., Thomas W. Copeland, Lucy S. Sutherland and George H. Guttridge, respectively, Cambridge University Press, 1958–61

———— *A Philosophical Enquiry into the Origin of our Ideas of the Sublime and the Beautiful,* ed., James T. Boulton, Oxford, Basil Blackwell, 1987

Campbell, Thomas, *An Essay on Perfecting the Fine Arts in Great Britain and Ireland,* Dublin, William Sleater, 1767

Crookshank, Anne and The Knight of Glin, *The Painters of Ireland, c. 1660–1920,* London, Barrie & Jenkins, 1978

———— *The Watercolours of Ireland: Works on Paper, in Pencil, Pastel and Paint, c. 1660–1914,* London, Barrie and Jenkins, 1994

———— *Irish Portraits 1660–1860,* London, Paul Mellon Foundation for British Art, 1969

Cunningham, Allan, *The Life of Sir David Wilkie,* 3 vols., London, Murray, 1843

Davis, Thomas, *Essays Literary and Historical,* ed., D.J. O'Donoghue, Dundalk, Dundalgan Press, 1914

*The Drennan-McTier Letters,* ed. Jean Agnew, 3 vols., Dublin, The Women's History Project and Irish Manuscripts Commission, 1998–1999

Duddy, Tom, 'Irish Art Criticism. A Provincialism of the Right?' *Circa,* no. 35, July/August 1987, pp. 14–18

Elliott, Robert, *Art and Ireland,* Dublin, Sealy, Bryers & Walker, 1906 (reprint, Port Washington, New York and London, 1970)

Fowler, Joan, 'Speaking of Gender … Expressionism, Feminism and Sexuality', and 'Locating the Context-Art and Politics in the Eighties,' in *A New Tradition. Irish Art of the Eighties,* Dublin, The Douglas Hyde Gallery, 1991, pp. 53–67, 117–129

Gibbons, Luke, '"A Shadowy Narrator": History, Art and Romantic Nationalism in Ireland 1750–1850', in *Ideology and the Historians,* ed., Ciaran Brady, Dublin, The Lilliput Press, 1991, pp. 99–127

———— *Transformations in Irish Culture,* Cork University Press, 1996

Godwin, William (pseudonym Theophilius Marcliffe), *The Looking Glass. A True History of the Early Years of an Artist…,* London, Thomas Hodges, 1805 (facsimile reprint, Benrose & Sons, London, 1885, appendix by F.G. Stephens)

Haydon, Benjamin Robert, *The Diary of Benjamin Robert Haydon,* ed., W.B. Pope, 5 vols., Cambridge, MA, Harvard University Press, 1963

Henry, Paul, *An Irish Portrait,* London, Batsford, 1951

———— *Further Reminiscences,* Belfast, 1978

Historical Manuscripts Commission, *The MSS and Correspondence of James, 1st Earl of Charlemont,* 12th Report, Appendix, Part X, vols. 1 and 2, London, 1891–4

Irish Free State, *Official Handbook,* Dublin, Talbot Press, 1932

Kearney, Richard, *The Irish Mind, Exploring Intellectual Traditions,* Dublin, Wolfhound Press, 1985

———— *Transitions. Narratives in Modern Irish Culture,* Manchester University Press, and Dublin, Wolfhound Press, 1988

Lavery, John, *The Life of a Painter,* London, Casell & Co., 1940

MacCarville, Eileen, ed., *Mainie Jellett: The Artist's Vision,* Dundalk, Dundalgan Press, 1958

McGonagle, Declan, 'Looking Beyond Regionalism,' *Circa,* no. 53, September/October 1990, pp. 26–7

MacGreevy, Thomas, 'Picasso, Maimie Jellett and Dublin Criticism', *Klaxon*, 1923–4, pp. 23–7

——— *Jack B. Yeats: An Appreciation and An Interpretation,* Dublin, Victor Waddington and Colm O'Lochlainn at the Sign of the Three Candles, 1945

Madden, Richard Robert, *The United Irishmen, Their Lives and Times,* second series, second edition, Dublin, 1858

Madden, Samuel, *Reflections and Resolutions proper for the Gentlemen of Ireland, as to their Conduct for the Service of their Country…*, Dublin, 1738

——— *A Letter to the Dublin-Society, on Improving their Fund; and the Manufactures, Tillage, etc. in Ireland,* Dublin, 1739

Mahony, Francis Sylvester, *The Reliques of Father Prout, later P.P. of Watergrasshill, in the County of Cork, Ireland,* London, Bell & Daldy, 1873

Moore, George, *Vale,* vol. 3 of *Hail and Farewell!,* London, Heinemann, 1914

——— *Confessions of a Young Man,* ed., Susan Dick, Montreal, McGill-Queen's University Press, 1972

——— *Modern Painting,* London, 1893

Morgan, Lady (Sydney Owenson), *The Life and Times of Salvator Rosa,* 2 vols., London, 1824

——— *Lady Morgan's Memoirs,* 2 vols., eds., W. Hepworth Dixon and Geraldine Jewsbury, London, 1863

*Municipal Gallery of Modern Art, Illustrated Catalogue,* Dublin, Dollard, 1908 (reprinted by the Friends of the National Collections of Ireland and the Hugh Lane Municipal Gallery of Modern Art, Dublin, 1984)

Nash, Catherine, 'Re-mapping and re-naming: New Cartographies of Identity, Gender and Landscape in Ireland,' *Feminist Review,* no. 44, Summer 1993, pp. 39–57

——— *Irish Geographies: six contemporary artists,* Djanogly Art Gallery, University of Nottingham, 1997

O'Doherty, Brian, ed., *The Irish Imagination 1959–1971,* Dublin, Rosc, 1971

O'Driscoll, W. Justin, *A Memoir of Daniel Maclise, R.A.,* London, Longmans, Green & Co., 1871

O'Keeffe, John, *Recollections,* 2 vols., London, Henry Colburn, 1826

O'Malley, Ernie, 'The Paintings of Jack Yeats,' in *Jack B. Yeats. A Centenary Gathering,* ed., Roger McHugh, Dublin, The Dolmen Press, 1971, pp. 64–70

O'Nolan, Brian, *The Best of Myles,* ed., Kevin O'Nolan, London, Hart-Davis, MacGibbon, 1975

Pasquin, Anthony, *An Authentic History of the Professors of Painting, Sculpture and Architecture in Ireland,* facsimile reprint. ed. R. W. Lightbown, London, Cornmarket Press, 1970

*Rosc,* exhibition catalogues, Dublin, 1967–1988

Rossetti, Dante Gabriel, *Letters of Dante Gabriel Rossetti,* eds. Oswald Doughty and John Robert Wahl, 4 vols., Oxford, Clarendon Press, 1965

Stokes, William, *The Life and Labours in Art and Archeology of George Petrie, LL.D.,* London, 1868

Thompson, Elizabeth, (Butler, Lady) *An Autobiography,* London, Constable & Co., 1922

Twiss, Richard, *A Tour of Ireland in 1775,* London, 1776

Webb, Daniel, *An Inquiry into the Beauties of Painting and into the Merits of the Most Celebrated Painters, Ancient and Modern,* London, 1760

Weinglass, David H., ed., *The Collected English Letters of Henry Fuseli,* Millwood, New York, London and Nendeln, Liechtenstein, Krauss International Publications, 1982

Yeats, William Butler, *Essays and Introductions,* London, Macmillan & Co., 1961

——— *The Collected Poems,* ed., Richard J. Finneran, London, Macmillan, 1983

———— *Autobiographies*, London, Macmillan & Co., 1955

———— *Uncollected Prose*, collected and edited, John P. Frayne and Colton Johnson, 2 vols., London, Macmillan, 1975


## ADDITIONAL SOURCE MATERIAL FOR IRISH ART

Arnold, Bruce, *Mainie Jellett and the Modern Movement in Ireland*, New Haven and London, Yale University Press, 1991

———— *Jack Yeats,* New Haven and London, Yale University Press, 1998

Arts Council of Great Britain, *Daniel Maclise*, London, National Portrait Gallery, 1972

Campbell, Julian, *The Irish Impressionists*, Dublin, National Gallery of Ireland, 1984

Carey, William, *Some Memoirs of the Patronage and Progress of the Fine Arts in England and Ireland*, London, 1826

*Circa Art Magazine*, Belfast, 1981 – ongoing

*The Circa Index, 1981–1991*, compiled by Marion Khorshidian, Belfast, 1992

Coffey, Stella, *Visual Invisible: A Strategic Review of the Visual Art Market in Ireland: Recommendations for a Developmental Approach,* Dublin, Artists Association of Ireland, 1999

Crookshank, Anne, *Irish Sculpture from 1600 to the present day,* Dublin, Department of Foreign Affairs, 1984

Cullen, Fintan, *Visual Politics. The Representation of Ireland 1750–1930*, Cork University Press, 1997

———— 'The Oil Paintings of Hugh Douglas Hamilton,' *The Walpole Society*, 50, 1984, pp. 165–208

Curtis, Lewis Perry, Jr., *Apes and Angels. The Irishman in Victorian Caricature*, Washington, D.C. and London, Smithsonian Institution Press, 1997

de Courcy, Catherine, *The Foundation of the National Gallery of Ireland*, Dublin, National Gallery of Ireland, 1985

Dalsimer, Adele M., ed., *Visualizing Ireland. National Identity and the Pictorial Tradition,* Boston and London, Faber, 1993

Dobai, Johannes, *Die Kunstliteratur des Klassizismus und der Romantik in England*, 4 vols., Berlin, Bentali Verlag, 1974–84

Fallon, Brian, 'Irish Painting in the fifties,' *Arts in Ireland*, 3 (n.d.), pp. 24–36

———— *Irish Art, 1830–1990,* Belfast, Appletree Press, 1994

Frazer, Hugh, *Essay on Painting,* Belfast/Dublin, M. Jellett/ James Burnside, 1825

Gillespie, Raymond and Brian P. Kennedy, eds., *Ireland. Art into History,* Dublin, Town House, 1994

Graves, Algernon, *The Royal Academy of Arts: a complete Dictionary of Contributors and their work . . . 1769–1904*, 8 vols., London, 1905–6

Gregory, Augusta, Lady, *Hugh Lane's Life and Achievement*, London, 1921 (reprinted Gerrards Cross, Colin Smythe, 1973)

Hayes, Richard J., *Manuscript Sources for the History of Irish Civilization*, 11 vols., Boston, MA, G.K. Hall, 1965; 3-vol. supplement, Boston, MA, G.K. Hall, 1979

Herbert, John Dowling, *Irish Varieties for the last fifty years*, London, 1836

Herr, Cheryl, 'The Erotics of Irishness,' *Critical Inquiry*, 17, Autumn 1990, pp. 1–34 Hill, Judith, *Irish Public Sculpture – A History,* Dublin, Four Courts Press, 1998

Ingamells, John, *A Dictionary of British and Irish Travellers in Italy, 1701–1800*, New Haven and London, Yale University Press, 1997

*The Irish Industrial Exhibition of 1853: a detailed catalogue...*, eds., John Sproule, Dublin and
    London, 1854
Irish Museum of Modern Art, *Louis Le Brocquy*, Dublin, 1996
*Irish Women Artists: From the Eighteenth Century to the Present Day*, Dublin, The National
    Gallery of Ireland and the Douglas Hyde Gallery, 1987
Kelly, Liam, *Thinking Long. Contemporary Art in the North of Ireland*, Kinsale, Gandon Edi-
    tions, 1996
Kennedy, Brian, *Dreams and Responsibilities: The State and the Arts in Independent Ireland,*
    Dublin, The Arts Council of Ireland, 1990.
Kennedy, S.B., *Irish Art and Modernism 1880–1950*, Belfast, The Institute of Irish Studies
    at The Queen's University of Belfast, 1991
Knowles, Roderic, *Contemporary Irish Art*, Dublin, Wolfhound Press, 1982
Larmour, Paul, *The Arts and Crafts Movement in Ireland*, Belfast, Friar's Bush Press, 1992
*L'Imaginaire Irlandais*, Paris, Hazan, 1996
*Irish Arts Review*, Dublin, 1984–7
*Irish Arts Review Yearbook*, Dublin, 1988 – ongoing
Loftus, Belinda, *Mirrors. William III and Mother Ireland*, Dundrum, Co. Down, Picture Press,
    1990
———— *Mirrors: Orange and Green,* Dundrum, Co. Down, Picture Press, 1994
Loizeaux, Elizabeth Bergmann, *Yeats and the Visual Arts*, Rutgers University Press, New
    Brunswick and London, 1986
McAvera, Brian, *Art, Politics and Ireland*, Dublin, Open Air, 1989
McConkey, Kenneth, *A Free Spirit: Irish Art, 1860–1960,* Woodbridge, Antique Collectors'
    Club, 1990
McCormack, W.J., ed., *The Blackwell Companion to Modern Irish Culture,* Oxford, Blackwell,
    1999
Marshall, Catherine, *Irish Art Masterpieces*, Hugh Lauter Levin Associates, Inc., 1994
Murphy, William M., *Prodigal Father: The Life of John Butler Yeats*, Ithaca, and London, Cor-
    nell University Press, 1978
Orpen, William, *Stories of Old Ireland and Myself*, London, Williams and Norgate, 1924
Pointon, Marcia, *Mulready*, London, Victoria and Albert Museum, 1986
Pressly, William L., *The Life and Art of James Barry*, New Haven and London, Yale Univer-
    sity Press, 1981
Pyle, Hilary, *Irish Art. 1900–1950,* Cork, Rosc Teoranta, 1975
———— *Jack B. Yeats: A Biography*, London, André Deutsch, 1989
Raley, R., 'Beyond all Expectations. The Dublin Society's Drawing School in Dublin in
    the eighteenth Century,' (with a supplement by A.O. Crookshank), in *Academies of
    Art, Between Renaissance and Romanticism,* eds., Anton W.A. Boschloo et al., SDU
    Uitgeverij, (*Leids Kunsthistorisch Jaarboek V–VI,* 1986–7), 1989, pp. 493–510
*Re-dressing Cathleen, Contemporary Works from Irish Women Artists,* Boston, McMullen
    Museum of Art, 1997
Sheehy, Jeanne, *The Rediscovery of Ireland's Past: the Celtic Revival, 1830–1920,* London,
    Thames and Hudson, 1980
Snoddy, Theo, *Dictionary of Irish Artists, twentieth century*, Dublin, Wolfhound Press, 1996
Stairs, Susan, *The Irish Figuratists and Figurative Painters in Irish Art*, Dublin, The George
    Gallery Montague, Ltd., 1990
Steward, James Christen, *When Time Began to Rant and Rage: Figurative Painting from
    Twentieth-Century Ireland*, London, Merrell Holberton, 1998
Stewart, Ann, *Irish Art Loan Exhibitions 1765–1927*, 3 vols., Dublin, Manton Publishing,
    1990

———— *Irish Art Societies and Sketching Clubs, Index of Exhibitors, 1870–1980*, 2 vols., Dublin, Four Courts Press, 1997

———— *Royal Hibernian Academy of Arts, Index of exhibitors and their works, 1826–1979*, 3 vols., Dublin, Manton Publishing, 1985

Strickland, Walter, *A Dictionary of Irish Artists,* 2 vols., Dublin and London, Maunsel, 1913

Turpin, John, *John Hogan: Irish Neo-Classical Sculptor in Rome 1800–1858*, Dublin, 1982

———— *A School of Art in Dublin since the Eighteenth Century. A History of the National College of Art and Design*, Dublin, Gill & Macmillan, 1995

Walker, Joseph Cooper, *Outlines of a Plan for Promoting the Art of Painting in Ireland: with a List of Subjects for Painters drawn from the Romantic and Genuine Histories of Ireland,* 1790

Walker, Dorothy, *Modern Art in Ireland*, Dublin, The Lilliput Press, 1997

## PERMANENT HOLDINGS OF IRISH ART

*AIB Art. A Selection from the Allied Irish Bank Collection of Modern Irish Art*, introduction by Frances Ruane, Dublin, AIB, 1995

*America's Eye: Irish Paintings from the Collection of Brian P. Burns*, eds., Adele M. Dalsimer and Vera Kreilkamp, Boston College Museum of Art, Boston, 1996

Arnold, Bruce, *The Art Atlas of Britain and Ireland*, London, Viking, 1991

Black, Eileen, *Irish Oil Paintings 1572-c.1830*, Belfast, Ulster Museum, 1991

———— *Irish Oil Paintings, 1831–1900*, Belfast, Ulster Museum, 1997

———— *Paintings, Sculptures and Bronzes in the Collection of the Belfast Harbour Commissioners*, Belfast, 1983

*British Watercolours in the Victoria and Albert Museum: An Illustrated Summary Catalogue*, London, 1980

Brown, David Blaney, *Ashmolean Museum, Oxford. Catalogue of the Collection of Drawings, vol. 4. The Earlier British Drawings; British Artists and Foreigners working in Britain, born before c. 1775,* Oxford, Clarendon Press, 1982

Butler, Patricia, *The Brocas Collection. An Illustrated Selective Catalogue of Original Watercolours, Prints and Drawings in the National Library of Ireland*, National Library of Ireland, Dublin, 1997

Casey, Christine, *Folk Traditions in Irish Art … paintings from The Department of Irish Folklore*, University College Dublin, Dublin, 1993

Chamot, Mary, *The Tate Gallery, British School*, London, 1953

———— Dennis Farr and Martin Butlin, *Tate Gallery Catalogues, The Modern British Paintings, Drawings and Sculptures,* 2 vols., London, The Oldburne Press, 1964

Cormack, Malcolm, *A Concise Catalogue of Paintings in the Yale Center for British Art*, New Haven, CT. Yale Centre for British Art, 1985

Crookshank, Anne and David Webb, *Paintings and Sculptures in Trinity College Dublin,* Trinity College Dublin Press, 1990

Elmes, Rosalind M., *Catalogue of Engraved Irish Portraits mainly in the Joly Collection*, Dublin, National Library of Ireland, 1932

———— *Catalogue of Irish Topographical Prints and Original Drawings,* Dublin, National Library of Ireland, 1932 (new ed., with additions, Michael Hewson, Dublin, Malton Press for the National Library of Ireland Society, 1975)

Finlay, Sarah, ed., *National Self-Portrait Collection of Ireland,* University of Limerick Press, 1989

Gallagher, William, *The Modern Art Collection. University College Cork*, University Collge Cork, 1998

Goodison, J.W., *Fitzwilliam Museum, Cambridge. Catalogue of Paintings, vol. 3, British School*, Cambridge University Press, 1977

*Images and Insights*, Dublin, Hugh Lane Municipal Gallery of Modern Art, 1993

*Irish Art 1770–1995, History and Society*. A Touring Exhibition from the Collection of the Crawford Municipal Art Gallery, Cork, Cork, City of Cork VEC, 1995

Irish Museum of Modern Art, *Inheritance and Transformation*, Dublin, Irish Museum of Modern Art, 1991

—— *Catalogue of the Collection, 1991–1998*, Dublin, Irish Museum of Modern Art, 1998

Jacobs, Michael and Malcolm Warner, *The Phaidon Companion to Art and Artists in the British Isles*, Oxford, Phaidon, 1980

—— and Paul Stirton, *The Knopf Traveler's Guides to Art. Britain and Ireland*, New York, Knopf, 1984

Jordan, Peter, *Waterford Municipal Art Collection*, Waterford, Garter Lane Arts Centre, 1987

Kerslake, John, *National Portrait Gallery. Early Georgian Portraits*, 2 vols., London, HMSO, 1977

Le Harivel, Adrian, ed., *National Gallery of Ireland: Illustrated Summary Catalogue of Drawings, Watercolours and Miniatures*, Dublin, National Gallery of Ireland, 1983

—— *National Gallery of Ireland: Illustrated Summary Catalogue of Prints and Sculpture*, Dublin, National Gallery of Ireland, 1988

Loane, Erica, ed., *The Watercolour Society of Ireland Collection*, University of Limerick Press, 1993

Murray, Peter, *Illustrated Summary Catalogue of The Crawford Municipal Art Gallery*, City of Cork Vocational Education Committee, 1992

National Gallery of Ireland, *Illustrated Summary Catalogue of Paintings*, Dublin, Gill & Macmillan, 1981

—— *Master European Drawings from the Collection of the National Gallery of Ireland*, Washington, D.C., Smithsonian Institution, 1983

National Portrait Gallery, London, *Catalogue of Seventeenth-Century Portraits, 1625–1714*, London, 1963

Noon, Patrick J., *English Portrait Drawings and Miniatures*, New Haven, Yale Center for British Art, 1979

Office of Public Works, *Art in State Buildings 1985–1995*, Dublin, The Stationery Office, 1997

—— *Art in State Buildings 1970–1985*, Dublin, The Stationery Office, 1998

O hAodha, Micheál, *Pictures at the Abbey: the collection of the Irish National Theatre*, Dublin, The Dolmen Press, 1983

O'Reilly, Paul, ed., *National Collection of Contemporary Drawings, vol. 1, part of the permanent collection of Limerick City Gallery of Art*, Limerick, Limerick City Gallery of Art, 1996

Ormond, Richard, *Early Victorian Portraits, National Portrait Gallery*, 2 vols., London, HMSO, 1973

Parkinson, Ronald, *Catalogue of British Oil Paintings 1820–1860*, London, Victoria and Albert Museum, 1990

Popplewell, Seán, *Exploring Museums: Ireland*, London, HMSO, 1990

Rouse, Sarah, *Into the Light. An Illustrated Guide to the Photographic Collections in the National Library of Ireland*, Dublin, National Library of Ireland, 1998

Scott, David, *The Modern Collection, Trinity College Dublin*, Trinity College Dublin Press, 1989

Stephens, F.G. and M.D. George, *Catalogue of Political and Personal Satires Preserved in the Department of Prints and Drawings in the British Museum*, 12 vols., London, 1870–1954

Strong, Roy, *National Portrait Gallery. Tudor and Jacobean Portraits*, 2 vols., London, HMSO, 1969

Teahan, John, ed., *Irish Decorative Arts, 1550–1928*, Dublin, National Museum of Ireland/ Smithsonian Institution, 1990

Tinney, Donal, ed., *Jack B. Yeats at the Niland Gallery, Sligo*, Sligo County Library, 1998

Trench, Chalmers, *Drogheda Municipal Art Collection*, Corporation of Drogheda, 1995

Ulster Museum, Belfast, *A Concise Catalogue of the Drawings, Paintings and Sculptures in the Ulster Museum*, Belfast, 1986

———— *Portraits and Prospects, British and Irish Drawings and Watercolours from the Collection of the Ulster Museum, Belfast*, Belfast, The Ulster Museum and The Smithsonian Institution Traveling Exhibition Service, 1989

University College Dublin, *University College: A selection of works from the UCD art collection*, University College Dublin, 1983

Walker, Richard, *National Portrait Gallery: Regency Portraits*, 2 vols., London, National Portrait Gallery, 1985

Whelan, Kevin, *Fellowship of Freedom. The United Irishmen and 1798. Companion Volume to the Bicentenary Exhibition by The National Library and The National Museum of Ireland at Collins Barracks, Dublin, 1998*, Cork University Press, 1998

# INDEX